Shakespeare and the Political Way

Shakespeare and the Politics of War

Shakespeare and the Political Way

ELIZABETH FRAZER

OXFORD
UNIVERSITY PRESS

OXFORD
UNIVERSITY PRESS

Great Clarendon Street, Oxford, OX2 6DP,
United Kingdom

Oxford University Press is a department of the University of Oxford.
It furthers the University's objective of excellence in research, scholarship,
and education by publishing worldwide. Oxford is a registered trade mark of
Oxford University Press in the UK and in certain other countries

© Elizabeth Frazer 2020

The moral rights of the author have been asserted

First Edition published in 2020

Impression: 1

Published in the United States of America by Oxford University Press
198 Madison Avenue, New York, NY 10016, United States of America

British Library Cataloguing in Publication Data
Data available

Library of Congress Control Number: 2020933063

ISBN 978-0-19-884861-5

Printed and bound in Great Britain by
Clays Ltd, Elcograf S.p.A.

Preface and Acknowledgements

Over many years many people have helped me with criticism, advice, information, and encouragement. I am particularly indebted to Deana Rankin and
Wes Williams who prompted me to think about political power and
Shakespeare, and staff at the Royal Shakespeare Company for invitations to
participate in performance discussions in Stratford, Warwick, and London.
The late Julia Briggs and the late Tony Nuttall both offered kind responses to
very early drafts. I spent time at Sciences Po Paris/Maison Suger in 2007,
where I drafted a short version. I'm particularly grateful to Sophie Duchesne
for unwavering support. Simon Palfrey and Ewan Fernie responded to that
draft and to plans that didn't come off; I'm grateful for their interest in that
project and for helpful criticisms. Meryl Altman, Teresa Bejan, Chris Brooke,
Emma Claussen, Charles Dannreuther, Mark Hausgaard, Robin Lane Fox,
Jane Lightfoot, Mary Nuttall, Will Poole, Mori Reithmayer, Caroline Wintersgill,
and Catherine Zuckert have helped with information or made comments on
chapters and papers. Audience members at seminars joint with Alan Finlayson
at PSA Manchester, 2009, University of Ulster Belfast, 2009, University of
Nottingham, London, 2009; and at presentations at University of Cambridge,
Contemporary Political Theory seminar, 2014, University of Oxford Political
Demonology conference, 2016, University of York, Myth Violence and Unreason
conference, 2016, University of Leeds, Interdisciplinary Approaches to Politics
conference, 2016, University of Oxford, Political Thought seminar, 2018,
made helpful comments and asked challenging questions. Alan Finlayson read
the draft chapters of this volume as I produced them, and has been, as ever,
generous as well as insightful in his responses. Elizabeth Mullett, Stephen
Mulhall, and Kim Hutchings read and commented on the complete draft. I'm
particularly grateful to Dominic Byatt, at Oxford University Press, and to
anonymous reviewers of the proposal and the draft. Part of Chapters 1 and 6
follow the analysis of 'Shakespeare's Politics', *Review of Politics*, 78(4), 2016:
503-22; Chapter 7 follows the analysis of 'Political Power and Magic', *Journal
of Political Power* 11(3), 2018: 359-77; and the whole book is a development of
Alan Finlayson and Elizabeth Frazer. 2010. 'Fictions of Sovereignty: Shakespeare, theatre, and the representation of rule', *Parliamentary Affairs*, 64: 233-47.

Contents

Note on Texts and Citations

Shakespeare text citations are all to *The Oxford Shakespeare*. That will make checking and cross-referencing for readers with other editions difficult in some cases—for example, the Oxford *King Lear* (2000) and *Timon of Athens* (2004) are not divided into what became the conventional five act form. So I have re-imposed act and scene numbers in the 'traditional' twentieth-century way for those plays, following scene breaks in the Open Source Shakespeare online edition (http://www.opensourceshakespeare.org), and cite these as well as the Oxford scene numbers (but note that this makes line number citations for these plays unreliable). So that readers can readily find out where in history we are, notes and bibliography citations first show the date (in some cases approximate) of the first publication of the work; where that is not a good guide to context, approximate date of composition is shown. Where date of composition or first publication is unknown or disputed, I have given the (approximate) birth and death dates of the author.

Introduction

Political Power and the Political Way

Politics and Politic in Shakespeare's Drama

The words 'politics' and 'political' don't feature in Shakespeare's dramas, although the associated adjective 'politic' does. That meant what it does now—to be politic means to be cautious, conciliatory, strategic, conscious of consequences, taking all (or as much as possible) into account. It applies to situations where an individual or group have to decide what to do and try to do it, given that other individuals and groups are interested, involved, or affected. State rulers should be politic; and politic conduct is advisable in other social contexts too, wherever there are conflicting interests, preferences, desires, or values, such as at work, in social organizations, or in families. The term might be used in physical settings like tricky terrains, although if you advised someone to be politic in picking their way across a heath you'd be using the word metaphorically. Shakespeare's tragic dramas stage scenes of politic deliberation which frame the disaster and mayhem that follows. In Act 1 of *Othello* [1.3.1-48] the duke and senators have a long discussion, in light of conflicting intelligence reports, of Turkish strategy and tactics, and their threat to Venetian interests. In Act 1 of *Hamlet* [1.2.16-39] Claudius, the king, considers with advisors and ambassadors the ins and outs of the relationships between the king of Norway and Norway's nephew the young Fortinbras (whose uncle, old Fortinbras, had lost territory in Poland to Claudius's predecessor, old king Hamlet). Young Fortinbras is on the war path, but Claudius has guessed—rightly at the time of the conversation—that his uncle the king will wish to reach an amicable settlement between the two states.

On the face of it, one of Shakespeare's key take away messages seems to be that politic conduct and wise rule can do all they can, but they are not equal to the passions of jealousy and rage, the psychological conflicts of resentment and wish for revenge, and the overwhelming mayhem of violence which leaves lead characters dead. The irony of this dramatic structure of politic deliberation followed by chaotic disaster is echoed by Shakespeare's characters'

Shakespeare and the Political Way. Elizabeth Frazer, Oxford University Press (2020). © Elizabeth Frazer.
DOI: 10.1093/oso/9780198848615.001.0001

use of the term 'politic'. King Lear's retinue of knights are causing trouble in the household where they live: 'A hundred knights?' exclaims his daughter Gonoril, 'Tis politic, and safe, to let him keep at point a hundred knights...' [*King Lear* 1.4].[1] Timon's servants are dismayed at the way Timon's so-called friends betray him when he is in need, refusing to repay his earlier generosity: 'The devil knew not what he did when he made man politic', remarks one, 'he crossed himself by 't: and I cannot think but, in the end, the villainies of men will set him clear. How fairly this lord strives to appear foul!...Of such a nature is his politic love' [*Timon of Athens* 3.3.26-35]. Hamlet has killed the court advisor Polonius, and is being maddeningly riddling about where he's put the body: 'Not where he eats, but where he is eaten', he replies: 'A certain convocation of politic worms are e'en at him' [*Hamlet* 5.1]. Usages like this outnumber straight ones such as Mortimer's chiding Richard Plantagenet: 'With silence, nephew, be thou politic...' [*I Henry VI* 2.5.101] In addition to ironic and literal usage, there are conventional ethical evaluations of 'politicians' as 'vile' [*I Henry IV* 1.3.240], as unvalourous and heretical [*Twelfth Night* 3.2.28-9], and so on.

Politics, in Shakespeare's world, then, is a kind of conduct, and politicians take on a certain kind of role. Shakespeare's characters certainly get caught up in 'politics', and caught out by political power and the political conduct of others. But it's a way of acting, not, as in later contexts, a field of life and action into which one can enter and from which one can exit. This is not a world in which 'going in to politics', or keeping out of it, or not taking any notice of it has the meaning it has later. In Shakespeare's, early modern, era, from a late modern standpoint, we see an early stage of what was later understood to be the separation of life and society into distinct 'fields', or 'spheres'. In modern political science the focus, almost invariably, is on a more or less established system of political power—often in the form of a 'state', sometimes an empire or similar—which is distinct from and intertwined with an economy (a system of exchange and circulation of goods and money); religion and culture; and more (or less) organized and institutionalized military and civil force and violence. States, societies, economies, and cultures map (but very imperfectly) onto territory, the borders of which are more or less contested or secure. 'States' accordingly are oriented outward, to rivalry, defence, expansion, conquest, and the like; as well as inwardly to the maintenance of order

---

[1] William Shakespeare. 1605/1997. *King Lear*, ed. R.A. Foakes (Bloomsbury Academic: London); this line does not occur in the Oxford edition: William Shakespeare. 1605 (comp.)/2000. *The History of King Lear*, ed. Stanley Wells (Oxford University Press: Oxford).

on the 'home' territory. The study of politics, in political science, focuses on the competition between parties, and their individual leaders, for the power to govern; on the efforts of governments to govern successfully—whatever that means—and to maintain the support and allegiance necessary for them to do so; and on the dissent and contestation of those who resist the existing order of authority. The explanation, and rights and wrongs, of every bit of this scheme have been and still are researched, theorized, and argued over.[2]

All the elements of such a scheme, and lots of the questions about it, are there in Shakespeare's dramas. Here are the settings for scenes of rulership, whether relatively successful ones like those of the Venetian duke and senators, or Claudius in Denmark; disastrous ones, like King Lear's division of his kingdom between two rivalrous sons-in-law [*King Lear* 1.1]; or ineffectual ones like the Prince of Verona's warning to the warring households to stop disturbing the public peace with their violence, or else [*Romeo and Juliet* 1.1.79–96]. The duke and senators in *Othello*, and the duke in *Merchant of Venice*, are concerned with their role of safeguarding Venice as a trading society. Shakespeare's dramas don't explicitly individuate 'the economy', 'the culture', 'the polity', 'the household', 'the military'. But, they do dramatize roles, distinguishing merchants from kings and from soldiers, fathers from senators and dukes. They show how things can go wrong when individuals muddle up their roles, but how, all the same, things must be muddled—kings are fathers, after all. In *Coriolanus* the clash between 'the military way' and 'the political way' is dramatized, dwelled on, metaphorized, philosophized, and debated. The result of the contest in the end, I think, is a draw, or perhaps a stalemate. But what's important, from the point of view of this book, is how the play dramatizes political conduct and political power (exemplified by Martius's mother Volumnia, the family friend Menenius, the citizens of Rome, the senators, and the tribunes of the people) in relation to the conduct of the courageous, ruthless, soldier (Martius, later called Coriolanus), and the dedicated housekeeper (his wife Virgilia).

So, by 'politics', were Shakespeare to have used the term, he would not have meant what readers of this book mean. However, what readers of this book mean, I am willing to bet, is vague. The meaning of 'politics' is vague for political theorists and thinkers, too, and is contested. When political scientists identify the state's power as 'political', or a question as a political one rather than some other kind, what does that mean? This question is, perhaps,

---

[2] Michael Mann. 1986/2012. *The Sources of Social Power*. Vol. 1: *A History of Power from the Beginning to* AD 1760 (Cambridge University Press: Cambridge).

even more contested than is the meaning of 'law' for legal theorists, or what is included in and what excluded from 'the economy' that economists model and study. Three kinds of puzzle and dispute arise. First, what does and what does not count as political? Second, is political conduct good, or bad, or neither? Third, what, if anything, is particular about political power, political institutions, and political conduct? I want to clarify these questions—not offer definite answers—in a preliminary way here.

To begin with where are 'the boundaries of politics'? After all, questions of leadership, authority, and domination (like those that are dramatized in *Othello* and *Hamlet*) and permitted or required styles of dissent, resistance, and opposition arise in friendship groups and in work places, in kin groups and households, in churches and clubs, as well as at the level of state or empire. 'Domestic' disputes and struggles recur in the plays discussed here, from Juliet's disobedience to her father's instructions regarding her marriage, to Lear's and his daughters' arguments about how his men behave indoors. Edmund, the illegitimate son of the Duke of Gloucester in *Lear*, rails to the theatre audience about the injustice of legitimacy laws and norms. Are these matters 'political'? Since such arguments began, and that, clearly, was before Shakespeare's plays were written and performed, and right up into the twenty-first century, some political thinkers argue definitely that using 'political' of such issues is, at best, metaphorical, as, I suggested, is 'politicly picking one's way across the heath'. However, there are two distinct responses from those who argue that here, if anywhere, is politics.

First, we can argue that issues such as the extent of children's obligation to obey parents are publicly relevant issues. Established views are likely to be reflected or enforced in state law, and in social and cultural norms. Individual practices add up to general and public cultures. Parent-child relationships are absolutely central to what kind of society we have, and to what kind of government and laws. At a certain threshold of contention arguments about these matters are political, in the sense that they are 'decided', among other ways, in processes of public discussion, legislation, and legal judgement, and pressure on the state. Second, we can argue that just as the production and exchange of goods and services like housework, spending money, food, income, and wealth within families are a significant element of the wider social and political economy, so contentions about power, who rules, who has authority, over what and whom—whatever the social setting—are political. This is what people mean when they say, vaguely to be sure, that politics is about power, and conversely that if something is about power it is political. In response to such arguments it has been, and is, in the power interests of many political thinkers and actors, from explicit patriarchalists to liberals and neo-republicans, to deny that such issues are political. It generally suits those who benefit from how things are, and have authority, if others don't argue the toss or ask questions and challenge their right to rule. Defenders of inequalities often attempt to depoliticize them: the legitimacy of some sons and not others has been justified in terms of religious doctrine; the exclusion of daughters from inheritance of property, or from the freedom to marry or live as they will, has been defined as natural and therefore beyond argument. Poverty and want can be theorized to be necessary, or an aspect of the natural workings of the world, and therefore simply to be accepted, not up for political argument.[3] This takes us to the matter of the rights and wrongs of political power and authority. First, authors of the kind of systematic treatise that Shakespeare conspicuously did not write have often discussed 'the ideal society', or asked how justice could be fixed on and achieved. Who should have the authority to rule? By what means is it okay for them to obtain the capacity to rule? Who may, and who may not, resist, disobey, or otherwise argue about ruling and being ruled? Shakespeare's plays dramatize these questions about how things ought to be. They often make satirical adversions to utopian pictures of perfectly just societies. They particularly focus on claims in support of hierarchy—that it is ordained by God, or is rooted in a metaphysical order. They dramatize, particularly, resistance to established orders or constitutions—the rise and organization of groups competing for governing power; daughters and sons who resist the authority of fathers; members of new classes who assert their new values and ways.

Second, there is the matter of the ethical quality, and the nature, of political power itself. For many modern thinkers, political power just is the power that states or their equivalent wield in order to maintain order and security (and perhaps justice), independently of the cultural and religious authorities of the society, and autonomously of the economic clout of those who profit from the economy. This means that it consists of state law (not religious law, or cultural authority), state organized military and civil force, the organized systems of fiscal and financial management and redistribution that are governed by public authority, and whatever normative and persuasive means states have to secure their authority—from appeals to divine ordination, to symbolic displays, or rational appeal to those who submit or are coerced. There are problems with this identification of political power with the power of the state.

[3] Nancy Fraser. 1989. 'Struggle over needs', *Unruly Practices: Power, Discourse and Gender in Contemporary Social Theory* (Polity Press: Oxford).

It doesn't specify what is particular about political power as opposed to the legal, economic, cultural, religious, military power, and so on from which it is distinguished. Modern societies spend a lot of time distinguishing between political power and the power of judges, and the extent to which judges may or should pronounce on the legality of political reasons and actions. Effective economic actors distance themselves from politics. It's widely considered to be a bad, or at least a problematic, thing if military leaders rule. It is argued that religious, or ethical, principles should not, properly, be suffused with political considerations. And so on.

The most cogent and coherent responses to these questions, in my under-standing, detach political power from the power of the state as such, and take the view that political power is a peculiar human capacity—the one that we have to make rules about rules, to use power to regulate power. It is the power we summon up when we not only resist authority, but argue about the grounds of it. In some political theory stories, this is the power whose use is rationally agreed upon by people to set up institutions and offices that secure the condi-tions for society, culture, economy, religion, and the rest. That is, it is the power that generates and underpins the state, but not only that—it generates and underpins lots of other organized social institutions and networks too. It is the power that some governments, some rulers, some individuals, some groups have to generate allegiance and to secure cooperation. People and groups who are politically skilled and resourced can 'command assent' to their policies and their rule—and this is independent of their command of means of violence, or economic clout, or religious authority. Critically, a polit-ical decision is one that secures assent in full cognizance of dissent—that is, agreement is secured in circumstances where not everyone agrees and some may be flatly opposed. Allegiance, cooperation, making rules about rules, set-ting up offices, resisting authority, arguing about the rights and wrongs of structures of power, competing for the power to govern—these are all typical human processes, which occur in all kinds of human groups.

Shakespeare and the Political Way

In my interpretation, Shakespeare's dramas frequently stage disputes about 'the political way' in a typically complicated multi-dimensional set of conten-tions. To begin with, the political way is put into contest with other ways—'the military way'; or the ways of market relations, trade, commodity consump-tion, and the valuing of things in terms of monetary value; or the associational and sociable (generally homosocial) life of taverns and streets. Political power, the power both of rulers and of those who contest their rule publicly, is set in contrast with religious authority, or with magic power. It is contrasted with the imperatives and standards of nature. The political life of royal courts, or of public conduct and contention of government, or open challenges to authority are pitted against the untrammelled freedom of the individual to live outside polity, outside society and law—often symbolized by the natural world of heaths and forests, often focused on the individual voluntarism of soul to soul and erotic love, or articulated by the reflexive, self-examining individual. At issue here are the merits of political life as opposed to other ways of life, the merits of political conduct as opposed to thinking in terms of monetary exchange, or religious truth, or supernatural power, or military heroism, or love.

Further, though, given that we accept that political conduct is a kind of conduct that has its place in societies, the question is raised what kind of conduct that is and should be. What, exactly, does 'the political way' involve? Etymology signals the descent of the concept 'politics' from the ideas of the classical Greek polis. In addition to the connotations of judiciousness and so on, politics is associated with 'publicness'. There's room for a good deal of dispute about what, exactly, it is for a thing to be public, but it tends to suggest some combination of being shared or common, being visible and audible, being open rather than hidden, known rather than secret. Such themes were attractive to early modern humanist and civic republican philosophers, and familiar generally to sixteenth-century thinkers from classical works which were central to grammar school learning. However, there are other ways of thinking about rule that emphasize rather what is mysterious and occult, not to be gazed upon or openly discussed. Some thinking about the sovereignty of queens or kings is like this: the sovereign is associated with divinity, or with magic. Maintaining the authority to rule, in this frame, is associated more with being glimpsed, from afar, rather than being heard and seen, let alone scrutinized or argued with. In Shakespeare's time, such association of the monarch with divinity, familiar from medieval custom, political theology, and doctrine, was developed in elements of the cult of Elizabeth I (reigned 1558-1603) and was keenly promoted by James I (reigned 1603-25). A good deal of the drama of Shakespeare's tragedies and problem plays turns on these opposing pulls of republican and openly contested, versus monarchical, divine right, views of the power to govern societies and states.

Whether in republics or monarchies, an alternative story about political conduct can also be told. This is based on Elizabethan readings of Niccolo

Machiavelli's (1469–1527) ideas about state stability and rule, and they have particular significance in Shakespeare's drama. In this book we meet a number of 'machiavellians'. For example, in *Othello* Iago is a character who is a by-word for clever, tricky, manipulation of appearances, for the capacity to appear good while doing evil, and for ruthlessness in bringing about the downfall of his enemies. Shakespeare's Richard Gloucester (later Richard III) uses the term as condemnation: 'Alencon! that notorious Machiavel! It dies, an if it had a thousand lives' [*I Hen VI* (composed 1591) 5.5.74–5]; and he also uses it of himself: 'I can add colours to the chameleon, change shapes with Proteus for advantages, and set the murd'rous Machiavel to school. Can I do this, and cannot get a crown?' [*3 Hen VI* (composed 1592) 3.2.191–4]. The 'Machiavel' was a stock stage character throughout the Elizabethan era. More widely, the devilish 'Machiavelli' had a prominent part in Elizabethan popular and political imagination—'it became as acceptable to call the devil Machiavellian as it was to call Machiavelli diabolical.'[4] All this was due, probably, less to the distribution of Machiavelli's own writings than to the very popular 'Anti-Machiavel' by Innocent Gentillet,[5] translated into English in 1602 but widely circulated in the original French before that, and the widespread practice, which Gentillet participated in, of rendering Machiavelli's *Prince* (published posthumously in 1532) as a series of pithy maxims, taken out of context. In drawing on the tradition of 'the Machiavel' Shakespeare was deploying a vague, but very familiar, and enduring commonplace.[6]

The theme of 'machiavellian' and shadowy advisers, who counsel subterfuge and dissimulation, is common wherever there is government. Those who design and determine party strategy in modern polities are assumed to use hidden persuasion techniques and other ways that operate beyond the conscious cognition of those whose decisions are affected. Counsellors are also assumed to disguise and conceal themselves—the machiavellian art includes the appearance of effortless wisdom and accurate judgement. So the schemes, technique, and stratagems of the advisors are not, themselves, publicly observable. It can be suspected that the ostensible ruler is not really

  [4] George Bull. ed. 1532/1961. 'Introduction', in Niccolo Machiavelli, *The Prince* (Penguin: Harmondsworth), p. 9.
  [5] Innocent Gentillet. 1576/1602. *A Discourse upon the meanes of wel governing and maintaining in good peace, a kingdome, or other principalitie, against N. Machiavell [in his Il Principe]*, trans. S. Patericke (A. Islip: London).
  [6] N.W. Bawcutt. 1971. 'Policy, Machiavellianism, and the Earlier Tudor Drama', *English Literary Renaissance*, 1: 195–209; Michael Shortland. 1988. 'Setting Murderous Machiavel to School: Hypocrisy in politics and the novel', *Journal of European Studies*, xviii: 93–120; Sydney Anglo. 2005. *Machiavelli—The First Century: Studies in Enthusiasm, Hostility and Irrelevance* (Oxford University Press: Oxford).

in charge, but shadowy advisers are effectively ruling in their stead. Part of the art of the modern political party is, first, to claim that party interests are, actually, the public interest; second, to promote the ostensible, but not necessarily the actual, inclusion of members and supporters into positions of influence and decision making. This, for lots of people, is what 'politics' means, and it is why politics has a bad name, and why politicians are suspect: 'like a scurvy politician [who] seems to see the things thou dost not', as Lear chides [4.6/S.20:159–61].

Shakespeare's dramas, in my interpretation, play with rival ideas of the nature of the political way. First, authority to govern is frequently presented as a divine gift, or a metaphysically ordained order. The political way is the way of the wise, Christian, prince. Second, the sign of authority to govern is frequently symbolized, or depicted as, the capacity to use rightful, honorable violence—to prevail in open physical armed combat. The political way is based on physical might. Third, though, the governing art is presented as closer to the occult arts of the magician. The political way is that of the trickster, the machiavellian, or the magus ruler. All of these are put into play against the fourth, radical, idea that political power is a collectively based human property, and political organization a straightforward human product, the kind of thing that people will make, given the resources. The egalitarian idea of political power is that people together could deploy a non-violent power in order to regularize their lives together, to permit production and exchange, and reproduction of human life, to defend territory, to settle social disputes by legal judgement. People acting in concert construct the structures that govern them, and can reconstruct them when that is needful.

Republican thinkers, who focus on the possibilities and actualities of 'self-rule', spend a good deal of time thinking about what social relationships would have to be like if this fourth kind of polity were to be possible and actual. Central to ideal inter-citizen relations in this tradition is the idea of friendship. Not kinship, which is unchosen. Not employment or service such as servants render to those who pay or keep them. Not the bondage that means that apprentices and vassals are tied to a lord. Not straightforward commercial exchange. Friendship transcends both convenience and necessity. Friendship is egalitarian—there are levels of inequality that make friendship effectively impossible between two people. The ideal of friendship as the fundamental political relation pervades pacific versions of political order.

Another, less harmonious but still republican, vision of polity centres on freedom and contention. The story is that people, together and separately, seek freedom; and people collectively have a tendency not to tolerate abuse or lack of freedom. If elite governments press down too hard there will be resistance, and people will energetically defend freedom and rights, not to mention welfare levels. This contentious view of politics can be conducive to the sceptical view that 'agreement' among people to legitimate, regularize, and comply with governing institutions is only a recognition of the unevadable power of violence. On this view, generalized friendliness across a society is a sham. The 'sovereign' who achieves power is the one, or the group, that can successfully dominate a territory and the people and resources within it. So-called assent is more often submission. But, dissent is always possible; and can be organized as oppositional political power.

Shakespeare was not a systematic political thinker. But the questions of who counts in a polity, the legitimation of ruling authority, the possibilities of friendship as the basis of political relations in societies that are fissured by class, race, sex, and religion, the fate of those who are at the margins of the economy, kept there because they are materially valued as dispossessed sources of labour, but not valued as citizens - these are all explicitly thematized in his dramas. The political ideals and the political puzzles that he dramatizes and tackles were explicitly argued over by classical thinkers including Aristotle (384-322 BCE), and especially Cicero (106-43 BCE) whose texts were studied in Elizabethan grammar schools. Classical Greek and Latin sources were refracted and challenged by Christian thinkers who developed accounts of the proper relationship between civil and religious authority, and the ideal of the Christian prince—ideas that were very much part of political common sense even for individuals who did not have first hand acquaintance with the works of St Augustine (354-430 CE), or the work of early modern humanists such as Desiderius Erasmus (1466-1536). Machiavelli attacked the ideal of the Christian prince—this was one reason for his vilification—but also challenged a picture of social and political harmony that can be associated with readings of Aristotle. His classical sources, with their stories of dearth and riot, and popular claims to participate in the government of the Roman republic, are among Shakespeare's sources too for his dramas. As we shall see, Shakespeare can be understood also as a key articulator of a developing scepticism—about what we can know, who and what we can trust—which was rigorously set out, in the decades after his life, by Rene Descartes (1596-1650) and Thomas Hobbes (1588-1679), among other philosophers.

The political questions that Shakespeare plays with, especially in light of scepticism about the claims of established authorities, and in light of the claims of justice in worlds of exploitation, oppression, and violence, are still the questions of political theory. The problems that we meet in Shakespeare's dramas are wrestled with by thinkers associated with the developing tradition of republicanism; by those who later developed and promoted the claims of individual liberty and right that we associate with liberalism; by those who focus on how to dismantle structures of exploitation and oppression and achieve the egalitarian justice that we associate with modern socialism; and by the feminist challengers of all forms of hierarchical, sex- or gender-based authority whether conservative, liberal, republican, or socialist. The category republican, and the rival ideas of monarchy, clearly and explicitly were meaningful to Shakespeare. The other three are more modern categories. The study of political thought focuses on conceptual change—on how arguments about authority, say, or sovereignty, cannot be presumed to be about exactly the same thing across contexts and times. I discuss some tricky issues of interpretation in what follows. But the claims of individuals against established social and political authorities; the claims of women against men; and the opposing pulls of the egalitarian social justice later associated with socialism, and the established stable social order ever prized by conservatives, are puzzles that were recognizable to Shakespeare, and which turn up as themes, or as structures, in his plots. I emphasize these problems as puzzles. My aim is absolutely not to ask why, for instance, Shakespeare falls short according to the lights of modern or post-modern feminism, or socialism, or theories of freedom. The point of examining Shakespeare's treatments of the puzzles of political power is to ask why what seems to have made sense to him did make sense, and to examine how it was that what evidently was taken for granted was so, and why what are presented as problems are problems. This is an important element of the method of critical theory as that has developed since the mid-twentieth century. It is also to take advantage of his undoubted sensitivity to power, and his insight into the paradoxes and puzzles of political rule.

The treatment of Shakespeare and politics here, then, is somewhat different from a good many scholarly and critical studies that can be gathered under that heading. Much analysis of and commentary on the politics of Shakespeare's drama has focused on where the weight of his sympathy lies—with the oppressed, exploited, but nevertheless potentially tumultuous, claims-making people? Or with the claims of aristocratic fitness to rule, or of divinely ordained sovereignty? In this book, I consider less whether he is reactionary or revolutionary, proto-feminist or standard-issue misogynist, rather I try to emphasize the way that staging political dramas—about who should rule, how they should rule, the justification of their rule, and the form their rule takes (violence or agreement, occult power or open authority)—draws theatre audiences and readers into debate. Shakespeare's plays are famously multi-vocal, and complicated; there is a great deal of noise in relation to signal; indeed, which is signal and which is noise is a problem that readers and audiences have to struggle with. Getting involved in a Shakespeare play, especially in performance, in a theatre surrounded by fellow audience members, takes us beyond images and pictures of power to involvement in interpretation, debate, contention, and judgement.

Political Readings of Shakespeare's Dramas

In the chapters that follow, I set out political readings of (some of) Shakespeare's dramas. Not all of them, obviously: in particular, I do not here analyse the 'history plays', nor most of the 'comedies', and only one of the 'late romances' (if that is what it is)—*The Tempest*. My selection centres on 'the tragedies' with their stories of greatness (whether actual or possible) and fall on the part of a hero who is assailed by complex arrays and concatenations of forces, of only some of which he has any glimmer of understanding, among which are the strengths and the weaknesses of his own character. But analysis of the 'politics' of *Macbeth*, *King Lear*, *Hamlet*, and *Coriolanus*, and the development of my view of the way Shakespeare plays, as I have outlined above, with the merits and demerits of 'the political way' in competition with other ways, and also explores rival accounts of the nature of political power and conduct, has led me to include three plays that are uneasily comedic in their structure (in that order is regained in the end) while they deal with themes of the destruction of human beings that are usually associated with tragedy (the destruction of Shylock in *Merchant of Venice*, the enslavement of Caliban in *The Tempest*) or with conduct that is less action and more machination (Vincentio in *Measure for Measure*).

All of the plays I analyse have an explicitly, and conventionally, political frame: Othello's service to the state of Venice as commander in Cyprus (Chapter 1); Duke Vincentio's temporary abdication of his office (*Measure for Measure*, Chapter 2); Martius's run for the office of consul at a time of public contention over food policy, in *Coriolanus* (Chapter 3); the disruption of civic peace in a city republic by feuding families (*Romeo and Juliet*, Chapter 4); King Lear's retirement from office and his division of the ancient kingdom of Britain between two rivalrous sons-in-law (Chapter 5); legal disputes and contentions over justice, and the problem of the friendly basis of political relations, in republics, in *Merchant of Venice* and *Timon of Athens* (Chapter 6);

Macbeth's reliance on magic to achieve, and justify, his regicide, and Prospero's loss of his dukedom to a usurper and his regaining of it by magic (*Macbeth* and *Tempest*, Chapter 7); regicide, usurpation, and the dispossessed Prince's vengeance, in the midst of inter-state territorial dispute, in *Hamlet* (Chapter 8).

It is common for critics to take the view that the frame might well be political, as I have described, but these summaries of Shakespeare's plays are mistaken to the point of perversity. Focusing on politics is precisely to miss the drama's main point, as if one stood in front of a great and famous oil painting, and examined and spoke only of the frame, or the wall behind. The conventionally political elements could be subtracted, and we would still be left with profound human stories of psychological conflict, inter-personal contention, emotional pain, impossible ethical dilemmas, and destructive social, natural, and supernatural forces. Othello (for instance) could be a successful bank manager and the drama would still work: he could be an incomer to a village, or a new member of a sports team, and the resentment, jealousy, sexual ambivalence, communicative failures, murder, and suicide would be no less plausible, and would add up to a tragic drama of genius.

In my analysis, however, the conventionally political setting, while framing tragedy or problematic comedy with all their ethical dilemmas, psychological confusions, and emotional conflicts as they, obviously, do is also the signal that a deeper set of puzzles about political power are significant in what follows. The conventional settings of sovereign governmental authority, competitions for the authority to govern, and challenges to political order lead us to a set of questions about how governmental authority can cope with deep social conflict, about how the human political power to challenge established authority fares when it is met with violence, or economic clout, or religious authority, or magic. The plays ask whether an open political way of conduct—voiced argument, public persuasive speech, protest about how things are organized— is possibly productive in a world in which some are ducking and diving, plotting and planning, setting traps and pulling off tricks. They also ask whether the desire for a life free of political power—in seclusion, say, or just being left to get on with buying and selling and making a living—is a proper desire in a world in which politics might not be optional.

These dramas problematize and play with a range of kinds of power that human beings institutionalize and exert over one another. Patriarchal authority, which is often brought into close relation with republican or monarchical sovereign authority (Chapters 1, 4, 5, 6, 8); sexual domination, and resistance to it (Chapter 2); violence, whether 'civil' or military (Chapters 3, 4); open public speech and reason, which is often brought into close proximity with occult trickery and manoeuvring (Chapters 1, 2); religious authority used for political purposes, or magic, or, at any rate, a reputation for it (Chapters 2, 7); the egalitarian but also rivalrous and antagonistic relations of friendliness and enmity (Chapter 6). Apart from the ironies of 'politic' reasoning and conduct that I have already mentioned, I don't believe that Shakespeare's dramas give us any one synoptic or evaluative view of political power, reason, or conduct. However, unsurprisingly, the closeness of theatrical drama to political action, and the role of the team effort to produce appearances, to incorporate audiences into actions, to command a hearing, to generate applause, both in artistic theatre and in political life, is a pressing theme. So also is that, despite the irony, despite the ineffectuality, or the violent over-reach of uses of sovereign authority, despite the way economic and material interests tend to be undisturbed by either comic or tragic upheavals in the structure of power and authority, despite the pulls of natural human life outwith the ambit of social or political power, Shakespeare's dramas do emphasize that 'the political way'— the way of people acting in concert, in open process and relations, to bring about change or to stabilize justice—is a way, and it is one that we would do well to follow when we may.

My political theory reading of Shakespeare, then, goes beyond the terms of debates by early modern political thinkers to enduring puzzles about political power that people still frown over. Some of Shakespeare's depictions of state and social power uncannily anticipate later philosophical pictures. In some cases, later theorists explicitly cite Shakespeare's dramas as a resource for the development of their insights. In others, it's closer to later theorists finding in Shakespeare's imagery and tropes, and in the structures of the plots, vivid dramatizations of class struggle, sex war, inter-generational conflict, inter-state war (of course), ruthless and veiled machinations in pursuit of the power to govern, claims of free public speech, assertion of individual right and will— all problems of political theory, classical, early modern, and later. Shakespeare was a canny observer of the political scene, and a sensitive interpreter of the subtleties of power, both covert and open. So, we can treat his work as a body of political theory, beyond the more familiar traditions of asking what the plays say, exactly, about the questions such as the divine ordination of sovereignty, or the rights of aristocratic authority, or the justification of popular protest, or the virtues and vices of republican as opposed to monarchical constitutions, or the nature of gender and sex distinction.

The method I use to explicate, and defend, this project of political theory, is to tell the stories of some of the dramas as political stories. Sometimes individual characters stand for political positions (for instance, Kent, in *King Lear*, can be analysed as defender and spokesperson for aristocratic values and rights). More often, though, the contestations about what political power is and should be are not emblematically personified like this, but lie in the structure of the plot and the workings to dramatic resolution, as well as in the textual imagery and metaphor. So, the way to show this is to tell the story. This might be irksome to readers who have close knowledge already of characters, plot, scene structure, and text. But for others, I hope, whose prior expertise is more hazy and undeveloped, it will anchor my interpretation of the plays so that rival interpretations (some of which I cite as I go), and also the enduring puzzles of political theory, are intelligible.

I do not want to be understood as asserting that my interpretations of the plays are 'what Shakespeare meant'. Any one human individual could not possibly mean or intend all the connotations, allusions, citations, denotations, allegories, metaphors, images, inferences, and implications that are found in their texts. That they were not the content of one individual's head does not invalidate them. We cannot intend everything we mean. Indeed, this is a theme of which Shakespeare seems to have been quite cognizant, because it arises in connection with the words and utterances of characters, and forms part of the plots, of the plays analysed here. And the Shakespeare who is cognizant, and writes into his dramas, the gaps and slippages between what is said, what is received, what is signified, and 'the meaning' of what is said, doesn't have (for my purposes at least) to be a single individual at all. This is not to say that I don't believe there was a historical person designated by that name who authored the plays and poetry. But we do have to take the plays we have as something like approximations. A line that got me thinking about Shakespeare's ideas of politics and political power is Gonoril's: 'A hundred knights! Tis politic, and safe, to let him keep at point a hundred knights!' in *King Lear*. To my dismay, when I standardized my references to the Oxford Shakespeare editions, I found this line wasn't there! It is not in the first Quarto edition (first published 1608);[7] but it does appear in versions which are based in part on the later Folio versions (1623 and later seventeenth-century editions).[8]

Scholars tell us that some of the plays and scenes are definitely co-authored, for instance, in this volume, *Timon of Athens*, part of which was written by Thomas Middleton. More generally, there has to be doubt about 'authorship'

---

[7] William Shakespeare. 1605/1996. *The First Quarto of King Lear*, ed. Jay L. Halio (Cambridge University Press: Cambridge).

[8] Shakespeare, *King Lear*, 1605/1997; Open Source Shakespeare: http://opensourceshakespeare.org/

in the sense of the question what, exactly, was written by Shakespeare and what is due to actors' and stage managers' emendations, compositors' errors and corrections, whether we take the Quarto or Folio versions as the more authoritative. 'Shakespeare's writing', for my purposes, is the texts that we read (and see performed); 'Shakespeare's thinking' is an inference from those texts, and 'Shakespeare's world' also an inference—much contested by theorists and scholars—and we shall never know how it relates to whatever was going on in the head of the historical William Shakespeare.

Shakespeare's dramas do many things. They play with poetic forms and produce great poetry. They tell mythical and historical stories in ways that disrupt history and re-present myth. Shakespearean myth has a prominent place in popular understandings of the history of Britain, especially of its queens and kings and wars. The dramas tell stories of girl meets boy, taking to a new stage what later became the traditions of 'romantic comedy' and 'tragic love'. They consider the nature of natural and supernatural forces and their places in human lives. And there is also a political imagination at work in his art. The plays consider the nature of social and political forces, against the background of agents enforcing and resisting established structures of authority and power. What form should political power take? Who should exercise it? In particular, how does it and how should it interact with natural and supernatural forces, and the social processes of kinship, friendship, and economy? His dramas are notable for the way chaos is restored to order in the comedies, and how order descends into chaos and death in the tragedies. So the dramas both draw on and generate elements of what political and social theorists now call a 'public, political, imaginary'. Shakespeare shows us pictures of political power, how it works, what is wrong and right with it, and how it might be.

1

Political Power and *Othello*

Politics and *Othello*

I begin with *Othello* (composed about 1604) because it is a drama that has
seemed to some modern critics to cry out for psychological reading: what is
it about the character of Othello the man that accounts for the seeming
ease, and the speed, of his destruction by an admittedly evil mischief maker?
Ethically, it can be read as a study of good and evil. More subtly, it meditates
on breakdown of trust, failure of communication, and the moral importance
of keeping the whole person, and the whole social relationship, in view in
our encounters and dealings with others. These psychological and ethical
themes can make 'the politics' of the play look irrelevant. In this chapter,
I try to show two things. First, we can admit that this play is a peerless
study in psychology and emotion, and, for the sake of argument that that is
the proper focus of critical and interpretive concern, but also insist that we
can't begin to understand Othello's psychology without understanding the
political power structure that shapes it, and shapes his sexual expectations
and his jealousy. Second, if we remove our attention from the politics of
patriarchy, from the political formation of social distinctions of race and
class, from the power of politic and sovereign government, from machiavellian
trickery, and from the political value of public speech, then a good deal of the
structure and the substance of the plot, the prose, the poetry, the character,
and the action fizzles away.

Othello is a notably heroic character, mature, distinguished, respected, and
valued in a society (early modern Venice) to which he is an incomer. Othello
is a moor—so he is called in the play's title, and so he is referred to by other
characters [1.1.32, 39, 163; 1.2.57, 1.3.47, 188, 289]. He falls in love with a
young woman—Desdemona—and they elope and marry without the approval
of her father, Brabantio. At the outset of the dramatic action, Iago, a subordinate to Othello in the military, who resents Othello's distinction and feels
displaced by the outsider, followed by Roderigo, a rival suitor to Desdemona,
stir things up by anonymously alerting Brabantio to the elopement [1.1.74ff].

Shakespeare and the Political Way. Elizabeth Frazer, Oxford University Press (2020). © Elizabeth Frazer.
DOI: 10.1093/oso/9780198848615.001.0001

He reports the abuse and theft of his daughter to the city authorities, accusing Othello [1.3.60-5, 100-7]. Meanwhile, however, the Venetian government has an important job for Othello, who is to be appointed to head the government and security of a colony (Cyprus, a key trading port for Venetian merchants) which is threatened by a rival power (the Turks) [1.2.36-47; 1.3.1-40]. The Duke mollifies Brabantio, approves the marriage, and Othello and Desdemona are asked to leave for their new post immediately [1.3.273-6].

Racial and ethnic categories are invariably unclear, with vague reference and uncertain boundaries, but there is no doubt that, although the earliest accounts of the play don't mention race, Shakespeare here dramatized blackness in relation to the dominant white culture; Othello is African in European Venice; Desdemona is white, the daughter of a Venetian citizen, and he black.[1] Black and white, the racialization of ethnic diversity, was emerging as a social thing, and, just as importantly, as an ideological one, serving to justify judgements and practices of white superiority. Fascination with the exotic and the strange served to emphasize the rightness of European norms. It also, though, offered a frame through which humanist ethicists could show how strange European ways are. Thomas More's *Utopia* (1516) was a sixteenth-century best seller about an imaginary society—the narrative poses the question why English society had such high levels of crime and cruel punishment, and also represented a possible harmonious and happy society.[2] Montaigne's essay 'Of the Caniballes' (1580) (which, scholars agree, Shakespeare had read—there are many affinities between Montaigne's thought and Shakespeare's[3]) constructs a vision of peace, a new golden age, in a new world, where there is no fear of punishment.[4] The exotic or strange, with racial difference as a critical idea making these intelligible, generated in European thinkers and society members also hostility, violence, or at least anxiety about the integrity of state and society. Characters in the play, including Othello himself, articulate the

---

[1] Wilhelm Hortmann. 2002. 'Shakespeare on the Political Stage in the Twentieth Century', in Sarah Stanton and Stanley Wells (eds.), *The Cambridge Companion to Shakespeare on Stage* (Cambridge University Press: Cambridge), p. 216; Michael Neill. ed. 2006. 'Introduction', William Shakespeare, *Othello* (Oxford University Press: Oxford), pp. 1, 8.

[2] Thomas More. 1516/2002. *Utopia* (Cambridge University Press: Cambridge).

[3] Stephen Orgel. ed. 1987. 'Introduction', William Shakespeare, *The Tempest* (Oxford University Press: Oxford): Appendix; Hugh Grady. 2000. 'Shakespeare's Links to Machiavelli and Montaigne: Constructing intellectual modernity in early modern Europe', *Comparative Literature*, 52: 119-42; Peter Mack, *Reading and Rhetoric in Montaigne and Shakespeare* 2010, Bloomsbury Academic; William M. Hamlin. 2013. *Montaigne's English Journey: Reading the Essays in Shakespeare's Day* (Oxford University Press: Oxford).

[4] Michel de Montaigne. 2006c. 'Of the Caniballes', in John Florio (trans. and ed.), *The Essayes*, Vol. 1 (The Folio Society: London).

black:foul, white:fair scheme. Elizabeth I issued proclamations to the effect that there were excessive numbers of 'blackamoors' in England.[5]

Othello tells fascinating travellers' tales, about strange lands and strange men [1.3.128-45]. But, of course, he is part strange himself.[6] Brabantio thinks he must have used witchcraft to ensnare Desdemona [1.3.65, 105-7]. Brabantio, Roderigo, and Iago are crudely racist in their speech about Othello [1.1.66-7, 86-9; 1.2.71-80], and the marriage, the sexual relationship, between white Desdemona and black Othello is a particular obsession [1.1.108-13, 129-36]. The Duke and senators are respectful; but they refer to him as 'the moor' as often as by his name [e.g. 1.3.48, 289]. The arc of the play is that Othello is 'the moor' in the opening scenes, he is personalized and elevated in the middle acts (Desdemona most often refers to him as 'my lord'), and then at the end, disgraced, he is once again 'the moor' [5.2.165, 239, 365]. The language racializes the story, as well as more generally signalling origins, belonging or not belonging. Iago refers to Cassio as a 'Florentine'—signalling Cassio's book-learning [I.1.18-25]; ironically he is a Florentine himself, as Cassio remarks (ironically) [III.1.39-40]. This is a nice Shakespearean disruption of clear views of who belongs where, and how origins relate to worth.

Cassio is Othello's lieutenant, and Iago his ensign.[7] Iago resents Cassio and Othello alike, and recruits Roderigo, a weak character and victim of Iago's exploitation, into a plan to bring them down [2.1.255-73, 2.3.349-54, 4.2.174-244, 5.1.1-24]. His intentions to 'play the villain' and 'enmesh them all' [2.3.321-47, 367-73] are made clear to the theatre audience. Playing a friendly, trustworthy fellow, Iago lures Cassio into drinking too much and fighting, provoking Othello's anger [2.3.30-57, 127-40, 145-56, 160-80]. Iago advises Cassio tfo seek Desdemona's help and mediation with Othello [2.3.301-20]. He succeeds in planting in Othello's mind the possibility that Desdemona is false [3.3.33-40]— after all, she deceived her father in order to marry Othello [3.3.209-11]—and Othello's suspicion and jealousy grows. He asks Iago to obtain 'ocular proof' of Desdemona's infidelity [3.3.361-5, 396-8]. Meanwhile, Iago's wife Emilia, maid and companion to Desdemona, at his request takes, and gives to him, a handkerchief of Desdemona's, one that had been a gift from Othello [3.3.293-302, 3.4.54-67]. He plants the handkerchief in Cassio's room [3.3.323-4].

---

[5] Kim F. Hall. 1992/2004. 'Guess Who's Coming to Dinner? Colonisation and miscegenation in The Merchant of Venice', in Emma Smith (ed.), *Shakespeare's Comedies* (Blackwell Publishing: Oxford.; Emily C. Bartels. 2006. 'Too Many Blackamoors: Deportation, discrimination, and Elizabeth I', *Studies in English Literature 1500-1900*, 46: 305-22.; Neill, 'Intro', 2006: 26-8.

[6] Neill, 'Intro', 2006: App. F.

[7] Neill, 'Intro', 2006: App. F, 461-4.

Othello's conviction that Desdemona is false grows with shocking rapidity. As with other Shakespeare plays, elapsed time, as opposed to chronology, is vague and contradictory, and is confounded with psychological and emotional processes.[8] The action seems to be compressed into very few days, and events to move with a rapidity that reflects and symbolizes the violence of the culmination. But, if we take into account the speed of communications and travel—messages and visitors arrive from Venice [4.1.205-12]—and the usual timescale for development of social relationships, we must conclude that the plot develops over a much longer period. This temporal ambiguity matters because there is doubt, in Shakespeare's play, whether Othello's and Desdemona's marriage has actually been consummated.[9] On one reading of the calendar and clock time their elopement is immediately punctuated with the summons to see the Duke, their immediate departure for Cyprus by separate ships, Iago's mischievous engineering of the fight [2.3.127-40], Othello's arousal to jealousy, and Iago's staged scene which gives Othello the impression that Cassio has the lost handkerchief [3.3.70-163, 433-9]. Othello is now murderous, numb—'my heart is turned to stone' [4.1.175-6]—and when Desdemona pleads for Cassio he hits her [4.1.231].

Obviously, we might think that time elapsed is the least interesting aspect of all this. How long it all takes is of next to no significance compared to the moral and psychological force of the change in Othello. Psychological readings can understand Iago the character as an aspect of Othello's own personality— after all what messages we receive from others can be less a function of what they actually say, or intend to say, than of our own filters and feelings, our propensity to interpret one way rather than another.[10] Whether from inside Othello's head or from outside, Iago sets out to change Othello [3.3.329].[11] Focus on Othello, his psychological conflict and struggle with himself, his transformations, his emotional turmoil, his estrangement from those who are on his side, is obviously encouraged by the sheer prominence of his role in the drama.[12] Like other Shakespearean tragic heroes, the number of lines the actor has to speak, the number of scenes in which they are present, the difficulty of representation of inner turmoil make these roles challenges for actors with stamina, experience, and exceptional dramatic skills. Where theatre and

---

[8] Janet Adelman. 1992. *Suffocating Mothers: Fantasies of Origin in Shakespeare's Plays* (Routledge: London); Geoffrey Bullough. ed. 1973. 'Othello', *Narrative and Dramatic Sources of Shakespeare*, Vol. 7 (Routlege and Kegan Paul: London), pp. 228–32; Neill, 'Intro', 2006: 2–23, 434–44.

[9] Adelman, *Suffocating Mothers*, 1992: 271, n.47.

[10] Neill, 'Intro', 2006: 92–4.

[11] Jonathan Bate. 1993. *Shakespeare and Ovid* (Clarendon Press: Oxford), p. 181.

[12] Neill, 'Intro', 2006: 71.

acting are organized around a star system, with famous actors taking title roles, the focus on the individual character is undoubtedly exaggerated by the charisma of the star and their prominence on stage. But even in ensemble companies the sheer challenge of the eponymous roles mean that audience attention, and thus interpretive emphasis, focuses on individual character and criticism on the performance of lead actors. The speed of the transformations in fictional time is far less significant than the visible and audible transformations achieved by the actor in audience time. Of course time is all awry in theatre and cinema: whether we think of *Othello* as spanning a period of weeks or a couple of days is far less significant than the artistic, literary, and theatrical achievement of producing any social time as a two- or three-hour performance.

From the psychological, and the political, points of view, though, the question whether Desdemona and Othello actually do have sexual intercourse, and therefore the ambiguity of calendar, emotional, social, and theatre times, matters. Stanley Cavell (1926-2018) focuses on the double bind of Othello's shame. As he comes to see himself through Iago's frame, he is shamed if his marriage is consummated, and shamed if it is not.[13] Othello's grief, fury—whatever violent emotion he is gripped by—focuses on Desdemona's sexual virtue [3.3.347-9; 3.3.347-9; 4.2.20-3, 385-90]. Othello tells her that Cassio has confessed to having sex with her (Othello is quite wrong, but Iago has engineered appearances to trap Cassio and convince Othello that this is the case [4.1.89-140]), he determines that she must die [4.1.175-6, 197-204], and kills her by suffocation [5.2.23-86]. Desdemona, in advance of Othello coming to their chamber, has her wedding sheets put on the bed [4.2.104-6, 4.3.20]. An obvious interpretation is that this is Desdemona's opportunity to prove her virginity, and hence her innocence of fornication; but that supposes that she has not had sexual intercourse with Othello either. Cavell's interpretation of the ethics of the play focuses on how Othello goes wrong two ways. He equates (female) virtue with sexual innocence, and constructs Desdemona, in his imagination, as perfect, as pure, meaning 'sexually pure' and 'non-carnal', failing to treat with her fully as a whole person.[14] He also demands certainty about her qualities.

Cavell's reading of *Othello*, like his readings of other Shakespeare tragedies, emphasizes the philosophical theme of 'doubt', the focus, rather than on how things are and how they should be, on what we can know. The questioning

[13] Stanley Cavell. 1979/2003. 'Othello and the Stake of the Other', *Disowning Knowledge in Seven Plays of Shakespeare*, updated edn (Cambridge University Press: Cambridge), pp. 130-5.
[14] Cavell, 'Othello', 1979/2003: 134-7; Adelman, *Suffocating Mothers*, 1992: 273, n.48.

of claims to knowledge, dwelling on how the way things appear is not a good guide to how they are, was a long established philosophical and cultural theme—very evident in Shakespeare's plots and stagecraft.[15] Rene Descartes's very clear articulation of the theme was published in 1641.[16] In Cavell's view this emphasis, in philosophy and ethics, leads to a new kind of estrangement between individuals in society; it disrupts and undermines the security of shared understanding between people who live together and share a world. Shakespeare's plots frequently turn on such dilemmas—on mistakes about appearances, on miscommunications. Othello's demand for 'ocular proof' of Desdemona's infidelity, on the one hand, endorses the unique epistemological significance of first person, sense-based experience as the guarantor of knowledge. Paradoxically on the other hand, it serves only to enmesh him further in Iago's web of manufactured appearances, false professions of loyalty, and lies [3.3.415-27, 462-70]. He is estranged from Desdemona by suspicion and jealousy, an emotional burden which he cannot share with her.

He is distanced by what Lisa Jardine (1944-2015) calls the 'peculiarly patriarchal question': can this woman be trusted?[17] Feminist theory focuses on the way such demand for certainty involves extraordinary amounts of discipline and constraint of girls and women. The distinction between women's virtue and men's, the importance of virginity as the sign of female virtue and as a good which is exchanged between men—father and potential husband—in patriarchal societies and polities, are themes that Shakespeare's characters obsess about at length, whether in serious suspicion about the value of women as goods, in violence, in doubt about their genuine (biological) paternity of women's children, in jest, or in more or less encoded slurs—designed mostly to get a laugh from a collusive audience—on women characters in particular and women in general.[18]

The question whether Desdemona and Othello do consummate the marriage—and therefore the matter of time in the plot—matters also if we focus on the intersection of racial and sexual relations in the play. Doubt and scepticism about other people intersect with fears and hostility, and with the conflicting sexual feelings that are so often disclosed by individuals' actions

---

[15] Stanley Cavell. 2003. *Disowning Knowledge in Seven Plays of Shakespeare*, updated edn (Cambria Press: Cambridge), pp. 3–5.

[16] Rene Descartes. 1641/1954. 'Meditations on First Philosophy: Wherein are demonstrated the existence of God and the distinction of soul from body', in Elizabeth Anscombe and Peter Thomas Geach (eds.), *Descartes Philosophical Writings* (Thomas Nelson and Sons: Sunbury on Thames).

[17] Lisa Jardine. 1983/1989. *Still Harping on Daughters: Women and Drama in the Age of Shakespeare* (Columbia University Press: New York), pp. 68–9, 74–5.

[18] Jardine, *Harping on Daughters*, 1983/1989: 120–2.

and words. A black man who kills a white woman confirms white racist stereotypes and fears of predatory black men. Miscegenation—racial mixing in marriage and in reproduction—in some versions of white racism is the worst thing; so the question whether Othello and Desdemona have, or haven't, had sexual intercourse is weirdly more anxiety generating than the violence and murder. Shakespeare's Othello articulates anxiety about racial mixing, in particular Desdemona having been sullied by the intimate relationship with him [3.3.388-90].[19] The death of a woman at the hands of a jealous and controlling man is commonplace. It is easily rationalized—although not, of course, justified—by accounts of women's guilt.[20] Although authorities from Venice come on the scene and attempt to prevent Othello from laying hold of any weapon, he manages to kill himself with a blade, describing himself, at the last, as like the 'Turkish dog' who must have his throat slit. At his death Othello takes the position of the white, civilized power which kills the beast-like, uncivilized, 'black' dog [3.3.266; 5.2.350-5].

So far, my telling of this story is consistent with individualist interpretation—with focus on emotions, psychology, and what happens to an individual when he misplaces trust, is prey to doubts about his social relations, is subject to forces of evil, and undergoes a disintegration of personality, losing his dignified sense of his own worth, putting hate where there was love. He is reduced to the destructive emotions of jealousy and wish for revenge, to violence, eventually to murder and suicide. But Othello's psychology—the interactions between his character, his cultivated demeanour as hero, dignified public figure, responsible leader; and his feelings and sensibly based beliefs about the world—can only be understood in light of *Othello* as a play about networks of persons related to each other in familial, gendered, social, economic, and political institutions.[21] In the following sections, I pick out the diverse ideas of politics that are played with in *Othello*.

Political Power and Social Divisions

To begin with, *Othello* is a play about, among other things, race, gender, and class. This twentieth-century trio has always to be treated with care because there are numerous, rival views about how we should think of and study

[19] Adelman, *Suffocating Mothers*, 1992: 275, n.53; Hall, Guess Who's Coming to Dinner, 1992/2004.
[20] Jardine, *Harping on Daughters*, 1983/1989: 74-5, 120.
[21] Rhodri Lewis. 2017. *Hamlet and the Vision of Darkness* (Princeton University Press: Princeton), pp. 1-2.

them, and what part they actually play in valid understandings and explanations of the worlds we inhabit and know about. And we must take care not to
attribute to Shakespeare understandings that are the product of twentieth-
century experience and thinking. But, as I have discussed, although we could
understand Othello's disintegration under the force of Iago's insinuations and
cruel tricks whatever Othello's ethnicity, the text insists that race is a factor in
Iago's animus, and in Othello's position in Venetian society. Underpinning Iago's
capacity to whip up Brabantio's ire against Othello, and explicit in his hostility
to Othello is racism—a white person's anti-black animosity of a familiar, crude
kind, mixed with sexual salaciousness [I.1.88-9]. Iago's relationship with his
wife Emilia is a familiarly brutal and controlling one. He tells the audience he
suspects Othello of having sex with Emilia—his jealousy is mixed up with his
racism [1.3.375-9; 2.1.285-90]. The play opens with Iago's class resentment—
his consciousness of the interaction of status and rank (military and social)
with income and wealth. 'Spinsterish, bookish' Cassio has been appointed
lieutenant while Iago is ensign. Iago is resentful of the demands for obsequy
from the lower status to the higher [1.1.40-54]. He is scornful of the dissimulation that is demanded in these hierarchies with their basis in false accounting. Iago's diatribe against the hierarchy mixes resentment at those who are
not what they seem, with assertions that he will not reveal his true feelings
about the matter—other than to Roderigo to whom the speech is addressed.
But Iago, as we soon learn, is not what he seems to Roderigo, who takes him
for a friend but is being materially exploited. Iago lures him on, taking advantage of Roderigo's spending power, with false promises and hopes that Othello
can be got rid of and the way cleared for Roderigo to win Desdemona, in a
familiar confidence trick from which, although he is half aware of it, Roderigo
cannot extricate himself [4.2.174-244].

Iago protests at and dissents from the system of values that dominate his
world. But his views of class, race, and gender division are not entirely personal or pathological. His misogyny is vulgar and his racism profane—but
not at odds with the values of the society in which he operates. Distinction,
ranks, barriers do structure societies according to income and social status.
This is the society for which the state exists, and the property distribution is
relied on, by the state, for its own stability. Othello's destruction, and the murder of Desdemona, is wrought by his taking up the position of the beast who
kills, in a process which turns on racial distinction and indistinction. But it is
completed symbolically, less by Othello's death, and more by the transfer of
his property to Gratiano's and Brabantio's family—to the man he wronged at
the outset by marrying his daughter without permission.

Patriarchal Power

Shakespeare's Venice, in common with the reality of early modern societies, whether governed by kings or republican officers, is patriarchal. Desdemona is subject to her father's will, as well as under his protection. On the other hand, her disobedience in eloping with Othello into a voluntary love marriage makes just as much sense in the context of Shakespeare's world as does the principle that they need her father's permission to marry. By patriarchalism is meant a system of authority in which fathers have rights over their wives, children, and wider households, which are enshrined in law and in custom. In early modern political thinking the sources for this were complex, including the classical Roman principle that the paterfamilias had the power of life and death over his women and sons, but also Christian theology and scripture such as St Augustine's account, in *The City of God* (composed early fifth century CE), of the relationship between a father's domestic rule and the civic order.[22] In early modern England, biblical justifications were various—Adam's authority over Eve, or Moses' commandment 'honour thy father and thy mother'.[23] Other religions and ethical systems have similar prescriptions. I will say more about the specific relationship of republican rule with patriarchalism in Chapter 4 on *Romeo and Juliet*, and discuss how the rights of fathers and the rights of kings relate in Chapter 5 on *King Lear*. Here I want to emphasize how closely such models of 'the family' relate to models of 'the state'. This goes further than fathers like Brabantio being as much entitled to seek the aid of the state to retrieve a disobedient daughter, as they are entitled to aid in finding a kidnapped one.

There are several distinct versions of the theory that the authority of fathers over family is the basis or model for the authority of state rulers over society and law. First, there is the view that God ordains that fathers, in general, should rule over women and sons. Second, there is the rival view that the sovereignty of king-the-father comes first (ordained by God-the-father), and patriarchal power is then bequeathed, by the king, to the heads of families. Third, there is the Aristotelian, non-theological view that families, presided over by male

[22] St Augustine. *c*.426 CE/1984. *The City of God*, trans. Henry Bettenson, ed. and intro. John O'Meara (Oxford University Press: Oxford), Bk. 19, Ch. 16.

[23] Gordon J. Schochet. 1969. 'Patriarchalism, Politics and Mass Attitudes in Stuart England', *The Historical Journal*, 12: 413–41; Gordon J. Schochet. 1975/1988. *The Authoritarian Family and Political Attitudes in 17th Century England: Patriarchalism in Political Thought* (Transaction Books: New Brunswick); Mark Hulliung. 1974. 'Patriarchalism and Its Early Enemies', *Political Theory*, 2: 410–19; Marilyn L. Williamson. 1986. *The Patriarchy of Shakespeare's Comedies* (Wayne State University Press: Detroit, MI).

heads, are the primary unit of social and political order, although in the Aristotelian scheme there is more to polity than a collection of families and neighbourly relations between households.[24] The idea of 'natural' right of male over female was rearticulated in the seventeenth century by thinkers who resisted theological accounts of patriarchalism, including King James I's defence of the second view in support of his developing thought about his rights of monarch vis-à-vis the law.[25] For example, against Robert Filmer (1588-1653) whose work *Patriarcha* circulated during his lifetime but was only published posthumously, John Locke (1632-1704) denied that Adam's authority over Eve was political, or derived by authority from God.[26] But Locke takes for granted men's natural authority over women.[27]

So, the relationship between patriarchalism and state authority changes over time. Feminists argue, though, that the generalized oppression, exploitation, and devalorization of women relative to men (to fathers, brothers, and husbands, but also the male heads of and participants in social organizations) is a form that survives all the theoretical transformations from Aristotelian naturalism, to divine right, to modern theories of nature and right. It is undamaged by modern social and political achievements including the general approval of individual choice and will, and the achievement by women of political rights (e.g. to vote, to participate in governing office), of civil rights (to own property, to earn income, to divorce, to marry or not according to their own choice), and of social rights (to participate in public cultures on more or less equal terms). In Carole Pateman's terms, strict patriarchal right gives way to the rights of brothers to overthrow fathers, and to take possession of women, and other goods, for themselves.[28] Harassment of women (and other disadvantaged groups) in public settings is a sign that their rights are not securely achieved; and material inequalities between group members

[24] Aristotle. 1932. *Politics*, trans. H. Rackham (Harvard University Press: Cambridge, MA), III.v.13–15, 1280b–1281a.

[25] James VI and I. 1598/1982. 'The True Law of Free Monarchies; or the Reciprock and mutuall duetie betwixt a free King and his natural subjects', in James Craigie (ed.), *Minor Prose Works of James VI and I* (Scottish Text Society: Edinburgh), pp. 61–2; James VI and I. 1603/1944. *Basilicon Doron*, ed. James Craigie, 2 vols (William Blackwood and Sons Ltd: Edinburgh), pp. 25, 60–1, 65–7, 135; J.W. Allen. 1938. *English Political Thought 1603–1660* (Methuen and Co. Ltd: London), pp. 5, 98.

[26] Robert Filmer. 1680/1991. 'Patriarcha', in Johann P. Sommerville (ed.), *Patriarcha and other Writings* (Cambridge University Press: Cambridge); John Locke. 1690/1960. *Two Treatises of Government* (Cambridge University Press: Cambridge), T2, Ch. VI,

[27] Locke, *Two Treatises*, 1690/1960: T2, Ch. VII, s82; Carole Pateman. 1989. 'The Fraternal Social Contract', *The Disorder of Women* (Polity Press: Cambridge), pp. 38–40.

[28] Carole Pateman. 1988. *The Sexual Contract* (Polity Press: Cambridge).

both licence and validate sex and gender domination. Feminist theorist Veronica Beechey terms this 'modern patriarchy'.[29]

Desdemona is 'betrayed and undone' [5.2.78] by the generalized association of women with wantonness or prostitution—Iago's success in his destructive project owes a lot to his capacity to envelop all the characters in a misogynistic discourse of women's sexuality, which would have been recognized and accepted by theatre audiences, both in general and because of the particular popular Elizabethan association of Venetian women with licentiousness.[30] She is doomed also, from the point of view of late modern audiences at any rate, by her voluntary and involuntary subjection to Othello. She addresses and refers to him as 'my lord' affirming his social status as a patriarch among other patriarchs. She endorses his rights vis-à-vis her virginity, and demonstrates unwavering loyalty even after he has suffocated her: to Emilia, Iago's wife, who tends her as she dies, she declares herself to be guiltless [5.2.123] but does not betray Othello. To Emilia's 'who hath done this deed?' she replies 'Nobody—I myself. Farewell—commend me to my kind lord' [5.2.124–5]. Othello's commentary on his killing of Desdemona contrasts with hers: in her last minutes she speaks of guilt and innocence (hers, and Cassio's), of truth and mercy [5.2.59–61, 69]. By contrast, Othello speaks in a judicial mode about confession, warning Desdemona of perjury [5.2.55–6, 65, 70], pronouncing sentence [5.2.58]. He also plays the role of the priest anxious for her soul [5.2.30–2]. In all of this, Othello is acting out sovereignty vis-à-vis Desdemona. He is the paterfamilias whose authority encompasses the power of life and death. Certainly, Desdemona has not voluntarily submitted to that. From the point of view of individual freedom she could not. But, of course, more cultures than Shakespeare's are ambivalent about the justifiability of killing a woman for infidelity.

Iago's misogyny, then, the plausibility of the tale he tells about Desdemona, depends for its effectiveness on Othello's similarly aligned understanding of female sexuality. Further, Iago's trick, his framing of Cassio, relies on Cassio's alignment with the sexual story also. Bianca, the third female character in the play, is similarly implicated by the social misogyny. Iago stages a conversation with Cassio, which Othello, overhearing, infers to be about Desdemona; but Cassio is speaking about Bianca, denigrating Bianca as a prostitute, laughing at Iago's suggestion that he should marry her [4.1.116–39]. Gender (norms of

[29] Veronica Beechey. 1979. 'On Patriarchy', *Feminist Review*, 3: 66–82.
[30] Mark Matheson. 1995/2004. 'Venetian Culture and the Politics of *Othello*', in Catherine M.S. Alexander (ed.), *Shakespeare and Politics* (Cambridge University Press: Cambridge).

masculine v. feminine) is imbricated (held together in a structure of overlapping elements) with norms of sexual desire and eroticism. The denigrated
female whore sells nevertheless desired sexual service to a male customer.
Valerie Traub warns that we must take care not to confound what Shakespeare's
dramas say about gender (masculine-feminine, male-female) with what they
say, and do, about eroticism.[31] The point is well taken, and I further discuss its
implications later in connection with the cross-dressing of female characters in
men's garb and guise, and the complication of the fact that, on the Elizabethan
stage, all female characters were played by cross-dressed boys. For now, though,
we see how patriarchal right (Othello vis-à-vis Desdemona; Iago in relation to
Emilia) maps onto misogynistic jokes, gibes, insinuations, and accusations
about female sexuality and conduct, and also onto the heterosexual desire of
men for sex with wife or prostitute, in a compound series of substitutions which
culminates in the perfectly intelligible scene of a killing which is a substitute for
(or is it a form of?), sexual intimacy and congress.[32]

Politic Government

The order of the opening scenes gives us, as I have set out here, Iago's class
resentment and racism as the first frame for the drama, followed by Brabantio's
fear and confusion at Desdemona's 'treason of the blood' [1.1.168]. Brabantio
confronts Othello simultaneously with Othello being summoned to see the
Duke [1.2.55-87, 88-95]. We witness the Duke and senators' discussion about
Turkish strategy and tactics and their threat to Venetian interests [1.3.1-48].
When Othello and Brabantio enter together [1.3.47], the Duke's immediate
welcome consists of 'Valiant Othello, we must straight employ you against the
general enemy Ottoman' [1.3.48-9]. He doesn't see Brabantio, Iago, and the
others. This is a scene of statesmanship. If directors are looking for cuts, it
must be tempting to shorten the exchanges between duke, senators, and mes-
sengers about intelligence and strategy, and move quickly to Brabantio's entrance
and his appeal about his daughter's elopement [1.3.48-76].

   The Duke, to be sure, quickly gives Brabantio his full attention. This switch
from foreign policy to concern about a citizen's family conflict suggests that in
Shakespeare's world there is seamlessness between inter-state and domestic

---

[31] Valerie Traub. 1992/2004. 'The Homoerotics of Shakespearian Comedy', in Emma Smith (ed.),
Shakespeare's Comedies (Blackwell Publishing: Oxford).
[32] Deborah Cameron and Elizabeth Frazer. 1987. *The Lust to Kill: A Feminist Investigation of Sexual
Murder* (Polity: Cambridge).

social relations; patriarchal authority is a governmental concern as much as invasion and naval warfare is. But, if the foreign policy detail is cut, the Duke here can look less like a statesman and more like a trusted authority figure of no particular status. In dramatic terms he can function simply as an inter-locutor who feeds lines which allow the audience to hear Brabantio's feelings about Desdemona and Othello, setting the scene for the family and individual drama of passion. Politics, in the sense of the detail of statecraft, strategy, diplomacy, office, gives way to inter-personal emotion and depoliticized psy-chological drama. Performing these lines, on the other hand, emphasizes that the frame for the play is, indeed, state and foreign policy, and a hierarchical society structured by race, class, and kinship. This interpretation emphasizes that political power in the restrictive sense of state governing power impacts directly on the personal, familial, and social lives of the characters. The for-eign policy of the state of Venice means that troops and traders are deployed to Cyprus; war, like peace, has a direct effect on family, personal, and profes-sional lives.[33] The Duke has the moral, but also presumably the political, authority to pronounce on the rightness of Brabantio's claim that the mar-riage between Othello and Desdemona be stopped.

Sovereign Authority

At the beginning of *Othello* we see the sovereign functions of deployment of resources in defence of the state and in the interests of the society. The story arcs to its conclusion with sovereign judgement and punishment. The concept sovereignty is contested in political thought. As I use it here, and in most usage, it signals final, decisive power. What the Duke and senators say shall happen, happens—Brabantio has to acquiesce in Othello's and Desdemona's marriage, they embark on the journey to Cyprus. In the end, Iago is found out, apprehended, and judged by the officers of the state. Between them they articulate a range of voices—outraged shock at the violence and evil [4.1.231-40, 5.2.185], reason and caution in their attempts to intervene with Othello [5.2.254-5], the moral voice of reasoned sorrowful judgement regarding Othello's fall [5.2.289-91]. They can finally explain to Othello—'Here is a letter...' [5.2.306-17]—the powers that have assailed and ruined him and Desdemona. But finally, they are the bearers of sovereign state power. They reallocate Othello's authority: 'You must forsake this room and go with us:

[33] Matheson, 'Venetian Culture', 1995/2004.

your power and your command is taken off, and Cassio rules in Cyprus'
[5.2.329-31]. Lodovico's closing lines pass sentence of torture on Iago: 'to you,
lord governor, remains the censure of this hellish villain—the time, the place,
the torture—O enforce it', and the final rhyming couplet affirms the sovereign
state as the final authority to which account must be made: 'myself will straight
aboard, and to the state this heavy act with heavy heart relate' [5.2.366-70].

Government has 'final' power. Commonsensically, there's not much to see
here: in certain contexts, and states are one of those, it makes sense that 'highest' or 'final' power should be located somewhere definite—there has to be a
last word about legislation and the execution of laws, about what is and what
is not lawful. This does not apply in all contexts, by any means: in friendship
networks, for instance, 'sovereignty' has no place. If anyone were to aspire to
or try to institute it, the group would be something other than a friendship
group. But Shakespeare's Venice is a republic, a particular kind of polity, based
on the idea that governmental institutions and offices are sovereign. They
have been set up that way, in order that conflicts within the society can be
subjected to final judgement and settlement, and also so that the state has
resources to defend itself against invasion or domination by any external
power. In republics, the idea is that processes of government are open and
understood by all who participate in them and are subject to them. Deliberation
about policy should be reasonable and based on good evidence and intelligence and reasoning. All of these ideals and principles of republicanism were
familiar to early modern philosophers and political thinkers, part and parcel of
political culture; and can be traced back to the classical tradition of Aristotle
and Cicero, which was refracted first by Christian philosophy and then by
early modern humanism.[34] The senators and duke have something to hide
from Turkish powers, in their deliberation about what to do about the threats
to their merchant shipping; but they should have nothing to hide from the
Venetian people. Disputes—about who should be next duke, for instance—are
resolved by discussion of candidates and established procedures for selection
and appointment. Disagreements about public policy—what to do about the
Turks—would be resolved by the merchants whose cargoes are at risk making
representations to the government, and the government deciding what to do
and then deploying sovereign resources to doing it.

---

[34] Quentin Skinner. 1978. *The Foundations of Modern Political Thought*. Vol. 1: *The Renaissance*
(Cambridge University Press: Cambridge); Andrew Hadfield. 2004. *Shakespeare and Renaissance
Politics* (Thomson Learning: London).

However, the idea of sovereignty is always problematic and always puzzling. In political controversy and Shakespeare's dramas alike, people are frequently at cross-purposes regarding what they are talking about and what they mean.[35] In monarchies, like that of early modern England and Scotland, the idea that people, or some people, simply agree on 'sovereign' institutions cannot work: the principle of divine ordination, or the special destiny of certain individuals as rulers, has to be fitted in. This is at the basis of one set of sovereignty puzzles, and Shakespeare plays with them at length, as I shall discuss in relation to *King Lear* in Chapter 5 and Ha*mlet* in Chapter 8. *King Lear* also raises, very vividly, the question whether sovereignty must be unified, at a single point, or whether it can be divided and distributed—a problem in the story of the unification of the Tudor and then the Stuart state, and a live one in current twenty-first-century national states.

Othello is a brilliant example of play with models of sovereignty. On the one hand, politic reasoning by those with sovereign authority and a measured approach to foreign policy conducted through the good offices of trustworthy figures like Othello; on the other, vicious inter-personal mischief, murder, and suicide, which make state power irrelevant, and to which the state response is sovereign punishment—the excess of torture. In political thinking, claims of sovereignty are frequently suspect because they seem inevitably to be in the service of oppressive, overweening, coercive, and violent power. Republicans theorize about the logical and real possibilities of uncoerced agreement to locate decisive judgemental power in publicly accountable institutions. But critics focus on sovereignty's violent origins, its excessively violent means, and the way it operates to reduce persons with social status, cultural identity, moral standing, and the augmented physical health and strength of the sheltered, clothed, nourished person. Sovereign power amounts to the power to make such individuals abject.[36] It is notable that Iago is to be punished by torture—the exercise of sovereignty as the power of life or death, as the infliction of violent pain and injury to the point where both death and life are withheld. Given the history and conduct of states, both in their domination of denizens and citizens, and in their conquest of territories and markets, such uses of excessive violence are at issue. This being so, the only defensible sovereignty is

---

[35] Raia Prokhovnik. 1999. *Rational Woman: A Feminist Critique of Dichotomy* (Routledge: London); Daniel Philpott. 2011. 'Sovereignty', in George Klosko (ed.), *The Oxford Handbook of the History of Political Philosophy* (Oxford University Press: Oxford).

[36] Curtis C. Breight. 1996. *Surveillance, Militarism and Drama in the Elizabethan Era* (Macmillan Press Ltd: Basingstoke); Daniel Juan Gil. 2013. *Shakespeare's Anti-Politics: Sovereign Power and the Life of the Flesh* (Palgrave Macmillan: Basingstoke), pp. 1–2.

the individual's sovereignty over self, as John Stuart Mill (1806-73) explicitly put it, an idea that had been implied by eighteenth-century thinkers such as Jean-Jacques Rousseau (1712-78).[37]

Politics in *Othello* is more than sovereignty and its paradoxes, patriarchy and its limits. In the next section, I deal with Iago as one of Shakespeare's most notable 'machiavellians'. I admit, this doesn't do much to further my argument that there is a 'pro-politics' strain in Shakespeare too. But, in the final section of this chapter, I turn to 'public speech'. And that introduces a political theme which we meet again in relation to *Measure for Measure* and to *Coriolanus*, and which, in my submission, casts Shakespeare's politics in a different light.

Machiavellian Trickery

Othello's appointment as governor of Cyprus, and head of the military forces that will defend the port, and serve the Venetian merchants, is made openly. His authority is allocated to him by the state. It is undermined by Iago's machiavellianism. I refer to Iago, like the other Shakespeare characters I identify as machiavellian, with a small 'm': they are not characters that Machiavelli himself would approve. He recommends Machiavellianism to princes whose aim is the glory and everlasting reputation of their states and their rule, not nasty, resentful, vengeful bullies like Iago.[38] For Shakespeare, though, machiavellians serve structurally to cast the possibilities of politics, and ethics, into doubt. The plays articulate doubt about the claims of monarchs, about the claims of republican dukes, and about the political ideals of openness and truth. Openness and truth certainly are human ideals which Shakespeare's stories of soul mates—Beatrice and Benedict in *Much Ado about Nothing* [4.1.255-88], Juliet and Romeo [2.1.169-78]—turn on. Their relationships are centred on moments of simple truth and honesty, albeit Beatrice and Benedict are still caught up in all the social 'ado', and Juliet and Romeo are doomed by violence and their families' projects of urban domination. If these are ideals and values that should guide relationships of rule and

---

[37] Jean-Jacques Rousseau. 1762/1997. 'The Social Contract', in Victor Gourevitch (trans. and ed.), *The Social Contract and Other Later Political Writings* (Cambridge University Press: Cambridge), Bk. 1, Ch. 1, Ch. 5; John Stuart Mill. 1859/1989. 'On Liberty', in Stefan Collini (ed.), *On Liberty and other Writings* (Cambridge University Press: Cambridge), Ch. 1, p. 13.

[38] Niccolo Machiavelli. 1532/1961. *The Prince*, trans. George Bull (Penguin: Harmondsworth), Chs. VIII, XIX.

order, though, it's clear that Shakespeare's dramas cast their realizability into doubt. Life, human relationships, and the competition for the power to govern are messy and opaque, and subject to a whole series of human patterns of conduct based on strategy, hypocrisy of various kinds, concealment, and confusion. Othello is appointed openly by the Duke and senators; he is ruined by trickery incomprehensible to him, including the tricks of his own understanding. Iago's power to bring down a virtuous officer of state works by interacting with Othello's own fears and doubts; and by working with the animus of class, and with the malevolent powers of misogyny and racism. Above all, it works through Iago's powers of dissimulation, of acting a part which diverges from his inner motivations.

Having told Brabantio about Desdemona's elopement with Othello, Iago goes back to Othello and acts as loyal ensign [1.1.67-81, 86-91; 1.2.1-17]. He conceals his own actions, for instance instigating a physical fight and making it look as though injuries he inflicts are the work of others [5.1.11-28]. He is ruthless, goading Othello into suspicion and jealousy of Desdemona, encouraging and conniving in violence by Othello against Desdemona [3.3.196-216, 463-79]. Iago is manipulative. He understands Othello's commitment to traditional values of loyalty and service.[39] He exploits this commitment for his own ends, by acting out his own service and allegiance to Othello [3.3.463-9], by casting doubt on Cassio's loyalty while protesting that he does not wish to cast doubt on the character of a friend [3.3.474]. He echoes Brabantio's view that a daughter who disobeys her father will become a wife who betrays her husband [1.3.290-1, 3.3.209-11]. Iago is cynical about political and ethical values [1.1.42-65, 1.3.315-27]. The political values of allegiance and loyalty are shattered ruthlessly by him; the modern values of freedom, equality, and friendship are twisted into a discourse of monetary exchange.[40]

In all polities that I know anything about, anti-political criticism is common. Shakespeare's dramas are replete with politicians who are full only of themselves and hot air, who talk talk talk but don't get anything done, or who pretend to be something they are not. A difficulty for normative political theory, for the project of working out how politics ought to be, is that it is hard to draw a bright line between ideals of politics, such as modern theories of democracy, or classical theories of the polis, and this machiavellian, broadly dishonest model. The political way, ideally, consists of public action in concert, to institute and then uphold offices whose incumbents are publicly accountable. The problem is that

[39] Matheson, 'Venetian Culture', 1995/2004: 77.
[40] Matheson, 'Venetian Culture', 1995/2004: 76-8.

any such open system is susceptible to corruption, and to people getting muddled about what is politics and what is its corruption.[41] After all, in politics, the very ideal of open, speech-based, deliberative, policy making means that political speakers have to watch what they say, weigh their words, orient their message to the relevant audience. There is no point speaking absolutely spontaneously or honestly, and consequently being misunderstood or reviled. But this means that the practice of political rhetoric can seem to be very close to dishonesty, to inauthenticity, to non-spontaneous rehearsal.[42] And, this being so, it can look as though Iago's machiavellian concealment, dissimulation, rhetorical skill, persuasive capacity—and talent at playing a part—are the essence of politics, an enactment of what politics really involves rather than a corruption of it. The idea that all politicians are dishonest can come to have force in political cultures.

We do not have to accept any such inference. To begin with, Iago's view of the world is based on misogyny and racism, his talent is for exploiting other people's weakness, and violence. He might be a political actor, but we can tell the difference between a good and an evil political actor. This makes of 'political action' a mode of action that itself is morally neutral, that can be used for good ends or for bad. That is one answer. An alternative answer—one that I try to develop and defend in this book—is that, although politic, prudential, action is certainly an element of politics, 'politics' constrains ends and means together; it is not a question of deploying neutral means for good or bad ends, but that, in order to count as 'political', action has to be of a certain kind, in a certain context, and with specific directionality. In brief, politics, if it is to be genuine, has to be for genuine assent, and continued dissent, not for submission to violence or trickery. This rules Iago out from the start. It constrains properly political action to action with an orientation to inclusion of all, not exclusion. It has to be for conciliation proper, not simply buying people off, or silencing them. It invariably involves contention, but puts absolute limits on violence. This 'model' of politics, discussed further in future chapters, is based on elements of Aristotle and neo-Aristotelianism, and on developing theories of popular sovereignty and freedom (including those of Machiavelli) which were elements of political thought, and indeed of political culture, in the early modern period, and were developed by twentieth-century political thinkers. Shakespeare's plays don't stage this complex kind of politics explicitly. However,

---

[41] Mark Philp. 1994. 'On Politics and its Corruption', *Political Theory Newsletter*, 6: 1–18.
[42] Martin Jay. 2010. *The Virtues of Mendacity: On Lying in Politics* (University of Virginia Press: Charlottesville, VA).

elements of it are present, as hints about what is lost from a world without politics proper, as the counterpart to the explicit denigration of Iago, and the doubts and aspersions that are cast, in other plays, on claims to various kinds of authority.

Public Speech

In *Othello* we hear two distinct streams of free speech, with different political implications. First, Desdemona's open, unguarded, speech which reveals her friendly, trusting, and egalitarian character. Second, Emilia's open speaking of the truth—to officers of the state of Venice—about Iago, about where blame lies, about what has actually happened. If Iago's machiavellianism destroys Desdemona, Emilia's speech destroys Iago—although, too late, and not in time to save herself, or Desdemona, nor to prevent the harm that Iago does.

Free, open speech is not a value, only, of late modern liberal democratic polities, where it has, to be sure, a specific place, and where questions about the limits of free speech are among the most prominent of public controversies. In the classical republican tradition 'parrhesia'—the fearless, artless, open speaking of truth, in the context of polity—was understood to be a characteristic of Athenian democracy.[43] Athenian citizens were equal participants in power, with equal rights to speak, and they discussed public affairs openly—that was the ideal, at least.[44] The idea that in politics we deliberate, each with each, to a decision and its implementation, involves open speech, among the decision makers, about possibilities, probabilities, bad and good ideas, hopes and fears. Hannah Arendt (1906-75) is a notable twentieth-century political thinker for whom this principle is key to a normative theory of politics. Compare it with a setting like a managerially administered organization, where extended debate about possibilities and probabilities, hopes and fears is taken to be an inefficient diversion from proper business, at best, a damaging subversion of authority at worst. Authoritarian rule is like that—free speech is not open. But 'speaking truth to power' does have a place in authoritarian polities, and in monarchies where sovereignty is associated with the incumbent of the office of king. In these settings, 'speaking truth to power' is premissed, rather, on inequality between speaker and spoken to. The counsellor, to

[43] Foucault, Michel. 1983/1985. 'The Meaning and Evolution of the Word Parrhesia', *Discourse & Truth: The Problematization of Parrhesia. Six lectures at the University of California at Berkeley CA Oct–Nov 1983*, ed. Joseph Pearson, https://foucault.info/parrhesia/ p. 7.
[44] Hannah Arendt. 1954/1990. 'Philosophy and Politics', *Social Research*, 57: 427–54.

be sure, should be able to speak truth to the king. It is one mark of tyranny that the tyrant disregards honest advice—or even punishes those who bring bad news.[45] Similarly, it is a mark of failure of popular sovereignty that relevant truth escapes, or is ignored by, governments.

Iago and Emilia conduct Desdemona to Cyprus, with Othello on a separate ship [2.1.87-90]. At the happy arrival—for the voyage has been through bad weather—and Cassio's welcome, there is joking about women's speech. Iago, in his jovial, good hearted guise, jokes about Emilia's tongue. The repartee, in which Desdemona engages in a spirited way, is occasion for Iago to articulate numerous *double entendres*—about black and white, with connotations of ordinary variation in skin tone and hair colour, and of race, and of good and bad—and to deliver a good deal of sexual innuendo, with sexual congress equated, by him, with commercial transaction [2.1.109-15, 125-58]. The extent to which the full sexual and racial connotations of his quips are clear or opaque to Desdemona can be a matter of artistic interpretation. So can the degree of good humour with which she plays the straight part to Iago's comic performance. The lewd innuendo of the puns and quips about women's tongues turns on the ambiguity of tongue in relation both to speech and to sexual congress. The jokes would provoke laughter from audience members, who may or may not get the sexual connotations. We can add here that part of the meaning of 'Venice' for Anglo-Saxon culture, in addition to its serene republican government, was its licentiousness and in particular the freedom of Venetian women.[46]

Jardine argues that, in combination with the sexual ambiguity of women like Emilia and Desdemona being played by boys, the whole effect of this aspect of the plot and action, and Emilia's death as punishment for speaking, would affirm cultural and social prejudices.[47] And any twenty-first-century reader or audience member who knows how the plot works out listens to these exchanges with a heavy heart. Desdemona's free speech (whether she is enjoying the banter or resenting Iago's presumption and rudeness) entangles her in a series of compromises, setting the foundation for Iago's subsequent destruction of her character. Unguarded speech, in situations of radical inequality, as between women and men in misogynistic patriarchal cultures, or between black and white, ethnic minority and dominant individuals, is not politic. Yet, open, free speech is a political value for any society that prizes

[45] Foucault, 'The Meaning and Evolution', 1983/1985: 8.
[46] Matheson, 'Venetian Culture', 1995/2004: 181.
[47] Jardine, *Harping on Daughters*, 1983/1989: 121–2.

social change that is understood by its members. Michel Foucault's (1926-84) analyses in numerous articles and studies of speech, discourse, freedom, and truth reveal how speech is as much bound up with power as with freedom.[48] Desdemona's dilemma—as we audiences see it—is a vivid example of this double bind.

Emilia, like Desdemona, is undone by the patriarchal values which deprive her of independent voice and autonomous judgement. In 3.3, Emilia gives Iago the handkerchief as he has asked her to ('what he will do with it heaven knows, not I', 'I nothing but to please his fancy' [3.3.293-302]) at a point when she seems to be utterly controlled by Iago's dominating violence supported by the patriarchal norms of marriage. But she has a friendship with Desdemona, signalled by her ability to sympathize with Cassio and give him assurances from Desdemona regarding her intercession with Othello about Cassio's job [3.1.41-55]. The friendship between the two women comes to a climax in their political and intimate conversation about men, women, sex, and marriage [4.3.55-98]. Emilia sees how male dominance in marriage is premised on women being either saints or whores [4.3.93-103].[49] Here, by contrast to the way Desdemona's speech, when Iago's view of the world and his capacity for manipulation dominates compromises her, is a case of a new kind of truthful understanding emerging from safe speech and trust.

Between obeying Iago in the matter of the handkerchief and being killed by him, Emilia begins to suspect, to understand, that Desdemona is calumnied. When she first arrives on Cyprus, Emilia is silent and diffident in response to Iago's misogynist 'jest' about her tongue. Desdemona, at the time, takes the joke humorously: 'Desdemona: Alas, she has no speech; Iago: In faith, too much...' [2.1.100-13]. Emilia comes to understand that her and Desdemona's free speech on behalf of Cassio has provoked or generated Othello's jealousy [3.4.154-7] but that the fault must lie elsewhere, not in the speech. During her confrontation with Othello after he has fatally injured Desdemona, Emilia switches from her initial deferential address to him as 'my lord' to calling him a devil as a riposte to his accusation that Desdemona is a whore [5.2.131-5]. When Othello tells her that Iago 'knew' that Cassio and Desdemona were false to him, that Iago was the informant, then Emilia understands [5.2.140,

[48] Michel Foucault. 1973/1978. *I, Pierre Riviere, Having Slaughtered My Mother, My Sister, and My Brother: A Case of Parricide in the 19th Century* (Penguin: Harmondsworth); Foucault, Michel. 2002. *Essential Works of Foucault 1954-1984*. Vol. 3: *Power*, ed. James D. Faubion (Penguin: Harmondsworth).

[49] Coppelia Kahn. 1981. *Man's Estate: Masculine Identity in Shakespeare* (University of California Press: Berkeley, CA), pp. 119-21,127-46.

144-55]. She challenges Iago; he tells her to be quiet [5.2.170-90], but Emilia has a right to speak. She asks the representatives of the state of Venice, directly, for permission to speak, irrespective of Iago's orders or interests: 'Good gentlemen, let me have leave to speak: 'tis proper I obey him, but not now' [5.2.193-5]. As Othello's distressed account to the Venetian officers continues, she goes on, taking implicit permission, or right, from the state of Venice: 'Twill out, 'twill out; I peace! No, I will speak as liberal as the north: let heaven and men and devils, let them all, all, all cry shame against me, yet I'll speak' [5.2.217-21]. Emilia dies speaking: 'So come my soul to bliss, as I speak true; so speaking as I think, alas, I die' [5.2.249-50], poignantly echoing Desdemona's 'alas, she has no speech' in their earlier confused encounter with Iago [2.1.103].

Othello and the Political Way

When we act politically there is a gap between being and seeming. This can be for good—as when we consider the effects of our words on our audience, and tailor our speech accordingly. Or, in corruption of political action, as in the case of Iago, it can be for bad. Emilia's speech—embodying and articulating the assertion of right, as well as statement of fact—is a brilliant example of a paradox of free speech as a political value. Free speech requires an appropriate political and social context, if it is to be heard, and heard in time. The political way, ideally, is open for voices, for listening and hearing. By speaking up and speaking out, people and their claims can propel themselves into the polity. Emilia, in her last words, politicizes—nearly—the personal tangle of misunderstanding between Othello, Iago, Desdemona, Cassio, and herself, revealing how the power and authority of patriarchal marriage had the effect not only of silencing her, but also of forcing the women to speak in such a way that they were further enmeshed in that power and authority. She brings it into the open, and brings Iago's crimes, and all the ways he has wronged others, into public view. She pushes—nearly—the conditions of Othello's murderousness to the level of public consideration. She does this by asserting her right to speak, and to be heard, in the context of, and by, state authority. The tragedy of the play, according to this reading, lies as much in the failure of a formation of political authority to recognize and empower all who should be able to exert political agency; as much in the ways public speech is forced and manipulated by corrupt power; as much in the destruction of two women, as it is in the fall of a noble person to ignominy.

The 'political context' for the moral, social, and personal tragedies of Emilia, Desdemona, and Othello is the Venetian state and its foreign trading interests. Were we to focus simply on this, moralists and literary critics could be forgiven for their annoyance and insistence that it is a travesty to read *Othello* as a political fable. However, if we focus, as I have tried to do, on the characters' exertions of power, and their appeals to public values in order to deepen, and then justify, those exertions, then the politics of the play in relation to the ethics and sheer human interest comes closer into view. The state power to which Emilia appeals is not, actually, equal to the enormity of the social conflicts—the racism, the misogyny—that fissure the society the state relies on and is for.

2

Political power and *Measure for Measure*

Politics in *Measure for Measure*

In the opening lines of *Measure for Measure* (composed *c*.1604) Vincentio, Duke of Vienna, distances himself personally from the art and science of politics, attributing to his adviser Escalus knowledge and skill greater than his own: 'Of government the properties to unfold would seem in me to affect speech and discourse, since I am put to know that your own science exceeds in that the lists of all advice my strength can give you' [1.1.3-7]. This deprecation of his capacity to advise, his confession that government, as a topic, adversely affects his capacities for speech and expression puts us, in this play, into a typically ambiguous Shakespearean relationship to the world of politics. Politics, after all, is preeminently a practice, a world, of speech—counsellors advise, protesters argue and sloganize, debaters persuade, rulers consult and pronounce. But for Vincentio, government incapacitates speech.

The terms politics or policy don't occur anywhere in the text of *Measure for Measure*, but government, governor, governs are repeated. In any case, here is a play that is, most obviously, 'political' in the sense that it is about a ruler, of a city state, who appoints deputy officers to govern in his absence. The plot follows what happens to and what is done by these officers, focusing on their political shortcomings and errors, and those of the Duke himself. Other key characters are subjected to various kinds of authoritative power—legal, abusive, punitive—and find various ways of resisting, challenging, or subverting those powers. People's lives are directly affected by decisions about public policy, law, and enforcement, and by the implementation of those decisions. Conal Condren warns against the anachronism of reading Shakespeare through the frame of the much later distinction between what is private (and should be the concern only of the individuals involved), and what is public, and potentially or properly the concern of other people, or of the government.[1] It's true

---

[1] Conal Condren. 2009. 'Unfolding the Properties of Government: The case of *Measure for Measure* and the history of political thought', in David Armitage, Conal Condren, and Andrew Fitzmaurice (eds.), *Shakespeare and Early Modern Political Thought* (Cambridge University Press: Cambridge).

Shakespeare and the Political Way. Elizabeth Frazer, Oxford University Press (2020). © Elizabeth Frazer.
DOI: 10.1093/oso/9780198848615.001.0001

that in the nineteenth and twentieth centuries the public v. private distinction came to centre on whether infrastructure like railways, or productive capital generally, or violence against wives, for instance, should be the business only of the individual owners ('in the private sector'), or public in the sense of the property or business of the state. It is fair enough to be clear that early modern drama does not play with those controversies. But the way personal and social lives are, or are not, impacted on by governmental authority and sovereign power, and the way government and public politics are affected by how people relate to each other and to authority, is central to Shakespeare's drama, as it is, or should be, to any thinking about politics.

The Duke deprecates his own political capacities. 'I love the people', so he says, 'but do not like to stage me to their eyes. Though it do well, I do not relish well their loud applause and aves vehement, nor do I think the man of safe discretion that does affect it' [1.1.68-73]. In Chapter 1 we began to discuss the political significance of public speech, and that is relevant for this play too. But the Duke draws our attention to how visibility and the theme of public appearance—being seen, being looked at—is also a problem. The idea that the political world is prominently a space of appearances, as much as it is a space in which things are said, can be drawn from classical sources, as it is by twentieth-century theorists such as Hannah Arendt, who develop its implications for liberal and for republican polities.[2]

We cannot quarrel with someone who simply does not want to, or cannot, act publicly, get up on the public stage, to be focused on and stared at. On the other hand, it's a real drawback in a duke, or any ruler—for them politics is non-optional, although Vincentio is neither the first nor the last ruler to try to depoliticize rule. We also cannot quarrel with someone who has misgivings about affecting to like adulation when really they don't. Vincentio here is articulating a familiar criticism of hypocrisy. In a world which values truth and authenticity the practice of seeming to be what one is not is not a good look. To this extent, reluctance or incapacity to act politically is understandable and even admirable. On the other hand, seeming to be what one is not can be the moral, the sociable, or the effective course, in daily life as well as in political.[3] It's important to tailor the way you speak to your audience or interlocutors.

---

[2] Hannah Arendt. 1958. *The Human Condition* (University of Chicago Press: Chicago); Bernard Crick. 1962/2005. *In Defence of Politics* (Continuum: London); Jeffrey Green. 2010. *The Eyes of the People: Democracy in an Age of Spectatorship* (Oxford University Press: Oxford).

[3] David Runciman. 2008. *Political Hypocrisy: The Mask of Power, from Hobbes to Orwell and Beyond* (Princeton University Press: Princeton, NJ); Martin Jay. 2010. *The Virtues of Mendacity: On Lying in Politics* (University of Virginia Press: Charlottesville, VA).

But these aspects—having to get up in public, to be applauded (or jeered at), and having to act otherwise than your real feelings dictate—are among those that give politics a bad name, for lots of us, not only Duke Vincentio.

In Act I we hear also that the Duke has discerned a problem in the government of Vienna—one of his own making.

> We have strict statutes and most biting laws, the needful bits and curbs to headstrong weeds, which for this fourteen years we have let slip…so our decrees, dead to infliction, to themselves are dead, and liberty plucks justice by the nose.   [1.3.19-31]

Vincentio goes on—because it was he who presided over a regime in which the laws weren't enforced, and the city has come to the point where the laws, therefore, are not respected, it can't be he who now becomes a strict enforcer: 'Twould be my tyranny to strike and gall them for what I bid them do' [1.3.35-9]; 'Tyrannical' rule is not only severe—it is arbitrary, dictated by the will and whims of the tyrant rather than by predictable lawful rules.[4] So, 'I have on Angelo imposed the office, who may in the ambush of my name strike home, and yet my nature never in the fight…' [1.3.41-3].

In other words, the Duke has appointed Angelo to do the dirty work.

Duke Vincentio is not keen on the public gaze, doesn't like being stared at. However, he does want to see, for himself—to be the unseen seer. In particular, he is embarking on an experiment. How will government of the city go under Angelo? How will having this power to enforce the laws affect him? So, having told his deputies that he is journeying to Poland [1.3.14, 1.2.1-5] he disguises himself, as a friar, so that he can stay in the city and 'behold his sway'. 'Hence shall we see if power change purpose, what our seemers be' [1.3.43, 53-4].

The 'strict statutes' and 'biting laws' are all about sexual conduct. Under Angelo's rule Claudio is arrested for fornication. Julietta, to whom he considers himself bound although 'we do the denunciation lack of outward order', is pregnant. They couldn't achieve a formal betrothal or marriage because Julietta's dowry was under the control of her family [1.2.143-51]. Claudio is condemned to be executed—and first must be 'shown to the world' as an example [1.2.115-20]. The new regime has also issued a proclamation that all the houses—brothels—are to be pulled down. 'Here's a change indeed in the

---

[4] Aristotle. 1932. *Politics*, trans. H. Rackham (Harvard University Press: Cambridge, MA), VIII.1-3, 1295a.

commonwealth! What shall become of me?' exclaims Mistress Overdone, the proprietress of one such house [1.2.94–104].

So by the end of the first three scenes the play has set up a number of political theory issues. The Duke's withdrawal from the proper exercise of his office raises the question whether his dislike of political life is a sign of admirable acknowledgement of who and what he really is, and a proper renunciation of the 'hypocrisy' of political life, or whether, rather, the constraints of the duties of office on the individual, and the imperatives of politic care, are themselves ethical values. But anyway, Vincentio does not really withdraw from political life at all. He positions himself as an intervening, clandestine, spectator. He substitutes a kind of machiavellian version of the political way for the open republican one.

We can note that *Measure for Measure* is very suggestive for twenty-first-century readers and audiences because of the themes of secrecy and surveillance.[5] But, should we, do we actually, associate politics with openness? It is an ideal that immediately generates paradoxes and problems. Is openness a matter of acting upon a public stage—in full view? Or is it a matter of truth and authenticity? Ordinary political language can be equivocal and undecided between these two. Being in full view means that not everything can be seen; revealing everything relevant is difficult, if not impossible, in the frame of any public stage. In any case, even in an open society, as critics point out, the voices and articulated views in public discussion are not complete. Lots of interested and affected parties and individuals are excluded, effectively suppressed—formally barred, made invisible, discounted.[6] From a point of view of justice, the question is whether such exclusions are justifiable; if they are not, the question is how the hitherto discounted can be properly counted. However, from a governing power and order point of view—the one Vincentio takes up in *Measure for Measure*—the question is how to find out about those people, for the purposes of social control as much as for justice. Like numerous rulers and regimes, the Duke has recourse to secrecy and surveillance. He goes out in disguise among the people and learns, for instance from Lucio, something of 'public opinion' about himself that he would not have learned in open discussion [3.1.350–420]. Forms of surveillance, too, are also needed in

---

[5] Jonathan Dollimore. 1985b. 'Transgression and Surveillance in Measure for Measure', in Jonathan Dollimore and Alan Sinfield (eds.), *Political Shakespeare: New Essays in Cultural Materialism* (Manchester University Press: Manchester); Robin Headlam Wells. 2009. *Shakespeare's Politics* (Continuum: London), pp. 202–3.

[6] Jacques Ranciere. 1995/1999. *Disagreement: Politics and Philosophy*, trans. Julie Rose (University of Minnesota Press: Minneapolis, MN); Lynn M. Sanders. 1997. 'Against Deliberation', *Political Theory*, 25: 347–76.

Angelo's law enforcement: closing brothels requires seeing where the brothels are, and, as Escalus finds, whether Pompey is Mistress Overdone's tapster or is a 'bawd' (an illegal occupation) is not a straightforward fact to establish by interview or discussion [2.1.202–20].

There can be no doubt that social class is a theme in *Measure for Measure*. Jonathan Dollimore notes that commentators from left, right, and centre broadly concur in accepting at face value the play's narrative that the practice of ille-galized sexual occupations and statuses really are a sign of disorder in the state.[7] He takes this as a sign that critics and audiences—lots of them, at any rate—share the Shakespearean conservative premise that sexuality must be controlled, which, in the logic of play, leads to the comedic conclusion with all the problems resolved in a series of marriages. In this book, I take this conservative v. radical, right v. left frame to be less productive, from the point of view of political theory, than reading Shakespeare's juxtapositions of sexual, racial, economic, and cultural constraints and freedoms as posing a series of political problems. Julietta's and Claudio's freedom to voluntarily love and marry, after all, is juxtaposed in Shakespeare's Vienna with the freedom of men to buy sexual services and women to sell them.[8] Mistress Overdone invokes 'the commonwealth' [1.2.103–4]—a term which has definite 'republi-can' connotations, although it is also consistent with government by a mon-arch.[9] She is speaking of the whole body, or overlapping communities, of people who share markets, goods, and ways of living, as well as laws and gov-ernment. She does not mean a society governed by secret surveillance. But she does seem to take for granted that this is what we would call a 'sex-gender' order—men demand, women supply. If the sexual culture of Shakespeare's Vienna does include a non-heterosexual scene or market, there is no hint of it in the text.

The text in 1.2 introduces the religious dimension of this morality. This play is understood to be one of Shakespeare's most overtly 'religious'.[10] The title quotes St Matthew: 'For with what judgement ye judge, ye shall be judged:

[7] Dollimore, 'Trangression and Surveillance', 1985b.

[8] Kathleen McLuskie. 1985. 'The Patriarchal Bard: Feminist criticism and Shakespeare—King Lear and Measure for Measure', in Jonathan Dollimore and Alan Sinfield (eds.), *Political Shakespeare: New Essays in Cultural Materialism* (Manchester University Press: Manchester), pp. 94–7.

[9] J.G.A. Pocock. 1975. *The Machiavellian Moment: Florentine Political Thought and the Atlantic Republican Tradition* (Princeton University Press: Princeton), pp. 80, 326, 347–8; David Armitage, Conal Condren, and Andrew Fitzmaurice. eds. 2009. 'Introduction', *Shakespeare and Early Modern Political Thought* (Cambridge University Press: Cambridge), p. 9.

[10] Debora Kuller Shuger. 2001. *Political Theologies in Shakespeare's England: The Sacred and the State in Measure for Measure* (Palgrave: Houndmills); A.D. Nuttall. 2007. *Shakespeare the Thinker* (Yale University Press: London), pp. 262–76; Peter C. Meilaender. 2012. 'Marriage and the Law: Politics and theology in Measure for Measure', *Perspectives on Political Science*, 41: 195–200.

and with what measure ye mete, it shall be measured to you again.'[11] This is the chapter that also warns about hypocrisy: 'Thou hypocrite, first cast the beam out of thine own eye; and then shalt thou see clearly to cast the mote out of thy brother's eye.'[12] Lucio—described in the list of persons as 'a fantastic' (an eccentric, at least in appearance)—and his friends (two other 'like gentlemen' as they are described) joke about sanctimony, the commandments, grace and vice. This irreligious joking and repartee is interspersed with bawdy jeering at each other, at Mistress Overdone, and with jokes about Claudio and Julietta [1.2.51-7, 86-90]. We can see these as anticipating, and contextualizing, the themes of sexual abuse and exploitation that are to come, and also as putting Isabella's religiosity into jeopardy [1.4.38].[13]

Isabella is Claudio's sister. She is about to enter a convent, and we meet her in 1.4 speaking with one of the nuns about the strictness of the rules, Isabella making clear that she isn't anxious about being constrained but 'rather wishing a more strict restraint' [1.4.4]. Lucio comes to explain Claudio's predicament, and to ask her to plead with Angelo [1.4.56-84]. Isabella then, who seeks seclusion, a life of strict rule in an enclosed order, has to engage with government. At the end of her meeting with Angelo—Lucio and the Provost are present—he asks her to return to see him the next day [2.2.158]. At their next meeting Angelo propositions her. If she has sex with him ('lay down the treasures of your body' [2.4.96], 'give me love' [2.4.145]), he will pardon Claudio. Isabella, horrified, refuses: 'I'll tell the world aloud what man thou art', to which Angelo replies, 'Who will believe thee Isabel?' [2.4.152-5].

The plot now gets very convoluted. Claudio pleads with Isabella to comply. The Duke (disguised as Friar Lodowick) hears about the matter. He arranges that Marianna (previously betrothed to Angelo, who had broken the betrothal when Marianna lost her dowry) should substitute for Isabella in the assignation with Angelo (which will have the effect of obliging Angelo to marry Marianna). Angelo, meanwhile, having bargained with Isabella that she exchange sex for her brother's pardon, then orders that Claudio be executed early, before the sexual assignation which takes place according to the Duke's plan. The Duke in disguise arranges with the Provost that Claudio be substituted by another prisoner (Barnardine), and thus spared execution. (In the end the Provost substitutes another prisoner, who has died of natural causes, for

[11] St Matthew. n.d. *Holy Bible*, Authorised (King James) version (Cambridge University Press: Cambridge), 7:2.

[12] St Matthew, *Holy Bible*, n.d.: 7:5.

[13] N.W. Bawcutt. 1991. 'Introduction', *Shakespeare Measure for Measure* (Oxford University Press: Oxford), p. 35.

Barnardine.) Meanwhile Vincentio disguised has encountered Lucio who gossips and jests about the absent Duke's lechery and theft. Openly, as Duke, he then announces his return to the city. He is met by Marianna and Isabella who denounce Angelo. The Duke affects not to believe them. Angelo suggests that they have been influenced by someone else (Friar Lodowick). They are arrested. The Duke, now as Friar Lodowick again, appears, and, as officers attempt to arrest him, is unmasked by Lucio who pulls off his hood. Angelo admits his guilt and asks for punishment. The Duke pardons Isabella, but continues to let her believe that Claudio has been executed. Marianna and Isabella plead for mercy for Angelo, which the Duke grants. Finally it is revealed that Claudio is still alive.

Many scholars and commentators read *Measure for Measure*, and Shakespeare's dramas in general, in the context of the concrete allusions to contemporary events and controversies that Shakespeare seems to be making, and to past and current (for him) reports and histories. Vincentio, in this frame, looks very like King James I, who also engaged in mock executions—in 1603 he sent the convicted conspirators of the Bye plot, including Walter Raleigh, to the scaffold twice, with last minute reprieves. James fretted over the laxity of cities, and was mocked for being 'a poor prince'.[14] Such allusions can be satirical—a way of passing comment on current events (safely deniably, of course) by a caricatural representation. From the point of view of simple stagecraft they are a way of bringing the audience into collusion with the theatre—the intrinsic enjoyment of laughter at a joke is enhanced by the pleasure of getting the joke, understanding the references. Socially, the getting or not getting of such allusions divides the audience too. Those closer to court life and gossip will understand allusions that escape those who are more distant. Vice versa, Pompey's protest in the midst of a dispute with the state officers who seek to close the brothel—'Truly, sir, I am a poor fellow that would live' [2.1.212]— will strike those who identify his quips and patter on the themes of exchange, value, criminalization, and state punishment as a smart commentary on poverty, class, and economy, as a kind of crux in the play. All city audience members would recognize references to the spatial-social divisions of the city, and the concentration of sex-trades. I return to this issue of theatre audiences, the multi-vocality of Shakespeare's dramas, and the contribution of theatre to political culture, in Chapters 7 and 8.

---

[14] Carolyn E. Brown. 1996. 'Duke Vincentio of "Measure for Measure" and King James of England: The poorest princes in Christendom', *Clio: A Journal of Literature, History and the History of Philosophy*, 26: 51–79; Andrew Hadfield. 2004. *Shakespeare and Renaissance Politics* (Thomson Learning: London), pp. 189–93; Andrew Hadfield. 2005. *Shakespeare and Republicanism* (Cambridge University Press: Cambridge), pp. 167–71.

By contrast to these comparisons of Vincentio with King James, there is a tradition of criticism which identifies Duke Vincentio as an exceptionally wise and powerful ruler—magnanimous in his forgiveness, the physician of the ailing city, the architect of a harmonious solution to disorder.[15] Plato (*c*.429–*c*.348 BCE) and Aristotle consider a range of rival metaphors in characterizing 'politikos', the statesman: ship's captain, the weaver of 'the fabric of the state', father, master, peacemaker, despot.[16] Plato also argued that philosopher-kings will have to generate 'noble lies' if those who are to be subject to their rule, but are incapable of grasping the philosophical justification of their subordination, are to accept the political order.[17] In the twentieth century, Leo Strauss (1899–1973), tracing these insights into the nature of political rule through the Jewish and Christian traditions, emphasized how the theorist of political power and the ruler alike must engage in strategic concealment of what they are really doing and saying, because the truth can be threatening or frightening or incomprehensible, in order that truths can continue to be told between those who are equal to them, and further because persecuting authorities and enemies have to be evaded.[18] The direct and indirect effects of thought, and on the practice of government, in the United States in the late twentieth century, are matters of controversy.[19] What is not particularly controversial is that readers and commentators who follow, broadly, Strauss's methods in political thought and theory are very struck by Shakespeare's representations of the self-concealing practices of wise rule by figures who seem to have access to a level of understanding that escapes the characters who are subject to their actions.[20] I agree that that is a significant element of 'Shakespeare's politics'; but I part company from such commentators when they commend Duke Vincentio

---

[15] Allan Bloom and Henry Jaffa. 1964. *Shakespeare's Politics* (Chicago University Press: Chicago); Barbara Tovey. 1996. 'Wisdom and the Law: Thoughts on the Political Philosophy of Measure for Measure', in Joseph Alulis and Vickie Sullivan (eds.), *Shakespeare's Political Pageant: Essays in Literature and Politics* (Rowman and Littlefield: London); Pamela K. Jensen. 2006. 'Vienna Vice: Invisible leadership and deep politics in Shakespeare's Measure for Measure', in John A. Murley and Sean D. Sutton (eds.), *Perspectives on Politics in Shakespeare* (Lexington Books: Oxford); Bernard J. Dobski and Dustin A. Gish. 2012. 'Shakespeare, the Body Politic, and Liberal Democracy', *Perspectives on Political Science*, 41: 181–9.

[16] Plato. 1930–1935. *Republic* (Harvard University Press: Cambridge, MA), Bk 6: 488; Plato. 1925. 'The Statesman/Politicos', *Plato*, Vol. VIII, trans. Harold N. Fowler (Harvard University Press: Cambridge, MA), S. 305–6; Aristotle. 1932. *Politics*, trans. H. Rackham (Harvard University Press: Cambridge, MA), pp. 1258a–1259a; 1265b; 1308a; 1324b–1325b.

[17] Plato, *Republic*, 1930–1935: Bk 2: 414.

[18] Leo Strauss. 1952. *Persecution and the Art of Writing* (The Free Press: Glencoe, IL).

[19] Shadia B. Drury. 1988. *The Political Ideas of Leo Strauss* (St. Martin's Press: New York); Mark Lilla. 2016. *The Shipwrecked Mind: On Political Reaction* (New York Review Books: New York).

[20] Joseph Alulis and Vickie Sullivan. eds. 1996. *Shakespeare's Political Pageant: Essays in Literature and Politics* (Rowman and Littlefield: London); John A. Murley and Sean D. Sutton. eds. 2006. *Perspectives on Politics in Shakespeare* (Lexington Books: Oxford).

as an acme of wisdom. He is no more a wise statesman than he is a modest Christian prince. His political conduct leaves a trail of human destruction and reduction in his wake.

In my interpretation, the play poses two basic questions about political life. First, whether it is worthy, whether individuals should aspire to evade or opt out of it. Second, given that politics is non-optional, which kind of political culture and mode of government we should favour. The play certainly does not offer clear answers to these questions; but it poses them in a vivid way, and stages the competition between rival answers. From the point of view of those engaged in government—the Duke, the officers such as Elbow the naive, malapropistic constable, Escalus, who assists Angelo in the Duke's absence, and the Provost of the prison—the problem is how to keep order. From the point of view of denizens of the city, caught up by government, the problem is that the order enforced is materially costly for them—how are they to live where their livings are illegalized? From the point of view of Claudio and Julietta, Isabella and Marianna, their personal lives and projects are arrested by the eruption of political power into them, and the need to conduct themselves in a new way.

First, the stories of Isabella and of the Duke put political life and action into contradistinction from seclusion. Isabella craves the seclusion of the convent and contemplative religious life, away from the city culture and its politics, and also, presumably, from the obligations of patriarchy. The Duke withdraws from public life and into the seclusion of clandestinity. Second, government, the contestation of governmental authority, and political action, contrast with the untrammelled operation of markets—the markets in sex, and alcohol, and other trades that people will construct in urban settings. Third, there are the pulls of voluntaristic sexual love, ideally untrammelled by authority whether sovereign or patriarchal. In this play, that is represented by Julietta and Claudio. On the one hand, the play takes the political setting of the city for granted—of course, city life requires regulation and government, and that will involve conflict or, at least, contention. On the other hand, government is liable to be oppressive and punitive; political action is ethically dubious, and in this as in other Shakespeare dramas there is a deep sceptical text about politics as such. The first dimension of analysis, then, focuses on the question 'whether politics, or some other way'.

The second dimension is premised on the acceptance that politics and government are an unsubtractable element of the world. The questions then are: what standards of government? What kind of constitution? Which politics? The framework is republican: a city, a commonwealth, and a duke whose office includes the exercise and administration of sovereign power. Republican ideals are by no means explicitly articulated by any of the characters. However, Lucio's mischievous allegation that the Duke had stolen from the state and left Vienna incognito can be read as a statement of the norms governing a sovereign office holder [3.1.355-8]. They should be present, visibly doing their job; and they should not embezzle funds or use them for personal purposes. By contrast, his view that the Duke would be more lenient than Angelo is to lechery [3.1.376-93] expresses the desire for rulers to share the ways of the (male) common people.

In contrast to republicanism, male dominated or otherwise, several other styles of political conduct are also shown in this play. Most obvious is Angelo's authoritarianism. An authoritarian constitution is one which articulates or legislates the principle of obedience, rather than, as some constitutions do, making provision for reflection on and challenge to the laws as they are written and enforced by judicial, political, or cultural means, or which guarantee rights and freedoms, including those to dissent and oppose the government. An authoritarian system gives to the wielder of sovereign authority the power to pronounce what the law is, and how it should be enforced. Then we have the Duke's subterfuge and manipulative trickery—his machiavellianism, which can also be understood as an instance of what I shall refer to later in the book as resort to a 'magic shortcut'. Vincentio transforms himself from duke to friar and back again with bewildering frequency. Like Prospero in *The Tempest* (Chapter 7) he can be read as a 'magus-ruler', a figure attractive to those political theories that idealize the mysterious qualities of rule. However, the quick change acts are more bewildering than Prospero's putting on and taking off his magic cloak [*Tempest* 1.2.23-4; 5.1.331-8]. The final unmasking by Lucio [5.1.350-6] is more like slapstick than like the grave philosopher king.

Next, we meet the comical, naive, malapropistic pretension of Elbow, the constable whose exercises of the authority of his office bring mockery from those he complains against; and, further, the humane insights and just impulses of Escalus and the Provost. Politics is not confined to this level of constitutions of governmental power and styles of rulership. It is also an aspect of social relations more generally, wherever the power and the right to dominate encounters contention or potential contention. *Measure for Measure* focuses on class—the frictional relationships between people trying to make a living on the margins of the city, and between them and the authorities that seek to control them. Most obviously, it raises the question of men's sexual power over women, and women's capacity to evade or confront it. Isabella challenges

Angelo's conduct to her, and she attempts to challenge the Duke to safeguard and deliver justice as the sovereign should.

The play also raises the questions of what kind of speech and action are properly associated with politics. Isabella's pleas and challenges to Angelo and the Duke can be interpreted as the open, public speaking of truth to power. But this interpretation is contested by readings of Isabella's speeches as for- malized rhetorical productions of a juridical cause.[21] If the first, Isabella tries to break through convention in order to speak freely. If the latter, she follows rules, of the kind that grammar school boys like Shakespeare learned (and, in his case, learned to break to great poetic and political effect). As we have seen, Isabella is thwarted first by the physically violent and abusive government of Angelo, and then by the machiavellian trickery of the Duke who delivers a per- haps just outcome, but certainly not by just means, and not by open political action. Isabella's public speech, arguing for justice—whether we class it as a species of truth and disobedience, or as a stylized form of rhetoric and obedi- ence to rules—contrasts with other modes of political conduct. These include the smart, resistant repartee of Pompey in conflict with the police, and Lucio's busybody quips as he attaches himself to 'Friar Lodowick' and tries to help Claudio. And there is the subterfuge and trickery of Duke Vincentio.

Bringing these styles of political conduct into relation with each other, and with the contestations over rival forms of constitution, and with the social- political conflicts of sex and class, produces a typically complicated—but, in my submission, enlightening—representation of the puzzling and elusive world of political power. Each political theme in this proliferation is relevant to each other one. It's difficult to know where to start; and any loose end you grasp in order to unravel the skein (if there is one) makes a knot. We could begin with Isabella's public speech, and trace why and how it is thwarted, and the political meaning of the play's finale. But this isn't a book about sexual politics as such; it's about Shakespeare's dramas. So I will begin by taking Shakespeare's own cue—the explicit message to his audience about the frame of the play: 'Of government the properties to unfold...'.

Of Government

The play begins with a conventional picture of statesmanship—instructions to officers, the Duke delegating duties. But when we see the Duke 'governing' it

[21] Quentin Skinner. 2014. *Forensic Shakespeare* (Oxford University Press: Oxford), pp. 60–2.

is by machiavellian means. In Book 7 of *The Prince*, Machiavelli tells a story which is paralleled—up to a point—by the story of Vincentio and Angelo.[22] This story is made much of by Gentillet in his scandalous Anti-Machiavel.[23] Cesare Borgia, who wished to subdue the Romagna, appointed his major-domo Ramiro d'Orco as governor.[24] D'Orco's methods were exceptionally cruel, and he succeeded in ruling by fear. Eventually, Cesare was given 'a pretext' and D'Orco's body was found in the piazza, cut in two pieces—the executor executed. This spectacle finally stupefied the population and the unfortunate people of the Romagna submitted to Borgia's rule. For Machiavelli, the point of the story is to show the possibilities that face a prince who comes to power over a state by chance or luck. In his chapter on 'the need to avoid contempt and hatred' he recommends that a prince 'should delegate to others the enactment of unpopular measures and keep in their own hands the distribution of favours.'[25]

The Duke's use of manipulation bewilders those subject to his machinations. Stephen Greenblatt speaks of an early modern governing style that consists in 'the distribution of anxiety.'[26] He relates the conduct of Prospero in *The Tempest* to Elizabethan discourses and practices of royal pardon. Duke Vincentio thoroughly outdoes Prospero in the anxiety distribution department. In the final act of *Measure for Measure*, all by order of the sovereign Duke, Isabella and Marianna are arrested and then released; Claudio continues to face punishment by death, although the sentence is not carried out; Angelo is arrested, imprisoned, and led to believe that he will be executed, then brought out and pardoned; Lucio is sentenced to whipping and hanging, and is then ordered to marry 'a punk' and pardoned. The Provost is sacked for having allowed Claudio to be executed early by order of Angelo, and then reinstated. Isabella continues to believe that Claudio has been executed almost to the end of the play. The pardons proliferate: Escalus is pardoned [5.1.362], and so too Isabella [5.1.386-9]—for having spoken to the Duke, when he was disguised, in a manner that they would not have used to a sovereign. In other words, for not having recognized sovereignty when it is concealed.

[22] Norman Holland. 1959. 'Measure for Measure: The duke and the prince', *Comparative Literature*, 11: 16–20.

[23] Innocent Gentillet. 1576/1602. *A Discourse upon the meanes of wel governing and maintaining in good peace, a kingdome, or other principalitie, against N. Machiavell (in his Il Principe]*, trans. S. Patericke (A. Islip: London), Part 3, Maxime 7: 184-98.

[24] Niccolo Machiavelli. 1532/1961. *The Prince*, trans. George Bull (Penguin: Harmondsworth), Ch. VII.

[25] Machiavelli, *Prince*, 1532/1961, Ch. XIX.

[26] Stephen Greenblatt. 1988. *Shakespearean Negotiations: The Circulation of Social Energy in Renaissance England* (University of California Press: Berkeley, CA), pp. 142–4.

Angelo's ruthlessness picks up the machiavellian theme that it is better to be feared than loved.[27] He voices strictures about punishment being the way to show mercy [2.2.101-6], and threatens that the Provost will lose his job if he does not execute Claudio as ordered [2.2.6-14]. So far, then, if we treat *Measure for Measure* as a 'how to govern' (or perhaps 'how not to govern') text, we see Escalus's humane administration of justice mocked by clownish policing and smart resistance by those who are policed. Where laws are enforced, this is done violently. Humane justice is eclipsed by Angelo's ruthlessness and Vincentio's manipulative subterfuge. We also see Vincentio, openly as Duke, forgiving and pardoning characters who should not have been criminalized in the first place, in a manner which personalizes his rule, as lawmaker, rather than emphasizing his office and its constraint. Vincentio combines personalized sovereignty with clandestinity, uses assumed religious authority, and engages in magus-like trickery, in order to respond to the pressures of the civic republic, and legitimate his actions.[28]

Sexual Politics

As Kathleen McLuskie points out, the text of *Measure for Measure* relentlessly presents female characters as sexualized, and women as confined to their established roles.[29] She emphasizes the comedic structure of the play, with its formal requirement of order restored, where the order, as Dollimore points out, is a sexual one, based on marriage.[30] The fornication that Claudio is prosecuted for will be ruled out. The prostitution that keeps Mistress Overdone and Pompey, is purchased by Lucio and his friends, and is supplied by unnamed women who have no part in the drama, will be eliminated. Marianna is married to Angelo, and the Duke restores to her her lost dowry, by gifting her Angelo's forfeit possessions [5.1.419-26]. Lucio is sentenced (for his slander of the Duke) to marrying a prostitute (no particular woman, but any one that he has 'wronged', i.e. impregnated, in the past) [5.1.507-26]. Vincentio, who has, as Friar Lodowick, conducted himself tenderly to Isabella, asks her to marry him. Her acquiescence is in doubt: the text licenses interpretations such as Isabella ignoring or not understanding 'the proposal', or turning away, or

---

[27] Machiavelli, *Prince*, 1532/1961: Ch. XVII.
[28] Compare Daniel Juan Gil. 2013. *Shakespeare's Anti-Politics: Sovereign Power and the Life of the Flesh* (Palgrave Macmillan: Basingstoke), p. 43.
[29] McLuskie, 'Patriarchal Bard', 1985: 93-8.
[30] Dollimore, 'Transgression and Surveillance', 1985b: 72-3.

refusing [5.1.493-6]. Either way, her bodily integrity is finally safeguarded—whether in her preferred life of religious seclusion or in marriage. Importantly, her public speech is ended: Isabella's final utterance is her plea for mercy for Angelo [5.1.445-55]. She doesn't speak during the play's final one hundred lines.

The sexual order, whether based on marriage or on the licentious sexual culture including prostitution is an order in which women are always sexualized, and in which their consent is always in doubt. Pompey jokes about Julietta and Claudio [1.2.84-92] and the Gentlemen ridicule and josh Mistress Overdone [1.2.43-57]. Lucio jokes that Marianna, if she is not maid, widow, or wife, must be a prostitute [5.1.179-80]. Marianna herself makes explicit reference to her body, which has had a sexual encounter with Angelo [5.1.209-12]. In particular, Isabella is sexualized. First, by Lucio, who when he visits her at the convent to ask her to intervene in the cause of Claudio, can't resist making a sexual joke: 'Hail, virgin, if you be—' [1.4.16-17]. Second, although she is not aware of this, by the disguised Duke, who when asking the Provost to leave them alone so that he can speak with Isabella privately, sees fit to assure the Provost: 'My mind promises with my habit no loss shall touch her by my company' [3.1.180-1]. Romantically (that is, in the modern sense, from the point of view of a boy meets girl love story), we can see this as a moment at which the Duke is developing tender feelings for Isabella. On the other hand, for the utterance to make any sense at all, it requires a view of sexual relations which takes it for granted that where a man and a woman are alone together the man is likely to molest the woman.

Whether Vincentio acts as a duke or as a friar, it ought to go without saying that he will not molest Isabella. If it does not go without saying—and, clearly, in the world of *Measure for Measure* it does not—then it cannot be obvious that Angelo has done wrong in importuning Isabella. By some lights, Angelo obviously has done wrong. By his own puritanical standards he can be charged with the hypocrisy that St Matthew warns against. Politically, using the sovereign office with which he has been entrusted for his own gain is corrupt. Morally his conduct is evil, as he himself understands and soliliquizes [2.2.165-90, 2.4.1-17]. But, culturally, whether fornication or forced sexual intimacy should be crimes are contested questions. Legally, as we all know, the matter of Isabella's consent will always be a problem, only decidable in the context of cultural contestation, and the struggle by women for full legal, social, and cultural subjectivity.

The sexualization of Isabella is nowhere more vivid than in her interviews with Angelo. Isabella has chosen seclusion in a convent. From this, she has to emerge not only to discharge the duties of kinship and to engage with life in society, but also to act publicly—she has to face and deal with public power, to challenge government. She meets Angelo in his governmental office. In Act 5, she meets the Duke, similarly, to complain about the conduct of a state officer. This encounter is at the gates of the city—in the open, and in the view and hearing of officers, citizens, and denizens. Isabella is positioned politically as subject of state authority, and the play gives to her the role of public speaker. The play takes a quizzically sceptical view of Isabella as either speaking truth to power or effectively deploying rhetoric to secure justice. Her political speech and her political agency are thwarted in several stages.

When she meets Angelo in his office, her plea for Claudio is at first ineffective as, by her own admission, she is in sympathy with the laws against fornication. At Lucio's urging, she steps up the poetry, sharpens the logic, and shifts ground in her forensic argument. Her rhetoric contrasts with Pompey's in the previous scene—he responds to charges with word play and trickery. Isabella invokes mercy, the golden rule (do as you would be done by), God's judgement, and the concept of tyranny. Two sexualizations unfold.

First, Lucio punctuates her speech with prompts, suggestions, encouragements, and asides to the audience. 'You are too cold' [2.2.56]; 'Ay touch him' [2.2.71]; 'O, to him … He's coming, I perceive't' [2.2.126-7]. The Lucio actor is certainly constrained to perform this as comic sexual innuendo—it is all of a piece with his irrepressible speech in other scenes. The humorous nature of the three way exchange stems not just from the intrinsically funny nature of references to sexual organs and so on, but also from the situation of the female character, the dupe, unwitting as to the sexual meaning of the words. Second, Isabella's speech—her theological argument with Angelo, her use of forensic rhetoric, her consideration of tyranny and law—takes on the kinds of appeals characteristic of political life. She appeals to an executive of the state law. But developing persuasiveness she appeals to Angelo personally: 'Isabella: Hark how I'll bribe you; good, my lord, turn back. Angelo: How? Bribe me? Isabella: Ay, with such gifts that heaven shall share with you' [2.2.146-8]. Her first words at their second meeting are: I am come to know your pleasure [2.4.31]. It's more than plausible that Shakespeare's audiences would have found Angelo's sexual proposition to Isabella, and Isabella's dilemma between submitting to sex or seeing her brother executed, with all the wit, banter, and unwittingness on her part that surrounds it, comical rather than evil or terrible. Isabella plays the straight comedian's part, and that's funny. In just the same way, the first appearance of Mistress Overdone—the dame—would provoke laughter or catcalls. Such sexualization of female characters—whether or not they are played by male actors in drag—is a feature of comic performance from Shakespeare to the twentieth-century 'Carry On' and its equivalents.

But the comic nature of *Measure for Measure* is problematic—not only for twenty-first-century audiences. It is clear that the meaning of Angelo's conduct, like the meaning of Isabella's attempts at public speech, are contested within the play. This is not least by Angelo himself, for whom his 'love' for Isabella [2.4.142] is mixed with his sense of himself as evil [2.4.4-8], and with confusion about 'false seeming' [2.4.15]. Funny or not, a matter of the confounding of good and evil or not, it's also clear that Angelo's treatment of Isabella is wrong. First, Angelo's proposition clearly proceeds from his sovereign office: 'I, now the voice of the recorded law, pronounce a sentence on your brother's life; might there not be a charity in sin to save this brother's life?' [2.4.61-4]. It's a while before Isabella gets it, but her theological commitments to her own bodily integrity and chastity mean that when she does understand Angelo's proposition, she is quite clear that she would rather die [2.4.99-104]. As the scene goes on she comes to understand it in the frame of men-women relations. 'Angelo: women are frail too. Isabella:...Women? Help heaven! Men their creation mar in profiting by them' [2.4.125-9]. Taking advantage of women's inferiority is as debasing to men as to the women they oppress. For Isabella, the wrong lies not only in the abuse of office, but in the general structure of sexual relations, and conduct of masculine gender men.

Such close intertwining of the social relations of sex, and the power to govern within those relationships, and the power to govern at the level of society and state, in my analysis, makes Shakespeare a significant figure for political theory. The question whether Shakespeare promotes any kind of proto-feminism in giving Isabella the role of speaking truth to power, or in writing for her character the eloquence of Renaissance rhetoric, is less interesting than the way the play relates inter-personal with state power, and makes of both a matter of contention.

Political Speech

In all the constructions of 'politics' that can be discerned and read in Shakespeare's dramas, speech in political action and events is central. This is unsurprising given that these are theatrical dramas and texts are our primary source. Some commentators insist, against the grain of scholarship and commentary on Shakespeare that focuses on his allusions to and rewritings of historical and local events and reports, and also against the grain of any exclusively literary focus on his engagement with literary forms and his particular capacities in poetry and wordplay, that the conventions and constraints of theatrical performance should be more prominent in our understandings of the dramas.[31] Analogously, some political theorists emphasize appearance or performance in political action. The focus should be on what people do rather than what they say. And theorists should understand how closely 'acting' in the theatrical sense and in the political and social senses are related.[32] For others, politicians' speeches, parliamentary disputations, and public comment are far less important than material, physical, struggles over resources and authority, and uses of violence to enforce order.[33] Nobody would entirely exclude the significance of speech—what is said and how and with what effects—from their conceptualizations of politics, or of the politics of Shakespeare's drama. However, the nature of political speech, what, if anything, is distinctive about it, is as contested as the nature of politics itself.

In the classical republican tradition persuasive speech is essential to the ideal of public political life. The grammar school education of Shakespeare's time had Ciceronian texts, with their articulation of the virtues of office, the threats of corruption, the art of argument, and the ties of civic and social life, at their heart.[34] Isabella's plea to Angelo begins with her admission that Claudio's crime is a foul one and that he is fully guilty [2.2.34-160]. She goes on to plead that the crime, not the criminal, should be condemned, and for mercy for the criminal. She justifies this plea by the need for all of us to acknowledge our own sins and participate in heavenly ways [2.2.74-80].[35] Her plea mounts in emotional intensity. This development, as Quentin Skinner emphasizes, is textbook Cicero and Quintilian (35-100 CE).[36] Effectively artful speech, which succeeds in persuading the people it intends to persuade while maintaining standards of validity and truthfulness, should be, according to republicans, the central vehicle of political power. This principle that the force of the better argument is the only force that must prevail, and therefore that the social conditions must be guaranteed that permit free and reasonable speech, dominates

---

[31] Robert Weimann. 1978. *Shakespeare and the Popular Tradition in Theater: Studies in the Social Dimension of Dramatic Form and Function* (Johns Hopkins University Press: Baltimore); Robert Weimann. 1988. 'Bifold Authority in Shakespeare's Theatre', *Shakespeare Quarterly*, 39: 401-17.

[32] Arendt, *Human Condition*, 1958: 184, 188.

[33] Karl Marx and Friedrich Engels. 1848/1977. *Manifesto of the Communist Party* (Progress Publishers: Moscow); Ranciere, *Disagreement*, 1995/1999: 26ff.

[34] T.W. Baldwin. 1944. *Shakspere's Small Latine and Lesse Greek* (University of Illinois Press: Champaign, IL), Vol. 2, pp. 1-97; Armitage, Condren, and Fitzmaurice, 'Introduction', 2009: 3-6; Skinner, *Forensic Shakespeare*, 2014: 11-47.

[35] Nuttall, *Shakespeare*, 2007: 267-8; Skinner, *Forensic Shakespeare*, 2014: 130-4.

[36] Cicero. 1949. *De Inventione* (Harvard University Press: Cambridge, MA), XVII.24; Quintilian. 2001. *The Orator's Education*, Books 1-12 (Loeb Classical Library, Harvard University Press: Cambridge, MA), Vol. 2, 4.1.33; Skinner, *Forensic Shakespeare*, 2014: 132-3.

twentieth-century republican and liberal theory, for instance in the work of Jurgen Habermas (b.1929).[37]

Isabella is not a political counsellor, but in her exchange with Angelo in 2.2, she interlards her plea for mercy for Claudio with spiritual-political advice: 'How would you be if He which is the top of judgement should but judge you as you are?' [2.2.76–8; also 2.2.108–10; 2.2.136–40]. As Foucault emphasizes, the speaker of truth to power speaks a truth which issues from within them, and is indissolubly connected to themselves.[38] This is the sign of authenticity which is a necessary condition of persuasiveness. In Isabella's case truth is a quality given to her speech by her own spiritual integrity and clear moral vision. A good deal of twentieth-century political philosophy focuses on the truth and logic of argument, independently, as it were, of the honesty of the speaker. In modern philosophy, evidence and logic, objectively evaluated, are the criteria for judging argument and utterance. Foucault contrasts this with the older criterion—to which Isabella seems to subscribe—that the truth speaker's truth is guaranteed 'by her possession of certain moral qualities'.[39] But as Foucault also emphasizes, the speaker of truth takes a risk.[40] The majority or a significant minority of an assembly of equals may dislike the truth that is spoken. The social setting for a truth speech has to be hospitable if it is to come off.

Playing the role of returning duke, Vincentio is displeased by Isabella's assertion that Angelo 'would not but by gift of my chaste body to his concupiscible intemperate lust release my brother' [5.1.98–100]. Typically, of course, Shakespeare has mixed things up. We know Vincentio to be dissembling, and we know Isabella's allegation about Angelo to be true. But, it is not completely true, however, that '...after much debatement, my sisterly remorse confutes mine honour, and I did yield to him' [5.1.100–2]. That is not true, because although Isabella had agreed to have sex with Angelo, Marianna had taken her place in a bed-trick which ambiguously makes a wrong less improper.[41] (St Augustine argued that although a wife does not have 'the power of her

---

[37] Jurgen Habermas. 1970. 'On Systematically Distorted Communication', *Inquiry: An Interdisciplinary Journal of Philosophy*, 13: 205–18; Jurgen Habermas. 1995. 'Reconciliation through the Public Use of Reason: Remarks on John Rawls' political liberalism', *Journal of Philosophy*, XC11: 109–31; Habermas is responding to John Rawls. 1995. 'Political Liberalism: Reply to Habermas', *Journal of Philosophy*, 92: 132–80; see also Rawls, 'Political Liberalism', 1995.

[38] Michel Foucault. 1983/1985. *Discourse & Truth: The Problematization of Parrhesia. Six Lectures at the University of California at Berkeley CA Oct–Nov 1983*, ed. Joseph Pearson, https://foucault.info/parrhesia/.

[39] Foucault, *Discourse and Truth*, 1983/1985: 3.

[40] Foucault, *Discourse and Truth*, 1983/1985: 2–3.

[41] Janet Adelman. 1992. *Suffocating Mothers: Fantasies of Origin in Shakespeare's Plays* (Routledge: London), pp. 77–9, 290n.41; David McCandless. 1994. 'Helena's Bed-trick: Gender and performance in All's Well that Ends Well', *Shakespeare Quarterly*, 45: 449–68.

own body', a wife who agreed to a trick of this kind, for the sake of saving her husband's honour, would not be condemned in the way that a trickster wife usually would.[42]) Neither is it true that '...the next morn betimes, his purpose surfeiting, he sends a warrant for my poor brother's head' [5.1.102-4]. Isabella thinks this is true, but—even worse—the audience knows that Angelo had sent the warrant before his assignation with Isabella. She is mistaken about Angelo in that she knows he has double-crossed her, but she does not know when he executed the cross. Isabella, in my interpretation, is appropriately understood in terms of parrhesia. However, she is mixed up in a trick, to which she is party. Both of these counter her integrity and her freedom.

All of this can be read as a representation of political power—how it really works. Rhetoric—carefully constructed judicious speech, delivered with full consciousness of audience and the words' likely effects—can be understood as continuous with the kind of subterfuge and downright mendacity that Vincentio engages in. The understanding of political speech, as such, as mendacious at worst, misleading at best, designed to bewilder or evade rather than to enlighten or to answer, runs deep in political cultures. The Duke's disguise as a friar, wearing a hood that covers his face, denying that Isabella can be telling the truth, and dealing with public problems in a way that seems to defer rather than to resolve social and governmental conflicts, can be understood as Shakespearean metaphors for political conduct. However, they are so close to how some actual political actors behave that they can also be understood as less metaphorical than literal.

But this is only one version of political power: another centres on the picture of a decisive, dominating authority who brooks no argument. The Duke's political language, Isabella's truth to power, and Pompey's smart talking back, all contrast with Angelo's authoritarian pronouncements. 'Authoritarian' thinking idealizes the transparency and finality of sovereign pronouncements. James I was keen on finality, but less clear about transparency.[43] Thomas Hobbes, forty years after *Measure for Measure*, set out a systematic rational defence of authoritarian and unified government which tolerates no opposition, repudiates rhetoric (and also trickery and 'conjuring'), arguing that we must recognize and defer to the conventional nature of the names of things, and accept the

---

    [42] St Augustine. 1958. 'De Sermone Domini in Monte Secundum Matthaeum', in Geoffrey Bullough (ed.), *Dramatic and Narrative Sources of Shakespeare*, Vol. 2 (Routledge and Kegan Paul: London), pp. 418–19.
    [43] James VI and I. 1598/1982. 'The True Law of Free Monarchies; or the Reciprock and mutuall duetie betwixt a free King and his natural subjects', in James Craigie (ed.), *Minor Prose Works of James VI and I* (Scottish Text Society: Edinburgh), pp. 69–76; James VI and I. 1603/1944. *Basilicon Doron*, ed. James Craigie, 2 vols (William Blackwood and Sons Ltd: Edinburgh), pp. 4–6.

need for authoritative arbitration or judgement in order to resolve disputes.[44] Paradoxically, Hobbes recognized, though, that scientific and rational truth alone would not persuade his readers, and in *Leviathan* had recourse to one of the most powerful metaphors in English language political writing—the state as a giant, inexorable, unopposable sea creature—and to other artful techniques, in order to push home to readers and to citizens the necessity of authoritarian power and sovereignty that is absolute.[45]

Angelo's language in 2.2 exactly enacts an authoritarian view of his legal sovereign power. Before Isabella's arrival the Provost asks 'Is it your will Claudio shall die tomorrow?' to which Angelo answers 'Did not I tell thee yea? Hadst thou not order? Why dost thou ask again?' [2.2.7-9]. To Isabella he repeatedly emphasizes that the law is the law, and that both the law and his pronouncement have priority over any other consideration. '…every fault's condemned ere it be done' [2.2.38]. 'Look what I will not, that I cannot do' [2.2.52, 2.2.48, 2.2.56]. Isabella does draw him into some longer engagements: but he repeats that though the law had been asleep it was now awake [2.2.90-100]. More philosophically, he retorts that pity is best shown by enforcing justice [2.2.101-5] and again utters the sovereign pronouncement 'Your brother dies tomorrow' [2.2.106].

Isabella's speech does 'affect' Angelo: he construes it as a matter of temptation—wondering in soliliquy 'Is this her fault or mine? The tempter or the tempted who sins most, ha? Not she, nor doth she tempt; but it is I…' and going on to a predictable consideration whether it is because of her very modesty and obvious integrity that Isabella is more alluring than a lewd woman [2.2.166-75]. But this engagement with his own sexual lust, and the theology and morality of sin, is reserved for soliloquy. His proposition (the text licenses physical assault of Isabella) is couched in the same imperative mood: 'Plainly conceive I love you' [2.4.142]. His exit line: 'As for you, say what you can; my false o'erweighs your true' [2.4.170-1] is a Shakespearean inversion of what later would be Hobbes's sovereign truth. That would be: What I say is true, is true. Angelo, by contrast, acknowledges that Isabella has truth on her side; but his sovereign power outweighs it. This fissure in Angelo's sovereign truth opens up assertions of sovereignty to Shakespeare's scepticism.

[44] Thomas Hobbes. 1651/1996. *Leviathan* (Oxford University Press: Oxford), Ch. XII, S12; Robert E. Stillman. 1995. 'Hobbes' Leviathan: Monsters, metaphors, magic', *ELH*, 62: 791-819; Quentin Skinner. 1996. *Reason and Rhetoric in the Philosophy of Hobbes* (Cambridge University Press: Cambridge); Quentin Skinner. 2002. *Visions of Politics: Hobbes and Civil Science* (Cambridge University Press: Cambridge), p. 78.
[45] Skinner, *Visions of Politics*, 2002: 86.

Isabella fails in her exertion of political power. Her attempts, while poetically, theatrically, and indeed formally impressive examples of their kind, are not successful. She is undermined by Lucio and his articulation and enactment of the values of their society. She succeeds in moving Angelo, but not in the right way. Her public plea to the Duke is first mocked and denigrated as madness [5.1.43-64] and then condemned as criminal lies [5.1.105-22]. Such responses to women's speech, of sexualization, mockery, denigration, and force, are culturally commonplace. For Isabella, we can surmise, the independent 'pull' of the secluded religious life which is her first choice must be pretty nearly matched in force by the 'push' of these values, bound up as they are with the sexual culture that positions women uneasily between marriage and prostitution. We can also surmise that her reluctant foray into public speech, against her preference for religious silence, is unlikely to inspire her to further adventures in politics: she now will be silent, whether in public (as through the last episodes of the drama) or behind the convent walls.

This interpretation focuses on Isabella's preferences and choices among the array of options that face her. Feminists have never been content with simply accepting the option set and choice context that is given in any setting. The political question is: how do we change the array of options that face people so that justice can be achieved? Among the factors that would have to change, were Isabella's voice to be heard in the right way, would be the habits and norms of conduct that govern the men she encounters. A longstanding tradition of analysis of language and truth focuses on the conditions that enjoin 'women's silence'. Among these—and they apply to structures of asymmetric power in general—are dominant understandings of how the world is which operate to authorize the views and voices of some (the powerful) and to denigrate and drown out any just reception of the voices of others (the subjugated). Twentieth-century philosophers emphasize that this is not a matter, simply, of some voices not being heard, it is also a matter of structures of knowledge and truth that operate so that those voices cannot, could not, be heard.[46]

One picture we might draw from this discussion of what Isabella tries to say, and the uptake of her speech, is that there's the thing Isabella is trying to say, and there is the context in which the meanings of her words can be

[46] Michel Foucault. 1976/1980. 'Two Lectures', in Colin Gordon (ed.), Power/Knowledge: Selected Interviews and other Writings 1972-1977 (Pantheon Books: New York);; Chandra Talpade Mohanty. 1984. 'Under Western Eyes: Feminist scholarship and colonial discourses', Boundary, 2(12): 333-58; Deborah Cameron. 1985. Feminism and Linguistic Theory (Macmillan: London), pp. 91-113; Gayatry Chakravorty Spivak. 1988. 'Can the Subaltern Speak?', in C. Nelson and L. Grossberg (eds.), Marxism and the Interpretation of Culture (Macmillan Education Basingstoke); Miranda Fricker. 2007. Epistemic Injustice (Oxford University Press: Oxford).

twisted, her testimony can be disbelieved and discounted. The political problem, on this picture, is: how can we construct and stabilize social and public contexts in which these systematic distortions don't take place?[47] This is a plausible ethical and political project, which owes a good deal to an ideal of reason in language that was developing in the early modern period. It is a difficult one that Shakespeare seemingly never tires of playing with. An alternative approach to politics takes a different approach to language also. As Cavell argues, Shakespeare's dramas insistently emphasize, and perform, the instability of meaning, the way that 'human language is inherently open to the repudiation of itself'.[48] For Arendt, in her reading of the possibilities of political life both in the classical tradition of the agora and the Ciceronian republic, and in the later Atlantic republican tradition, it is this openness that is the point, and the power, of political life.[49] How our words are taken up is not, cannot be, determined by us as speakers; and this is the heart of political life. It is here that, for Arendt, the possibility of political construction of new worlds—ways of living, institutions, and relationships—resides. This openness, that we cannot be secure in advance as to who will hear us saying what, authorizes us to speak for all when we speak publicly and politically, but also enjoins us to understand that we cannot authoritatively (that is, in the sense of sovereignty) speak for all. Political life involves us in encounter, which has to include full engagement with each other and the extended communication which alone might bring us to a point of concord.

Measure for Measure and the Political Way

Where do those ideals leave Isabella? If this interpretation of the phenomenology and ethics of political life is right, then Angelo's authoritarianism and Vincentio's machiavellian trickery and ruthlessness alike fall short of a normative understanding of politics. Trickery, and force, are kinds of human conduct, to be sure. They can be effective in social life, and they undeniably have political effects. They are among the features of public life that make people despair of politics. But they aren't political conduct as we know it ought to be.

---

[47] Habermas, 'Systematically Distorted Communication', 1970.

[48] Stanley Cavell. 2003. *Disowning Knowledge in Seven Plays of Shakespeare*, updated edn (Cambria Press: Cambridge), p. 16.

[49] Hannah Arendt. 1954/1990. 'Philosophy and Politics', *Social Research*, 57: 427–54; Arendt, *Human Condition*, 1958: e.g. 180–4.

Pompey's backchat, we think, might bring us somewhat nearer to the articulation of a truth of material want in relation to a 'commonwealth'. Both the modes of frank speaking of truth to power and the judicious use of rhetorical devices in order to (attempt to) secure audience assent are within the ambit of properly political speech. Their effects—such as they are—are fully political. For now, I want to note that this makes of Isabella, potentially, the fully political actor of this play. She uses rhetoric as artfully as she can, although she is thwarted by Angelo's, Lucio's, and Vincentio's sexualizations of her. Angelo's use of sovereign authority in order to dominate Isabella sexually falls short, to put it mildly, of what we can think of as proper political conduct. So too the Duke whose recourse to trickery brings about some semblance of 'justice' but by occult means—by surveillance and secrecy, rather than by liberty and public reason.

3

Political and Military Power

Coriolanus

Coriolanus and Politics

Coriolanus (composed *c.*1608) dramatizes a conflict that must be managed in polities, and is often discussed by political thinkers, between the political way and the military way. In modern political thought it is most often accepted that military power is for the security of states, and that political and civil domination of the military is critical to modern constitutions. Where princes or presidents or governmental ministers are effectively or formally 'commander-in-chief', obviously military reasoning and conduct can't be completely separated from political. Sometimes, of course, military officers take over the entire running of a state and society, to a greater or lesser degree applying military style discipline and procedures over governmental, judicial, and even social institutions. More often, the issue is that military officers and institutions have significant influence over or authority in government and society, and the question is whether this is beneficial or justifiable. Significant strains of social and political thought valorize military values and ways over others. The idea that physical combat, where death is a real possibility, is ennobling, whereas political manoeuvring is base, recurs in theory and in culture. The idea that the military organization of physical combat—based on physical discipline, hierarchical command, uniformity, and sequestration of the military from the wider social and cultural context—realizes the acme of masculine virtue, is a recognizable element of romanticism and some versions of republicanism, as well as fascism and some nationalisms.[1] Modern states' public political cultures are more or less 'militarist'—the prominence of military display at state and social events varies, as does the prestige of the military as an institution or as a career for individuals, and the influence of military styles in cultural pursuits and organizations.

---

[1] Alfred Vagts. 1959. *A History of Militarism: Civilian and Military* (Hollis and Carter: London); Andrew Alexandra. 1993. 'Militarism', *Social Theory and Practice*, 19: 205–23.

Shakespeare and the Political Way. Elizabeth Frazer, Oxford University Press (2020). © Elizabeth Frazer.
DOI: 10.1093/oso/9780198848615.001.0001

Disputes about exactly how military power should stand vis-à-vis state power take diverse forms, and the significance of military styles and disciplines for society is invariably a matter for contention. Early modern English history writings—which Shakespeare's historical dramas reflected and refracted, and to which they subsequently have made a popular contribution—tell a story of military distinction in battle progressively consolidating the English state. This story is vigorously contested from a number of viewpoints. Many thinkers and theorists emphasize that economic and related social changes were both pushing and pulling processes of centralization, and that the military story is at best a footnote to political economy. But, although history narratives are less heroic than many (not all) readings of Shakespeare's history plays are, historians continue to see military technology and organization as an independent and inter-dependent factor in complicated relationship with religion and culture, and polity, as well as economy.[2] The idea that territorial conquest and control found states and generate greatness is central to the story of the Roman republic and empire, as told through the works of Julius Caesar (100-44 BCE) and the historian Titus Livius (59 BCE-12? CE).[3] It was emphasized, in The Prince, the Discourses on Livy, and The Art of War, by Machiavelli. Machiavelli's Art of War, published in 1521, was translated into English and published with a dedication to Queen Elizabeth in 1560—it was reprinted in 1573 and 1588, so evidently a success.[4] Machiavelli insists that military valour and distinction must be among the first concerns of princes, that the republic must be armed, and it must be defended by its own citizens, not by the kind of mercenary and career soldiers from outside the city who defend the Venice of Othello. (Othello is not Venetian; neither are Iago and Cassio, both of whom are from Florence.) This ideal of citizen-soldiers is a key tenet of civic republicanism.

It is contested. In particular, a strain of pacific thinking, critical of military values, was current in the early modern period, connected with the Christian humanism of Thomas More (1478-1535) whose sketch of an anti-militarist society in Utopia is decidedly paradoxical and ironic; and Desierius Erasmus

---

[2] Philip Corrigan and Derek Sayer. 1985. The Great Arch: English State Formation as Cultural Revolution (Basil Blackwell: Oxford), pp. 1–5; Michael Mann. 1986/2012. The Sources of Social Power. Vol. 1: A History of Power from the Beginning to AD 1760 (Cambridge University Press: Cambridge), pp. 1–14, 22–8.

[3] Julius Caesar. 1917. The Gallic War, trans. H.J. Edwards (Harvard University Press: Cambridge, MA), Bk. VIII; Livy. 1919. Annales, Books 1–4 (a.k.a. Ad Urbe Condita), trans. B.O. Foster (Harvard University Press: Cambridge, MA).

[4] Peter Whitehorne. 1521/1964. 'Dedicatory Epistle to Elizabeth I', in Niccolo Machiavelli, Art of War, ed. Neal Wood (Perseus Books: Cambridge, MA), pp. 231–7.

(1466-1536).[5] For these thinkers, the ideal prince is a jurist and a philosopher, rather than a soldier-scholar.[6] It is important to note, though, that the vices as well as the virtues of military valour, and the tensions between military and civil power, are present also within the republican tradition. Later, in the eighteenth century, Mary Wollstonecraft took issue with Jean-Jacques Rousseau on, among other things, his principle that the republic must be militarily organized and defended by citizen-soldiers, who will, of course, be men, and, in her view, will be peculiarly susceptible to vice.[7] Before that eighteenth-century controversy, we find some knotty problems and puzzles about how the political and the military way can be squared. Machiavelli begins *The Art of War* remarking on the evident 'discordance' between civilian and military life, with their different standards of dress and manners, and the way that civilian ways seem effeminate from the point of view of military ways.[8] Cicero wants to emphasize the different but equal worth of political and military contributions to the life and security of the republic, but as we shall see, struggles to reconcile them, and to contain his concern about those who (like Julius Caesar) bring military power into the governmental life of the republic and threaten its civic values.[9]

In *Coriolanus* (and in the historical sources Plutarch (*c*.46-*c*.120 CE) and Livy (59 BCE-17 CE)[10]), Caius Martius is a Roman military general who, after his distinguished conquest of the Volscean city of Corioles, is known as Coriolanus. He is welcomed back to Rome by senators who ask him to stand for the office of consul. For Martius, the requirements of republican political conduct are both onerous and contemptible. As a partisan of the patrician or aristocratic policy position, he makes clear his opposition to popular policy measures such as the increase of the supply and the decrease of the price of grain in a time of hunger. He opposes the institution of the office of the tribunes,

---

[5] Thomas More. 1516/2002. *Utopia* (Cambridge University Press: Cambridge), Bk. 2, 109-17; Desiderius Erasmus. 1536/1946. *The Complaint of Peace*, trans. Thomas Paynell, Early English Books Online, https://eebo.chadwyck.com Stephen Marx. 1992. 'Shakespeare's Pacifism', *Renaissance Quarterly*, 45: 49-95.

[6] Marx, 'Shakespeare's Pacifism', 1992: 49-50; Theodor Meron. 2018. 'Shakespeare: A dove, a hawk, or simply a humanist', *American Journal of International Law*, III: 936-57.

[7] Jean-Jacques Rousseau. 1762/1997. *The Social Contract and Other Later Political Writings*, trans. and ed. Victor Gourevitch (Cambridge University Press: Cambridge) Bk II, Ch. 4; Bk III, Ch. 5; Mary Wollstonecraft. 1792/1994. 'A Vindication of the Rights of Woman', in Janet Todd (ed.), *Mary Wollstonecraft: Political Writings* (Oxford University Press: Oxford), Ch. IX:224-7; Jean Elshtain. 1987/1995. *Women and War* (Chicago University Press: Chicago).

[8] Niccolo Machiavelli. 1521/1965. 'Preface', *The Art of War*, ed. Neal Wood, trans. N. Farnsworth (Perseus Books: Cambridge, MA).

[9] Cicero. 1913. *On Duties (De Officiis)* (Harvard University Press: Cambridge, MA), Bk 1.

[10] Plutarch. 1916b. 'Caius Martius Coriolanus', *Plutarch's Lives*, Vol. 4, trans. Bernadotte Perrin (William Heinemann Ltd: London); Livy, *Annales*, 1919: Bk II: XXXIX-XL.

whose role is to represent the people's views to the senate and to represent senate policy to the people. He refuses to comply with the traditions of selection whereby a candidate for consul seeks the endorsement of the people for his appointment, presenting himself for questioning in a humble fashion with a deferential demeanour. He is accused of and tried for treason, and banished from Rome. At the heart of Martius's conflict with the Roman polity are, first, a deep antipathy to political values and ways at all; and, second, a deep antipathy to the inclusion of the common people in the institutions and political constitution of Rome. Martius values his ideal of Rome, the state; but he separates that decisively from Roman society, the real people, and from the existing governmental regime which, in his eyes, has betrayed Rome. Once banished, he joins forces with an erstwhile enemy, Aufidius, leader of the Volsceans with whom Rome is at war. They lay siege to Rome; eventually Martius, though, rather than destroying Rome settles a peace; so he is killed, as a traitor, by the Volsceans.

Martius raises the question whether society and the state, which the military is there to defend and to secure, are worthy of the sacrifice the military are called upon to make—a question that recurs in history. The valorization of the military way in contradistinction to those of civilians and politicians casts real doubt on the justice of the exchange. In Machiavelli's *Art of War* we find an ironic distinction between the city and the military camp.[11] Rationally designed and laid out, orderly, calm, disciplined and efficient, full of purpose and healthful activity, the camp is to be free of prostitutes, women generally, gambling, and conflict.[12] The city itself, with its dark narrow streets, taverns, and disorder, contrasts with the camp in every particular. 'The state' can be idealized. But the actual state consists of society, and cities; defence of the state involves defence of its people—including the disorderly undisciplined people. In the twentieth century, Samuel Huntingdon articulates the same thought: Highland Falls (the village in New York State) represents the spirit of the United States at its most tired, monotonous, commercial, and commonplace, while West Point (the nearby military academy) with its ordered beauty and serenity, its neatness and utility, epitomizes all that is good. Yet, according to Huntingdon, echoing the famous nineteenth-century, often revisited, formulation by Carl von Clausewitz (1780-1831): 'The military profession exists to serve the state. To render the highest possible service, the entire profession and the military forces which it leads must be constituted as an effective

---

[11] Elizabeth Frazer and Kimberly Hutchings. 2011. 'Virtuous Violence and the Politics of Statecraft in Machiavelli, Clausewitz and Weber', *Political Studies*, 59: 56–73.

[12] Machiavelli, *Art of War*, 1521/1965: Bk 6.

instrument of state policy.'[13] There is a problem if, like Martius, the military do not value the people of the society they are called upon to defend.

At one level *Coriolanus* is among the most obviously political of Shakespeare's dramas. It focuses on public disagreement about the inclusion of the common people in the polity (that is, about constitution) and about governmental policies which aim, or not, at egalitarianism and justice (public policy). It focuses, too, on the gulf between the militarist's ideal state and the actual political state and society—that is, on normative state theory. The alignment of Martius, the soldier, with an 'aristocratic', inegalitarian policy, and an idealization of the state is straightforward. This is a policy-party contest which, familiarly, is a structural feature in many polities. But the play also tackles politics at a deeper level—what has to be the case for there to be political organization of social relations at all?

Coriolanus poses this question in a number of ways. First, one quick answer is that there has to be a body politic—a constituted, organized population who somehow have become a unity, sharing social, cultural, and governmental institutions, and, in particular, sharing ways of making decisions about those institutions. This body, of course, includes some and excludes some, and inevitably who or what is a member must be at issue. Shakespeare gives the metaphor of the body politic—a productive trope that is among the most basic of the ontological metaphors that organize modern reason and understanding, as well as a cornerstone of republican and monarchical political thinking alike[14]—a characteristic run for its money. The play examines it from many points of view, including what happens when the body is starving, the nature of its sexuality, and crucially the question of how members are or are not related to each other and valued. A second answer to the question will disavow this body trope, and think of a polity as a population whose members relate to each other not as, for instance, limbs to trunk, but as individuals who interact with each other in a friendly and respectful way, governed by shared legal institutions and procedures of authority and the constraint of power. Members, in their roles such as citizen or candidate for office should

[13] Samuel P. Huntingdon. 1957/1967. *The Soldier and the State: The Theory and Politics of Civil-Military Relations* (Harvard University Press: Cambridge, MA), pp. 464–6, 73; Carl von Clausewitz. 1832/1976. *On War*, ed. and trans. Michael Howard and Peter Paret (Princeton University Press: Princeton, NJ), Bk 1.

[14] George Lakoff and Mark Johnson. 1980/2003. *Metaphors We Live By* (University of Chicago Press: Chicago), pp. 33–5; R.B. Parker. ed. 1994. 'Introduction', William Shakespeare, *Coriolanus* (Oxford University Press: Oxford), pp. 6–8.

witness and discuss, even if they don't directly deliberate about and decide on, matters of appointment, policy, and the conduct of government. These republican ideas, with their themes of cooperative ways of negotiation, and toleration of dissent, are repulsive to Martius.

Psychologically, in republican theory, individuals have to be the kind of subject who can engage in these kinds of interaction with fellow citizens and with strangers. Public life—crowds, political discussions—can be tumultuous; Martius's response to tumult is to draw his sword, turning civil political power to violence. Discussion with people you don't agree with can involve incomprehension or reactions of antipathy; Martius's response is vituperation. Appearances matter—the way you appear and behave to others will be read for its symbolism; body language will be interpreted. Jeffrey Green argues that late modern theories of democracy have over-emphasized 'voice' and 'vote', and under-emphasized the equally critical right of people to see, to hear, and to scrutinize those who (aspire to) govern. Individuals are, evidently, better and worse at this aspect of political life. Martius considers himself unable to act the part, and his shame at being exposed generates hostility to spectators and audience.[15] Shakespeare's play very clearly relates these aspects of Martius's temperament to his intimate relationships, with his wife, his child, his mother, and his warrior enemies and allies.

The play, then, can be read as asking about the deep subjective and social preconditions for politics. But what is this 'politics'? In *Coriolanus*, if we take seriously the setting of the contested Roman republic as that was understood by early modern thinkers (and, indeed, is still more or less understood by political theorists in the twenty-first century) we see conflict and strain between competing idealizations of public life. In my understanding, these are bound together by this principle of heterogeneity, of public encounter. But that idea of politics is ever contested by those who emphasize, rather, a structured, war-like conflict between classes, parties, or other structural formations like 'races' or 'genders'. It is contested also by those who focus on evasions of heterogeneous public encounter, by exercises of sovereign authority such as Angelo attempted in *Measure for Measure*, and—even more likely—the clandestine, behind the scenes, anything but open manipulation of appearances. All of these arise in the context of *Coriolanus*.

[15] Jeffrey Green. 2010. *The Eyes of the People: Democracy in an Age of Spectatorship* (Oxford University Press: Oxford), pp. 131–8.

Politics

We can begin with an idealizing strain of understanding of the value and virtues of political action from classical Greek thought, exemplified in Thucydides' (*c*.460–*c*.400 BCE) famous report of Pericles's (494–429 BCE) oration at the funeral of the first soldiers to die in the Peleponnesian wars: 'We do not say that a man who takes no interest in politics is a man who minds his own business; we say he has no business here at all'.[16] This principle is associated with an open, urban, pluralistic, free, and democratic society in which those who rule must also consent to be ruled, a principle that is institutionalized in the rotation and obligations of office.[17] There are two major sources of doubt about this ideal political way. First, the problem of the susceptibility of political ideals to corruption from external values, for example, their corruption by money, or by cultural traditions, or by violence. Here we focus on the question of the impact on politics of military values and power. Second, though, we repeatedly find scepticism, and even derision, about the validity of such political values and standards themselves.

In *On Duties*, Cicero, in the Periclean tradition, is concerned to emphasize that indifference to or scorn for public life is to the discredit of the scoffer. He also wants to draw a clear distinction between political and military conduct, to the credit of the former. Thinking that the achievements of war are more important than the achievements of peace is an error.[18] We have to take account of the context for his concerns. *On Duties* was written from his 'retirement' from Rome after the assassination of Julius Caesar in 44 BCE, and his text embodies all his worries for the future of the republic, and his own life, his ambivalence about his own relative lack of military experience or distinction, and his criticism, from the civic point of view, of the way Pompey, Caesar, Antony, and others had used military power and distinction for anti-republican purposes. Written to his son Marcus, about whose intellectual and civic seriousness Cicero had doubts, it also articulates his self-congratulation at his own civic achievements. He quotes his own poetry: 'Yield, you arms, to the toga; to civic praises, you laurels', and goes on

---

[16] Thucydides. 1972. *History of the Peloponnesian War*, ed. and intro. M.I. Finley, trans. R. Warner (Penguin: Harmondsworth), Bk 2, S40; T.W. Baldwin. 1944. *Shakspere's Small Latine and Lesse Greek* (University of Illinois Press: Champaign, IL), Vol. I: 106, 191–2 for place of Thucydides in Elizabethan education.

[17] Aristotle. 1932. *Politics*, trans. H. Rackham (Harvard University Press: Cambridge, MA), Bk III, 1278b–1279a.

[18] Cicero, *On Duties*, 1913: XXII, S74.

Did not arms yield to the toga when I was head of state? Thus, as the result of my counsels and my vigilance, their weapons slipped suddenly from the hands of the most desperate traitors.... What achievement in war, then, was ever so great?[19]

Wars, he emphasizes, must be under the control of statesmanship, and should be conducted in such a way as to make evident that it has no object other than peace.[20] Whereas physical fighting with an enemy is a 'barbarous and brutish kind of business,'[21] civil conduct does not involve enmity and there is no place for anger against political contestants.[22] If politics is conducted in a spirit of enmity, or partiality for one part only of the citizenry, the kind of breakdown that explains civil wars is a risk.[23] And so on. He wants to emphasize that affairs of state are just as dangerous as military campaigns, and take just as much courage—one's reputation, the good will of others, one's life (political assassination, after all, is a real threat for public figures), are all at stake. But the necessary skills and talents are quite different.[24]

Cicero cannot deny that military distinction counts as a mark of fitness for office and political power—nowhere can he say that Caesar's, or Pompey's, militarism unfits them for the consulship. The Roman system, for later commentators, serves as an ideal type of militarism: a society in which military values are socially dominant, in which education and socialization have a military cast, and in which military imperatives of conquest dominate public policy.[25] At the militaristic limit, it is soldiers who understand the real nature and interests of the state, soldiers rather than politicians who are the best promoters of the state's interests, and should govern. Cicero resists any such implication; but does understand military service itself to be an office: 'When the stress of circumstances demands it, we must gird on the sword and prefer death to slavery and disgrace.'[26]

Cicero's catalogue of points about the positive value of politics is interlarded with remarks on the problems of political conduct and institutions. There is corruption—the motivation to take on a public office can be more for

---

[19] Cicero, *On Duties*, 1913: XXII, S74.
[20] Cicero, *On Duties*, 1913: XXII, S80.
[21] Cicero, *On Duties*, 1913: XXII, S81.
[22] Cicero, *On Duties*, 1913: XXV, Ss87, 88.
[23] Cicero, *On Duties*, 1913: XXV, S86.
[24] Cicero, *On Duties*, 1913: XXIV, S83.
[25] Vagts, *Militarism*, 1959: 84.
[26] Cicero, *On Duties*, 1913: XXII, S81.

wealth than for serving the benefit of those entrusted to one's care.[27] There is the process of political office itself: electioneering and scrambling for office are wretched customs. Candidates quarrelling about who should hold office are like Plato's sailors who quarrel about who should steer the ship.[28] And so on. His argument ends with 'aporia'—not the feigned doubt that constructs a rhetorical platform from which a strong argument can be launched, but real doubt and uncertainty about what we should think.

We find the same tension in Machiavelli. Nobody should be allowed to make war or military life their business—it is a profession that obliges people to be 'rapacious, fraudulent and cruel'. Professional soldiers will be liable to sell their services to enemies, to set themselves up as soldiers of fortune.[29] Pompey and Caesar, who 'made war their sole occupation' according to Machiavelli's reading of the loss of the Roman republic, were not civic figures, although previous generations of Roman generals had been both great warriors and civic minded.[30] But key to Machiavelli's republicanism is that the prince or governor of a republic needs to be a constant soldier. Republics shouldn't give absolute power to the prince in any matter—except command of the military.[31] Citizens should do regular military training and be ready for battle; and—here is the point about life in a healthy well-governed republic—'Good men when war is over return cheerfully to their former way of life'.[32]

The conditions under which this happy participation by republican citizens in both military service and agriculture or urban trade can be achieved were subjected by later republican thinkers, for whom political economy was a more prominent theme, to greater scrutiny.[33] *Coriolanus* emphasizes the conflict between interests and needs of the urbanized plebeian class whose members are called upon to fight in the wars, and the failures of the economy to keep the supply and price of necessary food at levels that guarantee their health and welfare. The politics of overt, incipiently violent, public, protest, by hungry working and unemployed people, in an effort to exert both coercive and persuasive power in order to secure their favoured political outcome

---

[27] Cicero, *On Duties*, 1913: SVIII, SXXV.
[28] Cicero, *On Duties*, 1913: Bk I, SXXV; Plato. 1930–1935. *Republic* (Harvard University Press: Cambridge, MA), Bk VI, 488e–489d.
[29] Machiavelli, *Art of War*, 1521/1965: 14–15.
[30] Machiavelli, *Art of War*, 1521/1965: 14.
[31] Machiavelli, *Art of War*, 1521/1965: 19.
[32] Machiavelli, *Art of War*, 1521/1965: 18.
[33] Jean-Jacques Rousseau. 1755/1997. 'Discourse on Political Economy', in Victor Gourevitch (ed.), *Rousseau: The Social Contract and Other Later Political Writings* (Cambridge University Press: Cambridge); Rousseau, *Social Contract*, 1762/1997; J.G.A. Pocock. 1975. *The Machiavellian Moment: Florentine Political Thought and the Atlantic Republican Tradition* (Princeton University Press: Princeton).

(increase of the supply and decrease of the price of grain) has been prominent in theatrical interpretations of the play, as well as in historicist readings.[34] Berthold Brecht (1898-1956) translated, and hoped to stage, a production that would focus on the structure of class struggle rather than on individual character.[35] Class war, in parallel with inter-state war, with the incipient violence of the rioters, with the repressive violence of the state and in relation to military battle are eminently stageable.

Two further models of politics are in play in Shakespeare's text. Continuous with the tradition of Pericles and Cicero, politics means public conciliation, achieved through speech, as well as policy and action. Conciliation is not the same as representation of interests or social identities and statuses in government; nor is it the same as open democratic competition for office and participation in governing power. Shakespeare's Rome, to be sure, features elements of both of these. Public conciliation involves openly addressing the differences within the polity, and it involves accountability.[36] Martius thinks this is dangerously democratic, and will destroy the aristocratic structure of the city, destroy the state as such. Third, the tribunes engage in recognizable machiavellian manoeuvring—they manipulate political procedures and public opinion to bring about Martius's downfall. Volumnia, Martius's mother, can't see why her son refuses or is unable strategically to hide his real feelings about the common people in order to win their endorsement of his consulship. Martius, for his part, is as disgusted by the dissimulations of politics as he is by the bodies and the voices of the common people.

Class Protest

The material political problem that frames the plot, and opens the action, is dearth and political protest about it. Commentators emphasize Shakespeare's topical allusions to high prices after bad harvests, and to the Midlands corn

---

[34] David George. 2000/2004. 'Plutarch, Insurrection and Dearth in *Coriolanus*', in Catherine M.S. Alexander (ed.), *Shakespeare and Politics* (Cambridge University Press: Cambridge); Parker, 'Introduction', 1994: 6.

[35] John Willett. 1959/1977. *The Theatre of Bertold Brecht: A Study from Eight Aspects* (Methuen: London), pp. 121–3; Dollimore, Jonathan. 1984/2004. *Radical Tragedy: Religion, Ideology and Power in the Drama of Shakespeare and His Contemporaries* (Palgrave Macmillan: Basingstoke), pp. 226–7; Stanley Cavell. 1987/2003b. 'Coriolanus and the Interpretations of Politics (Who Does the Wolf Love?)', *Disowning Knowledge in Seven Plays of Shakespeare*, updated edn (Cambridge University Press: Cambridge), p. 146.

[36] Bernard Crick. 1962/2013. *In Defence of Politics* (Continuum: London), Ch. 1; Hannah Arendt. 1958. *The Human Condition* (University of Chicago Press: Chicago), Section V.

and anti-enclosure riots of 1607, and the claims that government, or owners of stocks, should release them in order to alleviate want.[37] Menenius—a family friend to Volumnia, who has been an avuncular figure to Martius—is a public participant, respected by the citizens [1.1.48-51], who doesn't hesitate to get involved. We first meet him in 1.1 speaking to plebeian citizens who are out to protest, armed with clubs. He argues with them—that the dearth is caused by the gods, not the patricians; that the patricians care for the state and everyone in it. Menenius is a courageous public speaker, but in the dialogic, rather than oratorical, style—speaking with, as much as at, interlocutors.

In *The Discourses* Machiavelli picks up Livy's account of Coriolanus.[38] Livy's account contains elements which evidence Shakespeare's having recourse to it as well as to Thomas North's (1535-1604) translation of Plutarch's *Lives* (1595).[39] Machiavelli's point, in telling Coriolanus's story, is the importance of procedures such as public indictments, and the exercise of limited public authority by officers such as the tribunes.[40] As Cathy Shrank argues, Shakespeare's audiences would have been familiar with such 'city offices'.[41] In Machiavelli's reading of history, a key style of political action is 'tumult'—riot, threats, and uses of violence that put coercive pressure on government, and that symbolize and enact popular refusal of elite domination of society.[42] Had the tribunes not cited Coriolanus to appear in court, he would have been tumultuously put to death, by the armed crowd, after his speech in which he argued that the senate should leave the people hungry [3.1.122-72]. The tribunes' final decision to banish Coriolanus rather than exact the death penalty had the tragic consequences of which Plutarch and Shakespeare tell. But, says Machiavelli, if he had been killed by a mob,

---

[37] George, 'Plutarch, Insurrection', 2000/2004: 128; R.B. Parker. ed. 1994. 'Appendix', William Shakespeare, *Coriolanus* (Oxford University Press: Oxford), pp. 375–6.

[38] Niccolo Machiavelli. 1531/1970. *The Discourses on the First Decade of Titus Livy*, ed. Bernard Crick, trans. Leslie J. Walker SJ (Penguin: Harmondsworth), Bk 6, Ch. 6.

[39] Livy, *Annales*, 1919: Vol. I, 1922: Vol. II; Thomas North. 1595/1998. *Plutarch: The Lives of the Noble Grecians and Romans*, ed. Judith Mossman (Wordsworth Editions: Ware); Walter W. Skeat. ed. 1875. *Shakespeare's Plutarch: Being a Selection from The Lives in North's Plutarch which Illustrate Shakespeare's Plays* (Macmillan and Co: London); Anne Barton. 1985/2004. 'Livy, Machiavelli and Shakespeare's *Coriolanus*', in Catherine M.S. Alexander (ed.), *Shakespeare and Politics* (Cambridge University Press: Cambridge), pp. 67, 77, 78–82; Parker, 'Introduction', 1994: 17–21; George, 'Plutarch, Insurrection', 2000/2004: 116.

[40] Machiavelli, *Discourses*, 1531/1970: Bk 1, Ch. 7.

[41] Cathy Shrank. 2003. 'Civility and the City in Coriolanus', *Shakespeare Quarterly*, 54: 407–8.

[42] Livy, *Annales*, 1919–22: Vol. I, Bk II, Ch. xxxv; Niccolo Machiavelli. 1525/1988. *Florentine Histories*, trans. Laura F. Banfield and Harvey C. Mansfield (Princeton University Press: Princeton, NJ), Bk III, Ch. 1; Machiavelli, *Discourses*, 1531/1970: Bk I, Ch. 4; Yves Winter. 2018. *Machiavelli and the Orders of Violence* (Cambridge University Press: Cambridge), pp. 167–91.

that would have given rise to private feuding, which would have aroused fear; and fear would have led to defensive action; this to the procuring of partisans; partisans would have meant the formation of factions in the city; and factions would have brought about its downfall.[43]

That is, the republican political answer to tumultuous protest is public conciliation, political procedure, and office.

Conciliation

The tribunate was designed to give the common people a voice, to furnish an institution both for representation to the senate of the common people's views and for representation of the senate's decisions to the common people. This constitutional and political innovation is made in the course of the plot of *Coriolanus* [1.1.211-19].[44] From the point of view of class justice (that the Roman republic failed to secure) institutions like the tribunate, the inclusion of relatively many people in the election of officers, and so on, can make conciliation look very much like buying off the dispossessed with superficial political reforms instead of meeting needs with deep economic justice. This superficiality-depth trope is common in modern political thinking; for instance, Marx condemns political reform as a swindle.[45] However, Jacques Ranciere argues that to interpret these events in terms of economic justice (as, according to him, Livy does) is to overlook, and suppress, exactly the claims of the plebeians to be included in the polity—to count politically.[46] I return in future chapters—and in relation especially to *King Lear* in Chapter 5—to this question of whether politics, in particular of the ideal kind, is of any significance in a world in which money talks and the interests of the economically dominant will dominate over all. At this point I want to focus on conciliation as both a political function of institutions and also as a personal political style which Shakespeare puts into juxtaposition with others.

After his conversation with the protestors in 1.1, Menenius accompanies Martius, after he has been made consul by the senate [2.2.130-1], to meet the

---

[43] Machiavelli, *Discourses*, 1531/1970: Bk 1, Ch. 7; Barton, 'Livy, Machiavelli', 1985/2004: 79–80.

[44] Livy, *Annales*, 1919–22: Bk II, Ch. xxxiii.

[45] Karl Marx. 1843/1975. 'Critique of Hegel's Doctrine of the State', *Karl Marx Early Writings*, trans. Rodney Livingstone and Gregor Benton (Penguin: Harmondsworth).

[46] Jacques Ranciere. 1995/1999. *Disagreement: Politics and Philosophy*, trans. Julie Rose (University of Minnesota Press: Minneapolis, MN), p. 23.

people and solicit their endorsement of his appointment. He attempts to keep Martius's speech in check. As he and other senators attempt to get Martius away from the streets, from the tribunes' and the people's indignation and anger at Martius's continued defiance and invective, he challenges Martius's desire to physically fight [3.1.229-42]. He goes, on embassy from Rome, to try to negotiate with Martius when he is laying siege to Rome [5.1, 5.2] He is the Ciceronian, courageous politician who (tries to) avert violence. I hasten to say that this is not all that Menenius is. Later, I discuss the merits of other ways of evaluating his speech and his class identity, which bring him closer to Stephen Greenblatt's characterization of him as an unabashed conservative, a kind of classical or Shakespearean equivalent of Karl Marx's 'Mr Moneybags'.[47]

Machiavellianism

The tribunes, Sicinius and Brutus, use machiavellian strategies to bring about Martius's downfall. They seek to exert their own judgement and will—but to have it articulated as the will of the common people by the people themselves [2.1.239-55, 2.3.173-213]. In Plutarch's story they manipulate the voting system to ensure that Martius is found guilty of treason and of designing to establish monarchical government.[48] This voting system business doesn't feature prominently in Shakespeare's plot, although it is referred to obliquely when the tribunes distinguish between a count of votes by head, and a count by tribes [3.3.8-11].[49] Rather, Sicinius and Brutus work effectively on the people's understandings and feelings (as they do also in Plutarch's account)[50] to get them to change their decisions. They constantly use, and discuss, their foresight—calculating the consequences of various courses of action, as they attempt to control and drive events. They understand very well the structure of the polity, the nature of the class and party divisions within it, and the distribution of interests. They also understand very well the constitutional settlement that has instituted their own office. They are ruthless in calling for and being ready to go forward with a death sentence—although their concern with office, procedure, constitution, and a political concern to be associated

---

[47] Stephen Greenblatt. 2018. *Tyrant: Shakespeare on Power* (Penguin Random House: London), pp. 160-1; Karl Marx. 1867/1954. *Capital*, Vol. 1 (Lawrence and Wishart: London), Ch. VI:172.

[48] Skeat, 'Coriolanus', *Shakespeare's Plutarch*, 1875: S.12, p. 21.

[49] Geoffrey Bullough. ed. 1964. 'Coriolanus', *Narrative and Dramatic Sources of Shakespeare*, Vol. 5 (Routledge and Kegan Paul: London), pp. 468-70; Parker, 'Introduction', 1994: 246n.

[50] Skeat, 'Coriolanus', *Shakespeare's Plutarch*, 1875: S.8, p. 13.

with justice persuades them to change the sentence to banishment [3.3.75-168]. This turns out to be a critical decision.

This kind of strategic action, in which one is dishonest about one's aims the better to realize them, in which one considers which procedure will best bring about the result one desires, in which individual advantage is always pursued under the guise of public and collective interest is recognized by Martius and it infuriates him. His response is to condemn it wholesale. Political action and relationships, in this sense, should be swept away in favour of transparent aristocracy, in which the rich patricians rule—by force, violently—in the interest of the state as such and without pandering to the demands of the plebeians. Audiences will feel some sympathy with Martius's rage about political intrigue, if they don't with his violence. Nobody likes a machiavellian. And the deep association of politics with this style of action is among the reason why politicians are liable to be considered suspect as to their characters. It is a reason why it can never be a source of shame for a person to say that they are unsuited to politics.

Body Politic

Martius is disgusted by all three styles of political conduct: protest, conciliation, and machiavellianism alike. Political conduct, political institutions, have to be premised on a particular kind of relationship between persons— and Martius is disgusted by this too. The relevant kind of relationship has often been thought in terms of 'body', and accordingly Shakespeare is able to make much of numerous elements and aspects of Martius's alienation from some kinds of bodily life, together, as we shall see, with his paradoxical engulfment and incapacity to achieve healthy distance from intimates.

Martius's anti-politics has to be understood in the frame of the Roman republican fear that authoritarian figures like Coriolanus, especially with military valour and military resources at their disposal, might successfully proclaim kingship.[51] Interestingly, this charge of kingship is not at issue in Shakespeare's play (he uses the term 'tyranny' [3.3.1-2, 63-6]). But it is in North's Plutarch.[52] In *Julius Caesar* (1599) much is made of Caesar's aspiration to kingship [1.2.230-46, 3.1.123-33]. Questioning kingship was much more risky in the reign of James I than it had been in the reign of Elizabeth

---

[51] Parker, 'Appendix', 1994: App. B, pp. 367–8.
[52] Skeat, 'Coriolanus', *Shakespeare's Plutarch*, 1875: Ss.11, 12, pp. 19–21.

I, when the Roman antipathy to it was a matter of classical scholarship. James complained in 1606, as he tried to assert absolute sovereignty, that he was assailed by 'tribunes of the people whose mouths could not be stopped'. He was sensitive, in a different way and to a different degree than Elizabeth, to challenges to monarchy.[53]

But Shakespeare's concerns go beyond 'who rules' to the matter of how political power is conceptualized. The calls of public speech, office, and processes of the power to govern are also put into opposition to the wordless relations of marriage, parenthood, and sexual passion. And, this being Shakespeare, there is another side to family and kinship—dynastic, partial ambition that a family name should come to prominence in the state, which requires a particular style of parenting. Volumnia's ambition for family distinction is not in itself at odds with Roman republicanism, any more than is the principle that a successful general like Martius should be influential in the senate and elected consul. However, dynasty and kinship, as much as military distinction, can also be understood to be at odds with the public political ideals of conciliation. Family inheritance as a criterion or justification for political authority and spoils can generate oligarchy.[54]

Action v. Speech

Martius's military courage and performance is constructed by him as exceptionally pure. Military valour traditionally is praised with trumpets, hurrahs, garlands, and so on. But Martius, after the attack on Corioles, repudiates the praise [1.10.28-9], the music, and the flattery, and refuses to accept any exceptional share of the booty as prize [1.10.36-40]. He distances himself from the political values—flattery, lies, softness, hypocrisy—of the city, and from the corruption of military values by them. He is as reluctant to hear praise as he is to speak formally and publicly: 'I have some wounds upon me, and they smart to hear themselves remembered' [1.10.28-9]. Martius is styled as a man of action, not a politic talker. Menenius—who is a talker—argues to a fellow patrician that 'His nature is too noble for the world.... What his breast forges, that his tongue must vent' [3.1.257-62]. Later he shifts ground to argue to the tribunes that Martius had been taught to be a soldier: 'he has been bred i' th' wars since a could draw a sword, and is ill-schooled in bolted language'

---

[53] Annabel Patterson. 1989. *Shakespeare and the Popular Voice* (Basil Blackwell: Oxford), pp. 122–4.
[54] Aristotle, *Politics*, 1932: IV.iv.6, 1292a-b.

[3.1.323-5]; and 'Consider further that when he speaks not like a citizen you find him like a soldier' [3.3.50-5].

Martius's professed alienation from language—'when blows have made me stay I fled from words' [2.2.69-70]—is not quite correct though. It's not words, as such, that are Martius's problem; he is very fluent with them. His invective is unrivalled in Shakespeare—he wishes boils and plagues on the soldiers [1.5.2-8], loathes their physicality [2.3.58-9]; he calls the people slaves [1.1.196], and 'superfluous' [1.1.224], a herd [3.1.35], rank-scented [3.1.69], a hydra [3.1.95], crows [3.1.141], curs [1.1.165], hares, foxes, geese, where they should be lions [1.1.167-9] and much more.[55] His fluency is strong on insult— his speeches of invective are long, piling metaphor upon metaphor. The speeches in which he argues against giving in to plebeian demands for redistribution, or condemns their representation in the political process [3.1.67-77, 3.1.92-114, 3.1.121-41], are furious, indistinguishable stylistically from his tirades directly at the plebeians and the soldiers [1.1.165-85, 1.5.1-11].[56] This is rhetoric alright, but without any conciliatory quality.[57] It is civil speech and conversation, rather than words as such, that are beyond Martius.

Martius's speech contrasts with several other styles and characters. Earlier, I characterized Menenius's as dialogic and conciliatory. Less kindly, he can be heard also as the endless, ineffectual, and above all irrelevant, 'talk talk talk' kind of political speaker. His argument that the patricians care for the whole state fails to address the citizens' complaint that there are storehouses 'crammed with grain' which should be distributed to relieve hunger [1.1.76-81]. His telling of the 'fable of the belly and members' [1.1.93-159]—listened to patiently enough by the citizens—is boringly sententious, as well as beside the point and insulting [1.1.154-60]. He has a personal interest in Martius's career, and is involved and complicit in Volumnia's family ambition. He is the kind of person who knows who's on the way up and who's out; gossip is his currency. Menenius's public courage and willingness to speak and to negotiate is twinned with the partial and partisan ambition which lay politicians open to the charge that their engagement with the public interest is really engagement in private interest.

The tribunes similarly can be suspected. Their criticism of Martius's position regarding grain distribution is bound up with their concern that, should

---

[55] Parker, 'Introduction', 1994: 79-81.

[56] Parker, 'Introduction', 1994: 71-3, 75-6.

[57] Markku Peltonen. 2009. 'Political Rhetoric and Citizenship in Coriolanus', in David Armitage, Conal Condren, and Andrew Fitzmaurice (eds.), Shakespeare and Early Modern Political Thought (Cambridge University Press: Cambridge).

he be consul, their own office would be abolished [2.1.218-19]. The real opposition between the aristocratic and the popular parties, and principled disagreement about distributive policy and constitution, is compromised by the protagonists' personal interests. Martius is appointed consul by the senate and, reluctantly, at the tribunes' insistence and Menenius's behest, faces the people in the market place and secures their endorsement. The tribunes remind the people, newly enamoured of Martius because of his military distinction, of their older dislike of his policy position and of his contemptuous conduct. They bet that sooner or later Martius's insolence will set the people ablaze [2.1.249-54]. They advise the people to rescind their endorsement: 'Sicinius: Lay the fault on us. Brutus: Ay, spare us not. Say we read lectures to you...' [2.3.222-50]. The plebeians consequently 'repent in their election' [2.3.250-1]. The tribunes then have to hurry to get to the capitol before the people arrive— so that it seems that the people have streamed there on their own, not that they have been 'goaded onward' [2.3.256-9].

The speech of the citizens can be contrasted with all these styles—Martius's invective, Menenius's sententiousness, the tribunes' strategy. Continuous with a tradition of reading Shakespeare as taking the aristocratic part in political dramas, interpreters can see the citizens as contributing a comic element to the play, confused about how to proceed vis-à-vis endorsing Martius as consul, and suggestible and easily led by the machinations of the tribunes.[58] Commentators observe, though, that the citizens in *Coriolanus* are individuated to a degree that the members of crowds in other Shakespearean dramas are not. We hear them voice opinions, disagree with each other, question procedures and conventions, and revise their decisions [2.3.1-45, 153-69, 205-8].[59] The theme of 'uprising' and 'riot' can be interpreted in terms of agency in response to material need. The later tradition of Marxist analysis of class struggle can be seen as being prefigured in Shakespeare's stories—not least by Marx himself for whom Shakespeare was an important literary source.[60] But this picture of economic motivation and action is incomplete if the interest of the people in the political institutions themselves is discounted. Ranciere insists that the question of politics is the question of who does, and who does not, have

[58] Patterson, *Shakespeare and Popular Voice*, 1989: 3-5, 122-4.
[59] George, 'Plutarch, Insurrection', 2000/2004: 117-18; Patterson, *Shakespeare and Popular Voice*, 1989: 128-32; Dollimore, *Radical Tragedy*, 1984/2004: 225.
[60] David Leopold. 2014. 'Karl Marx and British Socialism', in W. J. Mander (ed.), *The Oxford Handbook of British Philosophy in the Nineteenth Century* (Oxford University Press: Oxford), p. 404; Sean Ledwith. 2016. 'Marx's Shakespeare', *Counterfire*, https://www.counterfire.org/articles/analysis/18300-marx-s-shakespeare

speech.[61] The citizens in *Coriolanus* 'have speech'—but their speech is, of course, contested: unheard, derided as noise, as unreasonable and therefore inadmissible to political discourse.

In this frame of the question 'who has speech', how it is produced and how engaged, how counted, in Ranciere's term, there is no doubt that this is a play that is about the deep conditions of politics. And there also seems to be no doubt that Shakespeare here considers the nature of a 'body politic' without an aristocratic 'head'.[62]

Individual and Polity

The Ciceronian argument and the Machiavellian one alike both focus on the way individuals are called, in a polity, to take up a range of roles, and conduct themselves in specific ways. Martius refuses numerous social relationships and roles, and asserts himself as an individual who would rule by violence: 'Would the nobility lay aside their ruth and let me use my sword, I'd make a quarry with thousands of those quartered slaves as high as I could pitch my lance' [1.1.194-7]. When his banishment is proclaimed by the tribunes he asserts his own individual agency against any social or political authority:

'You common cry of curs, whose breath I hate as reek o' th' rotten fens... that do corrupt my air; I banish you!'.... 'Despising for you the city, thus I turn my back. There is a world elsewhere'.   [3.3.121-36]

The senators, tribunes and people are horrified and afraid when Martius leads the Volsceans in a siege on Rome. Cominius, then Menenius, and finally Volumnia, Virgilia, neighbour Valeria, and the young Martius go to plead with Martius to make peace with Rome. He is, finally, persuaded by his mother. At his death, as a traitor to the Volsceans, he defiantly, and finally, proclaims: 'Alone I did it'—like the 'eagle in the dovecote', he alone took Corioles [5.6.115-17].

Shakespeare's Martius, we must note, is much more individualistic and alone than Plutarch's. Plutarch emphasizes Martius's leadership of a faction of young nobles and senators—or, at least, their followership of him. In North's translation 'specially they flocked about him and kept him company...'[63]

[61] Ranciere, *Disagreement*, 1995/1999: 26–8.
[62] Patterson, *Shakespeare and Popular Voice*, 1989: 143.
[63] Skeat, 'Coriolanus', *Shakespeare's Plutarch*, 1875: S.9.

There is a political theory problem of what kind of friendship 'factionalism' and party loyalty actually involves—whether it is consistent with or conducive to the kind of generalized and open friendliness that a republican polity requires. Although it can be used neutrally, for Shakespeare 'factionalism' is a derogatory epithet. In *Timon of Athens* a senator associates 'faction' with crime [3.5/S.10:24-30]; in *Julius Caesar* Brutus associates it with conspiracy [2.1.77-9; see also *Titus Andronicus* 1.1.23-4]. Later in republican thought faction is a dreaded thing.[64] Plutarch's account of a partisan, political faction with a charismatic leader, is also interpretable in the frame of a band of brothers who exert masculine domination over public spaces. I take up the question of this particular style of gendering political life and public space in Chapter 4 on *Romeo and Juliet*.

Sex and Gender

Shakespeare's Martius is not a member or leader of a gang, but an individualist; and his individualism makes others suspicious. His body is trained for glory—but 'what he hath done famously, he did it to that end' thinks one of the citizens [1.1.32-3]. Though fame is a good thing, aiming at fame is not. But Martius's individualism is also suspect, not so much because it is ethically bad, but because it is bogus. The same citizen also says 'he did it to please his mother' [1.1.35-6]—the outward masculinity is a mask for inward childishness and effeminacy. The ties of intimate relationships, in particular the parent-child, mother-son, relationship, are inescapably taken as key to Martius's character, and as with Shakespeare's other great tragic heroes audiences and readers are asked to consider how character and relationships to others interact to bring about his downfall.

Individualistic resistance to social and political norms can be taken as a sign of depth of feeling. In that key, throughout the drama, the silence, the intimacy, and the inexpressibility of romantic and familial love is contrasted with the publicity, the hubbub, the intrigue, the manipulation, violence, and speech of politics. Shakespeare is, of course, a key figure in the claims of voluntaristic romantic love which frequently, in comedies and in tragedies, operates as a challenge to established forms of power and modes of domination, and as a source of authenticity and simple truth. Martius's wife Virgilia infuriates her political mother-in-law with her wilful self-seclusion [1.3.28-30,

---

[64] Pocock, *Machiavellian Moment*, 1975: 361-2, 483.

72-84] This refusal to engage in public sociable life underlines exaggerated sexual difference, and is for her a symbolic expression of her bond to Martius. Home from war, he addresses Virgilia: 'My gracious silence, hail' [2.1.171].[65] For her, and for him, the inarticulacy of military valour and the wounded soldierly body, on the one hand, and the inarticulacy of voluntaristic sexual love and the erotically active body, on the other—he as strongly silent man of action, she as modestly silent woman—is a dichotomy which encompasses their world, and excludes the civilly clothed and active body of the polity. Such depth of feeling, expressed in silence, is key to another famous moment: his mother Volumnia's plea to him not to destroy Rome leaves him wordless [5.3.183].

Volumnia is fluent and argumentative [3.2.16-94, 5.3.95-183] and in their conversations Martius is often close to monosyllabic [2.1.165]. She can be interpreted, in a psychoanalytic frame, as a smothering, cold, mother—the performer of a gendered, sexualized, parent-child relationship of a kind that is fateful for adult pain and patterns of conduct.[66] She is the archetypical Roman (or Spartan) matron of the classical tradition, glad when their sons are dead in battle (in Volumnia's case, glad that Martius is severely wounded [1.3.18-25; 2.1.115-22, 143-52]).[67] Feminist critique focuses on the fantasy and archetypical aspects of this representation of Volumnia as castrating, or as unnaturally phallic, a fearsome monster, to blame for Martius's intemperance and violence.[68]

Without wanting to deny these meanings (which may be amplified in a theatre where the part is played by a cross-dressed male actor) we must note further political meanings that also attach to Volumnia. To begin with, she endorses the conventions, and dissimulations, of politics. Trying to get Martius back to the market place to solicit the people's votes, she points out that publicly he must not speak as his feelings prompt him; he should use his anger advantageously [3.2.28-31], speak less 'absolutely' [3.2.41]. This is no more dishonourable than taking an enemy city peacefully rather than violently [3.2.60-3]. In war, it is honourable to 'seem the same you are not, to adapt policy to ends' [3.2.48-53]. For Volumnia, as for many other thinkers, politics and war are continuous.

But they are not the same. In politics, the strategy is to build and maintain state, relationships, 'a world' as Hannah Arendt, in her reading of republicanism,

[65] Parker, 'Introduction', 1994: 102.
[66] Parker, 'Introduction', 1994: 48–51; Janet Adelman. 1992. *Suffocating Mothers: Fantasies of Origin in Shakespeare's Plays* (Routledge: London), Ch. 6; Cavell, 'Coriolanus', 1987/2003b: 145ff.
[67] Plutarch. 1931. 'Sayings of Spartan Women', *Plutarch, Moralia*, Vol. III (Loeb Classical Library, Harvard University Press: Cambridge, MA), nos. 5–8.
[68] Coppelia Kahn. 1981. *Man's Estate: Masculine Identity in Shakespeare* (University of California Press: Berkeley, CA), pp. 153–5; Adelman, *Suffocating Mothers*, 1992: 130–64.

put it.[69] The people whose world this is, to be sure, will have to be wary of threats to it. In war, enemy worlds are destroyed. In the end, Volumnia voices and enacts a truly political commitment to her world—in striking contrast to the commitment to strategy and machiavellian dissimulation. The embassy of three women from Rome—from the world that Martius has rejected— consists of Martius's mother, wife and young son and also their neighbour Valeria. It might be tempting to cut Valeria from productions. The structure of individual, and kinship, in relation to state, could squeeze out the civil society element of Shakespeare's drama. But Volumnia's commitments are to her society. Her anger with Virgilia who does not want to join in this life is an endorsement of the communal commitment of neighbours needing to care for neighbours [1.3.74-91].

Having failed (she thinks) to prevail upon Martius to lift the siege of Rome and desist from its destruction, Volumnia says: 'So, we will home to Rome, to die among our neighbours' [5.3.173-4]. This can, to be sure, plausibly be read as emotional manipulation of Martius. Furthermore, it works; Martius crumbles. But it seems to me that the politics of the line is more than simple manipulativeness. She doesn't simply say: 'if you don't do as I ask I'll be dead and you'll be sorry.' She invokes a genuinely political value—community, neighbourhood, civil society—in her invocation of what is at stake in the loss of Rome.[70]

Throughout, it is true, Volumnia speaks of 'blood' [1.3.35, 43; 3.2.63; 5.3.119]. The ambiguity of wounds and kinship can plausibly be read as a deep symbolic structure to the play.[71] But in my interpretation the blood tie, and the soldierly body turned inside out, at last gives way to the tie that rests only on mutual good will—the tie of neighbourliness, the solidarity that keeps you together with people with whom you have relations of sociability, mutuality, and exchange. These are the relations that underpin the building and maintenance of public institutions. Volumnia lives the relationships that Cominius, the army general, invokes at the very beginning of Martius's troubles. Cominius tells Martius that he is going to report his (Martius's) deeds, in public:

Where senators shall mingle tears with smiles, where great patricians shall attend, and shrug, i' th' end admire; where ladies shall be frighted and, gladly quaked, hear more; where the dull tribunes, that with the fusty plebeians hate thine honours, shall say....   [1.10.1-10]

[69] Arendt, *Human Condition*, 1958: 173–4; Hannah Arendt. 1969. *On Violence* (Harcourt Brace: New York), p. 80.
[70] Dollimore, *Radical Tragedy*, 1984/2004: 219.
[71] Adelman, *Suffocating Mothers*, 1992: 148–50; Kahn, *Man's Estate*, 1981: 154–5.

Let us overlook Cominius's stereotyping here, and note that what he is telling Martius, which Martius cannot bear, is about difference. Different positions and viewpoints, different views, different embodiments. The state is heterogeneous. The plural state is all that commands any loyalty. Volumnia returns to Rome as a confirmed political actor: making a triumphal entry, as 'patroness, the life of Rome!' with flowers strewn before her [5.5]. She is 'worth of consuls, senators, patricians, a city full' [5.4.52–5].

The city's plurality and diversity repel Martius who voices longing for phallic, solitary unity, which he cannot (really) instantiate. What he gets, instead, is engulfment: his wordless love for Virgilia; the engulfment and domination by his mother; and, we cannot overlook, his intimate tie with Aufidius, the Volscean leader. Their combat is, we might say, unconsummated throughout the drama. When they meet at Antium, Aufidius reaches for the metaphor of marriage, and then a more explicit sexual image: 'more dances my rapt heart than when I first my wedded mistress saw bestride my threshold.... We have been down together in my sleep, unbuckling helms, fisting each other's throats...' [4.5.116–26]. It has to be said that this passionate metaphor of gladness and sexuality does not appear only in the relationship between these two. Martius greets Cominius in the course of the Volscean war: 'O let me clip ye in arms as sound as when I wooed, in heart as merry as when our nuptial day was done, and tapers burnt to bedward' [1.7.29–32].

This masculine, band of brothers' articulation of the relations between military comrades tells us much about idealizations of military life and its susceptibility both to homoeroticism and, as we shall see, to rape, in Shakespearean and other cultural representations. Martius's anxiety to engage in combat with Aufidius raises the emotional temperature of relations with the enemy as high as that of relations between comrades [1.7.55–63]. The direct fight between them during the Volscean war (their fifth encounter, as we hear [1.11.7–10], although Aufidius also says it is twelve times [4.5.122–4]) is muddled by Aufidius's soldiers coming to his aid—not a fair combat, and one that shames Aufidius [1.9.14–15]. Frustration, in Act 1, turns Aufidius's admiration for Martius to a destructive desire to beat him whatever it takes. 'Mine emulation hath not that honour in't it had, for where I thought to crush him in an equal force, true sword to sword, I'll potch at him some way, or wrath or craft may get him' [1.11.10–16]. Aufidius here declares himself a machiavellian opponent to Martius. When Martius hears that Aufidius has retired to Antium, after the defeat of Corioles, he asks 'Spoke he of me?' [3.1.12] and remarks that he wishes he had cause to seek him at Antium [3.1.20–1]. Which, on his banishment, he does have. He seeks him out, and offers his service.

Despite their passionate meeting, things don't go well between Aufidius and Martius. Aufidius is taken aback at Martius's pride [4.7.8-10], and Martius's popularity with the Volscean soldiers is a matter of concern for the Volscean command [4.7.1-6, 12-16]. Aufidius now reverts from trying to find a technique or 'craft' for his encounter with Martius, back to the theme of equal and opposing forces:

> Power, unto itself most commendable, hath not a tomb so evident as a chair t'extol what it hath done. One fire drives out one fire, one nail one nail; rights by rights falter, strengths by strengths do fail. [4.7.49-55]

The chair Aufidius refers to here is the rostrum from which public orations are declaimed. Power, advertised, invites resistance. It is politics—his inability to conciliate, to consider or adjust his conduct and speech, his refusal of his position in the public polity of Rome, and then his mismanagement of his position in the political society of the Volsces—that brings about Martius's tragic death. Martius repudiates politics, proclaims truth, and seeks revenge on Rome. But, he takes up a prominent position in the Volscean's polity. That generates, inevitably, opposition. His death is tragic in the sense that it is inevitable, and there is nothing Martius could do to evade it. But it is not the fates, nor the gods, nor even luck, which ordain his downfall. In my reading, it is Martius's refusal of the reality of a world in which politics—Ciceronian, Machiavellian, or popular—is not optional.

Membership

Shakespeare's dramas frequently ask whether we have to engage politically or whether there is another way. Why can't we have society without rostrums? True love, friendship, market exchanges, religious devotion, military defence—aren't these enough? In *Coriolanus* this fundamental question is addressed via the extended metaphor of the body politic—a 'body' ironically divided by class, and sex. Menenius, in response to the people's militant protest at prices and hunger, argues that their action against the senate is misguided, because the senators are like the belly of the body—sending sustenance to all the members. Everything that the members make and obtain goes through the belly—but all of it goes back to them, the belly retaining 'but the bran' [1.1.139-60]. What's brilliant about this episode is, first, the patience with which the citizens let Menenius have his say; and, second, the way this trope is a hackneyed commonplace. The head is 'kingly and crowned', the arm is the soldier, is quoted back at him [1.1.111-16]. Isn't the stomach a cormorant [1.1.118-19]? As usual, Shakespeare ensures that fables and metaphors are contested in their very telling.

Class division makes of the polity a structure of contestation the outcomes of which cannot be encompassed in the metaphor of a self-regulating system. Class justice will require restructuring. As Martius sees, if the citizens win rights that means the senate must change its constitution; the plebeians cannot gain without loss to the patricians. Second, sex distinction can, of course, be understood functionally. But Shakespeare always problematizes it—often by making female characters more stoical, or more masculine, than male ones. Volumnia fits into this pattern. Otherwise by showing the impossibility of maintaining a clear distinction. Virgilia will not go out to help a neighbour in childbirth because, as a woman—insisting on the feminine-private scheme of gender—she should be secluded, keeping vigil against her husband's return. But, if so, who will help Virgilia if she finds herself without kin?

A dominant metaphor that runs through and around Shakespeare's consideration of the body politic here is that of health and starvation.[72] The association is 'literal' with respect to the hungry citizens. It is reprised in imagery such as Volumnia's associations of suckling with blood [1.3.40-4], or her feeding on anger: she sups 'upon myself and so shall starve with feeding' [4.2.53-4]. Menenius likens Martius to the lamb who is devoured by the wolf (the kind of lamb that baas like a bear, says Brutus) [2.1.7-11]. In Martius's imagery, curs scavenge, rats attack the corn in the granaries. The citizens are the disease and the poison of the body politic—boils, sores, plagues [1.5.1-5, 3.1.8] The Roman 'rats' will be let loose on the Volsceans' granaries, so the Volsceans shall starve [1.1.246-8]; the citizens are the Romans' grain—but they are musty [1.1.223-4]. For Martius, virtuous soldier-citizens—stoical in hardship, courageous in battle, and willing to follow their leaders—should sustain the state.[73] But at the gates of Corioles, the soldiers do not follow him and he enters 'alone to answer all the city' [1.5.24-5]. For the plebeians, the wars are not for them.[74] The state needs functioning markets before they can play the role of citizen-soldiers, so that they can consume what is necessary for city life. This ideal of the body politic—members connected by market relations

---

[72] Cavell, 'Coriolanus', 1987/2003b: 148–53; Parker, 'Introduction', 1994: 77–80.
[73] Geoffrey Miles. 1996. *Shakespeare and the Constant Romans* (Oxford University Press: Oxford), pp. 150–3.
[74] Willett, *Theatre of Brecht*, 1959/1977: 122.

and friendship, underpinned by family—with its distribution among 'parts' of functions and roles is problematized at every turn.

Martius is associated with blood—'Enter Martius, bloody' [1.7.21] is a key moment. He looks as though he has been flayed [1.7.22]. The symbolism of this has been much analysed. Adelman emphasizes reproduction and mothering.[75] Cavell too, but he also emphasizes the sacrificial (and Christian religious) motifs—Martius is the sacrificial lamb ('Who does the wolf love?' [2.1.7]). The language of the play repeats metaphors of starvation, hunger, eating, and cannibalism—invoking imagery of Christ and the Eucharist.[76] The blood can be associated straightforwardly with military valour and courage. However, that cannot be separated from the blood of kinship and, especially, of the female-male, mother-son, husband-wife bonds. For Martius—and, indeed, for his patrician admirers—the blood of the soldier is a sign of personal standing, and service to the state. For Volumnia it is the sign of her family's greatness. For Virgilia it is the injury that has to be tended.

The nature of Martius's masculinity, the counterpart to Virgilia's feminity, is in question throughout. His individualism, his contempt for the citizens, sets him apart from his society. This enacts a kind of hyper-masculinity that is articulated by him in the commonsense association of warfare with rape. To motivate his soldiers through the gates of Corioles he urges them 'If you stand fast, we'll beat them to their wives, as they us to our trenches' [1.5.12-13]. The threat of the Volscean invasion of Rome is the threat of Rome's daughters being raped [4.6.85-7]. From the point of view of theories of militarization, this articulation of rape as an incentive to military courage, and a sign of masculine comradeship, is a commonplace.[77]

Martius's rapacious masculinity is juxtaposed with the association of him with boyhood—Volumnia's and Valeria's memories of him as a child, and the sense that he remains his mother's boy. Finally, in the showdown, Aufidius uses 'boy' as the insult to express his rage and to put Martius in his place [5.6.99-100, 102]. This is the insult that is finally Martius's undoing: 'Alone I did it, boy!' he draws his sword [5.6.112-17, 128]. Taking all in all, the other versions of Martius's masculinity—his tenderness to his wife, for instance; his stoicism when injured—are overshadowed by this pairing of rapist and small boy. He lacks the political body that engages in public life and encounter. The

[75] Adelman, *Suffocating Mothers*, 1992: 148–52.

[76] Cavell, 'Coriolanus', 1987/2003b: 147–51, 155–6, 165.

[77] Elshtain, *Women and War*, 1987/1995: 200–2; Cynthia Enloe. 2000. *Maneuvers: The International Politics of Militarising Women's Lives* (University of California Press: Berkeley), pp. 108–11ff; Josh Goldstein. 2001. *War and Gender* (Cambridge University Press: Cambridge), pp. 362–71.

idea of patrician status, of aristocratic domination, of noble martiality, that he tries to articulate in words, tries to embody in himself, takes him out of the public and social body. In the end we see him borne aloft by his enemies, a corpse [5.6.142–4, 154].

Military Violence and the Political Way

This chapter has explored the relationship, the competing calls, of, on the one hand, noble violence and virtuous military power, and, on the other, a variety of versions of the political way. The tribunes' machiavellian manoeuvres and manipulation of political offices and procedures interact with class-based claims for justice prosecuted in the streets of the city, among its warehouses. Volumnia represents the dynastic, self- and family-serving climb to social and political prominence; but she also notably articulates the values of the city and neighbourhood, the solidarities between people who live together, share a life, and need to maintain their world. All of these forms of politics arise, also, in Chapter 4 on *Romeo and Juliet*. But there the violence is not militarily organized or armed state power, nor the incipient violence of class protest, but the 'civil' violence of feuding families. As in *Coriolanus*, Shakespeare's play hints at the virtues of non-violent republican political life as he dramatizes the many forces that militate against it.

4

Violence and Political Authority

Romeo and Juliet

Romeo and Juliet and Civil Power

Romeo and Juliet (composed 1593) is framed, by Chorus in the Prologue, by
city life, civility, and civil violence:

> Two households both alike in dignity, in fair Verona, where we lay our scene,
> from ancient grudge break to new mutiny, where civil blood makes civil
> hands unclean.   [Prologue 1-4]

Romeo Montague and Juliet Capulet become lovers, although Juliet is betrothed
by her father to marry Paris. The violence between the two households reaches
a level where, fights having broken out despite the Prince's warnings that the
punishment of death will be inflicted on those responsible, Romeo's friend
Mercutio dies; and in a fight with Romeo, so does Tybalt from the Capulets.
Friar Laurence helps Romeo and Juliet secretly marry, believing that their
union may eventually end the enmity. Romeo is banished from Verona.
Juliet's father seeks to hasten the marriage between her and Paris. Laurence
arranges that Juliet take a sleeping potion that will make her seem to be dead,
with the plan that Romeo come back to Verona to take her away from her
family tomb and out of the city until the feud can be ended and the families
reconciled. But messages go astray, and Romeo returns believing that Juliet
really has died. He kills himself with poison. She awakes to find him dead, so
kills herself with his dagger. The finale sees the two families, as Chorus tells
us, 'bury their strife' [Prologue 8], agreeing to raise gold statues of Romeo and
Juliet as a sign of the new civil peace of the city.

   Romeo and Juliet is understood, above all, as a great love story. It is received,
in contemporary cultures, in the tradition of romance in the sense of 'girl
meets boy'. In Shakespeare's own context, 'romance' indicated fable and fantasy written as a story in a vernacular language. The theme of idealized erotic
and intimate love and friendship came later, although a strand of unattainable

Shakespeare and the Political Way. Elizabeth Frazer, Oxford University Press (2020). © Elizabeth Frazer.
DOI: 10.1093/oso/9780198848615.001.0001

love, or chivalric heroism for the sake of a woman, was part of the tradition. In relation to Shakespeare, we can intelligibly use the term in part with its later connotations because *Romeo and Juliet*, and indeed Shakespeare's love stories in general, are works which transform older romantic themes of quest and codes of chivalry to the intimate context of inter-personal, heterosexual, great love. His works can be seen as formative contributions to the development of the later genres of tragic (which is to say, hopeless or doomed) love, and of romantic comedy.

Morally, from some standpoints, *Romeo and Juliet* can be read as a warning about the terrible consequences of authoritarian parenting, from others about the terrible consequences of disobedience to parents. The French and English translators of the play's Italian source narrative prefaced the work with moral warnings of the latter sort.[1] Critics and interpreters, in accounting for the tragedy, have often focused on the psychology and character flaws of Juliet, Romeo, and other characters. Juliet might not have lied to her parents about having met Romeo; Romeo might not have acted so impetuously throughout; Juliet's father might have been less violent and impatient to marry her off; Mercutio might not have been so mischievous and determined to pick a fight; and so on.[2] The psychological themes of family drama—the deep need for maternal connection, the struggle with paternal authority, the quest for, or the fear of, adult independent identity—also press on twentieth-century critics and interpreters.[3]

The great love is connected explicitly, by Shakespeare, to the theme of fate. Chorus, in the Prologue, announces to us 'A pair of star-crossed lovers' [Prologue 6]. This locates the workings of fate in 'the heavens'. But 'fate' is located also in parentage: the star-crossed lovers are 'From forth the fatal loins of these two foes' [5]. They are born to feuding patriarchs, are members of warring households, their worlds are infused with hate. There's nothing heavenly about accident of birth and such social conflict, a materialist will say. But 'the stars' are a repeated image. Before his first meeting with Juliet, Romeo has forebodings about 'a consequence yet hanging in the stars' [1.4.104-5]; the love poetry of their illicit meeting on Juliet's balcony repeats the imagery of night and starlight as metaphor for physical beauty and passion [2.1.58-65, 150-4; also 3.2.20-5]. Later, when catastrophe strikes, and he has (false) news of Juliet's

[1] Geoffrey Bullough. ed. 1957. 'Romeo and Juliet', *Narrative and Dramatic Sources of Shakespeare*, Vol. 1 (Routledge and Kegan Paul: London), pp. 271, 276-7, 284-5.

[2] Paul N. Siegel. 1961. 'Christianity and the Religion of Love in Romeo and Juliet', *Shakespeare Quarterly*, 12(4): 379-82.

[3] Coppelia Kahn. 1977. 'Coming of Age in Verona', *Modern Language Studies*, 8(1): 12-15.

death, Romeo's immediate response is: 'Is it even so? then I defy you, stars!' [5.1.24]. The heavens, as a transcendent, unreachable, realm, and as a mysterious determinant of human fate, symbolize the qualities of Juliet's and Romeo's love.

This image of heaven can also be read theologically. The love isn't only heavenly and fated; it shares the universality of Christian love. Allen Bloom emphasizes that in Shakespeare's art love is, or can be, boundless. Renaissance theology emphasized God's all-pervading love. Human love participates in the divine. It won't be constrained by conventions of city, family, or society; it will defy political power of state, or party.[4] Christian theological themes of death and resurrection are also prominent in the plot and imagery. The drug that Friar Laurence gives to Juliet will send her into a deep death-like sleep for forty-two hours [4.1.104-6]; she will be laid in the family tomb on day one, and on the third day will be spirited away [4.1.113-17]. The theme of suicide inserts a tension or complication here though—it is a sin for which punishment can be expected.[5]

Recent critics have emphasized more material, political, economic, and social themes. Feminist readings insist that Juliet's and Romeo's fates are determined not by 'the stars' but by the inexorable logic of feud and patriarchy.[6] In Chapter 1 we saw how patriarchy was a normative structure of power and authority in the state, and also an important moral, theological, and legal principle, connected to the pervasive and generalized dominating and denigrating power of men over women in household, economy, culture, and society.[7] The clowning of the Capulet servants who open the action centres on jokes about their courage and anger (or their cowardice), and their prowess (or not) with weapons and sex:

SAMSON: When I have fought with the men, I will be civil with the maids, I will cut off their heads.

GREGORY: The heads of the maids?

SAMSON: Ay, the heads of the maids, or their maidenheads, take it in what sense thou wilt.

GREGORY: They must take it in sense that feel it.

SAMSON: Me they shall feel while I am able to stand... [etc. etc.; 1.1.20-8]

---

[4] Allan Bloom. 2000. *Shakespeare on Love and Friendship* (University of Chicago Press: Chicago), pp. 9–15.

[5] Siegel, 'Christianity and Religion of Love', 1961: 382–5.

[6] Kahn, 'Coming of Age', 1977: 6.

[7] Gordon J. Schochet. 1969. 'Patriarchalism, Politics and Mass Attitudes in Stuart England', *The Historical Journal*, 12: 413–41; Marilyn L. Williamson. 1986. *The Patriarchy of Shakespeare's Comedies* (Wayne State University Press: Detroit, MI).

The bawdy and misogyny of this repartee flows into the pervasive misogyny of the young men's culture of violence with swords (articulated in particular in the scene when Juliet's nurse goes to meet Romeo, and is teased by his friends [2.3.96-134]), and into the violence of the patriarchal power that Capulet exerts over Juliet [3.5.140-95].[8] Critics also point to religious—liturgical and theological—allusions here, most obviously in Samson's and Gregory's names, but also in the way sexual connotations (such as Samson's 'stand') are entwined with religious ones.[9] Sex, religion, and politics are all bound up in Samson's 'I will be civil with the maids' [1.1.21], which ironically echoes, only twenty or so lines later, Chorus's 'civil blood makes civil hands unclean' [Prologue 4].

So, the first political problem of the play is what civility can mean in a setting dominated by feud and patriarchy. The association of feud and Italian life is commonplace. The complicated twelfth- and thirteenth-century factionalism and conflict between Ghibellines and Guelphs originated in rival support for the Holy Roman Emperor and the Pope respectively—and there really was a feud between 'the Montecchi' and the 'Cappetti' in Verona, which is reported by Dante in *The Divine Comedy* (composed 1308-20).[10] From those city conflicts to the organized clan and family violence that we associate with mafia crime and domination, Italian societies have been a source for understanding and modelling the logic of social relations of hostility, hate, and violence that endure over generations. (Unfair, of course, as most societies feature similar dynamics to some degree; and in any case the medieval Italian city states are also originators of the values of republican rule.)[11] As generations pass the original disagreement—whether disputes and insults were about religion, or women, or property—can become hazy, issues other than the original one can become more salient, new schisms and factions can obscure the original contention. By the time Dante himself was involved in Guelph politics, the Guelphs had divided into two factions, the Blacks and the Whites—antagonisms can

    [8] Kahn, 'Coming of Age', 1977: 12–13; Jill H. Levenson. ed. 2000. 'Introduction', in William Shakespeare, *Romeo and Juliet* (Oxford University Press: Oxford), pp. 143–7.
    [9] Angela Ward. 2017. 'Symbols of the Sacred: Religious tension in Act I Scene 1 of Romeo and Juliet', *Literature and Theology*, 31(1): 64–77.
    [10] Dante Alighieri. 1978. *The Divine Comedy*. Vol. 2: *Purgatorio*, trans. and ed. John D. Sinclair (Oxford University Press: New York), Canto 6.106; Skinner, Quentin. 1978. *The Foundations of Modern Political Thought*. Vol. 1: *The Renaissance* (Cambridge University Press: Cambridge), pp. 17–8, 23; see also Machiavelli, Niccolo. 1532/1961. *The Prince*, trans. George Bull (Penguin: Harmondsworth), Ch. XX.
    [11] Carlo Levi. 1947/1963. *Christ Stopped at Eboli*, trans. Frances Frenaye (Farrar, Strauss, Inc.: New York); Edward C. Banfield. 1958. *The Moral Basis of a Backward Society* (Chicago: The Free Press), p. 11; Skinner, *Foundations*, 1978: Ch. 1; Robert D. Putnam, Robert Leonardi, and Raffaella Nanetti. 1993. *Making Democracy Work: Civic Traditions in Modern Italy* (Princeton University Press: Princeton, NJ).

be complicated, as well as sharpened, by brand new interests, in territory or markets. The signs and symbols of membership can become as powerful an incitement to hostility as any substantial rivalry over goods. In the history of Ghibellines and Guelphs marks of membership such as hats were occasions for violence. The Montague boys' hostility to Tybalt focuses a good deal on Tybalt's style of sword fighting.[12] The densely solidaristic networks of hierarchically organized families, dominated by patriarchs, who have the power of patronage, and thus command allegiance by tying young men into their households—as Tybalt seems to be incorporated into the Capulets—make for an exaggeratedly inward orientation by individuals, and an exaggeratedly hostile and fearful attitude to outsiders.

All of these factors—the significance of signs and symbols, the prominence of family and household allegiance—can be understood as indicators of Shakespeare's Verona's 'political immaturity', which can be connected, as far as the play's imagery and symbolism goes, to Juliet's and Romeo's permanent immaturity.[13] But focus on political immaturity suggests that Verona simply had not, yet, developed the kind of constitution and institutions that mellow out social and cultural antagonisms. In this book, I want to emphasize the moments in Shakespeare's drama which seem to say that the political way is the better way, and, perhaps, that in late modern polities we all have to be a bit grown up about it. But we cannot overlook the way political power always is in tension with other power claims, and this is not a matter of the age or maturity or 'development' of political institutions. In *Romeo and Juliet*, the power of the state (and its claims for civility on the part of citizens and denizens, as well as its enforcement of law), comes into a tense relationship with patriarchal authority, and with machiavellian ingenuity and manoeuvring. We have met this trio before, in connection with *Othello*, and we will meet it again. But in Verona these three forms of political power in competition are variously reinforced, challenged, and undermined, by, first, violence—civil violence this time, not the military discipline and punishing authority favoured by Martius in *Coriolanus*; second, by the forces and pulls of market exchange.

---

[12] Jill H. Levenson. 1995. 'Alla Stoccado Carries It Away: Codes of Violence in Romeo and Juliet', *Shakespeare's Romeo and Juliet: Texts, Contexts and Interpretation*, ed. Jay L. Halio (University of Delaware Press: Newark, NJ), pp. 90–2; Levenson, 'Introduction', 2000: 36–8.

[13] Mera J. Flaumenhaft. 2017. 'Romeo and Juliet for Grownups', *Review of Politics*, 79: 548–9; Kahn, 'Coming of Age', 1977: 5–7.

Sovereign Power

The play is punctuated with the exertion of sovereign, princely power. In Scene 1, Prince Escalus addresses Montague and Capulet with an assertion of civic values in the face of uncivilized men:

> What ho! You men, you beasts; that quench the fire of your pernicious rage....On pain of torture, from those bloody hands throw your mis-tempered weapons to the ground, and hear the sentence of your moved Prince....If ever you disturb our streets again, your lives shall pay the forfeit of the peace. For this time all the rest depart away. You, Capulet, shall go along with me; and Montague, come you this afternoon, to know our farther pleasure in this case, to old Freetown, our common judgement place. Once more, on pain of death, all men depart.   [1.1.77–99]

This speech succinctly performs the executive and police functions of a polity—quashing the disturbance, dispersing the participants, arresting the leaders, and summoning them for judgement. It makes reference to the city's estab-lished places and institutions: 'old Freetown, our common judgement place' invokes authoritative, evolving institutions that pre-exist the present inhabit-ants and will live on after them, emphasizing the communal nature of political and legal institutions.[14]

Of course, the irony of the play, perhaps an irony of sovereignty itself, is that this sovereign pronouncement and action has no effect whatsoever. The old men, despite their patriarchal power, are unable to control the young men of their households, and the violence continues. We might wish that sover-eign power were more effective than Prince Escalus manages to make it. There wouldn't be much of a play, to be sure, if his pronouncement had the effect he intended—drama as well as deaths would have been avoided. But there are a number of reasons, in any case, to be sceptical of the very idea that there can be this final and decisive power, really. Shakespeare's representations of sover-eign power often play with the idea that absolute sovereignty, than which there is no higher, is an illusion. Sovereignty has an intelligible meaning, but the thing it invokes is fantastic, like a unicorn. Shakespeare shows us sover-eign rulers—Escalus; the monarchs of England—repetitively attempting to exert sovereignty. We are not at all surprised that they repeatedly fail in the

---

[14] Levenson, 'Introduction', 2000: 150n.98.

face of social forces, ruthless enemies, unintended consequences, sheer incapacity, and so on.

Sovereignty in this play describes a similar arc as in *Othello*. In this first scene we see well-ordered, as it were, sovereign authority attending to matters of state, and exerting unambiguous, final, and overweening authority over Montague and Capulet. In 3.1, Mercutio is killed, in a fight, by Tybalt, and Tybalt in turn by Romeo. A citizen performs an arrest, and the Prince is summoned. Despite having told Montague and Capulet that they were responsible for the conduct of the younger men of their households, and despite having threatened them with death, he now exacts a fine, a financial penalty, from them [3.1.190-1], and for Romeo's offence the punishment is exile [3.1.186-7]. The sovereign threat in 1.1, fails to prevent further violence; and at this point he draws back from the penalty he had promised. In the final scene, sovereign authority comes on stage, too late to prevent tragedy, but ready to dispense justice. When the watchmen find Juliet dead they send for the Prince [5.3.174-8]; Escalus takes charge. He elicits from Friar Laurence the full story of what has happened. Laurence tells all: 'if aught in this miscarried by my fault, let my old life be sacrificed, some hour before his time, unto the rigour of the severest law' [5.3.266-9]. Escalus judges: 'We still have known thee for a holy man' [5.3.270]. To the news that Balthazar has brought a letter from Romeo addressed to his father, Escalus exercises sovereign authority over private relations, intercepting it: 'Give me the letter; I will look on it' [5.3.278]. It is he who reads Romeo's account of events, including that he had bought poison with which to kill himself and to be with Juliet [5.3.286-90].

The tragedy is a sign, among other things, of the limits and failings of sovereign power. In light of Laurence's and Romeo's accounts of the events, the Prince can do nothing. His is still the moral and political voice that can utter reproach to Montague and Capulet: 'see what a scourge is laid upon your hate, that heaven finds means to kill your joys with love' [5.3.292-3], but this moral function is hardly all that traditional theorists were thinking of when they talked of sovereign power. He also is a man and a citizen himself. As such he utters a self-reproach at his exercise of sovereignty which has fallen short: '...I, for winking at your discords, too, have lost a brace of kinsmen. All are punished' [5.3.294-5]. *Romeo and Juliet* articulates the failings and the futility of so-called sovereign power. It is over-ridden by the workings of chance, fate, and heaven. It is exercised by men who are merely men. It is also ironized by the reasoning and actions of machiavellians, whose plots and devices evade and undermine the open pronouncements of authority and dispensations of

justice such as Escalus attempts. It is thwarted, by passions, and by the organization of social relations, in particular the power of patriarchs.

Patriarchal Power

We can understand the limits of sovereignty in Verona by seeing that patriarchy does not give way. But it is not quite secure. If fathers stand in relation
to their households as heads of state stand in relation to society and the law
that governs it, that raises the thorny question of the patriarchal—or other—
nature of the power of the head of state over the patriarchs.[15] In political and
social thought this conundrum is often resolved in the idea of 'spheres' of
power and authority. But *Romeo and Juliet* depicts a world in which the
spheres of authority of the patriarchs, and the conflict between the households, severely constrains the Prince's authority over the city. The patriarchs
need the city streets and squares as the setting for their feud.

Exercising their power as fathers, Montague and Capulet, we can assume,
command loyalty not only from their servants, the young men attached to the
household and their friends, but also from allies and parties with whom they
are engaged in exchange. Capulet is engaged with Paris for the exchange of
Juliet in marriage, which, we understand, will bring Capulet into enhanced
relations with Prince Escalus (Paris is listed in the 'Persons of the Play' as a
kinsman of the Prince). In the first conversation between Capulet and Paris to
which we are witness, Capulet demurs in the matter of Juliet's marriage. She is
a good, to be exchanged, to be sure; in particular he speaks to her as of fruit
on a tree: 'She hath not seen the change of fourteen years; let two more sum-
mers wither in their pride ere we may think her ripe to be a bride' [1.2.9-11]. In
their second conversation, while Paris seems to accept that the household and
civic turmoil will delay his suit to Juliet, Capulet is suddenly 'desperate': 'Sir
Paris, I will make a desperate tender of my child's love. I think she will be ruled
in all respects by me. Nay, more, I doubt it not' [3.4.12-14]. This combines the
material relationship of pricing and proffering for sale ('I will make a tender...')
with the overweening importance of exchange in social life ('desperate tender')
and the patriarchal imperative, the necessity that Juliet is ruled by him.

Juliet, like other Shakespearean daughters, finds ways of evading and
opposing her fathers' authority—in her case, by lies and trickery. But her
ultimate form of resistance and evasion is suicide. In patriarchal households,
wives and husbands, while each deploys their own form of power, are not

---

[15] Williamson, *Patriarchy*, 1986: 149.

symmetrically situated or equal as partners. The patriarch and his wife, though, are central in the household—Juliet's mother tries to exert influence over her husband, is engaged in the family feud, considers herself to have agency and capacity for action (e.g. in procuring poison with which to murder Romeo [3.5.88–92]). But Shakespeare's list of the 'Persons of the Play' names her only 'Capulet's wife'.

This assertion of untrammelled patriarchal authority contrasts with the ambiguity of the Prince's rule over Capulet and Montague. At the outset of 1.2, we catch Capulet and Paris mid-conversation: 'But Montague is bound as well as I, in penalty alike, and 'tis not hard, I think, for men so old as we to keep the peace' [1.2.1–3]. We learn from this fragment of their conversation about the fight that Capulet does not like the sentence the Prince has pronounced, but acknowledges the even-handedness of the justice. He recognizes the reason in the Prince's sentence; as patriarchs, they should be able to do so. In these lines we see alignment between the republic and the families: the Prince is one patriarch among many, appointed to office whose sovereignty depends on his recognition of the authority of household heads.

Montague and Capulet are both invested in the state: they are engaged in competition for social dominance, and all the economic, cultural, and political advantages connected with it, and the city is the setting for their houses. But they both want to maintain an awful lot of personal and social power in reserve, and to deploy it in the feud which, in many ways—emotionally, libidinally, materially—transcends their investment in the state, in the rule of law, in civility and sovereignty. These are men who partly 'buy into' the civil order but reserve to themselves the rights of 'natural sociality' in such a way that effectively undermines that very civil order, even while one of the ends they have in view is power within that civil order.

In this sense, the Prince's charge that their men are beasts [1.1.79], at their masters' behests, violating civil and political values, both is and is not well-aimed. It might be tempting for some thinkers to see Montague and Capulet as essentially natural beings—top primates. But no matter how attractive to biologically minded social or political thinkers to see them as warring silverbacks, struggling for domination, Shakespeare figures them decidedly as members of a polity and a culture. Republican culture favours—or needs, according to Aristotle—friendship as a dominant model for relations between citizens.[16] But the patriarchs preside over a polity of enmity and alliance—solidaristic friendship and kinship within, but not between, the households.

---

[16] Aristotle). 1932. *Politics*, trans. H. Rackham (Harvard University Press: Cambridge, MA), pp. 1262b–1263b, 1280b.

They also participate in an economy of accumulation. Montague and Capulet and men like them are in a threshold position with regard to the state—both in and out. They wish to exploit state power while reserving for themselves their social power.

Machiavellian Strategy

Juliet and Romeo are caught between patriarchal power, futile sovereign authority, overweening economic interests, and social violence. Into this impasse, Friar Laurence acts. In Arthur Brooke's 'Tragicall Historye of Romeus and Juliet' (1562), one of Shakespeare's sources for the play, Laurence is said to be a wise counsellor to the Prince.[17] In general, the public political life of Verona is more prominent there than it is in Shakespeare's play.[18] Shakespeare's Laurence, in my reading, is more of a magus (this interpretation is at odds with Tony Nuttall's characterization of him as 'a sweet old man who picks flowers and medicinal herbs'[19]). His spiritual authority and reputation as a holy man are given a cryptic twist by his focus on the occult and contradictory properties of things. When we first meet him, he meditates on the ambiguity of the categories good and evil, virtue and vice by analogy with the qualities of plants that can be precious when used, with knowledge, for medicine, and baneful when used, unknowing or perversely, for poison [2.2.1-30]. Paradoxical antitheses like the ones in Laurence's soliloquy—and in Romeo's poetry—were popular poetic and philosophical devices in Elizabethan literature.[20] His speech also adverts to the themes of birth and death, the image of the tomb, and the ambiguity of bodily life in relation to death: 'The earth that's nature's mother is her tomb; what is her burying grave, that is her womb' [2.2.9-10].

Shakespeare's Laurence is confidant and teacher to Romeo, who in the early morning after his first encounters with Juliet comes immediately to him [2.1.234-5, 2.2.31-94]. Laurence sees, beyond the vaguely annoying, vaguely amusing, superficiality of Romeo's love—which seems to have more to do with his eyes than with his heart proper [2.2.67-72]—that, if the union is real, 'this alliance may so happy prove, to turn your households' rancour to pure

[17]   Bullough, 'Romeo and Juliet', 1957: 280-1.
[18]   Arthur Brooke. 1562/1977. 'The Tragicall Historye of Romeus and Juliet', in G. Bullough (ed.), Narrative and Dramatic Sources of Shakespeare, Vol. 1 (Routledge and Kegan Paul: London), pp. 280-1.
[19]   A.D. Nuttall. 2007. Shakespeare the Thinker (Yale University Press: London), p. 17.
[20]   Tom McAlindon. 1991. Shakespeare's Tragic Cosmos (Cambridge University Press: Cambridge), pp. 5-7; Peter G. Platt. 2009. Shakespeare and the Cuture of Paradox (Ashgate: Farnham).

love' [2.2.91-2]. Laurence transfers his understanding of the hidden qualities of plants to the hidden qualities of social relations.

His magus-like insight, though, cannot be pursued openly. He, Juliet, and Romeo will have to use trickery and pretence if the good outcome is to be secured. First, he agrees to marry them without their families' permission [2.2.63-4, 89-90; 2.5.35-7]. Juliet has the help of her nurse, who carries messages [2.3.151-205]. The same day, Romeo is involved in the death of Tybalt and the Prince sentences him to banishment [3.1.186-7]. Laurence brings Romeo the news of the Prince's judgement, which he considers a sign of Escalus's kindness [3.3.10-11, 25-8] but which Romeo considers worse than death [3.3.12-23]. Laurence, upbraiding Romeo and reminding him that it is happier for him that he had killed Tybalt than vice versa, that it is better to be sent into exile than be sent to die, that it is better that Juliet be still alive than she be dead, urges him to go secretly to be with Juliet, to leave before dawn in accordance with the Prince's sentence, and to go to Mantua 'where thou shalt live till we can find a time to blaze your marriage' [3.3.145-53]. Juliet's father, in the wake of Tybalt's death, and Juliet's barely accountable withdrawal from the household, decides to hasten her marriage to Paris—instead of waiting for her to agree, he tells her simply she is to be married, and sets the date for three days later. When she turns to Laurence for help, he comes up with the desperate plan that she should take a drug that will affect her like death—'stiff and stark and cold' [4.1.103]. Her body will be put in the Capulet family vault; meanwhile Laurence will have summoned Romeo back to Verona, they will be with Juliet when she awakes, and she and Romeo can go together to Mantua.

These episodes of ingenious planning and persuasion of others to follow his plan have several meanings for readers and audiences. First, they echo and reprise Laurence's signature theme of good and evil coexisting in the same substance or circumstance. In the context of Christian imagery, Laurence's insistence to both Juliet and Romeo—against their professed desires to die, to commit suicide—that life is better than death is counter-balanced by a version of the view that death will bring life. Both Juliet and Romeo will exchange suicidal despair for new life. Second, they echo Machiavelli's emphasis on the prizes for seizing the opportune moment—*kairos*—taking the chance. In Machiavelli's account of rule and politics, *kairos* is an aspect of time and history that is more significant than *chronos*. The passing of time, our understanding of cause and effect, of the flow of events of course is important in life, in technology, in maintaining political power. But seeing opportunities and taking them, acting against the natural flow of causes and effects, arguably is what sets 'political' action apart from related phenomena such as administration and legal judgement. Sovereignty also, according to some understandings, works against natural flow, interrupting, bringing processes of deliberation and bargaining to an end with decision. The one who seizes the moment is the one who can dominate in the contest with chance.[21]

Reading Laurence politically emphasizes the way he sees opportunities and takes them. But this aspect of his character and role in the action is countered by two other temporal phenomena. The first is fate. The tragic action of the play and the outcome of the drama are foretold in several ways. In the Prologue, Chorus relates to the audience the drama we are about to see or read, alerting us to the lovers being 'star-crossed', and their love 'death-marked' [Prologue 6, 9]. The script is written and nothing can evade the finale. The characters, in their words and reported feelings, also presage the fatal conclusion. Juliet's mother wishes her in her grave! [3.5.139]. Her father threatens to drag her to the church to marry Paris 'on a hurdle' [3.5.154]. Romeo is full of foreboding: 'I dream'd a dream tonight' [1.4.48]; 'my mind misgives some consequence yet hanging in the stars' [1.4.104-9]. Fatalism, the sense that there is nothing we can do, is politically—perhaps anti-politically—significant. Political action is an effort to exercise agency—over the structures that govern us, over the rules, and the rules about rules. Fatalistic cultures are antithetical to such aspiration. They can be marked by estrangement or alienation from those who do wield power—who dominate, or who extract. Fatalist thinking often engages, rather than with social and political relationships and realities, with supernatural forces, occult realities, myth and legend.[22] I return to these themes in Chapter 7.

In *Romeo and Juliet* the theme of fateful presage intersects with a further time theme: that of tragic coincidence, bad luck, accident. Capulet brings the wedding forward by twenty-four hours [4.2.21-37] thus giving much less time for the message about Juliet's feigned death to reach Romeo and for Romeo to get back to Verona. Friar John, in any case, is prevented from delivering the first letter to Romeo in Mantua [5.2.5-16]. Laurence sends a second, but Romeo is already on his way back to Verona because his servant Balthazar has brought (false) news of Juliet's death to him before the message from Laurence can reach him [5.1.17-24]. Laurence arrives just after Romeo has taken the poison, too late to tell him about Juliet [5.3.135-46]. Juliet awakes too late to see Romeo alive [5.3.147-50].

---

[21] Machiavelli, *Prince*, 1532/1961: Ch. XXV.
[22] Levi, *Christ Stopped*, 1947/1963: Ch. 14.

Violence and Political Power

The three forms of political power—sovereignty, patriarchy, machination—intersect and thwart one another, making a kind of backdrop of futility against which a human, emotional, relational drama is played out. In *Romeo and Juliet* love, the potent form of human connection, interacts and intersects with violence, a particularly potent form of human disconnection. Love and violence, connection and destruction also are ironized by a discourse that pervades the drama of economic exchange, this reflective, of course, of what the feud of the patriarchs is—at least in part, we can surmise—about. The relationship between violence and politics is, like everything about politics, contested. For many thinkers and political actors, violence is an instrument—perhaps the most potent one—of political power, whether that is thought of as sovereign authority, or persuasion, or manipulation. But an alternative tradition of political thought associates politics with pacification. The story of the imposition of, or the agreement to, political power (procedures for selecting governors and officers, settling public disputes, passing legislation, managing administration, and so on) is the story of a shift from inter-personal violence to public reasoning, negotiation, and conciliation—from swords to words. This does not mean that social actors are entirely pacified—but when they are permitted, or required, to use violence, and when they are forbidden, is a matter for the public authority to decide; and the public authority controls uses of violence for punishment or military action. The pacification story (emphasizing that in political societies violence is, if not overcome, then minimized) and the monopolization story (the idea that the means and rights of violence shift from individuals to centralized authorities) are differently weighted in rival traditions of political thought.[23] Some thinkers speak of governmental uses of police, military, and judicial violence as 'force'—hence emphasizing its legality, legitimacy, and 'pacific' quality; others emphasize the way ordinary common or garden violence, in all its varieties, is barely submerged beneath civil institutions and social manners. In particular, permissions—for instance, to fathers to use violence against children, wives, and servants—make the difference between a 'political' society and a non-political one indiscernible from the point of those who are subject to this violence. The same goes for those who are on the receiving end of permitted and legal economic coercion,

[23] Elizabeth Frazer and Kimberly Hutchings. 2011. 'Virtuous Violence and the Politics of Statecraft in Machiavelli, Clausewitz and Weber', *Political Studies*, 59: 56–73; 2020. *Violence and political theory*, Polity Press.

including being injured by exploitative work conditions or inadequately sustained when prices are too high; or those who are victims of culturally approved 'punishment' for those who don't conform.

Romeo and Juliet is a great play for thinking about these puzzles about the prospects for political society, and in particular how violence works in relation to other forms of power. The plot is carried along by violence.[24] First, and most obvious, the feud structures all the social and political relations and actions—exercises of sovereignty, exercises of patriarchal authority, Laurence's political subterfuge. The themes of enmity and hate pervade the text; and the feud is carried on by physical fighting with deadly weapons. Second, the friendship and camaraderie between the men and boys of the two households is suffused with imageries of violence and victory. Their sport incorporates the equation of fighting with weapons with sexuality, and their misogynistic play makes the streets an uncomfortable place for female characters. *Romeo and Juliet* focuses on a culture of violence; it is dynamic, and affects other areas of people's lives (their markets, their parties, their intimate relationships) just because it is governed by norms and standards, and because for the violent actors their skills and capacities are embodied—learned, practiced, habitual. Third, all the anger and combat of the feud, between families and out in the streets, is reprised in private—for example, in Capulet's treatment of Juliet when she fails to submit to his will, or when the sociable setting of Capulet's party is disturbed by the mischief of the gate-crashing boys. Fourth, audiences will vary in their judgements of the violence of suicide. We might see Juliet's killing herself with a dagger as itself a form of violence—a final transformation of the inter-personal violence of the play into violence against herself.

The feud is carried on with deadly weapons. It must be remembered that sword fighting, for sport and in play, has direct relevance to military service. The discipline and skill, and fruits of study, training, and practice, are straightforward social goods for the boys themselves; but capacity to fight, to the death, is also a public good—the kind of thing that, if it is not supplied in the ordinary course of socialization, should be supplied by the government. As discussed in Chapter 3, the question of how citizens can be made into soldiers, and then turned back again after the war is over into citizens, is a central question for republican political thinkers. All these considerations elevate fighting, socially and politically. Sword fights have an enduring place in entertainments such as theatre. For Shakespeare's early audiences, the allusions to weapons and styles would have been topical rather than of historical interest.

---

[24] Kahn, 'Coming of Age', 1977: 7–10; Levenson, 'Alla Stoccado', 1995.

The difference between the Montague boys' and Tybalt's fighting is marked by Tybalt's distinctive Spanish style, and also his high level of skill or, at any rate, the advantage of his distinctive way. It also marks him as influenced by foreign ways and therefore suspect as to his character and motivation [1.1.105-10, 2.3.17-34].[25] The physical violence is accompanied by insult—the intention always to injure, the object always the body. Insults in *Romeo and Juliet* are most often sexual, and inseparable from expression of misogyny. In 1.1, Samson equates sexual assault of the Montague women with physical assault of the men [1.1.14-17, 20-8]. Mercutio's insults of Tybalt connect Tybalt's sword fighting with sexuality [2.3.17-34]. Insults are also belittling—for instance, Tybalt's use of 'boy' [3.1.65, 130]—and the ones to the nurse are simply misogynistic [2.3.18-132].

The feud and the violence, first, require solidaristic friendship within the camps. In republican theory, friendly relations between citizens facilitate economic commerce and shared governmental institutions, and can transform easily into the comradely relationships between soldiers. But in *Romeo and Juliet*, generalized friendliness has been severed by the line of enmity between the Montagues and the Capulets. The concomitant of the supportive, joshing, relationships between the Montague boys is their destructive, insulting attitudes to the Capulets. Among the Capulets, hate is a dominating emotion. Tybalt hates the word peace 'as I hate hell, all Montagues, and thee'—he is addressing Romeo's friend Benvolio [1.1.66-8]. When Juliet finds out Romeo's identity she doesn't hesitate to articulate her own identity in this war:

NURSE: His name is Romeo, and a Montague, the only son of your great enemy.
JULIET: My only love sprung from my only hate.... [1.4.249-51]

Lady Capulet is quick to assign blame at the fight in 3.1, to call for exemplary punishment for Romeo [3.1.176-81]. She assumes that Juliet must be as vengeful, against Romeo and on behalf of Tybalt, as she is herself [3.5.78-84]. She plans, or promises, to have Romeo poisoned [3.5.88-92]. This level of hatred, and focus on who is friend and who enemy, is evident also in Tybalt's sensitivity at the party. He hears Romeo speak, recognizes him as a Montague 'by his voice', and, enraged, calls for his rapier [1.4.167-72].

[25] Levenson, 'Alla Stoccado', 1995: 90–2; Jerzy Limon. 1995. 'Rehabilitating Tybalt', in Jay L. Halio (ed.), *Shakespeare's Romeo and Juliet: Texts, Contexts and Interpretation* (University of Delaware Press: Newark, NJ), pp. 99, 102–4.

The gate-crashing, although it might seem to be trivial, and a manifestation of the boys' high spirits, is reckless, and can be interpreted as a sign of their arrogance. From the point of view of those who are intruded upon, gate-crashing certainly is one form of violence—a boundary has been crossed, and an injury is done to the event that the hosts have envisaged and organized. Tybalt's reaction—'Fetch me my rapier, boy…to strike him dead I hold it not a sin' [1.4.167-72] is overly violent, but the matter of honour is not all in his imagination.[26] Tybalt's construction of the honour of the house is, though, subject to the arbitrary authority of Capulet the patriarch. As we see in 1.1, the brawls between the households are with the licence, if not at the behest, of the two old men:

CAPULET: My sword, I say. Old Montague is come, and flourishes his blade in spite of me.
MONTAGUE: Thou villain, Capulet! (To his wife) Hold me not, let me go.
[1.1.71-5]

But at the party, Capulet wants a civil, hospitable atmosphere, and he disciplines Tybalt. At first, he tries to communicate his bonhomie: 'Young Romeo is it?…Content thee, gentle coz, let him alone. A bears him like a portly gentleman;…' [1.4.177-87]. Tybalt is defiant: 'I'll not endure him' [1.4.189] at which Capulet subjects him to an angry verbal exercise of authority: 'He shall be endured…; you are a princox, go, be quiet, or…I'll make you be quiet' [1.4.188-201]. The old men cannot, actually, control the young; but at this time Tybalt is, indeed, silenced.

This angry discipline is next used on Juliet when Capulet hears that she will not marry Paris. In response to his anger:

Thank me no thankings, nor proud me no prouds; but fettle your fine joints 'gainst Thursday next to go with Paris to St Peter's Church, or I will drag thee on a hurdle thither. Out, you green-sickness carrion! Out, you baggage, you tallow-face. [3.5.151-6]

Juliet kneels, or falls. It's hard to imagine this scene staged without an engagement of Capulet's body in his extreme emotion, and it's plausible that his 'outs' are accompanied by blows that send her to the ground. The actor could exhibit

---

[26] Limon, 'Rehabilitating Tybalt', 1995: 98.

cold, cutting anger—but that is less consistent with the insults than physically violent blows or near blows.

Juliet's mother is entirely incorporated into this patriarchal power. In the first scene, she attempts to restrain her husband with mockery—implying an affectionate relationship between them: 'A crutch, a crutch—why call you for a sword?' [1.1.72]. But she is entirely implicated in the violence, exaggerating the number of Montagues involved in the death of Tybalt [3.1.176-9], calling to the Prince for Romeo's death [3.1.180-1]. She makes some efforts to stem Capulet's anger to Juliet [3.1.156], and remonstrates at his attack on the nurse [3.5.174]. But she, too, has no sympathy at all for Juliet's demurral regarding the accelerated marriage to Paris [3.5.139]. Her remonstration with Capulet has no effect on his diatribe, which continues for a further twenty, uninterrupted, lines [3.5.175-95], culminating in an angry exit. To Juliet's plea 'O sweet my mother, cast me not away!' [3.5.198] she rejects her: 'Talk not to me, for I'll not speak a word. Do as thou wilt, for I have done with thee' [3.5.202-3].

These episodes of violence carry the plot along. In my interpretation, they supply an energy, establishing relationships, deciding patterns of subordination and hierarchy, making things happen, relevant to the life of the city. This being so, as political theorists we can say either of two things. First, that violence is a political power. It has these public effects, makes differences to how life is lived in the polity, affects and shapes the workings of the public institutions. Second, that violence is a destructive threat to political power. The power of people to establish institutions and offices which govern all, citizens, denizens, and aliens alike, and then to use that power to make and execute laws, to dispute over relationships and transactions, is threatened by violence.

Gender and Commerce

I have pointed out that Montague and Capulet are accumulators of economic and material goods and resources. Even without a stable state, they would preside over their households, dominate their women and younger kinsmen, maintain their fences and their fortifications, strike bargains, and make peace and pacts, or conduct feuds and war with their neighbours. In such a situation, though, they would have far less surplus with which to dispense hospitality and enjoy parties, and to live in the splendour that a city setting allows them. The city setting, and the tense relationship of the feuding families to the laws and the norms of civil public life, serves to emphasize the household wealth, as well as to emphasize the patriarchal power that dominates it.

The significance of wealth, as so often in Shakespeare's plots and settings, inserts a sceptical question about political power. The Prince is a patriarch and a notable, just like Montague and Capulet. We can infer that Capulet will benefit from a closer alliance with the Prince's kin group via the marriage of Juliet and Paris, and that this benefit will be both political and economic. According to some materialist thinkers—influenced by the work of Karl Marx (1818-83) or Max Weber (1864-1920)—the fiction of sovereign authority always and only disguises the power of a group based on shared material interests. One way of putting this is that political power is really only economic power organized to enforce the kind of systems of law and rule that safeguard established economic interests. Cultural institutions—religion, kinship, the public settings of the state—are the medium through which the legitimacy (in the broadest sense, not simply the legality) of the domination of economic interests in the political realm of the state and society is maintained.[27] With his focus on household and domestic relationships, on streets and taverns, on wealth and goods exchanged, Shakespeare's dramas show audiences this process of legitimation of rule, and also (as in Chapter 2) they show, and articulate, resistance to it.

One way that he articulates ironic comment on material exchange is by the imagery of worth and value that runs through the text. At its heart is Capulet's physical, material exchange of Juliet, in marriage, for the goods that accrue to a house from an alliance through kinship advantageous in terms of connections and wealth. For this, as we have seen, he relies on patriarchal power over his daughter, on an economy of accumulation and exchange, and also on the laws and institutions of the city—the church, the authority of the Prince. This recognition of the significance of the city is signalled rhetorically in the play by the concept 'civility'. His remonstration to Tybalt at the party, warning him not to use violence or other aggression against the Montague boys, makes direct reference to his citizenly reputation:

> to say truth, Verona brags of him [Romeo] to be a virtuous and well-governed
> youth. I would not for the wealth of all this town here in my house do him
> disparagement. Therefore be patient, take no note of him: it is my will, the
> which if thou respect, show a fair presence and put off these frowns, an
> ill-beseeming semblance for a feast.   [1.4.180-6]

---

[27] Jonathan Dollimore. 1985a. 'Introduction: Shakespeare, cultural materialism, and the new historicism', in Jonathan Dollimore and Alan Sinfield (eds.), *Political Shakespeare: New Essays in Cultural Materialism* (Manchester University Press: Manchester), pp. 3–4.

It matters to Capulet what Verona thinks. He is determined that his household should participate in the citizenly sociable norms. Of course, as a patriarch his idea is that compliance should be nothing more than a matter of his expressed will—'because I say so'—although that is tempered with reasoned argument.

Romeo's speech consistently emphasizes themes of value and exchange, but in a sense that emphasizes the paradoxical transformation of qualities of goods. His words echo Laurence's soliloquy on the mingling of qualities of poison and sustenance, vile and good, virtue and vice. Love is 'a choking gall and a preserving sweet' [1.1.186-90]. His images of exchange and value romanticize commerce and exchange, and intersect with another dominant theme in his poetry—quest. Romeo is first lovesick for Rosaline and later heartbroken for Juliet: 'mine own fortune is my misery' [1.2.59]. In his intimate encounter with Juliet on her balcony he combines the imagery of voyage and commerce: 'I am no pilot, yet wert thou as far as that vast shore washed with the farthest sea, I should adventure for such merchandise' [2.1.125-7]. The exchange that Romeo seeks with Juliet, unlike her father's with Paris, is 'The exchange of thy love's faithful vow for mine' [2.1.170]. But Juliet disavows exchange in favour of gift: 'I gave thee mine before thou didst request it; and yet I would it were to give again' [2.1.171-2].[28] Romeo's love for Juliet, on the occasion of their marriage, is such that any sorrow 'cannot countervail the exchange of joy' [2.5.4]. Later, though, his sorrow seems to overwhelm all else.

Finally, Romeo makes a fateful and final transaction, exchanging a large amount of gold for a dram of poison [5.1.59-60]. The poor apothecary sells him the poison, against the law of Mantua [5.1.66-7]. Romeo here asserts the power of material exchange over that of law and politics:

ROMEO: The world is not thy friend, nor the world's law; the world affords no
    law to make thee rich. Then be not poor, but break and take this.
APOTHECARY: 'My poverty, but not my will, consents.
ROMEO: I pray to thy poverty and not thy will. [5.1.72-6]

Here is commerce. The poor apothecary does not wish, or will, to sell Romeo the deadly poison. But in commercial relations, it is not our deliberative judgement, nor our moral convictions, that drive action, but our calculations about the satisfaction of our interests and needs.

---

[28] Jonathan Bate. 1993. *Shakespeare and Ovid* (Clarendon Press: Oxford), pp. 178-9.

However, this imperative of need is not the last word on the transaction. Romeo is cognizant of, and muses on, the ambiguity of this ostensibly rational exchange:

> There is thy gold, worse poison to men's souls, doing more murder in this loathsome world, than those poor compounds that they mayst not sell. I sell thee poison; thou has sold me none. Come, cordial and not poison, go with me to Juliet's grave, for there must I use thee.   [5.2.80-6]

These paradoxical anthitheses—that gold is poison, that gold does more murder than poison, that poison is cordial—emphasize the transformation of qualities of commodities as they circulate around the economy. The poison has a straightforward use for Romeo—he is going to use it to kill himself. This use value is also a transformative value—it will transform his relationship with Juliet.

Romeo's poetry, and the drama generally, plays with the implications of a world in which everything is for sale, and in which emotions and feelings ricochet between transcendence and despair. Juliet's and Romeo's relationship is imagined and articulated in terms of stars, heavens, night, and day—the transcendent, eternal structures of the universe and the world [3.2.1-33]. He thinks of her and their relationship in terms of precious and rare commodities, valuable goods for which voyages and quests are justified. Finally, the two of them are to be realized in gold as statues [5.3.298-304]. The obverse of this soaring imagination, and image of bounteous value, is despair and death—of friends and enemies, Mercutio and Tybalt, and of Juliet and Romeo themselves.

I must note, in all of this, that between transcendence and despair, and after his marriage to Juliet, Romeo goes through a brief episode of civil responsibility, attempting to stop the fight between Mercutio and Tybalt: 'Gentlemen, for shame forbear this outrage. Tybalt, Mercutio, the Prince expressly hath forbid this bandying in Verona streets' [3.1.85-7]. But with the death of Mercutio he is overtaken, once again, with his fatalism: 'This day's black fate on more days doth depend; this but begins the woe others must end' [3.1.119-20]. But that thought is accompanied by regret at the way he has let himself be taken up with paradoxes and transformations, with the transcendence of feminine heavenly love rather than the masculine life of the feuding city: 'O sweet Juliet, thy beauty hath made me effeminate, and in my temper softened valour's steel' [3.1.113-15].

Clear distinctions between male and female, masculine and feminine run through the text of *Romeo and Juliet* while Shakespeare also shows us, as he does elsewhere, the blurred nature of the gender boundary. Juliet's parents, as we have seen, live the clear distinctions between husband and wife, and unambiguously endorse and enforce the particular sex-fate of their daughter. The culture of the city, in particular the joshing and teasing of the men and boys, turns on sexuality and eroticism in general, and on heterosexual male to female sexual action in particular [1.1.10-35; 1.4.23-30, 51-92; 2.3.100-30]. Laurence, who emphasizes the ambiguous qualities of substances and entities, nevertheless insists on a clear sexual distinction ('women may fall when there's no strength in men' [2.2.80]) and an unalloyed standard of manliness from Romeo. '...come forth, thou fearful man' [3.3.1]. 'Art thou a man? Thy form cries out thou art. Thy tears are womanish;...unseemly woman in a seeming man' [3.3.108-13]. At this point, the nurse also calls on Romeo to be a man: 'blubb'ring and weeping, weeping and blubb'ring—Stand up, stand up, stand an you be a man; for Juliet's sake, for her sake, rise and stand' [3.3.88-90]. But Laurence also demands manliness of Juliet. When he gives her the sleeping drug he tells her she must be brave—not womanish: 'And this shall free thee from this present shame, if no inconstant toy nor womanish fear abate thy valour in the acting it' [4.1.118-20].

In the end, Romeo's consciousness of ambiguity is confirmed in their conduct. Juliet, indeed, is valorous in taking the drug. She is afraid, to be sure is seized with terror [4.3.15-56] but drinks the potion [4.3.57]. Romeo's violence is 'manly' enough: he kills Tybalt with a sword, and similarly Paris, although not knowing it is he, who tries to prevent him entering the Capulet tomb [5.3.70-3]. Romeo drinks his poison [5.3.119-20]. Juliet kills herself with a dagger [5.3.170], dying the more 'manly' death.

Political Economy, Violence, and Emotion

I have argued that, in *Romeo and Juliet*, civic and political values are swept away by violence—obviously enough—and also by the imperatives of feeling and emotion in a world in which everything is for sale, and it is the exchange and circulation of goods, and bads, as commodities that allow characters to make sense of their world. I return to the theme of 'the poitics of emotion and feeling' in Chapter 5, on *King Lear*.

5

Sovereignty, Justice, and Political Power

King Lear

Political Power and *King Lear*

In *King Lear* (composed 1605) two family stories intertwine. First, that of old King Lear, his three daughters, and the outcome of his division of the unified kingdom of Britain (the traditional story of Lear is set in a mythical time before the founding of Rome[1]) between the husbands of two of them—Gonoril and Regan—and his disinheritance of the third, Cordelia. Second, that of Lear's counsellor, the Earl of Gloucester, his two sons, legitimate Edgar and illegitimate Edmund, and the outcomes of Edmund's vengeful victimization of Edgar, in payback for the injustice he has suffered, from his father, as an illegitimate boy. These emotional and ethical stories of inheritance, paternity, inter-generational conflict, familial love, grief, and vengeance, deepened by Shakespeare's imagery of nature, suffering, and redemption, make for the most powerful of his dramas. But we can narrate the play also as a skein of political stories. The threads pick up and develop the familiar themes that we have met in previous chapters—sovereignty, patriarchy, machiavellian political action, violence—and also justice. I begin by telling these five stories.

Sovereignty and Succession

Sovereignty, in the modern world, is often identified with state sovereignty, and that means territory and borders.[2] Scene 1 sees King Lear displaying a map of the kingdom to a council of courtiers and family members. He intends

[1] Geoffrey Bullough. ed. 1973. 'King Lear', *Narrative and Dramatic Sources of Shakespeare*, Vol. 7 (Routledge and Kegan Paul: London), pp. 269–74.
[2] Dan Brayton. 2003. 'Angling in the Lake of Darkness: Possession, dispossession and the politics of discovery in King Lear', *ELH*, 70: 70.

Shakespeare and the Political Way. Elizabeth Frazer, Oxford University Press (2020). © Elizabeth Frazer.
DOI: 10.1093/oso/9780198848615.001.0001

to split the territory of Britain into three, allotting one part as dowry to each of his three daughters. Gonoril's husband is the Duke of Albany (Albany is an ancient name in English, of Welsh and Scots Gaelic derivation, for the north of the island of Britain including what is now Scotland). Regan is married to the Duke of Cornwall (implying that he is lord of lands in the southwest). The names underline the closeness of sovereign power, persons, and territory. Stuart Elden points out that this is the only Shakespeare play that features the word 'territory'—with its meaning familiar to us—as opposed to 'territories'.[3] Cordelia, Lear's youngest daughter, is not yet married. Two suitors are present at the court—the Duke of Burgundy who is favourite to marry her and the King of France. Lear's plan is to retire from the daily work of the monarchy, deputing Albany, Cornwall, and the new husband of Cordelia to take on the 'cares and business of our state' [1.1/S.1: 39].

His plan goes wrong at the point of announcement. He couches the distribution of dowry and territory in terms of a 'love contest', demanding that his daughters tell him how much they love him, in order that 'our largest bounty may extend where merit doth most challenge it' [1.1/S.1: 44-7]. Whether he intends this as a jocular merry game, or whether it is an instance of paternal control and manipulation, Gonoril and Regan respond by assuring him of the extent and quality of their esteem and love for him, while Cordelia refuses to answer in the spirit that he wishes. Lear's response is fury. He immediately withdraws Cordelia's dowry, reallocating her portion between Cornwall and Albany, investing them jointly with his 'power, pre-eminence, and all the large effects that troop with majesty' [1.1/S.1: 119-23]. He also announces that he will live with each of them by turns, one month at a time, reserving to himself one hundred knights to be sustained by the household in which he is dwelling.

An obvious first interpretation of these decisions is that Lear has muddled up sovereign decision making with familial emotional motivation and reaction, and thereby has destabilized sovereign authority vis-à-vis the state. As monarch, Lear has sovereign authority over the organization and conduct of government, and, as ruler, must take responsibility for orderly transfer of power on his death or, as in this case, abdication or retirement. Sovereignty over state intersects complicatedly with the sovereignty of a father over his family. In a system of inherited property and status, in particular in a world in which women may not inherit monarchical power in their own right, matters of family and kinship are intimately intertwined with matters of state sovereignty and

---

[3] Stuart Elden. 2013. 'The Geopolitics of King Lear: Territory, land, earth', *Law and Literature*, 25: 148–9; Stuart Elden. 2018. *Shakespearean Territories* (University of Chicago Press: Chicago).

political succession. The French 'Salic Law' which explicitly proscribed female inheritance was a matter of fascination during Elizabeth I's reign; it entered into disputes about the legitimacy of English monarchical inheritances, and is alluded to by Shakespeare, for instance in *Henry V* [1.2.35-100]. That Lear has daughters, not sons, confounds the convention and laws of male primogeniture; but it also introduces the theme of property, inheritance, and legacy becoming a matter of the testator's will and choice. The judgement that Lear errs in confounding demands for filial love (rather than political allegiance) with rights of inheritance of property and sovereignty is common: according to one interpretation of Lear, in the theoretical frame of the Platonic wise ruler, wisdom and power part company at this moment.[4] Jaffa argues, to the contrary, that Lear has a clever and rational plan. By posing the love test, Lear elicits Gonoril's and Regan's testimony of their allegiance and his worth, and their endorsement of his authority over them as father and as king. This would leave them unable to dissent from his (larger) allocation to Cordelia when her turn to answer came.[5] In other words, muddling up familial love with political allegiance is a strategically canny thing to do.

Consequent to Albany and Cornwall taking up authority, it quickly transpires that there is conflict—'likely wars'—between them [2.1/S.6: 10-11, 3.1/S.8.19-21]. This is a matter of 'internal' sovereign instability. We should not draw the 'internal-external' distinction too clearly, obviously, and *King Lear* shows how entwined they are; but his actions have direct 'foreign policy' implications.[6] His first plan seems to be that Cordelia will marry the Duke of Burgundy, and that they should rule the central and by implication largest part of the territory. But once Cordelia's dowry is withdrawn Burgundy declines to marry her. Cordelia responds that, since he loves money rather than the person, she will not be his wife [1.1/S.1: 238-9]. The King of France—with praise of Cordelia's virtue, and protestations at Lear's treatment of her—declares his wish to make her Queen of France [1.1/S.1: 240-51]. The alliance with Burgundy would have had the effect of enhancing Britain's resources against France, which by the sixteenth century was the more powerful. Instead the subsequent domestic, emotional, and political conflict between Regan, Cornwall, Gonoril, Albany,

[4] Paul A. Cantor. 1996. 'King Lear: The tragic disjunction of wisdom and power', in Joseph Alulis and Vickie Sullivan (eds.), *Shakespeare's Political Pageant: Essays in Literature and Politics* (Rowman and Littlefield: London), pp. 189–92.

[5] Harry V. Jaffa. 1957. 'The Limits of Politics: An interpretation of King Lear, Act I, Scene 1', *The American Political Science Review*, 51(2): 417–18.

[6] Daniel Philpott. 2011. 'Sovereignty', in George Klosko (ed.), *The Oxford Handbook of the History of Political Philosophy* (Oxford University Press: Oxford); R.B.J. Walker. 1993. *Inside/Outside: International Relations as Political Theory* (Cambridge University Press: Cambridge).

and Lear is responded to by France sending 'a power into this scattered kingdom' [3.1/S.8:21.5].

There are differences between the Quarto (first printed 1608) and Folio (printed 1623) versions of the text with regard to the nature of the invasion with Cordelia at its head. Is she a woman warrior? Or, alternatively, is she a caring daughter returned to help her father?[7] Either way, the sovereignty story is that Lear, in trying to order the succession, and to secure the state of Britain, actually brings it into crisis both internally and externally. As with *Othello* there are puzzles in the timescale. According to some schemes of elapsed time the whole action can be compressed into four days; but there are indications of a much longer period—the Fool 'pines' for Cordelia [1.4/S.4: 68-9], rumours and intelligence circulate. Armies march. Whether Cordelia returns at the head of a foreign force, or whether she comes back with a security escort to help her father, matters, in one crucial way. Foreign invasion is decidedly distinct from governmental and constitutional crisis at home. Staging a French invasion is also a riskier theatrical venture for Shakespeare's company.

Patriarchal Power and Resistance

This is the second political story. We have seen the complications that follow on Lear's doubled or muddled exercises of patriarchal power over his daughters and sovereign power over his heirs, successors, and subjects. After Cordelia and France leave the court, so too do the others—Cornwall and Regan to their estate; Gonoril, Albany, Lear, and his followers to Albany's. Quickly, household relations at Albany's deteriorate. There is conflict between Lear's knights and Gonoril's household; one of Gonoril's gentlemen chides Lear's Fool, so Lear strikes the gentleman [1.3/S.3: 1-2]. When Lear returns from hunting, Gonoril confronts him. Reprising a theme from her discussion with her sister Regan following Cordelia's departure [1.1/S.1: 278-96], she is concerned about his poor judgement: 'Come, sir, I would you would make use of that good wisdom whereof I know you are fraught, and put away those dispositions that of late transform you from what you rightly are' [1.4/S.4: 211-14].

Diverse interpretations of the Gonoril-Regan-Lear relationship are possible. Lear could be an erstwhile fine man whose late poor judgement is an effect of ageing. Accordingly, we can interpret Gonoril's and Regan's responses as seeking simply to reassure, to normalize, and to remind him of their family

---

[7] W.W. Greg. 1940. 'Time, Place and Politics in King Lear', *The Modern Language Review*, 35: 439ff.

history. They are ordinary women dealing with a difficult parent (and will command the sympathy of many members of modern audiences!). Alternatively, he might be a controlling tyrannical father whose manipulative behaviour is familiar to and feared by his daughters—the Gonoril and Regan actors can react to his demands for testimony of love, in 1.1, with anxiety and uncertainty. To twentieth- and twenty-first-century audiences the sexual abuse interpretation of Lear's demands for declarations of love is pressing. Cavell emphasizes 'shame' as central to the emotional and epistemological economy of the play, while the sexual nature of Lear's curses of, and evident fantasies about, Gonoril are striking.[8] Or, of course, Regan and Gonoril can be interpreted as Shakespeare's 'ugly sisters'[9]—grasping, hypocritical about their love for their father, vicious in contrast to Cordelia's virtue and wisdom. Directorial and production decisions about the early scenes will make a difference to audience interpretations of this family drama.[10]

What is not ambiguous is Lear's retaliation to Gonoril. He does not focus on her hypocrisy, or cupidity, but instead curses her as a woman, in a grotesque account of her as an ugly sister and worse [1.4/S.4: 265-80]. This curse is reprised by him later in the action, when Lear is described in the stage directions as 'mad', and his obsession with his daughters is articulated in misogynistic terms:

> Down from the waist they're centaurs, though women all above. But to the girdle do the gods inherit; beneath is all the fiend's. There's hell, there's darkness, there's the sulphury pit, burning, scalding....   [4.6/S.20: 105-27]

Patriarchy, as a way of organizing political power, is particularly fixated on sex, because inheritance, therefore the legitimacy of sons, and therefore the control of women's sexuality, is central to it.[11]

The Earl of Gloucester has two sons. Edmund the bastard (as the scripts style him) resents, and challenges, the constructs of legitimacy and nobility, bastardy and baseness. In a soliloquy which is likely to command the sympathy

[8] Stanley Cavell. 1969/2003. 'The Avoidance of Love: A reading of King Lear', *Disowning Knowledge in Seven Plays of Shakespeare*, updated edn (Cambridge University Press: Cambridge), pp. 57–9, 69–71; Daniel Juan Gil. 2013. *Shakespeare's Anti-Politics: Sovereign Power and the Life of the Flesh* (Palgrave Macmillan: Basingstoke), pp. 108–9; Janet Adelman. 1992. *Suffocating Mothers: Fantasies of Origin in Shakespeare's Plays* (Routledge: London), p. 109.

[9] Bullough, 'Lear', 1973: 271.

[10] Felix Budelmann, Laura Maguire, and Ben Teasdale. 2013. 'Audience Reactions to Greek and Shakespearean Tragedy' (Oxford: Oxford University Research Archive), http://ora.ox.ac.uk/objects/uuid:da99b8a5-1102-4d47-aabb-118ca658722d pp. 13–15.

[11] Adelman, *Suffocating Mothers*, 1992: 107, 296n.8.

of modern audiences for whom 'accident of birth' cannot be a signal of virtue or desert, and which appeals directly to the groundlings in the theatre—who similarly were stigmatized with 'baseness'[12]—he declares that he rejects the imperatives of 'tradition' and is obedient only to the rule of 'nature'. 'Nature' is a central symbol and image of the whole drama. The idea of 'natural' man, stripped of his social and political trappings, revealed in bare existence, is a key theme. Structurally, nature serves to contrast with the artificiality and corruption of sovereignty and with social relationships; but disorders and exceptional events in nature—'these late eclipses of the sun and moon' [1.2.101-4], and the storm—echo or presage the disorder of the state. As usual, Shakespeare inserts a good deal of ambiguity into the matter of what is natural. Edmund's appeal to nature manifests in his evil designs—but modern audiences will be sensitive to the role of society in nurturing that capacity. Edmund has forged a letter which purports to be in Edgar's hand and to evidence a plot to murder his father and secure his fortune, which, the letter promises, will be shared with Edmund [1.2/S.2: 45-57]. Gloucester is eventually convinced of Edgar's guilt—Edmund wounds himself, and tells their father that Edgar was responsible—so Edgar has to flee, and goes into hiding, in a hovel on the heath, disguised as a beggar 'Poor Tom' [2.3/S.7: 166-86].

Meanwhile, Lear has left Gonoril's house, bound for Cornwall's and Regan [1.5/S.5]. Regan forestalls him [2.1/S.6: 120-8; 2.4/S.7: 187-8]; and they all eventually meet at Gloucester's [2.4/S.7: 286]. Lear appeals to Regan—gentler than her unkind sister [2.4/S.7: 327-30]. But the upshot of the extended, passionate dispute about Lear's conduct and that of his knights [2.4/S.7: 358-440] is that Lear leaves and goes out into the storm, accompanied by the Fool [2.4/S.7: 443ff]. The plot has now brought Regan, Gonoril, and Edmund together at Gloucester's house, the three of them forming an 'anti-patriarchy' party in opposition to Lear, Gloucester, and Lear's faithful ally the Duke of Kent.[13] (Albany is unhappy with the way Lear is treated, and eventually critical and condemnatory of Gonoril's conduct [1.4/S.4: 302-4, 4.2/S.16: 29-66]). Lear, Gloucester, and Kent represent traditional values of kingship, personal allegiance, and service. The Fool, whose presence and role is 'at the pleasure' purely of Lear, represents one form of personal service; Kent a different one. Lear and Gloucester also stand for (failed) patriarchal family authority— repudiated by the younger generation. Edmund has declared himself an

---

[12] Chris Fitter. 2016. ‘"The Art of Known and Feeling Sorrows": Rethinking capitalist transition, and the performance of class politics, in King Lear’, *Early Modern Literary Studies*, 19: 1.
[13] Paul Delany. 1977. ‘King Lear and the Decline of Feudalism’, *PMLA*, 92: 431.

individual, master only of himself, servant only to nature [1.2/S.2: 1–2]. Gonoril and Regan can be interpreted as insisting upon newer ideas of the autonomy of households, with a daughter's marriage breaking the authority and rights of her father. In their dispute with Lear about his knights, Regan and Gonoril appeal to household efficiency: why does he need a hundred? Isn't fifty enough? Or twenty-five?

GONORIL: What need you five-and-twenty, ten, or five…?
REGAN: What needs one?' [2.4/S.7: 418–21]

We can interpret this quantitative, calculative theme as presaging the new, non-traditional world of economic rationality.[14] 'O, reason not the need!' exclaims Lear, struggling between anger and grief, '…nature needs not what thou, gorgeous, wearest, which scarcely keeps thee warm' [2.4/S.7: 422–8]. Regan and Gonoril resist Lear's monarchical and aristocratic manners with an assertion of calculative sufficiency. By contrast, Cordelia's resistance to Lear's patriarchal authority consists in her refusal to engage in excessive effusion, as opposed to proportionate public expression of loyalty and love [1.1/S.1: 93–5]. For lack of excess they all are rejected.

Machiavellian Subterfuge

Two machiavellians are at work in *King Lear*. Paul Delaney cites Machiavelli's theme of the lion's courage versus the cunning of the fox, identifying Edmund as the foxy character.[15] But he overlooks that Kent is a foxy manipulator too. They can be conventionally assigned as bad and good. *Lear* is one of the plays that, on the face of it, most readily lines its characters up as good versus evil.[16] However, Kent's performance as good involves cruelty to those he considers inferior; and Edmund finally (although too late) tries to make amends for his evil.

The Earl of Kent understands the error that Lear makes in 1.1, and attempts to intervene to prevent him from banishing Cordelia and endangering himself

---

[14] Delany, 'Lear and Decline of Feudalism', 1977; Fitter, 'Art of Known', 2016; Peter Holbrook. 2000. 'The Left and King Lear', *Textual Practice*, 14: 343–62.

[15] Delany, 'Lear and Decline of Feudalism', 1977: 430–1; Niccolo Machiavelli. 1532/1961. *The Prince*, trans. George Bull (Penguin: Harmondsworth), Ch. XVIII.

[16] Stanley Wells. ed. 1605 (comp.)/2000. 'Introduction', in William Shakespeare, *The History of King Lear* (Oxford University Press: Oxford), p. 24; Cavell, 'Avoidance of Love', 1969/2003: 55.

[1.1/S.1: 130–44]. In response, Lear banishes him [1.1/S.1: 156–68]. Kent, however, disguises himself and remains. Embodying the old values of fidelity and allegiance, in disguise he gets back into Lear's service [1.4/S.4:21–39]. He also challenges and provokes Gonoril's staff, heightening the tension between them and Lear, and accelerating the development of the conflict [1.4/S.4:81-7, 2.2/S.7: 1–37]. In these encounters he articulates aristocratic and traditional disdain for upstart individuals. Meanwhile he is in clandestine communication with Cordelia and France; is party to the plan that French forces land at Dover, headed by Cordelia; and is embroiled in the circulation of secret intelligence in order to galvanize opposition to the new regime [3.1/S.8, 3.3/S.10, 4.3/S.17].

Edmund plays the part of dutiful son, and tricks his gullible father into believing in Edgar's parricidal plot. He is ruthless in his displacement of his brother; and then in his defeat and destruction of his father. Gloucester confides in him about his dissent from Cornwall's regime, and tells him that he has intelligence of the French landing at Dover. Edmund immediately betrays him to Cornwall, earning himself a prominent position in the new regime. He ingratiates himself with both Regan and Gonoril by sexual seduction.

Violence

The machiavel stories meld into a pair of violence stories. The first contrasts styles: Edmund's machiavellian sneaky cowardly violence with Edgar's chivalric, honest, open combat. Edmund convinces his father that a self-inflicted wound was the result of a sword fight with Edgar [2.1/S.6: 47–56]. Edgar, in the middle acts, is reduced to abjection and to base forms of violence. When he kills Oswald, it is with a 'baton', a much less virtuous weapon [4.6/S.20: 229–42],[17] but he emerges at the finale as a heroic heir to greatness, defeating Edmund in an open sword fight [5.3/S.24: 146-7]. It is only as he is dying, at the last, that Edmund confesses to his trickery and malice [5.3/S.24: 169–70, 239–43]. Edmund's violence stands in an ambivalent relation with Kent's. Kent insults and provokes Gonoril's servant, Oswald [2.2/S.7: 1–39]. His violence, like Edmund's, is strategic and crafty. Both conduct themselves viciously to

---

[17] Margot Heinemann. 1992. 'Demystifying the Mystery of State: King Lear and the world upside down', *Shakespeare Survey*, 44: 162; Alan C. Dessen. 1978. 'The Logic of Elizabethan Stage Violence: Some alarms and excursions for modern critics, editors, and directors', *Renaissance Drama*, 9: 54.

others—Kent from a position of aristocratic entitlement and loyalty to his sovereign; Edmund from a position of resentment.

The second is a story of 'sovereign violence'. Traditional pictures of sovereignty include both legitimacy and rightful submission to authority, and the use of the sword to enforce, if necessary, that recognition and submission. Forty years after Shakespeare's *King Lear* Thomas Hobbes had a hand in designing the frontispiece (engraved by Abraham Bosse) for his *Leviathan*—which shows 'the sovereign state' with the sceptre, the symbol of authority, in one hand, and the sword, the sign of sovereign violence, in the other.[18] Sovereigns seek out and punish criminals and traitors, they wage war, and take prisoners. All of these forms of violence pervade and punctuate the drama. Cornwall and Regan discover, from Edmund, that Gloucester is in communication with Kent and Cordelia, and is seeking to aid Lear, so they subject him to torture in order to extract information about the French landings, and as punishment for his treachery [3.7/S.14: 1-9]. After this they expel him, blinded, from his house [3.7/S.14: 91-2]. He is helped by his servants [3.7/S.14: 97-105], and one of the servants challenges Cornwall, and is killed by Regan [3.7/S.14: 69-80]. Eventually Gloucester is encountered by his son Edgar disguised as Poor Tom [4.1/S.15: 24-38, 53-76], who helps him towards Dover. The blinding of Gloucester is one of the most vivid scenes of violence in Shakespeare's drama, and the help he receives from his servants and son among the most poignant episodes of human compassion.

Eventually Lear, Gloucester, and Cordelia are reunited at Dover where Cordelia has landed with French troops [4.7/S.21, 5.2/S.23]. Of course, they have been betrayed by Edmund, and are pursued by Cornwall's forces, who, directed by Edmund, arrest and imprison them [5.3/S.24: 1-3]. Edgar fights Edmund and is victorious [5.3/S.24: 145]. Eventually Edmund, too late, admits that he has ordered the executions of Cordelia and of Lear [5.3/S.24: 239-43]. Cordelia is already dead, although Lear lives a while to lament his torment and his loss [5.3/S.24.253-70].

Social Justice

The story of social justice in *King Lear* is notably inconclusive and incomplete. Many commentators focus, though, on the issue of class inequality, deprivation, and need, and the role of king or government in the alleviation of want as key

---

[18]   Thomas Hobbes. 1651/1996. *Leviathan* (Oxford University Press: Oxford).

themes in the drama.[19] Lear's reduction, when he leaves Regan at Gloucester's house, and goes out into the storm with the Fool, can be understood as the crux of the play, both morally and politically.[20] Out in the storm, Lear raves at, or meditates on, nature and the kingdom [3.2/S.9.1-24]. In the cold and the wet, stripped of his majesty, sovereign authority, and his followers, he is 'reduced' to the condition of 'unaccommodated man', no more than a 'poor, bare, forked animal' [3.4/S.11: 96-7]. He is reduced to basic care and concern about himself: 'My wit begins to turn'; and about the Fool: 'Come on, my boy. How dost, my boy? Art cold? I am cold myself' [3.2/S.9: 68-70].[21] The Fool, however, continually twits him and quips, reproaching him, as he has since the move to Gonoril's, with having acted foolishly, put his daughters in the place of authority that he should inhabit, given up his crown, and reduced himself, therefore, to 'nothing', 'to a zero', a 0 [1.4/S.4: 177-9; 1.5/S.5: 24-9]. We can interpret the Fool's speech in the frame of 'speaking truth to power' with the special permission of personal service and function—a form, and not a form, of parrhesia.

Lear himself, conscious that he is losing his wit, is conscious also of cold and want. Kent guides them to the hovel where Edgar, as Poor Tom, is sheltering.

LEAR: Poor naked wretches, wheresoe'er you are, that bide the pelting of this pitiless night, how shall your houseless heads and unfed sides, your looped and windowed raggedness, defend you from seasons such as these? O, I have ta'en too little care of this. [3.4/S.11.25-33]

This delayed understanding of poverty and want, which comes to Lear only when he experiences it, puts his loss of majesty into a different frame: 'Take physic, pomp, expose thyself to feel what the wretches feel, that thou mayst shake the superflux to them and show the heavens more just' [3.4/S.11.30-4]. Edgar, for his part, had already understood something of the extent of poverty—it was his knowledge

The country gives me proof and precedent of Bedlam beggars who with roaring voices strike in their numbed and mortified bare arms pins, wooden pricks.... Sometime with lunatic bans, sometime with prayers enforce their charity. [2.3/S.7: 178-85]

---

[19] Jonathan Dollimore. 1984/2004. *Radical Tragedy: Religion, Ideology and Power in the Drama of Shakespeare and His Contemporaries* (Palgrave Macmillan: Basingstoke), p. 197; Holbrook, 'Left and King Lear', 2000.

[20] Heinemann, 'Demystifying', 1992; Fitter, 'Art of Known', 2016.

[21] Gil, *Shakespeare's Anti-Politics*, 2013: 105.

that made his decision to take on the guise of a beggar, in order to escape his father's forces, a sensible one. Gloucester too, blinded and unhoused, trying to reach Dover and Cordelia, is reduced, but comes to a new understanding of 'how the world goes'—'I see it feelingly' [4.6./S.20: 141-3]. Gloucester and Lear, out of their context of patriarchal authority, deference, and all the trappings of household service, experience want, and for the first time understand what inequality really means for human bodies and minds.

The social justice story in Lear is unresolved; but political analysis, in the sense of the strategic competition for the power to govern, goes on, as it always will. As Lear and Cordelia are reunited at Dover, Cordelia and Kent (who is still in disguise, but known to Cordelia) are preoccupied both with Lear's health [4.7/S.21: 11-22], and with the war [4.7/S.21: 8-11]. If Cordelia is an armed woman warrior, she is nevertheless actively engaged with care for her father. And to her, Lear's status still includes that of king. To his bewildered question: 'Am I in France?' Cordelia's answer combines personal response with political assertion: 'In your own kingdom, sir' [4.7/S.21: 73-4].[22] Kent and Cordelia's gentleman discuss who is wielding authority after Cornwall's death (it's Edmund); and the rumours that Kent is in Germany with Edgar. The battle between the forces of Edmund and Albany, Gonoril and Regan, and those of Cordelia and France, proceeds—the use of military means for political ends.

Meanwhile, Regan and Gonoril are in conflict over Edmund. Lear and Cordelia are taken prisoner. In tandem with events at the level of state politics the inter-personal relations—between Regan and Gonoril (who would rather lose the war than lose Edmund to her sister [5.1/S.22: 20-1]), between each of them and Edmund, and, in particular, between Lear and Cordelia—now structure the action. Lear identifies himself wholly with Cordelia at this point. The Fool can be interpreted psychologically as an aspect of Lear's own personality, his repartee Lear's own reproaches to himself for his errors. He disappears from the action (or, at least, does not speak) after 3.6/S.13 which means that one actor can play both the Fool and Cordelia, lending a very specific psychological slant to the play for modern audiences.[23] To Cordelia's question on their arrest: 'shall we not see these daughters and these sisters?' he answers: 'No, no. Come, let's away to prison. We two alone will sing like birds i'th'cage. When thou dost ask me blessing, I'll kneel down and ask of

---

[22] Gil, *Shakespeare's Anti-Politics*, 2013: 120-1.
[23] Wells, 'Introduction', 1605/2000: 39; Heinemann, 'Demystifying', 1992: 163-6; Cavell, 'Avoidance of Love', 1969/2003: 59.

thee forgiveness...' [5.3/S.24: 7-19]. The play ends on this note of the bond between father and daughter, whose deaths leave the state of Britain in the hands of Albany, or Edgar; and the fate of the poorest unchanged.

Sovereignty and Regime Change

King Lear is framed by an opening setting in which sovereign authority coincides with (literally, is mapped onto) territory and stable borders, and the person of the monarch. A conventional political interpretation reads it as a fable which shows what chaos and violence ensue when this unity is broken.[24] The obverse of Shakespeare's histories, which are readable as narratives of how the feuding dispersed powers of Britain came eventually to be unified under Tudor sovereignty, *King Lear* is a story of reverse, the reassertion of the conflicts of warring feudal lords, and threats from external powers. But, on the surface of the text are notes of irony and scepticism which problematize this story. Allusions to the question of succession at the death of Elizabeth, and dissent from and challenges to her rule, invoke the doctrine of 'the sovereign body' but ask which body that really is. The 'natural' human body suffers and is injured; it calls for the care that only social relationships can deliver. 'Sovereign' power, though, as it is shown in this play, is destructive of those relationships.

I don't want to suggest that Shakespeare, here or anywhere else, in any sense settles the political theory puzzle about the nature of sovereign power. Rather, he plays with the unsettled questions about its nature, source, and proper location—in particular with the commonsensical, functional idea that a polity is one of those social contexts in which the 'final' power to judge and decide has to reside somewhere, and that's all we mean by sovereignty. This idea sits uneasily in political thinking with the idea that sovereignty is divine, or at any rate transcendent in some way over concrete social relationships, and is paradoxically both of the political world and other than it.

The *King Lear* story seems to allude straightforwardly to anxieties about sovereignty, succession, and stability of the time of its composition and early performances. Elizabeth I inherited the monarchy in a contested process and died without a 'natural', that is to say biological, legitimate heir. The question of inheritance, both on her accession and on her death, was bound up with the question of religion, in particular the stability and authority of the Church

---

[24] Delany, 'Lear and Decline of Feudalism', 1977.

of England. James I, her successor, sought to assert the authority of the monarch over matters of doctrine and theology, against the reformed Scottish church and against puritan dissenters in England and Wales. He also enforced penalties against Catholics; but despite this his plan to marry his son Charles to a Spanish princess raised fears of Catholic power, and renewed anxiety about succession. Religious controversy is not a problem for Lear as monarch—Shakespeare sketches a pagan religious sensibility, with characters invoking Jupiter (or, in the Folio, Apollo) [1.1/S.1: 167] and 'gods' [1.1.171, 1.2/S.2:21]. But foreign policy certainly is a problem. The Essex rebellion in 1601 was a challenge to the dominating powers in Elizabeth's court, and impacted on foreign and colonial policy following Essex's truce with Irish rebels. Lear's plan, redrawing the internal boundaries of authority between his three daughters' three husbands, is bound up with the maintenance of external alliances. The switch from Burgundy to France as Cordelia's husband, and France's disapproval of Cordelia's treatment, obviously changes the foreign policy scene.

The theory that sovereignty cannot or must not be divided can be attributed to Jean Bodin (1530–96) whose *Six Books of the Republic* (1576; translated into English by Richard Knolles and published as *Six Bookes of the Commonweale*, 1606) set out a legally based theory of sovereignty.[25] He worked out the ideas of the power of state as absolute and perpetual, the monarch as accountable only to God, and the principle that only passive resistance to sovereign authority is permissible. In the French context of conflict between reformation Protestantism and Catholicism, and anxiety about witchcraft and demonology (about which more in Chapter 7), Bodin arrived at the thesis that ultimate rule must be located at the level of government. It was from this idea that followed the view that such 'high' or 'highest' powers of government could not be shared or distributed, because to do so would be to dilute and weaken them. This theme of centralization and concentration is emphasized and elaborated by Hobbes and in the later republican tradition.[26]

Whether Bodin intentionally and consciously set out to promulgate a theory of absolutist monarchism is doubtful. That his work has been read in that frame, and was influential for later formulations of monarchical absolutism

---

[25] Confusingly, the edition of Bodin that I cite is entitled *On Sovereignty*, rather than 'six books'— Jean Bodin. 1576/1992. *On Sovereignty*, ed. Julian Franklin (Cambridge University Press: Cambridge; selection from *Six Livres de la Republique*, trans. Richard Knolles, 1606).

[26] Hobbes, *Leviathan*, 1651/1996; Jean-Jacques Rousseau. 1762/1997. *The Social Contract and Other Later Political Writings*, trans. and ed. Victor Gourevitch (Cambridge University Press: Cambridge).

and 'divine right', is not in doubt. Similar ideas of course can stem from different premises. James I himself developed theologically (rather than legally) based ideas of monarchical absolutism, the specific relationship between God and king, the impermissibility of disobedience and dissent, and the necessity of all authority being coalesced and concentrated in the monarch.[27] Whether the monarch, the site of governmental power, has to be a single body in the sense of a single human individual, is also a question. The medieval doctrine of the monarch's 'two bodies'—the distinction between the human body or person of the queen or king, which dies, and the body politic which is, while a property of the selfsame monarch, also a public property and eternal—resolves anxiety about the death of the monarch, up to a point.[28] Ernst Kantorowicz reads Shakespeare's *Richard II* (1597) as one of the most vivid literary illustrations of this thesis.[29]

The point of monarchy is that the king, or queen, is a single human individual, and is the sole bearer of sovereignty. Kent articulates the idea that this is what Lear is:

LEAR: Dost thou know me, fellow?
KENT: No, sir, but you have that in your countenance which I would fain call master.
LEAR: What's that?
KENT: Authority'. [1.4/S.4: 21-8]

Kent is behaving strategically—he wants to be able to stay close to Lear, to safeguard his interests and those of the state; but nevertheless this idea that Lear embodies sovereignty runs through the play. The Fool, as we have seen, reproaches Lear with the correlative idea: once he has given up sovereignty he is nothing [1.4/S.4: 122-8]. That is, being a 'mere man' without status is nothing. But beyond this theme of loss and dispossession there are intimations in the plot and the dialogue that perhaps sovereignty is nothing beyond the potentialities of social relationships anyway. Has Lear become nothing in giving up sovereignty? Or was sovereignty nothing, apart from social relations and symbols, after all?[30]

[27] James VI and I. 1603/1944. *Basilicon Doron*, ed. James Craigie, 2 vols (William Blackwood and Sons Ltd: Edinburgh).
[28] Ernst H. Kantorowicz. 1957/1997. *The King's Two Bodies: A Study in Medieval Political Theology* (Princeton University Press: Princeton, NJ), pp. 13, 14, 407–8.
[29] Kantorowicz, *King's Two Bodies*, 1957/1997: Ch. 2.
[30] Brayton, 'Angling in the Lake', 2003: 421.

King Lear invites the interpretation that it is really about materially based social change, old ways coming into conflict with new relationships.[31] The story of state unification and disunification, of the fantasies and performances of monarchical power and right, is imbricated with a story of transformation of social relations, the inexorable realities of material and social change, and within those processes the role of class conflict. According to this interpretation, to read the story as about a sovereign transfer of power is to mistake appearances for reality, to be dazzled by the political disputes between elites into overlooking the economic changes that proceed irrespective of who governs, and that really are fateful for people. Commentators and critics like Karl Marx (1818–83) are struck by the way Shakespeare tells stories of the class conflicts that were later theorized in scientific and historical terms.[32] Materialist historical analysis emphasizes that the dynamics of technological and economic transformations are independent (relatively, at any rate) of government and political power. Those who have an interest in new technologies, new modes of production, and the new social organizations and laws that are necessary to secure them will come into conflict with those who preside over old ways, old laws, and who wield established political authority. This conflict will have the appearance of political crisis; but it is generated by something much more fundamental than problems or failure of government.

In England in the early modern period, changes were leaving behind a world in which landlords were lords, rural denizens tended to have fixed places in hierarchical village and estate order, and work in agricultural production was oriented towards subsistence for rural families, and payment of rent and tribute in kind to the landlord. In its place, agriculture and manufacture alike were industrialized, there was a dramatic shift of population from country to town, workers worked for wages rather than subsistence, and individuals' origins were less likely to be identical to their end of life destinations. One dramatic symptom of these shifts is the poverty of those who are dispossessed, and lack either employment security or the personal capital that is now necessary.

In the view of Marx and other modern historians, the critical category in this story is 'capital'.[33] Land, estate, domination of territory, and command of

---

[31] Laurence Fontaine. 2018. 'Prodigality, Avarice and Anger: Passions and emotions at the heart of the encounter between aristocratic economy and market economy', *European Journal of Sociology*, 59: 39–61.

[32] Sean Ledwith. 2016. 'Marx's Shakespeare', *Counterfire*, https://www.counterfire.org/articles/analysis/18300-marx-s-shakespeare

[33] Karl Marx. 1867/1954. *Capital*, Vol. 1 (Lawrence and Wishart: London); Max Weber. 1921/1978. *Economy and Society*, trans. and ed. Geunther Roth and Claus Wittich (University of California Press:

the people and resources in it had been the major source of power. Feudal lords, with territorial power, tended to be in conflictual relations with each other. Dominant monarchs, with sovereign authority, tried to unify countries, to regulate the relations between lords, the church, and the common people, and to personify 'the state'. But, over time, financial capital, which was necessary for cargo, traffic, and commerce, for building up cities and towns, and later on for the large-scale reorganization of manufacture and trade came to count as a source of prestige, and to be usable as a power resource as well as an instrument of material production and profit. Individuals, no longer tied to the village or to the trade of their father, were more free to make their own way, in a variety of occupations, using their personal human, intellectual, and social (as well as financial) capital for themselves. On the other hand, as Marx tells it, through the words of nineteenth-century English factory inspectors and others, having nothing but one's own labour power generates unprecedented levels of want, injury, and misery.[34]

Theoretically, the point about the category capital, in contrast to other 'resource' terms, is that it can be invested so that it grows. Whereas with other resources—things, money savings, labour power—'spending' them consumes them (so they have to be replaced); with capital (whether financial, social, cultural, symbolic, or other), investing it makes more of it—it reproduces. So, just as some people make money with their money (while others simply spend theirs), people who 'invest' in friendships, and mutually helpful and sustaining relationships with others, will make more such important social relationships and will reap lots of social benefits. The more you love and trust others, the more love and trust you will enjoy, and the more secure and successful society will be.[35] This has been elaborated in the 'social capital' approach to political theory and social life. It is commonsensical. Of course, it works for bads as well as goods. People who 'invest' in their reputations for violence might, as a result, not have to use (expend) as much violence because their personal symbolic capital will buy them credit. But the more people use violence the more violence tends to spiral. Society in general does not benefit from the cultivation of this kind of bad. The general point is that capital, of all sorts, can be frittered or gambled away, wasted or lost; but potentially it is productive, for the individual, society, or both in this sense. Problems and

Berkeley, CA); Michael Mann. 1986/2012. *The Sources of Social Power*. Vol. 1: *A History of Power from the Beginning to* A D *1760* (Cambridge University Press: Cambridge).

[34] Marx, *Capital*, 1867/1954: Vol. I, esp. Ch. XV.
[35] Robert D. Putnam, Robert Leonardi, and Raffaella Nanetti. 1993. *Making Democracy Work: Civic Traditions in Modern Italy* (Princeton University Press: Princeton, NJ), Ch. 6.

paradoxes arise, though, if it is calculation and expectation of return and interest that drives one's expenditure of, say, love, or one's investment in friendship. Loving in order to get love, one might think, is not really loving at all. It will be as self-defeating as would be trying to be cool or unconcerned.

According to capitalist ideology, the difference between making more and losing all lies in rational understanding of how the world works. In *King Lear*, Shakespeare tells a typically ambiguous and complicated story of clashing understandings of 'how the world goes' [4.6/S.20: 141–3]. Edmund, with his determination to make his own way, against the value judgements and rules of his time, displacing those who stand in his way, and accruing property and power is emblematic of a new kind of individualism. He is determined to overturn the old rules about who is legitimate and what people are worth. Gonoril and Regan, in their conflict with Lear, speak of household economy in terms of what is needed, what is reasonable; whereas for Lear his attachment to his knights is not about 'need' in that material sense [2.4/S.7: 418–22]. Their complaints about the conduct of Lear's men—there are too many of them for the household, their behaviour is riotous—bespeaks a view of household life based on prudence, on harmony, on sufficiency, at odds with the older feudal norms of combat and carousing as the mark of a man.

The conflict between Kent and Gonoril's servant Oswald heightens this clash, expressing it in physical assault. When Kent arrives at Gonoril's, he rails at Oswald, insulting him as 'an eater of broken meats, a base, proud, shallow, beggarly, three-suited, hundred-pound, filthy worsted-stocking knave', etc. [2.2/S.7: 13–22]. This is a combination, as Stanley Wells remarks, of accusations that Oswald is a despised menial, and that he is a pampered favourite who has more than he is worth.[36] Kent's understanding of how the world works is shot through with values, with affect (he is affronted and disgusted by Oswald), and emotion. Hatred of the poor and the upstarts, disgust at their being poor, simultaneous resentment at their having too much is familiar throughout modern times. Kent is challenged by Cornwall for his attack on Oswald: 'Why art thou angry?

KENT: That such a slave as this should wear a sword, that wears no honesty. Such smiling rogues as these, like rats, oft bite those cords in twain which are too entrenched to unloose... [etc.; 2.2/S.7: 69–81]

---

[36] Wells, 'Introduction', 1605/2000: 153n.14.

Kent's exposition of disgust comes close to matching Martius's (Chapter 3). I hasten to say that, of course, Kent is also here acting provocatively in order to heighten conflict and, machiavellian-style, to move the action on. So we can't take his actions to be prompted purely by his feeling—calculation enters. But by contrast, Gonoril's defence of Oswald can be read as a signal of her commitment to the idea that a person is to be judged by their performance in their acquired position, not by their birth. (This is in contrast to reading it as a signal of her evil nature—the ugly sister aided and abetted by her obsequious servant.) Gonoril relies on Oswald for the running of the household; she speaks to him about the problems with Lear's knights, treating personal relationships of kinship as on a par with other household relationships, undermining the idea that there are clear, natural, barriers and boundaries between classes of person.

The play's play between sovereignty and materiality is complicated by further play with the contrast between sovereignty and 'natural' relationships. The king is nothing but a man, and the question is what that means. Aristotle distinguishes between natural life and social, interactional (eventually political) life.[37] Modern political theory frequently offers a choice between sovereignty and nature—either a hierarchical state organized around sceptre, sword, and all, or a state of nature which is variously threatening (as in Hobbes, for whom, without the sovereign state man's life would be brutish),[38] or idyllic but lost (as in ideals of the 'golden age' or the prelapsarian 'Eden'),[39] or, at best, somewhat 'inconvenient' (as in Locke and Rousseau, who emphasize the enhanced security but also opportunities for new kinds of freedom that are afforded by political agreement).[40] In early modern thought, clear boundaries between the wilderness and the civilized and urban spaces meant that the world of beasts and that of men were demarcated—by walls, by ditches, by hedges. This meant that human life and, especially, traffic involved a series of passages, boundary crossings.[41] The idea of the natural wilderness less as threatening, more as threatened by man's own practices of despoliation

[37] Aristotle. 1932. *Politics*, trans. H. Rackham (Harvard University Press: Cambridge, MA), pp. 1252a–1253b.

[38] Hobbes, *Leviathan*, 1651/1996: Ch. XIII, S.9.

[39] Ovid. 1916/1977. *Metamorphoses* (Harvard University Press: Cambridge, MA), Bk 1; Genesis. n.d. *Holy Bible*, Authorised (King James) version (Cambridge University Press: Cambridge), Ch. 2.

[40] John Locke. 1690/1960. *Two Treatises of Government* (Cambridge University Press: Cambridge); Rousseau, *Social Contract*, 1762/1997.

[41] Annabel S. Brett. 2011. *Changes of State: Nature and the Limits of the City in Early Modern Natural Law* (Princeton University Press: Princeton), pp. 3–8; Annabel S. Brett. 2018. 'Is There Any Place for Environmental Thinking in Early Modern European Political Thought?', in Katrina Forrester and Sophie Smith (eds.), *Nature, Action and the Future: Political Thought and the Environment* (Cambridge University Press: Cambridge), p. 23.

were already current. Equally important, and significant in Shakespeare's drama, are ideas connected to the thought that in the wilderness people can find their true nature, untrammelled by social conventions and constraints. But, the question is, what kind of nature is this? In Shakespeare's comedies we meet women in the forest or journeying between cities who are freed of the constraints of femininity. (I discuss this possibility further in Chapter 6, in connection with *Merchant of Venice*.)

In *King Lear* the question is whether loss of sovereignty (in Lear's case), loss of aristocratic status (in Gloucester's), loss of noble persona (in the case of Edgar) really do reduce us to 'bare' life. The category 'bare life' has come to prominence in late twentieth- and twenty-first-century political theory, and has been applied to this play.[42] Politically, the point is that whereas the older post-Renaissance picture of power posed the choice between full subjection to sovereignty and the various authorities of city life, or bare or animal life in nature, modern theories of how political power actually works emphasize that it is a characteristic of the overweening nature of sovereignty that it, itself, can, and is liable to, reduce human beings to bare life. When human beings are punished by sovereign state power—in the form of prisons, detention camps, torture units—they are reduced, symbolically and physically.[43] Similarly when human beings are rejected by sovereign states—when they have to flee, when they land in the limbo of refugee camps.

Such extreme reduction—so familiar in the twentieth and twenty-first centuries—is, first, significantly but insufficiently, countered by reassertions of human dignity and agency on the part of the punished and deprived individuals themselves. Second, in the late twentieth century at least, the political and legal assertions of 'human rights' (such as they are) discursively raise refugees and others to the status of equal humanity. But Hannah Arendt argued that the problem with human rights, absent a state-like power to defend and enforce them, is that they are only asserted when individuals have already been reduced and no longer have any effective right to have rights.[44] Developing Arendt's thought, theorists such as Michel Foucault and Giorgio Agamben (b.1942), echoing also points made by Karl Marx and Friedrich Engels about the treatment of human beings in capitalist states and systems of economy, focus on the way states as such—not just the systems of camps and prisons— reduce human beings. According to this line of thought, it is not loss of

---

[42]   Giorgio Agamben. 1995/1998. *Homo Sacer: Sovereign Power and Bare Life*, trans. Daniel Heller-Roazen (Stanford, CA: Stanford University Press); Gil, *Shakespeare's Anti-Politics*, 2013: 103–9.

[43]   Achille Mbembe. 2003. 'Necropolitics', *Public Culture*, 15: 15.

[44]   Hannah Arendt. 1951. *The Origins of Totalitarianism* (Harcourt Inc: San Diego), Ch. 9 esp. 295–7.

sovereignty that reduces Lear, but the workings of the sovereignty that he has transferred to his daughter's husbands.

These themes have some continuity with older, twentieth-century artistic and philosophical interpretations of Shakespeare, influenced by the philosophy of existentialism,[45] which emphasize 'bareness' in the sense of lack of social and cultural complexity, loneliness, meaninglessness, absurdity. In these representations, the forces that assail individuals are unintelligible as well as frightening.[46] These themes can be reflected in production values in which 'the bare stage' is prominent, and characters encounter each other unadorned by social status.

But between loss of sovereignty and reduction to bare life, and sovereignty working to wreak that reduction, there is the always present possibility that human relations are a social matter, whether we are within or without the ambit of sovereignty or city.[47] It is from this that we can derive the possibility of politics that escapes the logic of overweening sovereignty. Lear, the Fool, and Edgar are cold and unsheltered. So is Gloucester, and he is also maimed and must be in pain. Gloucester has literally lost a sense on which he relied. Edgar is afraid, of being recognized, or being apprehended, of being close to the now fugitive king, so he is playing at demonic possession and madness.[48] Lear is finding it difficult to keep his mind focused, his speech reasonable, his emotions in check. In the hovel, Lear and the others play-act (in the Quarto, but not the Folio version) an arraignment and trial of Gonoril and Regan [3.6/S.13: 42–51].[49] Either we can juxtapose this acting out of sovereignty with the opening scene in which Lear is 'really' judge and deliverer of justice or we can interpret it as raising the question how authentic Lear's sovereignty could ever have been. Either because the characters are reduced to the bare life of the flesh they are driven to fantasize and play the power, and the social, political, and cultural furnishings that are lost; or, perhaps, even when Lear was bolstered by the significant quantities of social, cultural, material, and political support of a king, the enactment of 'sovereignty' was actually fictional and theatrical.[50] When was sovereignty not 'acted out'? But, crucially,

[45] Jean-Paul Sartre. 1946/2007. *Existentialism Is a Humanism*, trans. Carol Macomber (Yale Univeristy Press: New Haven).

[46] Jan Kott. 1964. *Shakespeare our Contemporary*, trans. Boleslaw Taborski (W. W. Norton: New York), pp. 127–68; Martin Esslin. 1968. *The Theatre of the Absurd* (Penguin: Harmondsworth) ; Wells, 'Introduction', 1605/2000: 74–8.

[47] Brett, *Changes of State*, 2011: 6–7.

[48] Stephen Greenblatt. 1988. *Shakespearean Negotiations: The Circulation of Social Energy in Renaissance England* (University of California Press: Berkeley, CA), pp. 116, 122.

[49] Wells, 'Introduction', 1605/2000: 55–6.

[50] Heinemann, 'Demystifying', 1992: 79; Gil, *Shakespeare's Anti-Politics*, 2013: 106–7.

such acting presupposes that we are in social relations with an audience, with interlocutors, with fellow actors.

There is also an ambiguous theme of 'care' in this unsheltered scene. Lear comes to care about the poor, but of course does nothing (can do nothing) to care for them. Yet we see real mutual care. Servants and strangers care for Gloucester [3.7/S.14: 101–5, 4.1/S.15: 7–21]; Lear and the Fool look after each other [3.2/S.9: 69–79]. Edgar (disguised as Poor Tom) then takes care of Gloucester, promising to lead him to Dover, to the height of the cliff from where Gloucester 'shall no leading need' [4.1/S.15: 71–6]. On the way, he tells Gloucester that he is indeed at the edge the cliff; Gloucester 'jumps', lives, is confused about what has happened [4.6/S.20: 11–79]. Edgar, as Poor Tom, has been playing at demonic possession; in the aftermath of Gloucester's 'fall', Edgar pretends that an evil spirit has departed Gloucester's body [4.6/S.20: 67–74]. Greenblatt relates these circumstances and episodes to the more general phenomenon of 'counterfeiting'.[51] Like other plays of Shakespeare, *Lear* disorients our taken for granted understanding of what is real, what feigned, what acted, what play-acted. But Edgar's capacity to trick Gloucester (like Iago's capacity to trick Othello, the tribunes' to trip up Martius, Laurence's to stage Juliet's death) presupposes that social relations between them are real alright. There is nothing 'magic' in these tricks.

To this group Kent stands in an ironic relation. He too is play-acting, but by comparison with the others he is in full possession of himself. Edgar's understanding and experience of how the world goes is metamorphosed by his time as Tom, and Gloucester's injuries mean his world is transformed. Kent is unchanged by his roles and disguises. All this is far from 'sovereignty', the public final power to decide, whether that is thought of as a metaphysical property of kings (as James I was inclined to do), or as the rational construction of people in agreement about self-rule.[52] Critical theorists are sceptical about both these models of sovereignty. But they often equate the power of the state with unconstrained permissions and capacity. Kent, acting on behalf of indivisible, concentrated, final power, has recourse to machiavellian and secretive politics. He is enmeshed in a world of spies, secret missions, messages, and plots.

[51] Greenblatt, *Shakespearean Negotiations*, 1988: 115–19.

[52] Hobbes, *Leviathan*, 1651/1996: Ch. XVIII; Carl Schmitt. 1922/1985. *Political Theology: Four Chapters on the Concept of Sovereignty*, trans. George Schwab (MIT Press: Cambridge, MA); Carl Schmitt. 1927/1996. *The Concept of the Political*, trans. George Schwab (Chicago University Press: Chicago).

Sovereign and Social Violence

I have mentioned *King Lear*'s exploration of styles of socially entrenched, legitimated, normal patterns of violence in relation to sovereign violence. These are the basis for a story of extreme suffering and redemption. Together, they raise questions about the naturalness or otherwise of various kinds of violence. The storm [3.1/S.8, 3.2/S.9, 3.4/S.11] at the centre of the drama is natural, but it symbolizes the extremity of characters' suffering, and ironizes the social and sovereign violences. Is war for the domination of territory—as that between the metonymically named Kent, Albany, Cornwall, and France— also natural? It has its counterpart in other species, of course. But Lear's cruel, misogynistic attack on Gonoril; the torture and punishment of Gloucester; the execution of Cordelia—these take us into a realm of violence that is human, non-natural, and excessive.

The questions of what human violence, if any, is natural, and what justifiable or legitimate are central in political thought. In Chapter 4, I outlined two contrasting theories. According to one, politics displaces violence—the point of political authority, settled states and boundaries, and sovereign power internal to a state, and mutual recognition of foreign powers is the peace and security of individuals and communities. By a mixture of agreement, generalized consent to the propriety of the organization and institutions, by the melioration of the suffering of those who are subordinate or relatively deprived, by legislation and enforcement that is in the interests (ostensibly so, at least) of all—by all these means, the costs and hurts of violence can be avoided. According to the other theory, enforcement, mutual protection, the establishment of constitution and institutions of government, and agreed procedures for the transmission of power, are just so many thin disguises for the domination and violence held in reserve by those in power. Either way, the maintenance of territory, the patrolling of boundaries, the repulsion of invaders; the regulation of social and inter-personal violences, the punishment of criminality, treachery, or treason—these are the functions of sovereignty, and violence is its means for fulfilling them.

One way of reading *King Lear* is that the political power that displaces general violence is destroyed with Lear's disastrous allocation of sovereign authority to warring rivals, and violence rushes in to fill the void. Similarly, social civility, and filial and parental duty should displace violence. But Gloucester's carelessness of Edmund unleashes Edmund's vengeful violence against his brother, and the consequent pursuit of Edgar by his father's forces. Another way to read it is not so much violence unleashed as violence disclosed. In patriarchal societies, treatment of an illegitimate son like Gloucester's treatment of Edmund is normal, and Edmund's violence mirrors the violence that is normalized. Lear's misogynistic attack on Gonoril—as a sea-monster, a kite; he calls on the 'goddess' to dry up her womb—to be sure shakes him emotionally to a degree where, as McLuskie puts it about a point later in the play, 'the hardest hearted feminist' cannot fail to have sympathy for his pain.[53] But even the softest hearted feminist cannot overlook the clear violence, and perhaps more importantly the clear normality, of these lines and his attack on Gonoril. Such violence, symbolic or physical, or both, from father to daughter, is unsurprising, and this tells us that it is well within the norms of power and order.

Kent sees fit to attack Oswald physically, because he (Kent) dislikes Oswald's appearance, manner, and position in Regan's household. He can intelligibly, so it seems, offer his dislike and disapproval as an explanation and justification of his assault. The poor are reviled and rejected—Edgar tells us so when he decides to adopt the persona of Poor Tom in order to evade his pursuers [2.3/S.7: 166-86]. Lear himself knows, or discovers, that the 'respectable', those with property to lose, will loose their dogs to bark at beggars [4.6/S.20: 148-52], and that parish beadles use the lash against the poor [4.6/S.20: 154-7]. As we have seen, Lear's experience of the violence of the world against a resourceless human being tells him that 'we should have ta'en more care of this' when he was wielding sovereign authority. But it also tells him that what passed for authority was violence: 'An the creature run from the cur, there thou mightst behold the great image of authority. A dog's obeyed in office', he tells Gloucester [4.6/S.20: 151-3]. The contrast with Kent's view that 'authority' is written in the face, as a natural property of a noble man [1.4/S.4: 25-8] could not be greater.

The story of the violences of *King Lear* are also stories of extreme suffering. The final scene, in which Lear enters carrying Cordelia's dead body, and laments over her, can be performed as a gender inverted pieta: Cordelia in the place of Christ taken down from the cross, Lear as the grieving parent, Cordelia's death a kind of expiation for all the suffering that the play's characters have inflicted on one another and on the poor of Britain.[54] We can subtract this explicitly Christian imagery, and leave a humanist account of the enactment

---

[53] Kathleen McLuskie. 1985. 'The Patriarchal Bard: Feminist criticism and Shakespeare—King Lear and Measure for Measure', in Jonathan Dollimore and Alan Sinfield (eds.), *Political Shakespeare: New Essays in Cultural Materialism* (Manchester University Press: Manchester), p. 102.

[54] Gil, *Shakespeare's Anti-Politics*, 2013: 120-1; Cavell, 'Avoidance of Love', 1969/2003: 73-80.

of extreme violence, extreme injustice, and extreme suffering, eventuating in a redemptive moment when, at Lear's death, and Kent's anticipation of his own, with old Gloucester, Edmund, Gonoril, Regan, and Cornwall all dead, Albany and Edgar inherit the rule of Britain—perhaps having learned the lessons of justice.

The redemption, if that is what it is, is the culmination of a drama that is both pervasively saturated with violence, and punctuated by episodes of extreme violence. Lear's rage to Cordelia and to Kent; Gonoril's passive-aggressive violence to Lear (when she instructs Oswald to upset the knights and escalate the household discord so as to hasten the crisis); Lear's violent attack on Gonoril; Regan's retaliation to Lear; Edgar's entering the world of the outcast beggars; the dogs barking at the poor. These episodes all work up towards two excessive episodes of 'sovereign violence'—first, the blinding of Gloucester by Cornwall; second, Edmund's execution of Cordelia without due process, and even when he knows that his regime has been defeated. This excessive sovereign violence contrasts both with the social violences I have enumerated and with the military power of France.

These episodes of violence fit into the category of 'cruelty' as that idea has been articulated in a variety of contexts.[55] In art, particularly in drama, practices and images of cruelty have been fascinating for artists. Greenblatt argues that Elizabethan audiences would have been 'less squeamish' than later ones about torture on stage.[56] Whether or not that is true, we are prompted to ask how the dramatic and artistic representation of cruelty interacts with the workings of cruelty in politics. Leonard Tennenhouse focuses on the symbolism of the mutilation of human bodies on stage, and the underlying association of the (metaphysical) body politic or sovereign body with the physical body of the monarch, the symbols of state with the effective power of institutions and offices.[57] But violence on stage or screen goes beyond symbols and meanings to experience. In the twentieth-century 'theatre of cruelty' meant less the overt representation of extreme violence, more assaulting audiences with overwhelming sensory experience, engendering something of the anxiety that can be associated with situations of extreme violence.[58] Several of Shakespeare's dramas, including *King Lear*, can be staged with that audience effect.

---

[55] Leonard Tennenhouse. 1986/2005. *Power on Display: The Politics of Shakespeare's Genres* (Methuen: London), Ch. 3.

[56] Stephen Greenblatt. 2009. 'Shakespeare and the Ethics of Authority', in David Armitage, Conal Condren, and Andrew Fitzmaurice (eds.), *Shakespeare and Early Modern Political Thought* (Cambridge University Press: Cambridge), p. 74.

[57] Tennenhouse, *Power on Display*, 1986/2005: 115–22.

[58] Albert Bermel. 2001. *Artaud's Theatre of Cruelty* (Methuen: London), pp. 7–14; Gil, *Shakespeare's Anti-Politics*, 2013: 109–11.

For Machiavelli, cruelty was a specific use and practice of violence which, in his theory, could have political effects that other forms of violence—military warfare, popular riots and brawls, feuds conducted in public spaces, legal punishment—could not have.[59] Strategic uses of cruel violence, especially when they are spectacularly staged, have a stupefying effect on populations, generating a reputation for the perpetrator as overwhelmingly powerful and unconstrained, and, critically, damping down or chilling elite competitors. All this contrasts with later pacific, ethical, and political theories according to which cruelty is the worst thing.[60] Some political theories are oriented to the concrete realization of justice, equality, virtue, right, and good; others are less ambitious, even sceptical about the validity of such perfectionist aims. But the elimination of cruelty and other evils from the fundamental principles and organizations of society and polity, and from inter-personal relations is widely (not universally) accepted as an ethical and political imperative. Shakespeare's humanist visions of love, his championing of freedom, his questioning of established inequalities, his ironic and satirical depictions of sovereign authority, of course, makes him a source for such political and ethical ideals.

We can put his representation of Cornwall's and Regan's blinding of Gloucester into this complex interpretive frame. Edmund has informed Cornwall that his father, Gloucester, is in touch with Cordelia and with Lear; and has been rewarded by Cornwall who orders him to find his father and arrest him, and who tells him that he is now Earl [3.5/S.12: 15]. Gonoril is excluded from the scene of torture although it is she who exclaims 'Pluck out his eyes' as a rejoinder to Regan's 'Hang him instantly'. Cornwall's order is 'Leave him to my displeasure' [3.7/S.14: 3–5], ironically emphasizing the imperative of action at the pleasure of the sovereign actor.[61] The blinding is a political strategy as much as a wilful act of extreme cruelty.[62] Servants are ordered by Cornwall to bind Gloucester to a chair for an interrogation about his knowledge of the French invasion, and about Lear's journey to Dover. Gloucester is defiant: 'All cruels I'll subscribe. But I shall see the winged vengeance overtake such children' [3.7/S.14: 61-4] to which Cornwall answers: 'See't thou shalt never.—Fellows, hold the chair. —Upon those eyes of thine I'll set my foot' [3.7/S.14: 64-5].

[59] Yves Winter. 2018. *Machiavelli and the Orders of Violence* (Cambridge University Press: Cambridge), pp. 155–6.

[60] Judith Shklar. 'The Liberalism of Fear', in Nancy L. Rosenblum (ed.), *Liberalism and the Moral Life* (Harvard University Press: Cambridge, MA).

[61] Fontaine, 'Prodigality, Avarice and Anger', 2018: 49.

[62] Greenblatt, 'Ethics of Authority', 2009: 73.

Perhaps this act of hiding from Gloucester's sight is, as Cavell has it, a sign of Cornwall's shame despite his assertion of sovereign prerogative.[63] To the extent that Cornwall is now bearer of sovereignty, he is in an ambiguous position with regards to 'laws' which operate as the criterial arbiters of what is right and what is wrong, what admirable and what shameful. If the sovereign is author of laws, on one interpretation, the sovereign will cannot be bound by them. James I claimed absolute power as ruler over the body politic, including that of life and death over the body's members, but came progressively to accept that he did not have illimitable authority, and indeed was bound by the law and custom of which the monarchy was a part.[64] But, nevertheless, sovereigns can kill (authorize executions, for instance, that could not legally be authorized or carried out by anyone else; or send soldiers to their deaths without incurring liability for murder).[65] Torture, as Gil points out, could not be allowed in any circumstances in common law, because the debasement and humiliation of the victim dehumanizes them; so it could only be a royal prerogative. The ambiguity vis-à-vis law is clarified (if that's not too paradoxical a way of putting it) by the twin rules that information obtained under torture cannot be admissible in common law proceedings, while torturers with sovereign authorization cannot be subject to common law prosecution for their actions.[66]

Whether we read Cornwall as enacting for us the truth of sovereignty, or whether we read him as committing an outrage, staging the scene raises obvious difficulties. The stage direction: 'Cornwall puts out one of Gloucester's eyes and stamps on it' seems to call for verisimilitude, and for Cornwall to use his hand, or, as in some productions, surgical implements or other weapons.[67] As Dessen points out, though, the scene could be played symbolically, in particular focusing on 'Upon those eyes of thine I'll set my foot' [3I.7/S.14: 65]. If Gloucester is supine, and bound, and Cornwall does use his foot or heel, the representation of overweening state sovereignty in relation to a bound individual is clearer than a representation of the scene as one either of Cornwall's uncontrolled and uninhibited physical violence or of his cold sadistic surgical cruelty. Dessen's point is that the symbolic strategy avoids the risk of laughter and charges of 'unreality'. It is, in any case, consistent with the conventions of

---

[63] Cavell, 'Avoidance of Love', 1969/2003: 47.
[64] J.W. Allen. 1938. *English Political Thought 1603–1660* (Methuen and Co. Ltd: London), pp. 4–6.
[65] Curtis C. Breight. 1996. *Surveillance, Militarism and Drama in the Elizabethan Era* (Macmillan Press Ltd: Basingstoke), pp. 34–6.
[66] Gil, *Shakespeare's Anti-Politics*, 2013: 112–13; Mathias Thaler. 2019. *Naming Violence: A Critical Theory of Genocide, Torture, and Terrorism* (Columbia University Press: New York), pp. 88–92.
[67] Dessen, 'Logic of Stage Violence', 1978: 59–60.

synecdochic stage craft in which half a dozen actors represent an army, two or four pairs of swordfighters represent a battle. Audience anxiety and horror is maintained not by the verisimilitude of any episode of violence but by the inexorability of the flow of action, one episode flowing horrifically on to another. The rage in the aftermath of the love auction; the banishing of Kent and Cordelia; the rows with Gonoril and Regan; Kent's beating of Oswald; Kent's punishment by Cornwall in the stocks; the storm—all leading to this scene of torture and extreme injury. From the point of view of political theory the point is that sovereign will and violence (Lear can banish Kent and does) finds its epitome in torture, but is also continuous with the more mundane normalized forms of violence. From the point of view of the drama's structure, this scene is a crux or a turning point. Cornwall is injured by a servant (who is killed by Regan) and later dies of his injuries. Is this a scene of sovereign over-reach, that tells us that Cornwall is not a fit ruler? Or, rather, does it tell us something about the nature of the final power to 'govern' when that is organized around the ideas of 'state' and 'sovereignty'?[68]

The execution of Cordelia takes place off-stage.[69] Edmund has been beaten by Edgar in a sword fight and, fatally wounded, participates in the final conversations that make all clear and tie up the loose ends [5.3/S.24: 146-289]. Gonoril attempts to rally Edmund; Edgar and Edmund reveal all; Albany professes that he always believed that Edgar (despite the disguise as Poor Tom) was royally noble [5.3/S.24: 171-2]; Gonoril and Regan die together—Gonoril poisons Regan and then kills herself, for love of Edmund ('I was contracted to them both; all three now marry in an instant' [5.3/S.24: 223-4]). Finally Albany remembers Lear and Cordelia: 'Great thing of us forgot!—Speak Edmund; where's the King and where's Cordelia?'—and finally after further delay and explanations about Gonoril and Regan, Edmund tries to save them:

EDMUND: Some good I mean to do, despite of my own nature. Quickly send, be brief in't, to th' castle; for my writ is on the life of Lear and on Cordelia. Nay, send in time.
ALBANY: Run, run, O run! [5.3/S.24: 240-43]

But it is too late for Cordelia, whose body is carried in by Lear. All the women characters die; only men are left. In Cohen's interpretation, Gonoril and Regan die because of their participation in the excesses of sovereign power, whereas

---

[68] Gil, *Shakespeare's Anti-Politics*, 2013: 113–16.
[69] Derek Cohen. 1993. *Shakespeare's Culture of Violence* (Macmillan Press Ltd: Basingstoke), p. 94.

Cordelia dies because she asserts the value of public proportionality and challenges excess.[70] The meaning of her death would be one thing if she is a woman warrior—the bearer of honourable might; it is arguably different if she is a dedicated, caring daughter. We can't decide between these two—they are both intelligible. But we should note that the frustrating delay and its awful finale—the wrongful writ of execution, the failure to correct it—tell us something else about the nature of state power. Not only can it 'legitimate' extreme violence, in the name of sovereignty, of the sort that Cornwall perpetrates. It is also bureaucratic and horribly slow, with authoritative directives operating under their own inertia and energy.

Politics, Emotion, and Justice

King Lear treats of injustice, without a doubt—the injustice of legitimacy laws and norms that stigmatize and injure the illegitimate, and that justify careless or cruel conduct to them; the injustice of material distributions that leave the homeless, the workless, the ill to the cold and the violence of the weather, and to the predations of violent human beings. As we have seen, this injustice can be put into the context of materialist history of social change—the rise and decline of classes—which looks historically very much more significant than the rise and decline of monarchs like Lear, while the transformational and effective power of economic exchange seems more irresistible even than the violence of sovereign will. Accordingly, many critics offer readings of King Lear that focus primarily on social and political structures of inequality and injustice—sexual, generational, class.[71]

Others dissent, arguing that such readings overlook the interaction between poetry and feeling, the way King Lear is above all a literary work, and a tragedy of the emotions. Tom McAlindon argues that if 'tragedy' is political it is because it moves 'the hardened heart' (the phrase is from Phillip Sydney's 'Apology for Poetry' published in 1595).[72] This way tyrants lose any legitimacy or justification that they command, and are revealed as the causes of great human suffering. Focusing on political economy and class struggle misses the point, and misrepresents the force of Shakespeare's art by marginalizing the

---

[70] Cohen, Shakespeare's Culture of Violence, 1993: 94-109.
[71] Dollimore, Radical Tragedy, 1984/2004: 195-202; Heinemann, 'Demystifying', 1992: 199; Holbrook, 'Left and King Lear', 2000.
[72] Tom McAlindon. 1992. 'Tragedy, King Lear, and the Politics of the Heart', Shakespeare Survey, 44: 85.

centrality of feeling, and by discussing Shakespeare coldly. 'Compassionate, unselfish love is the supreme virtue of the play'; Albany's stand against Gonoril and Edmund is motivated by his horror of cruelty; 'heart' is a key image. The audience to the drama has a political role to play—as witnesses to how much misery human beings can inflict on each other, and what is needed to bring this suffering to an end.[73] Gloucester's and Lear's refocused perceptions of 'how the world goes' [4.6/S.20: 140-9] and their understanding of the suffering of the poor and outcast are matters above all of feeling. It is Cordelia's concern for her father's welfare that motivates her landing at Dover. She comes to rescue her father from ill-treatment by Gonoril and Regan, rather than to seize sovereign power from Albany and Cornwall. Her heart contrasts with the marble heart of Gonoril [1.4/S.4: 251]. But Jonathan Dollimore argues that this humanist reading cannot do justice, as it were, to the nature of the injustice that the play shows.[74]

I argue that this opposition, according to which we focus either on human feeling or on social justice, itself must be misleading. As the political narratives recounted in this chapter make clear, the feelings of the characters, vividly articulated and expressed in their words, are part and parcel of the power relations between them, and of their negotiation of the background conditions of state, local powers and rivalries, and society. Cordelia's emotional motivation in coming to rescue Lear does not, itself, impugn an account of what she actually did that makes reference to sovereignty and inter-state conflict. If what she did was to come to rescue Lear out of compassion, Cordelia, in the selfsame act, was at the head of, or, at any rate, accompanied by, the forces of a foreign power. The two descriptions of the action should not crowd each other out. Any telling of the stories of justice and sovereignty that thread through the drama have to be tellings also of feeling and emotion—from Lear's demand for professions of love, and his daughters' confusion and resentment, and Edmund's resentment and hate onward. The feelings are not separate from the politics in any way. The experiences of the characters in interaction with one another involve bodily affect—they are moved to tears, to anxiety, to rage, to hatred, to pity, to love, and so on. Lear's demand for professions of love—whether it is strategic and canny, or an inept confounding of intimate with public motivation and conduct—is political, in the sense of being a power play.

---

[73] McAlindon, 'Tragedy', 1992: 88-9.
[74] Dollimore, *Radical Tragedy*, 1984/2004: 190-5.

There is more to 'feeling' than pure bodily affect. Emotions are also intentional—that is, they are oriented towards an object, they are 'about' something. They aren't only bodily perturbations; they are a cognitive matter, themselves subject to judgement and evaluation, and contributing elements of our judgements about the world.[75] A number of points follow. The expression or articulation of feelings is public or inter-subjective—trying to name our bodily feelings is not simply a matter for us individually. Words can, indeed, often fail us when we try to tell what we are feeling. By the same token, whether we are sad or angry or anxious is a matter of judgement, and also a matter of language. Among the judgements we have to make as we struggle to articulate emotion are judgements of what the emotion is about, and whether it is appropriate. Lear expresses this when he struggles to feel the anger that is fitting (in his view) and to fight off the sadness, frustration, and tears that are overwhelming:

> Touch me with noble anger. O, let not women's weapons, water-drops, stain my man's cheeks!...You think I'll weep. No, I'll not weep. I have full cause of weeping, but this heart shall break into a hundred thousand flaws or ere I'll weep.   [2.4/S.7: 434-44]

Dollimore argues that focus on individual characters' feelings and inter-personal emotions itself is a deeply 'political' programme because it studiedly refuses to consider the structures and distributions that position us where we are.[76] For Lear to feel empathy with and sympathy for the poor, for him to regret that he had not done more to address human need is one thing. Getting to grips with the social, economic, and political mechanisms that account for his position such that, first, he had no idea, and that, second, people are positioned in poverty to begin with is quite a different matter. Shakespeare does not present us with class differences that are simply given, as it were. The plays focus again and again on the political decisions, economic and market shifts, and cultural conflicts that structure and restructure classes.

But, we can add, understanding new patterns of land ownership and the development of towns, and the displacement of people from the countryside, cannot in itself tell us why the rich and the entitled hate the poor so much.

---

[75] Raia Prokhovnik. 1999. *Rational Woman: A Feminist Critique of Dichotomy* (Routledge: London), pp. 71–8; Martha Nussbaum. 2001. *Upheavals of Thought: The Intelligence of Emotions* (Cambridge University Press: Cambridge), pp. 19–88; Sara Ahmed. 2014. *The Cultural Politics of Emotion* (Edinburgh University Press: Edinburgh), pp. 191–229.

[76] Dollimore, *Radical Tragedy*, 1984/2004: 191.

Clearly, affects like disgust enter into Kent's violence to Oswald; but his anger is built on much more than affect. Kent's feelings are intertwined with his beliefs about individuals in Oswald's position. His understanding that Oswald is a fit victim of violence builds emotion, motivation, action, and justification into a complex thing. What 'things' are called and labelled is, itself, a matter of public contention, and the political power to make meanings stick is a very important power. Is Oswald 'the composition of a knave, beggar, coward, pander, and the son and heir of a mongrel bitch' [2.2/S.7: 19-20]? Or is he the servant who can be entrusted to discretion, as he is in Gonoril's world [1.3/S.3: 8-10]? Political and cultural change is relevant, clearly, to feelings like disgust. We can't doubt that Kent is disgusted by Oswald. It takes a complex account of an aristocratic and radically unequal society for us to understand why, and how, that can be so.

The dispute about the propriety and value of focusing either on the feeling heart, or on the class structure, in *King Lear*, then, is particularly unproductive. Shakespeare consistently problematizes dichotomies such as these. McAlindon organizes his argument as between those who interpret Shakespeare's drama from the point of view of material, social, and economic analysis, and those who focus on emotion, affect, and poetry. Dollimore (whose work is explicitly cited by McAlindon) focuses on what is missed if we take up the point of view of individual agency, emotions like pity, action, and belief, as opposed to getting to grips with structures, systems, and the problems of restructuring.[77] But these dichotomies, like body and mind, appearance and reality, masculinity and femininity, being a woman warrior or a caring daughter are consistently mixed up by Shakespeare. We can see this by examining how *King Lear*, in addition to saying a good deal about sovereignty, violence, and economy, has a good deal to say about the 'politics of emotion'.

To repeat, emotion is intentional in the sense of being about something; it goes beyond the individual's own body and mind subjectively felt, and is oriented to a world of objects, which can include the individual's own body and mind, reflexively experienced. When Lear is emotional—grieving, angry—about the threat to his men and his new life in retirement, he tries to say, both to himself, and to Regan and Gonoril, and (this is a theatrical drama) to the audience, what he is feeling and what he is angry and sad about. This articulation, of course, is 'public', in the sense that it is expressed out loud, and in the sense that Regan and Gonoril can both argue back, tell him he's wrong to be feeling what he says he's feeling. As is clear, in another idiom, another context,

---

[77] Dollimore, *Radical Tragedy*, 1984/2004: 191-2.

in another family, they might more empathetically and helpfully ask him what he's really grieving, or angry, or resentful, or enraged, or whatever, about. Such reflexive, communicative capability is a crucial element of 'emotional literacy' and healthy relationships.[78] But Regan and Gonoril respond to Lear's feeling with rational calculation about what he really needs—and perhaps they do this out of justified, but not well articulated or communicated, resentment.

At issue in *King Lear* is the gendered distribution of emotions. In much political thinking, there has been a deep association of men with rationality and women with emotions, rationality and emotionality marked masculine and feminine respectively.[79] This accepted and pervasive sex gender difference definitely pre-dates Shakespeare's context—it arises in classical philosophy.[80] Here as elsewhere he plays with the normative distinction: Lear is all feeling, and Regan and Gonoril are obdurately rationalistic and calculative in their dealings with him. This is one reason why interpretations of Gonoril and Regan hold them to be unnatural, unwomanly, ugly sisters. Be that as it may, Lear has to deal with the degree to which his overwhelming feelings are, as we might say, sex gender appropriate [2.4/S.7: 435–6]. Anger, revenge, insult, curses are fit conduct for a man; tears are womanish and unfit. Kent is angry as well as contemptuous at Oswald's person, conduct, and relationship in Gonoril's household. Gloucester is angered as well as disappointed when he believes that Edgar is plotting against him.

There is a class (or status) marker of emotion here, as well as sex and gender. The noble anger of the lion hearted contrasts with the base, calculating, heartless, conduct of the foxes—the machiavellian plotters like Edmund, those who are out to win the contest, like Gonoril and Regan.[81] It also contrasts with the impoverished oppression of the suffering commoner (Poor Tom) who can only rave.[82] Edmund's resentment at the way accusations of baseness and the like justify oppressive treatment and the effective ignoring of the victim's feeling, can be addressed, as Fitter suggests, to those of the theatrical audience who identify with that sense of being outcast and denigrated, and whose indignation at such treatment is first person, personal.[83] Resentment, and a feeling of injury, rather than sheer pain, can only be 'felt', certainly only

[78] Daniel Goleman. 1995. *Emotional Intelligence: Why It Can Matter More Than IQ* (Bloomsbury Publishing: London).
[79] Genevieve Lloyd. 1984. *The Man of Reason: 'Male' and 'Female' in Western Philosophy* (Methuen: London); Prokhovnik, *Rational Woman*, 1999.
[80] Aristotle, *Politics*, 1932: 1254b13–14; Lloyd, *Man of Reason*, 1984: 2–9, 18–28.
[81] Delany, 'Lear and Decline of Feudalism', 1977: 431.
[82] Fitter, 'Art of Known', 2016.   [83] Fitter, 'Art of Known', 2016.

articulated, in a world in which the entitlement of the propertied to feel disgust and to denigrate the unpropertied does not go without saying—a world in which a different, more egalitarian, more needs-meeting, more individualistic state can, at least, be imagined. It is to that imagination that Edmund appeals.

All of this addresses the politics of emotion in the sense of how political power shapes individual lives and feelings; and the strategic effects of acting out emotions. A further dimension of the politics of emotion focuses on the uses of emotion language, and the performance of emotion not by individuals but by institutions and states. In the world of late modern (sovereign) states expressions of happiness, anger, or disappointment, on the part of the state or government themselves, make perfect sense. The validity or otherwise of such expressions of corporate emotion are not a matter of whether the spokesperson feels the happiness, anger, or disappointment themselves.[84] The articulation of emotion (the long-felt resentment of a nation, the anger or indignation of a class) both can work backwards from articulation, first, to feeling by individuals; and, second—independent of feelings in the bodies of individuals—can motivate collective action. Now, we do not find such complexities in *King Lear*, where the king of France is named France, and is a human man who has feelings of respect, love, and sympathy for Cordelia, which he articulates in his persona and office of king [1.1/S.1: 240–51]. He departs from Britain, according to Gloucester, 'in choler', or angrily [1.2/S2: 22–3], and is described by Lear later as 'hot-blooded' [2.4/S.7: 369]. Everything to do with France is strictly personal as well as metonymic. Similarly, I suggest, Kent's intrigue and political machinations disclose intimations of 'wisdom' and 'secrecy' which are characteristics of 'a power' [3.1/S.8: 21–5]. Kent's emotions of disgust for Oswald, his esteem for Lear, show how intimately state politics are bound up with emotion.

The ambiguity of personalism and abstraction in sovereign emotion is also evident in Cornwall. In response to Regan's 'Hang him instantly' and Gonoril's 'Pluck out his eyes' [3.7/S.14: 4] Cornwall's reply is 'Leave him to my displeasure' [3.7/S.14: 4]. The 'my' here is part personal, part sovereign: 'The revenges we are bound to take upon your traitorous father are not fit for your beholding' he tells Edmund. 'Though we may not pass upon his life without the form of justice, yet our power shall do a curtsy to our wrath, which men may blame but not control' [3.7/S.14: 5–6, 23–6]. Cornwall here explicitly assumes sovereignty; and constructs a sovereignty, at that, which is constrained by justice and due process. But it also licenses feeling—wrath—which may not be

[84] George E. Marcus. 'Emotions in Politics', *Annual Review of Political Science*, 3: 221–50.

controlled. Gloucester is a traitor, who may, therefore, be 'pinioned like a thief' [3.7/S.14: 21-2]. Cornwall's is a wrathful, angry, sovereignty, which takes revenge on traitors, and inflicts extreme violence.

Lear's flawed judgement allocates sovereignty to this extraordinarily violent couple, Cornwall and Regan. In the end, Cornwall dies from a wound inflicted on him by a servant, a 'villein' [3.7: S.14: 69-76]. Regan is appalled by the servant's challenge to Cornwall's actions: 'A peasant stand up thus!' she exclaims, and kills him with a sword from behind [3.7/S.14: 78]. Regan here contrasts with Gonoril's democratic relationship with Oswald (if that is what it is; it is tempting for directors to stage that relationship as corruptly sexual). As we have seen, Albany has from early on had misgivings about the way Lear is treated by his daughters. At the end of the action, the tyrants (Cornwall, Edmund) are dead, and we look forward to more pacific rule by Albany and Edgar. We have evidence that they two both have more 'heart' than Cornwall and Edmund, and perhaps will learn from Edgar's empathetic experience of poverty. But, we also know that problems of social justice require political solutions of rights, obligations, state, and social power organized and concerted.

Violence, Passion, and the Political Way

The violence of *King Lear* can instructively be compared with the social violence and the suicides of *Romeo and Juliet*; just as the emotion of Lear—resentment, hatred, fear, grief—can be compared with the way *Romeo and Juliet* juxtaposes Romeo's being gripped by romantic love and erotic longing with the hatred between the two houses, and with the economy in which everything can be traded. In such contexts, 'the political way' seems doomed to take only its machiavellian route, or to being captured by interests which have economic dominance, or physical might, at their behest. In Chapter 6 we explore further what happens when polity is overtaken by economy. We also explore further the prospects for the political way in societies which are structured by ethnic and racial inequality. Both *Merchant of Venice* and *Timon of Athens* question the possibilities of political friendship.

6

Friendship and Justice

Merchant of Venice and Timon of Athens

Politics and Friendship

The classical idea that friendship—friendly relations, at any rate, between members of a polity, and between states which are allies—is a necessary condition of cooperative, non-violent, political government is plausible. We can read Aristotle as arguing that it is the human relation of friendship which makes political relations, institutions, and procedures possible. Cicero suggests, though, that it is because of the human capacity for politics (in the ideal sense) that friendship in society is possible and its value evident.[1] The point, either way, is that political antagonists—opponents in the competition for the power to govern, or those with rival visions of the constitution or public policy—can conduct their rivalry in a way that is consistent with civility, even with sociability and affability.

Friendship is voluntary, rather than involuntary as our kin relations are; so in friendship we act freely. In friendship we give valuable things to each other—support, in particular; and we share goods. But we don't do this for instrumental, material reasons, as we do when we buy and sell in the market place. In friendship, we encounter each other as full persons, which contrasts with the impersonal, partial relationships we have in public and work life. Of course, we might be friends with co-workers, or with people we buy from, but to be a co-worker or a customer, simply, we don't have to know much about the other person beyond the transaction. In these ways, friendship looks as though it is an important symbolization and instantiation of a political, as opposed to an economic, or a kin relationship.

---

[1] Aristotle. 1934. *Nicomachean Ethics*, trans. H. Rackham (Harvard University Press: Cambridge, MA), VIII, i.1–4; ix.3–6; Cicero. 1923. 'Laelius: On friendship', *Cicero*, Vol. XX, ed. and trans. W.A. Falconer (Harvard University Press: Cambridge, MA), xxiii.86; Horst Hutter. 1978. *Politics as Friendship: The Origins of Classical Notions of Politics in the Theory and Practice of Friendship* (Wilfried Laurier University Press: Waterloo, Ontario).

Shakespeare and the Political Way. Elizabeth Frazer, Oxford University Press (2020). © Elizabeth Frazer.
DOI: 10.1093/oso/9780198848615.001.0001

But this thought raises puzzles—about the nature of friendship, and about its place in the wide array of other relationships that feature in human societies.[2] In particular, another meaning, or kind, of friendship connects it with gangs, with cronies, with bands of brothers. They might be political in the sense that they compete for dominance or the power to govern. But, as we saw with *Romeo and Juliet* this competitive group structure involves levels of hostility and disruption of the public space that are antithetical to politics properly speaking.

Early modern thinkers articulated an ideal of friendship which set it apart from civility. Aristotle had emphasized the ethical quality of 'true friendship'—which is between equals, between mutually virtuous parties, who care for the other as they care for themselves.[3] Michel de Montaigne (1533-92) emphasized that the tie, in true friendship, transcends ordinary relationship. Friends relate to each other authentically, without artifice or pretence, without acting.[4] Such ideas were later very influential. In discourses of love, like those of the erotic, romantic ties that defy social norms, established laws, and the judgements of authorities (such as we met also in *Romeo and Juliet*), humdrum and political materiality is transcended. Aristophanes' account of love, as reported by Plato in *The Symposium*, is that Zeus originally created hermaphrodites, who tried to set upon the gods, so they were all cut in half. Each of them now suffers from a desperate yearning to find their other half: 'love is always trying to reintegrate our former nature, to make two into one, and to bridge the gulf between one human being and another.'[5] This romantic idea resurfaces in many meditations on love—despite the fact that Aristophanes is a joker and a satirist.

Montaigne elevated the idea of 'true' friendship into 'affinity' which is to be distinguished from passion and desire (because it is deep, constant, and serene, not agitating), and from bargains or compromises. Later republican thinkers, like Mary Wollstonecraft (1759-97), inspired by Montaigne's account of friendship as the meeting of souls, emphasized the sacred nature

[2] Preston King. 1999. 'Introduction: The challenge of friendship in modernity', *Critical Review of International Social and Political Philosophy*, 2: 1–14; Preston King. 2007. 'Friendship in Politics', *Critical Review of International Social and Political Philosophy*, 10: 125–45.

[3] Cicero. 1913. *On Duties (De Officiis)* (Harvard University Press: Cambridge, MA), Bk I.XVII.56; Cicero, 'On friendship', 1923: V.18–19; Aristotle, *Nicomachean Ethics*, 1934: VIII.ii.3–4, VIII.iii.6; John M. Cooper. 1977. 'Aristotle on the Forms of Friendship', *Review of Metaphysics*, 30: 619–48; Sybil Schwarzenbach. 1996. 'On Civic Friendship', *Ethics*, 107(1): 97–128; Susan Bickford. 1996. 'Beyond Friendship: Aristotle on conflict, deliberation and attention', *The Journal of Politics*, 58(2): 398–421.

[4] Michel de Montaigne. 1580/1603 (in English)/2006a. 'On Friendship', *The Essays*, Vol. 1, trans. John Florio (The Folio Society: London), pp. 184, 186–9.

[5] Plato. 1938. 'Symposium', *Plato: Five Dialogues*, trans. Michael Joyce (J.M. Dent and Sons: London), S.3.

of the friendship tie.[6] She would have been shocked and indignant, but not surprised, to discover, though, that numerous thinkers and writers after her time followed Montaigne in opining that women are incapable of the holy bond of true friendship.[7] This idea of real friendship being possible for men only is remarkably persistent.[8] Looking back to the Greek tradition of Plato's *Symposium* among other texts, modern thinkers find a model of intimately friendly relations between men predicated on homocentrism that encompasses homoeroticism. Women's friendships, passionate, political, or both, are erased from this story.[9]

A further important controversy focuses on whether commercial, instrumental, self-interested relations of exchange are consistent with friendship. 'In friendship there is no traffic or commerce but with itself', said Montaigne.[10] Wollstonecraft saw traffic and exchange, transactional society and commercial economy, as inevitably debasing friendship.[11] Aristotle, though, includes instrumental friendship as a kind of friendship—the relationship is for something else (because we share common pursuits, or are otherwise contiguous with each other), or is simply enjoyable and we therefore are motivated to continue it, but were the pleasure, the pursuits, or the contiguity to end, the friendship would be over. This kind of friendship is possible between individuals who are not particularly virtuous, or, even, are bad. Aristotle distinguishes it clearly, though, from true, ethical, friendship.[12] Wollstonecraft's view was that commercial trading societies foster rivalry and doing other people down, grubby self-interest, and fixation on profit. They are inconsistent with the kind of friendship necessary for civilized society and politics. She was here setting herself against an earlier theory that friendship is as valuable economically as it is politically and socially. Friendship, good office, and the softening of manners go together with public exchanges, with the voluntary taking on of obligations and the trust that are necessary for trade, in the view of David Hume (1711-76) and Adam Smith (1723-90).[13]

---

[6] Mary Wollstonecraft. 1792/1994. 'A Vindication of the Rights of Woman', in Janet Todd (ed.), *Mary Wollstonecraft: Political Writings* (Oxford University Press: Oxford), Chs. 4, 5; Elizabeth Frazer. 2008. 'Mary Wollstonecraft on Politics and Friendship', *Political Studies*, 56(1): 240.

[7] Montaigne, 'Friendship', 1580/1603: 184.

[8] For example, C.S. Lewis. 1960. *The Four Loves* (Geoffrey Bles: London): Ch. IV.

[9] Lilian Faderman. 1981. *Surpassing the Love of Men: Romantic Friendship and Love between Women from the Renaissance to the Present* (Morrow: New York); Janice Raymond. 1986. *A Passion for Friends: Towards a Philosophy of Female Affection* (Women's Press: London), p. 4.

[10] Montaigne, 'Friendship', 1580/1603: 188-90.

[11] Mary Wollstonecraft. 1796/1987. *A Short Residence in Sweden, Norway and Denmark* (Penguin: Harmondsworth), pp. 136-7, 191-5; Frazer, 'Wollstonecraft on Friendship', 2008: 247.

[12] Aristotle, *Nicomachean Ethics*, 1934: VII.ii.3-4.

[13] David Hume. 1741-2. 'Of Refinement in the Arts', *Essays, Literary, Moral and Political* (Ward, Lock and Co: London); David Hume. 1751/1975. 'Enquiry Concerning the Principles of Morals', in

Finally, and relatedly, is the question of the equality between friends. There can be friendship relations between unequals, especially older and younger, but also richer and poorer, and those with honour and those without. But, there are limits to the distance between the parties that friendship can withstand.[14] There might be a tension between the view that equality is necessary before there can be friendship (many republican thinkers, including Rousseau and Wollstonecraft, insist that the mutuality, civility, and cooperation that is politically necessary cannot survive in societies with high degrees of inequality), and the idea that friendship equalizes—that intimacy and confidence can overcome distinctions. Either way, because friends are equalized, deference, authority, and submission are not, properly, characteristics of friendship. Friends find ways to agree with each other; citizens are able and willing both to be ruled and to rule when their turn comes.[15] In this political strain of thought about friendship, friendship is generalizable—friendliness can characterize relationships between co-citizens, between those who meet in market transactions, between strangers. This cannot be the case if we think of friendship as a transcendent bond, or as peculiarly intense. The 'true' kind of friendship—deeply personal, based on intimacy and extended time together, between equal, virtuous parties for whom the other's good is as important as their own—must obviously be quantitatively limited. You simply can't have that many of that kind of friend.[16] But acquaintances, people with whom you enjoy friendly, convivial, comradely, relations can be very numerous.

This discussion has not settled the questions of how we should think of friendship, or what kind is relevant to polity. Aristotle insists that the relationship between citizens must be ethically like the one between true friends, in the sense that friends care about each other's characters and are connected in a relationship of mutual virtue. Lawgivers must be interested in citizens being friends, and 'set more store by it than they do by justice, for to promote concord which seems akin to friendship is their chief aim, while faction, which is

---

L. A. Selby-Bigge (ed.), *Enquiries concerning Human Understanding and concerning the Principles of Morals* (Clarendon Press: Oxford): S.VII, VIII, 456-67; Adam Smith. 1776/1974. *The Wealth of Nations* (Penguin: Harmondsworth), Bk.3, Ch.4; John Jowett. ed. 2004. 'Introduction', William Shakespeare and Thomas Middleton, *Timon of Athens* (Oxford: Oxford University Press), p. 48n; Laurence Fontaine. 2018. 'Prodigality, Avarice and Anger: Passions and emotions at the heart of the encounter between aristocratic economy and market economy', *European Journal of Sociology*, 59: 45-8.

[14] Aristotle. 1932. *Politics*, trans. H. Rackham (Harvard University Press: Cambridge, MA), VIII. vi.7-vii.6.
[15] Aristotle, *Politics*, 1932: VIII.v.5; Aristotle, *Nicomachean Ethics*, 1934: III.ii.9, 1277b, IV.ix.5, 1295b.
[16] Aristotle, *Politics*, 1932: VIII.iii.8.

enmity, is what they are most anxious to banish.'[17] So although it seems that civic friendship must be an extension of, or a variation on, the true kind, it is a critical element of an Aristotelian theory of polity that citizens are not related to each other simply out of convenience.[18] The polity is the setting in which it is possible to achieve excellence, and in which justice can be realized. So civic friendship can't be a weaker case, in the way that friendships between evil people would be. But, to what degree and in what way civic friendship is friendship is not clear, because the degree of liking and the degree of voluntarism of inter-personal friendship are not present.[19]

Merchant of Venice (one of Shakespeare's earlier plays, composed 1595) explores how economic motivations and exchanges interact with socially, culturally, and religiously based divisions and structures, with state sovereignty in the form of law, and with ethical relations. Friendship, within groups of co-religionists, and between men, is explicitly thematized as a problem because some—in particular the Jewish Shylock and the female characters— are excluded from the friendly relations that constitute the mercantile republic. Shakespeare's Venice is a republic that—as we saw in *Othello*—it is fissured by race and, here, by religion. What can be the fate of friendship in societies that are divided by race or religion, and by sex? *Timon of Athens* (co-authored with Thomas Middleton, 1608), explores the relationship between republican politics, economic exchange and profit, and (failed) friendship. The relationships between character, the institutions and procedures of credit, and the fate of society and polity were clearly part of Elizabethan and Jacobean public imagination. They are articulated as such in Thomas Middleton's 'city comedies', and in *Merchant* and *Timon* among other Shakespearean sources.[20] What is the fate of friendship in a world in which everything has a price?

Politics, Friendship, and *Timon of Athens*

The plot of *Timon of Athens* is very simple, and the play we have has a linear structure, featuring two intersecting stories: that of Timon, friendship, and misanthropy; and that of Alcibiades, a military hero in conflict with the senate.

---

[17] Aristotle, *Politics*, 1932: VIII.i.4.

[18] Aristotle, *Nicomachean Ethics*, 1934: III.v.12–15, 1280b.

[19] Sybil Schwarzenbach. 1996. 'On Civic Friendship', *Ethics*, 107(1): 107–9; Bickford, 'Beyond Friendship', 1996: 407.

[20] Aaron Kitch. 2009. *Political Economy and the States of Literature in Early Modern England* (Ashgate: Farnham).

According to scholars, Shakespeare was very interested in Alcibiades the character, but switched his attention to Coriolanus (who is paired in Plutarch's *Lives* with Alcibiades) as a better subject for tragedy.[21] Timon is mentioned in Plutarch's *Alcibiades*.[22] *Timon* could be thoroughly 'Shakespearified', with more complexity to characters and to the interweaving of stories and themes, a tragic or tragi-comic finale, and so on. As it is, the play's simplicity lends itself to interpretations and productions that emphasize existential loneliness and alienation, the absurdity of social norms, and the unachievability of justice in a materialistic society.[23]

At the beginning, Timon is a generous patron of the arts, a magnificent host, a willing lender to those who have financial need, and ready to write off debts. His consumption, gift giving, and entertainment can be interpreted as magnificent hospitality or as conspicuous show. Critics have associated Timon's gift giving with King James' reputation for 'Timonesque' generosity.[24] In Aristotle's analysis virtues have as their counterparts not one, but two, 'opposites'—an excess of the virtue, also a deficiency. So generosity or liberality, which is a virtue, has as its counterparts meanness and also prodigality.[25] Timon explicitly connects his hospitality—or prodigality—with citizenship: 'I take no heed to thee; thou'rt an Athenian, therefore welcome' [1.2/S.2: 35]. But the monetary values look like a corruption of ideal virtuous citizenship. Timon's gifts are of greater monetary value than those he receives [1.2/S.2: 157, 186–207, 222–5]. Perhaps no matter—in friendship and citizenship, after all, there should be no close reckoning.

Timon, then, articulates ambiguous citizenship virtue; and he is questioned by two prominent voices. First, his steward, Flavius, a figure of loyalty, care, and good sense believes that Timon is kind, and overly generous out of goodness [1.2/S.2: 191–205; 2.2/S.4: 226–7]. Second, the cynic Apemantus— labelled in the list of characters as 'a churlish philosopher'[26]—points out the depravity of Timon's sociability, and interprets Timon's hospitality and generosity as bribery [1.2/S.2: 242–5]. According to him 'Friendship's full of dregs'

---

[21] Geoffrey Bullough. ed. 1966. 'Timon of Athens', *Narrative and Dramatic Sources of Shakespeare*, Vol. 6 (Routledge and Kegan Paul: London), pp. 238–9; Jowett, 'Introduction', 2004: 71–2; Plutarch. 1916a. 'Alcibiades', *Plutarch's Lives*, Vol. IV, trans. Bernadotte Perrin (William Heinemann: London); Plutarch. 1916b. 'Caius Martius Coriolanus', *Plutarch's Lives*, Vol. IV, trans. Bernadotte Perrin (William Heinemann Ltd: London).

[22] Walter W. Skeat. ed. 1875. *Shakespeare's Plutarch: Being a Selection from The Lives in North's Plutarch which Illustrate Shakespeare's Plays* (Macmillan and Co: London), 'Alcibiades', S.4, p. 296; cf. Gerard Sargent. 2015. 'Timon, Sir Thomas North, and the Loup-Garou', *Notes and Queries*, 62: 572–4.

[23] Jowett, 'Introduction', 2004: 83–98.   [24] Jowett, 'Introduction', 2004: 7, 50.

[25] Aristotle, *Politics*, 1932: IV.i.1–50.

[26] The life and thought of Diogenes of Synope, the Cynic, is told by Diogenes Laertius. *c*.220 BCE/1925. 'Diogenes', in *Lives of Eminent Philosophers* (London: William Heinemann and Co.).

[1.2/S.2: 236-7]. On the one hand, Apemantus's anti-social manners reflect his cynicism about sociability, generosity, and friendship, and their place in citizenship and the city. On the other, he is a kind of real friend to Timon, criticizing his friend out of concern for the friend.[27]

A great banquet in scene 2 shows and ironizes Timon's magnificence and the Athenian culture. It features a theatrical show of ladies as amazons—the conventions of the court masque or pageant ironized as the dinner guests get to dance with the women [1.2/S.2: 117, 126, 141].[28] It also stages an ironic version of Plato's *Symposium*—a dinner table discussion of friendship. In Plato, Aristophanes delivers his hermaphroditic account of yearning love that I described earlier.[29] Alcibiades is the last to speak, arguing (with direct reference to Socrates (*c.*470-399 BCE) with whom Alcibiades was in love) that love, properly, focuses on the qualities within, not on external appearances of beauty and such.[30] In *Timon*, though, Alcibiades relates friendship to the death of enemies:

TIMON: You had rather be at a breakfast of enemies than a dinner of friends.
ALCIBIADES: So they were bleeding new, my lord, there's no meat like 'em. I could wish my best friend at such a feast. [1.2/S.2: 74-8]

Timon's speech on friendship associates it with the gods' provision, with 'heart', with joy, and with proper riches. He associates friends with need: 'what need we have any friends if we should ne'er have need of 'em?' He invokes the unique value of solidarity: 'O, what a precious comfort 'tis to have so many like brothers commanding one another's fortunes!' and is moved to tears by his own words [1.2/S.2: 85-104]. Timon's paean to friendship is mocked by Apemantus [1.2/S.2: 105], who also delivers a satirical grace: 'Grant that I never prove so fond to trust...my friends if I should need 'em' [1.2/S.2: 62-9]. All this satire and mockery suggests a crisis, or decline, of friendship in Athens.[31] Even if we resist Apemantus's cynicism, surely we must doubt what Timon says, and his belief in it. Then there is the ambiguity of Alcibiades' connection of friendship to the killing, and eating of enemies. Does the solidarity and love of friendship presuppose a hatred of foes? Twentieth-century thinkers are troubled by this paradox—some, like Jacques Derrida

[27] Cicero, 'On friendship', 1923: XXIV.   [28] Jowett, 'Introduction', 2004: 40-3.
[29] Plato, 'Symposium', 1938: Ss.189-93.   [30] Plato, 'Symposium', 1938: Ss.216-17.
[31] Jan H. Blits. 2016 'Philosophy (and Athens) in Decay: *Timon of Athens*', *The Review of Politics*, 78(4): 539-50.

(1930-2004),[32] are more troubled than others. Carl Schmitt (1888-1985) approved the idea that friendship between allies and co-members of a polity presupposes enmity of outsiders and of internal foes. Enmity is serious; it is existentially threatening, not metaphorical or symbolic.[33]

Over the next scenes, Timon's immoderate expenditure, his indebtedness (the land is mortgaged, to Flavius's great sorrow) [1.2/S.4: 126-40] and his neglect of his finances mean disaster. Timon thinks 'I am wealthy in my friends' [2.2/S.4: 179], but his friends and creditors refuse to help him. This is to the general disapproval of their servants, who count up how much their employers have taken from Timon [3.4/S.8: 15-34] and condemn their hypocrisy. 'Excellent' exclaims one of Timon's servants after a friend declines to help:

> Your lordship's a goodly villain. The devil knew not what he did when he made man politic—he crossed himself by't, and I cannot think but in the end the villainies of man will set him clear. How fairly this lord strives to appear foul! Takes virtuous copies to be the wicked, like those that under hot ardent zeal would set whole realms on fire; of such a nature is his politic love.   [3.3./S.7: 27-35]

The servant here associates 'politic' with strategic, hypocritical, action—with the appearance of friendship as a mask for self-interest.

Timon takes revenge—inviting his debtors to a feast and serving them dishes full of water and stones. He receives them as guests amicably and graciously, so it seems. But the grace that he delivers reiterates the theme of need from his speech in S.2: 'Lend to each man enough that one need not lend to another; for were your godheads to borrow of men, men would forsake the gods' [3.6/S.11: 72-4]. He ends in a cynical, angry voice reminiscent of Apemantus: 'For these my present friends, as they are to me nothing, so in nothing bless them; and to nothing they are welcome.—Uncover, dogs, and lap' [3.6/S.11: 81-4].

> Plagues incident to men, your potent and infectious fevers heap on Athens.... Itches, blains, sow all th'Athenian bosoms. Breath infect breath, that their society, as their friendship, may be merely poison. Nothing I'll bear from thee but nakedness, thou detestable town.   [4.1/S.12: 30-3]

---

[32] Jacques Derrida. 1988. 'The Politics of Friendship', *Journal of Philosophy*, 85: 632–44; Jacques Derrida. 1994/1997. *Politics of Friendship* (Verso: London).

[33] Carl Schmitt. 1927/1996. *The Concept of the Political*, trans. George Schwab (Chicago University Press: Chicago), Ch. 3: 27.

Tearing off his clothes, Timon goes to 'the woods, where he shall find th'unkindest beast more kinder than mankind' [4.1/S.12: 35-6]. He turns away not only from the society and the city, but from the human race:

> The gods confound—hear me you gods all—th'Athenians, both within and without that wall; and grant, as Timon grows, his hate may grow to the whole race of mankind, high and low.   [36-40]

In the woods, when Alcibiades and two women come to see him, Timon declares 'I am Misanthropos, and hate mankind' [4.3/S.14: 53].

His repudiation of all friendship and of all citizenship is underlined by his references to himself and to those who visit him in the woods—Alcibiades, the women Phrynia and Timandra, Flavius, the Senators, Apemantus—as 'beasts' [4.3/S.14: 49, 201, 423-5] echoing the Aristotelian principle that friendship, sociability, and polity are the ultimate human relationships, while those who do not or cannot have them are as if they are gods, or beasts.[34] In his essay on friendship, Francis Bacon invokes Aristotle's view that 'he that cannot abide to live in company, or through sufficiency hath need of nothing, is not esteemed a part or member of a city, but is either a beast or a god.'[35]

As Shakespeare's treatment of sovereign power dramatizes the philosophical conflict between constructions of it as an ultimate power of life and death, and as a mundane human production, so his treatments of friendship play between dramatization of its paradoxical quality, and its straightforward, socially ethical value. Timon's misanthropic beastliness is structured, in the play, in contrast to Alcibiades' cannibalistic joke. He would like to be eating the hearts of his newly killed enemies for breakfast; desire for one's enemy is as strong as desire for one's friends. Alcibiades is 'living among the dead', and all the lands he has 'lie in a pitched field' [1.2/S.2: 224-5]. Enmity involves the kind of love we have for food as much as it rests on hate; and in Alcibiades's world friendship presupposes this enmity and hate.

Economy, Friendship, and Justice in *Merchant of Venice*

Merchant of Venice tells the story of Antonio, a merchant, who borrows money from Shylock against the security of a cargo of goods that is on its way to

---

[34] Aristotle, *Nicomachean Ethics*, 1934: I.i.12, 1253a.
[35] Francis Bacon. 1753. 'Of Friendship', *The Works of Francis Bacon*, Vol. I (London: A. Millar), p. 70; Jowett, 'Introduction', 2004: 270n.

Venice. Antonio and the other merchants are Christian; Shylock is Jewish. Jews were tolerated in Venice although segregated in the ghetto; in England, Jews had been proscribed and expelled by Edward I; and in Shakespeare's time they had not been invited back (they were, later, by Oliver Cromwell (1599-1658, Protector 1653-8)).[36] Antonio objects, on cultural and religious grounds, to paying interest on loans, and in the end he and Shylock do a deal according to which instead of money interest Antonio will pay with a pound of his own flesh if he cannot repay the loan. The money is for Antonio's friend Bassanio, who needs it in order to attempt to marry Portia. Portia's late father has left her a large inheritance, but has specified certain conditions (the successful suitor has to choose the correct one of three caskets) that have to be met before she can marry. In the event, Bassanio wins the competition to marry her. But the ship carrying Antonio's cargo is lost. Shylock meanwhile has suffered loss also—his daughter Jessica elopes with Lorenzo, a Christian man of Bassanio's circle, and she takes with her a good deal of Shylock's money. Shylock enforces the contract, despite entreaties by the Duke that he show mercy. Bassanio goes, with money from Portia, to pay the debt for Antonio; Portia, disguised as a man, follows him. As Balthasar, she takes the place of the lawyer who had been appointed to hear the case. When her plea to Shylock to accept late payment, to show mercy, fails to move him, and it looks as though Antonio must pay the forfeit, she argues that the contract was for a pound of flesh, no blood. She argues that were Shylock to do any harm to Antonio in taking the flesh, he would be guilty of a capital crime [4.1.321-8]. Shylock desists and attempts to back out of the case. But Portia further argues that in planning to do harm to a citizen of Venice Shylock is guilty of a crime; all his goods and property are forfeit to the state and he is forced to convert from Judaism [4.1.343-59].

Merchant of Venice, similar to *Romeo and Juliet*, can be told as a story of republican sovereignty, or rather its failure. Like Prince Escalus, the Duke in *Merchant* can't, by using either his social-political power as a notable and a member of the oligarchy, or his formal sovereign power, settle without harm to anyone the dispute between Antonio and Shylock. The story can also be told as one of justice: how inter-personal justice between individuals, and between citizens and aliens interacts with legal and moral justice, and with state enforcement. A conventional interpretation is that Portia's success is based on her legal wisdom and rhetorical power.[37] Her speech about mercy represents the height of Shakespeare's humanist, ethical, and poetic appeal

[36] Jay L. Halio. ed. 1993. 'Introduction', William Shakespeare, *The Merchant of Venice* (Oxford University Press: Oxford), pp. 1–6.
[37] Quentin Skinner. 2014. *Forensic Shakespeare* (Oxford University Press: Oxford): 54, 143, 213.

[4.1.181-201]. However, the place of mercy, and of the moral or godly justice that transcends social relations and state power alike is unclear in the end. Should we take away the conclusion that, at a number of points in the plot, mercy should have been exercised? Or do we conclude that mercy is a vain hope where human antagonisms, and material interests are at stake?

Shylock is referred to, and directly addressed as, 'the Jew', and reviled as the devil [1.3.174-5, 3.1.19-20, 4.1.33]. In response, in an exchange with Antonio's friends, Shylock's

> I am a Jew. Hath not a Jew eyes?...If you poison us, do we not die? And if you wrong us, shall we not revenge? If we are like you in the rest, we will resemble you in that.   [3.1.50-69]

stands as one of great literary poems (although it is prose) of humanism. It emphasizes universal, common qualities and potentialities. It also emphasizes the relations of 'teaching' and 'learning' that are inevitable in structured societies, and that insert into the range of human qualities those that are of social, and local, origin. 'The villainy you teach me I will execute', Shylock ends, presaging his protest in court that he has done no wrong—according to the laws and the trading society of Venice—in enforcing his contract with Antonio:

> What have among you many a purchased slave which, like your asses and your dogs and mules you use in abject and in slavish parts because you bought them?   [4.1.88-102]

The wrong that Shylock has done is to be a member of a stigmatized and excluded group which nevertheless has a role in Venice's system. We can only understand these poems of justice, and of humanity in the context of that systemic structure of social, economic, and political relations.

Our thinking about the values of mercy, justice, and humanity must also be contextualized by the quality of Portia's power, which is first and foremost the power of trickery. Disguised as a male lawyer, Balthasar, rhetorically she establishes first that the bond is valid, and that the context of justice is prior to the mercy that she invites Shylock to exercise [4.1.174-9]. She thereby secures Shylock's endorsement of her reason [4.1.203-4, 220-1]. But having done this, she turns legal reason in a direction neither he nor the others in court anticipate, establishing both that the bond must be fulfilled and that Shylock must not physically injure Antonio. Having already refused to exercise mercy,

Shylock is trapped. An obvious resolution at this point would be for the Duke to dismiss the case on the grounds that the original contract is invalid because impossible to realize [4.1.103-6]. Obviously, there are dramatic reasons for that not to happen—it would make a boring play about a reasonable resolution of an unreasonable dispute. But beyond that we can note that such a dismissal of the legal case would anyway not resolve, or heal, the social antagonisms between merchants and financiers, in particular because those economic roles are mapped firmly on to the religious-ethnic antagonism of Christian and Jew in the context of anti-semitism and state sovereignty.

Portia/Balthasar's final strike is to invoke a law that holds that any plan by an alien that 'seeks the life' of a citizen is a crime for which the penalty is forfeiture of all goods and property [4.1.343-59]. Portia's ruthlessness is then developed by Antonio who, invited by Portia/Balthasar to exercise mercy, proposes that just one-half of Shylock's goods should be claimed as a fine by the sovereign, while the other half should be managed and used by Antonio (this would, of course, compensate Antonio for the loss of his cargo) before being left on Shylock's death to Lorenzo (Jessica's husband). Further, that Shylock, in recognition of this favour, should convert to Christianity [4.1.376-86]. The use of disguise; the cleverness; the ruthlessness; all put Portia into the category of Shakespeare's 'machiavellians'. She unflinchingly exacts violence. This is not the violence—the halter—for Shylock that is called for by Antonio's friend Graziano [4.1.374-5], but the deprivation of his means of living, and his enforced conversion which means, at the very least, the loss of his community. Sovereign justice fails in Venice; at least, what sovereign justice above all means is the exaction of violent punishment. Open political negotiation of social relations and laws also fails. Any ideal of a republic as based on friendship and civility, which underpins the conduct and enforcement of the law, and permits the resolution and public conciliation of conflicting winners and losers in political decision making, is shown to be hollow and false. What prevails is machiavellian trickery.

This story of a polity seems to me a plausible interpretation of Shakespeare's plot and treatment of his characters and themes. The tone is not thoroughgoingly sceptical about republican political values—those values are disclosed as their concrete manifestation in Shakespeare's Venice is shown to be contradictory, negated, or paradoxical. Further, the quality of political relations is complicated in interaction with personal, familial, legal, economic, and religious ones. As in other plays, this disclosure of political power and action is via characters' resistance to the power that constrains them.

Patriarchy and Resistance

In *Timon of Athens* women are present only as entertainers and as prostitutes. Phrynia and Timandra, with Alcibiades, visit Timon in the woods. 'Promise me friendship, but perform none!' he exclaims [4.3/S.14: 73-4]. Digging for roots to eat, Timon has found gold [4.3/S.14: 23-6]. He does not need it now, of course; but in an ironic reprise of his previous liberality, he gives it, violently, to those who visit him, including these three [4.3/S.14: 101-8, 130-6]. Timon identifies Phrynia and Timandra's whoredom as key to all that is rotten in Athens: 'They love thee not that use thee' but also sees it as a weapon to be used against the city: 'Give them diseases...' [4.3/S.14: 83-4, 133-48]. 'We'll do anything for gold'—including listening to Timon's repulsive views and insults—they say [4.3/S.14: 150, 167]. Alcibiades' planned military action against Athens is confounded, in Timon's speech, with this sexual attack.[38]

Alcibiades has come into conflict with the senators over a matter of criminal justice and law [3.5/S.10: 7-37]. His plea for mercy fails: 'Nothing emboldens sin so much as mercy' as a senator puts it [3.5/S.10: 18-22]. Alcibiades pleads that 'pity is the virtue of the law, and none but tyrants use it cruelly' [3.5/S.10: 8-9]. It was a crime of passion, of anger [3.5.18-22]. But the senators argue that this is a paradox too far—attempting to make crime look like virtue [24-5]. Alcibiades then shifts to the senate's indebtedness to him for his military service, and hence their, as he sees it, obligation to favour him in this matter [3.5/S.10: 77-84]. The upshot of this interview is that Alcibiades is banished [3.5/S.10: 94-8], to which, Martius-like, Alcibiades responds: 'I hate not to be banished' [3.5/S.10: 110].

Timon urges Alcibiades, and Timandra and Phrynia, to show no mercy to the Athenian people, in a diatribe which mixes the violence of the sword with misogynistic, sexual, violence [4.3/S.14: 140-66]. Timandra and Phrynia are explicit representations of masculine fantasy of women both as happy prostitutes and as pollutants of the body politic. *Timon of Athens* questions the ideals of republican friendship as the basis for citizenship. But it takes for granted the homosocial structure of citizen relations and the exclusion of women from that republic.

In *Merchant of Venice*, Portia is oppressed by her confinement at Belmont, and the situation her father has bequeathed whereby she has to await a marital partner who will win her in a game of chance. Perhaps there is an admixture

---

[38] Janet Adelman. 1992. *Suffocating Mothers: Fantasies of Origin in Shakespeare's Plays* (Routledge: London): 8-10, 13, 169-74, 331nn.

of skill or wisdom in this contest. The lyric of the song that is performed while Bassanio makes his choice can be interpreted as sending a coded message to choose the lead casket over the gold or silver ones. This choice responds to Plato's Alcibiades' warning in *Symposium* that appearances and superficial beauty are no guide to inner quality.[39] Portia may not choose, nor may she refuse a husband she dislikes, 'so is the will of a living daughter curbed by the will of a dead father' [1.2.22-4]. In voicing this complaint Portia makes plain the contradictions of patriarchy, proclaims her own status as agent with will, and states the negative effects of oppression on individuals—'my little body is aweary of this great world' [1.2.1-2]. Jessica, too, is subject to her father's authority—when he is out, and the masques are on, she is not to look out onto the public street [2.5.29-32]. His culture must be hers.

Both are deprived of freedom of choice; but they exercise their ability to make themselves and follow their own path. Jessica disguises herself as a boy in order to elope with Lorenzo [2.6.26-50]. Portia and her companion Nerissa disguise themselves as men in order to travel to Venice to observe Bassanio's and Antonio's fates, and to participate in the court case [3.4.45-84]. Some feminist criticism looks at these actions as signals of Shakespeare's female characters' psychological potentialities and exploitation of such social opportunities as they have. Lisa Jardine, though, argues that this feminist reading of Shakespeare's heroines is cast into doubt by the fact that the actors playing Jessica and Portia on the Elizabethan stage were boys.[40] Her reading is that Elizabethan audiences, at least, would have enthusiastically jeered at the women characters' appearance, and laughed at the sexual innuendo of the scripts, endorsing the fundamental misogyny of the drama and the wider society. In the homosocial context of the theatre, the cross-dressed actor is a spectacle, whether humorous or erotic or both, so that the characters, and the actors who play them, are close to the entertainers and prostitutes of *Timon of Athens*.[41] Politically, the point is that Shakespeare's narratives show the imperative of keeping women off the public, political stage.[42] Portia and Nerissa in male clothing suggest that Bassanio and Graziano are sexually emasculated. Jokes about cuckoldry and feminine domination over men express misogyny, albeit in a different way from the boys' insults and joshing

---

[39] Halio, 'Introduction', 1993: 35–6, 167–8n; Plato, 'Symposium', 1938: Ss.216–17.

[40] Lisa Jardine. 1983/1989. *Still Harping on Daughters: Women and Drama in the Age of Shakespeare* (Columbia University Press: New York), pp. 29–33.

[41] Valerie Traub. 1992/2004. 'The Homoerotics of Shakespearian Comedy', in Emma Smith (ed.), *Shakespeare's Comedies* (Blackwell Publishing: Oxford), pp. 165–7.

[42] Leonard Tennenhouse. 1986/2005. *Power on Display: The Politics of Shakespeare's Genres* (Methuen: London), pp. 15, 115–22.

of the nurse in *Romeo and Juliet*.[43] The position of women in early modern societies is only the given pretext for the erotics of theatricality; the position of women is a kind of infrastructure, a given, which is then played with for theatrical effect, and audience pleasure and laughter. The female characters are comical, in part, because resistance to established gender roles is futile.

Feminist critique analyses how, from a conventional sex-gender point of view, women's freedom involves taking the part of man or boy—the only way women can become agents is to take up a masculine structural position. Jardine's point is that the approach of psychological realism that is implied by a response to Jessica and Portia in terms of proto-feminist courage is an error. If we focus on structure, then we see 'characters' as positioned and constrained, rather than as free agents. The early modern theatre enacts and reenacts, iterates and reiterates that dramatic resistances serve only to reaffirm the rightful (masculine, patriarchal) pattern of domination.

But rather than getting stuck between agency and structure, we must focus on the diverse processes by which structure is achieved and maintained. One story we have met is that patterns of friendship are an important infrastructural element for polity—for a system of order and rule that publicly sets up and perpetually contends institutions and rules, commanding assent, up to a critical point. Like other Shakespearean comedies *Merchant of Venice* focuses on a group or network of partly chosen, partly thrown together individuals. Some are together out of liking; but you don't choose your friends' friends, or their sexual or romantic loves. *Timon of Athens* focuses on a network of 'friends' of Timon and his subsequent rejection of friendship, citizenship, and humanity. As we have also seen, a rival meaning of politics is the lone individual (or possibly group) who operate behind the backs of friends and enemies alike to manipulate the structure of power and influence, in order to further their own aims and position. The case of Portia shows very clearly how her trickery contributes to a personal, individual solution to some of her problems, but it does not exactly contribute to any political (public, shared) process of sexual justice.

Among the questions raised about how friendship works in the polity, the difference between men's and women's friendship in sex and gender structured societies, is key. Before Bassanio leaves Belmont to help Antonio, Portia gives him a ring which he swears to wear always: 'When this ring parts from

[43] Coppelia Kahn. 1981. *Man's Estate: Masculine Identity in Shakespeare* (University of California Press: Berkeley, CA), pp. 119–21; Marilyn L. Williamson. 1986. *The Patriarchy of Shakespeare's Comedies* (Wayne State University Press: Detroit, MI), pp. 40–51.

my finger, then parts life from hence' [3.2.183–5]. During the court proceedings Bassanio expresses his despairing devotion to Antonio: 'I would lose all, ay, sacrifice them all [life itself, wife, and all the world] to deliver you' [4.1.279–84]. Portia, disguised as the lawyer, remarks: 'Your wife would give you little thanks for that, if she were by, to hear you make the offer' [4.1.285–6]. Bassanio has made the same oath, on his life, to his wife and to his friend. After the court case, Shylock destroyed, Antonio's life and livelihood saved, Bassanio asks Balthasar/Portia what reward he can give in thanks. Portia/Balthasar first demurs and says, 'nothing'; and then, on Bassanio's pressing his gratitude, asks for the ring [4.1.417–25]. Of course, Bassanio refuses, but Portia is persuasive, and Antonio urges him to concede, and the interaction ends with his parting from the ring [4.1.445–50]. All is revealed in the final scene; how surprised Bassanio is, when after a good deal of reproachful teasing, Portia presents him with the ring again [5.1.254–7]. How surprised all are to discover that Portia was the lawyer and Nerissa the clerk [5.1.275–85].

Portia's marriage to Bassanio, in one reading, is voluntary, based on mutual love or liking. However, Bassanio and his friends do not conceal his pecuniary motives for attaining the 'golden fleece' [3.2.239]. Patriarchy, which in earlier chapters I have presented above all as a system of oppression, is also a system of extraction. In marriages traditional and modern, domestic labour is overwhelmingly performed by women and is not counted. In traditional marriage law—like that of Venice—a wife's property becomes her husband's on marriage. It is counted, as Bassanio counts it prior to the marriage; and then it disappears, becomes uncounted, when it is absorbed into the husband's assets after marriage.[44] From an individualist, voluntarist point of view, Portia's and Bassanio's chosen love relationship cancels out a series of inequalities. She is rich, he impecunious; he is a man with all the politically organized and legally enforced superiority over women that involves, while she is subject to father's and then husband's control. They are both young; they share a sense of humour and wit. Marriage between them instantiates the conjugal friendship that is developed—nowhere more clearly than in Shakespeare's comedies of love—as relevant to heterosexual marriage, and is consistent with a wider network of voluntaristic friendships such as the one centred on Portia and Bassanio at Belmont. Jessica and Lorenzo have fled to Belmont on their elopement; Lancelot, Shylock's servant, helps Jessica and follows her, joining

---

[44] Christine Delphy. 1978/1984. *Close to Home: A Materialist Analysis of Women's Oppression* (Hutchinson: London); Carole Pateman. 1988. 'Wives, Slaves and Wage-slaves', *The Sexual Contract* (Polity Press: Cambridge), Ch. 5.

the group at Belmont [3.5]. Portia's companion Nerissa falls in love with Bassanio's friend Graziano. The friendships and friendliness within this circle— a voluntary group, not kin—are characterized by trust, mutual aid, degrees of emotional equality consistent with Portia's being rich, Nerissa being employed by her, and Jessica being a 'stranger' [3.2.235]. Lancelot, the clown character, is free from social ties and conventions. Once he has broken from service to Shylock his discourse of dissent reflects freedom as much as it challenges authority, while his service to Jessica can continue under new conditions. This is a group of friends who are collusive with each other as regards marriage— welcoming each other's affianced, urging conjugal happiness.

But Bassanio's inability to square this conjugal friendship with Portia with the depth of his commitments and obligations to Antonio contrasts with this happy representation of friendships. Further, there is an ambiguity in the ideal of conjugal friendship. The term can also be analysed as friendship between men which is as if it were conjugal. In this frame, it is the loss of Bassanio that accounts for Antonio's sadness [1.1.1-64]. This is the opening theme of the play, discussed by Antonio's friends, and he attempts to account for it himself. He thinks his role is simply a sad one [1.1.79]. This later evolves into a more tragic story of fatedness 'I am the tainted wether of the flock, meetest for death. The weakest kind of fruit drops earliest to the ground' [4.1.113-15]. But Antonio, in the play, suffers loss after loss. First he loses Bassanio: Bassanio and Portia's conjugal friendship displaces Bassanio and Antonio's. He loses his cargo, and comes close, consequently, to losing his life.

He also suffers the loss that attaches to compromise of a social identity. As a Christian who reviles the Jews, Antonio's chosen role is to unambiguously, publicly, and violently, reject the financial services of the money lenders. New financial and market relations are emerging, and Antonio wants no part of them. His loss of Bassanio to marriage disrupts their friendship; but out of that friendship, he is obliged to compromise his political and social identity, and enter the contract with Shylock. The contract itself is a compromise, and Shylock's compromise compromises Antonio even further—he comes close to loss of self. Further, Portia shifts Bassanio's financial debt from Antonio to herself. The conventions and laws of patriarchy say that on their marriage her wealth is Bassanio's. But, from the point of view of individualism, there is no doubt that Bassanio's capacity to pay Antonio's debt is thanks to Portia. Her actions put Antonio himself directly in her debt. The three are linked by a chain of transfers and exchanges; and also by the chain of 'life oaths': Bassanio swears on his life to both Portia and to Antonio.

The cultural representation of evasion, wit, and disguise, voluntary friendships between men and women, and of individuals choosing their marriages contributes to the public imagination of voluntarism and freedom. As we have seen, to begin with, this imagination co-exists with legal, cultural, and political realities of patriarchal oppression and exploitation. Further, voluntarism and individualism make ambiguous the political significance of new cultures or new social relations. On the one hand dramatic theatrical heroines are exceptional, by definition, and their courage, passion, cleverness, and trickery exceptional too. There's nothing political, critics can say, about individual solutions to systematic or structural disadvantages and oppressions, especially when these solutions are based on mendacity and trickery (as women's power behind the throne, and the like, so often are said to be). On the other hand, these representations contribute to the politicization of sex and gender relations: Portia's, Nerissa's, and Jessica's resistances are in part disclosed in dialogue with other characters, but in part they are addressed directly to the theatre audience and beyond. These stories contribute to the process whereby problems are propelled onto public political agendas. And the individual struggles and solutions, dramatized, highlight the structural constraint that is struggled against. Further, these female characters have reason, incentive, and means to oppose the power of their fathers. But, as the dramas show, their projects come into conflict with the projects of others. Politics is a process of clashing projects and ideals.

According to political theory readings of the ebbs and flows of patriarchal power, men are as engaged in the project of the overthrow of fathers as women are. As sons and brothers, and as friends and co-citizens, men, too, have an interest in freedom from fathers.[45] If men are to be able to make contracts with each other, then they have to be formally free to engage in these transactions, and they have to live in a system of the rule of law which is able and organized to enforce contracts which conform to the new standards. As Carole Pateman argues, in order to engage in such a world, men have to be free from the patriarchal power of life and death. In Shakespeare's world, as I discussed in connection with *King Lear*, consciousness of the shifts from aristocratic and patriarchal ties and allegiances, to voluntarily struck bargains and individual expenditure and investment of their own resources and capital is evident and dramatically represented in the plays in sons' conflicts with

---

[45] Carole Pateman. 1989. 'The Fraternal Social Contract', *The Disorder of Women* (Polity Press: Cambridge).

fathers. But brothers need sovereign authority too. *Merchant of Venice* discusses the need for the rule of law to instil confidence in contracts struck in that state [3.3.26–31]. Sovereign authority in the mercantile republic enforces contracts between individuals. (We can contrast this with Lear's exercise of monarchical sovereignty as the allocation of territory to lords.)

However, this dispossession of patriarchy, and institution of a society of formal equals, who can transact with each in market relations and in friendship, simply substitutes one set of mechanisms of women's exclusions from civil society and state for another set—what Pateman calls 'fraternal power', and what other feminist thinkers call modern patriarchy.[46] There is a clear limit to the men's commitment to equality—the equality that is necessary between them, in order to allow the market economy and the republican polity, does not license any inference to any wider reaching social equality. Generalized citizen friendship is shown to be consistent with frontiers of inequality, antagonism, and exclusion. In *Merchant of Venice* there are two such lines. First, that between men and women, vividly shown by Portia's and Nerissa's need to disguise themselves as men in order to be safe on the road to Venice, and in order to gain admission to the public institutions of the city. Second, Shylock's and the other Jewish patriarchs' authority over their wives and daughters is thrown into relief by their exclusion from participation in the polity, and by their segregation from the society.

State and Economy

Indebtedness and 'bonds' operate as a master trope throughout *Merchant of Venice*.[47] Bassanio's debt to Antonio, Antonio's to Shylock, Antonio's and Bassanio's subsequent debt to Portia, operate as a chain that link the characters by financial transactions that are both explicit and transparent (the lending or giving of money under certain terms), and also occult and vague. Bonds and debts are on the one hand real links, and also they are breakable ones. Bassanio and Antonio are indebted to Portia when she gives the money to pay off Antonio's debt to Shylock; but her subsequent disguise and virtuosic legal performance indebt them further in ways they don't understand to an individual whose identity is opaque. When married, Portia and Bassanio are

[46] Pateman, 'Fraternal Social Contract', 1989; Veronica Beechey. 1979. 'On Patriarchy', *Feminist Review*, 3: 66–82; Williamson, *Patriarchy*, 1986: 27–40.
[47] Halio, 'Introduction', 1993: 29–38; Renato Rizzoli. 2017. 'Shakespeare and the Ideologies of the Market', *European Journal of English Studies*, 21(1): 14–15.

bound, as one person; Bassanio's commitment to Portia and his commitment to sacrifice himself and his wife for Antonio's life, though, are impossible to square, as Portia will not be sacrificed. Portia's father's will constrains her marriage choice, but Portia exercises agency which aligns her father's will with her own. The terms of Shylock's loan to Antonio are, on the one hand, 'a merry sport'—a play at what would normally be a serious bargain specifying interest payable on a financial loan [1.3.142]. On the other hand, the contract is sealed by a notary, is legally enforceable [1.3.141]. Jessica breaks the patriarchal bond between her and Shylock, defying his authority with regard to her social conduct and marriage; she also steals his wealth.

This is a point at which a political economic reading might seem impossibly superficial and inadequate to the depth psychology and symbolism of Shakespeare's plot and poetic art. Janet Adelman's interpretation focuses on how the Oedipal story of a child's destruction of the father is imbricated with Jessica's and Shylock's respective conversions from Judaism to Christianity, which in turn are imbricated with Judaism's 'paternity' with respect to Christianity, and the way that the themes of cutting and of the blood which is both the life material of the body, and the medium and vehicle of inheritance and parentage, underpin the explicit and the implicit anti-semitism of the drama.[48] But Adelman's psychoanalytic and symbolic account connects directly with, cannot be separated from, the socially expressed and politically settled anti-semitism of Venice. The hostility of the Christian traders towards the Jewish financiers, and the segregation of the Jewish people in the ghetto is the material and political counterpart of the deep psychology of parenting and inheritance, membership and exclusion, friendship and marriage, as well as bonds and debt. Shakespeare's imagination of Venice holds all these levels together.

Shakespeare's play also asks normative and critical questions about the meanings of debt and obligation, and, in particular, about the ethics and politics of a world in which 'things', including relationships like marriage and friendship, are cashed out in exchanges and contracts.[49] If the exchanges of love and friendship should be free from financial evaluation and meaning, we must ask how that is to be achieved. States and societies are the context for economy, and by the same token economy is the context for state and society; kinship and intimacy are imbricated with citizenship and full state membership, and

---

[48] Janet Adelman. 2003. 'Her Father's Blood: Race, conversion and nation in The Merchant of Venice', *Representations*, 81: 4–30; Janet Adelman. 2008. *Blood Relations: Christian and Jew in The Merchant of Venice* (University of Chicago Press: Chicago).

[49] Fontaine, 'Prodigality Avarice and Anger', 2018: 48–51; Richard Arneson. 1985. 'Shakespeare and the Jewish Question', *Political Theory*, 13: 85–111.

with the various degrees of allegiance between citizens and denizens, between the insiders and the liminal.

As *King Lear* does, *Merchant of Venice* sets its characters' social and psychological dilemmas in the context of a new order of voluntary transactions and exchanges, in which individual fortunes are determined by the individual's own way in the world. The Venetian trading republic deploys state power to guarantee legal contracts between commodity traders and those between traders and financiers. Currency value and exchange rates, imports and exports of commodities (including human slaves), financial loans, and commodity contracts with deferred payment, or receipt and delivery, terms were new, but established phenomena of Elizabeth I's rule.[50] Bodin, whose theory of sovereignty we met in connection with *King Lear*, had argued that stable currency, and an effective economic policy were necessary for a sovereign state.[51] His unpublished but widely circulated 'Colloquium of the Seven' concludes that the sovereign should refrain from enforcing faith and should prescribe toleration, in order to avoid sectarian disputes.[52] Queen Elizabeth visited the Royal Exchange in 1571, in which year there was also a relaxation of the usury laws.[53] This was instrumentally because the monarch needed loans to finance war and trading expeditions, which were closely bound up together; symbolically the visit showed trade to be an interest of the sovereign. James I's proposal to unify Scotland, England, and Wales was understood to be motivated partly by economic concerns. Concerns of power, in the traditional sense of the state of the state, and concerns of economy are bound up with questions of religious and cultural policy—who belongs?

Karl Marx said that *Timon of Athens* shows that Shakespeare understood money.[54] Money distorts—it distorts both individuals and the relationships, the bonds, of society. As Marx puts it:

I can be a brainless person, but if I have money I can pay clever people to think for me. If I am ugly, I can nevertheless buy the most beautiful of lovers. I might be lame, but 'money furnishes me with twenty four feet'. With

[50] Kitch, *Political Economy*, 2009: 2–5.
[51] Jean Bodin. 1576/1992. *On Sovereignty*, ed. Julian Franklin (Cambridge University Press: Cambridge; selection from *Six Livres de la Republique*, trans. Richard Knolles, 1606), Bk 1, Ch. 10.
[52] Jean Bodin. 2010. *Colloquium of the Seven about Secrets of the Sublime*, trans. Marion Leathers Kuntz (Pennsylvania State University Press: University Park); Teresa M. Bejan. 2018. *Mere Civility: Disagreement and the limits of toleration* (Harvard University Press: Cambridge MA), pp. 37, 45.
[53] Rizzoli, 'Shakespeare and Ideologies of Market', 2017: 13.
[54] Karl Marx. 1843/1975. 'On the Jewish Question', in Lucio Colletti (ed.), *Early Writings* (Penguin: Harmondsworth), pp. 376–8.

money, I am presumed to be honest (even if I am dishonest). 'Does not my money, therefore, transform all my incapacities into their contrary?'[55]

Money, as the existing and active concept of value, confounds and confuses all things. Exchange of values through the medium of money and contract, the circulation of goods, bring anxiety about what else will be exchanged, and, where parties are of different structural groups—religion, culture, race—anxiety about movement and mixing, loss of clarity and purity.[56] Such paradoxical antitheses are prominent at all levels of *Timon of Athens*. Most obviously, in Timon's speech. There is an obvious paradox in his finding gold at the point where it is valueless to him [S.14/4.3.23-6].[57] But, more than being valueless, he now (in a speech that has striking parallels with Romeo's characterization of the poison he buys from the Mantua apothecary as 'cordial' while the gold he gives for it is 'worse poison') considers it to be the author of his downfall: 'Gold...much of this will make black white, foul fair, wrong right, base noble, old young, coward valiant' [4.3.26-30]. 'It will 'bless th'accursed...give thieves title, knee and approbation...' [4.3.35-42]. This confounding of moral categories is at the heart of Marx's critique of commodity and capital economies, and the societies and states that are their counterparts: 'All that is solid melts in air' say Marx and Engels, echoing Hamlet [*Hamlet*, 1.129-32].[58]

In Shakespeare's time the notion of usury was transforming into interest. It was changing from a sin and an evil into a mundane aspect of existence. The vicious passion for money progressively, over the next century or so, became a 'rational passion'.[59] But biblical discourse and religious laws retain their cultural grip, and the link between the idea of usury and the making of human beings themselves into things that can be bought and sold, destroyed or let live, but at a price, runs deep in both *Merchant of Venice* and *Timon of Athens*. However, as Shylock neatly, smartly, and poetically points out, it doesn't take usury to permit or entrench slavery markets in human beings. The Christian

---

[55] Karl Marx. 1844/1975. 'Economic and Philosophical Manuscripts', *Karl Marx Early Writings*, trans. Rodney Livingstone and Gregor Benton (Penguin: Harmondsworth), p. 377.

[56] Kim F. Hall. 1992/2004. 'Guess Who's Coming to Dinner? Colonisation and miscegenation in The Merchant of Venice', in Emma Smith (ed.), *Shakespeare's Comedies* (Blackwell Publishing: Oxford), pp. 199-200.

[57] Jowett, 'Introduction', 2004: 53-9.

[58] Karl Marx and Friedrich Engels. 1848/1977. *Manifesto of the Communist Party* (Progress Publishers: Moscow), p. 39; Jacques Derrida. 1993/1994. *Specters of Marx: The State of Debt, the Work of Mourning and the New International* (Routledge: London), pp. 9-13.

[59] Albert O. Hirschman. 1977/1997. *The Passions and the Interests: Political Arguments for Capitalism before Its Triumph*, Twentieth Anniversary edn (Princeton University Press: Princeton, NJ) esp. pp. 32-41.

merchants had been trading human beings long before they got involved with new forms of finance and credit. By contrast, the financiers who buy and sell money don't buy or sell human beings directly [4.1.88–92].

Justice and Friendship

In *Merchant of Venice*, both the power of sovereignty and the nature of the society and economy are shown to be flawed in relation to the achievement of justice. The play asks how justice can be realized when a society is organized around antagonistic relations, in which a dominating economic and cultural group—the Christian traders—both rely on and denigrate an excluded group. Although the Jews are tolerated by the Venetian polity, and allowed to dwell in a sequestered space in the city, members of the society, characters in the play, persist in treating them as subjects for persecution and violence. Antonio is quite open about his contempt for Shylock; he clearly believes that public incivility at best, but also outright coarseness of manner and even physical violence are justified. It might be that the system of status differences that is characteristic of Venice as a traditional society licenses, or prescribes, defer- ence from Shylock to Antonio, and licenses contempt for Shylock on Antonio's part. Or, it might be that the assumption of 'equality' in the trading republic— in which one person's money is as good as another's—means that honour and status are not legally or culturally protected, and, by contrast, that the rough and tumble of the public space means individuals are unchecked in their speech. In spaces of freedom, individuals have to toughen up to insults.[60]

Or, it has been thought, Antonio's contempt is licensed by the fact that Shylock is evil. Shakespeare's Shylock is in many ways a straightforward ver- sion of a medieval figure, a stage villain, which identifies Jewishness with wickedness and stereotypes alleged Jewish traits and types.[61] Among promin- ent instances of this figure, Christopher Marlowe's Jew of Malta (*c.*1589) pre- sented, like Shylock, as a complicated character, and sympathetically in some scenes, is also figured as a machiavellian who is skilled in murderous art.[62] Shylock is less violent, but nevertheless the interpretation of his actions and strategies as designing Antonio's death is plausible. Kitch points out, however,

---

[60] Bejan, *Mere Civility*, 2017: 152–64.

[61] Geoffrey Bullough. ed. 1957. 'Merchant of Venice', *Narrative and Dramatic Sources of Shakespeare*, Vol. 1 (Routledge and Kegan Paul: London), pp. 449–50; Halio, 'Introduction', 1993: 7–9; Arneson, 'Shakespeare and the Jewish Question', 1985.

[62] Bullough, 'Merchant of Venice', 1957: 455.

that focus on this devilish stereotype overlooks the extent to which, in the early modern period, 'the Jewish nation', in many discourses and representations, overwhelmingly was understood in terms of trade and state economic policy.[63] From the point of view of critical political thinking, that is, we can see how stereotyped characterizations of group and class members can both be reinforced by popular understandings of economic and social flows, and also, to some degree, modified by them. If Shylock's financial trade should no longer be understood, as it is by Antonio, as transaction between enemies [1.3.131-3] but understood, in accordance with Shylock's articulated aspiration—'Why look you, how you storm! I would be friends with you and have your love, forget the shames that you have stained me with, supply your present wants' [1.3.134-6]—as a friendly transaction between co-participants in a voluntary economy, then what is left of Antonio's condemnation but crude dislike and contempt, based on cultural, or racial, hatred?

Shakespeare also unsettles the crude anti-semitism of the stage Jew with his humanist poetry, and its universalist appeal. Shylock's 'I am a Jew. Hath not a Jew eyes?' speech [3.1.55-69] beautifully emphasizes what is common to all human beings, what all need, what is universal in reaction to right and to wrong. Politically, such universalist appeals demand that societies organize the meeting of human needs as such. However, this universalism is in some tension with Shylock's own articulation of particular community values and the distance between religious groups. Among Shylock's complaints about Antonio are that he has 'scorned my nation' as well as mocking his gains, and heating his enemies [3.1.51-4]. Shylock asserts the ways of the Jews as opposed to the Christians, and expresses fear of and disgust at Christian ways [I.3.37-49]. He engages in a scriptural debate in defence of the principle of making more money out of money [I.3.68-92]. He wants to defend himself from the profane culture with which he is surrounded. We first hear Shylock, in response to Bassanio's courteous and friendly 'If it please you to dine with us' [1.3.30] expressing disgust ('to smell pork;' [1.3.31]), followed by a clear statement of cultural limits: 'I will buy with you, sell with you, talk with you, walk with you, and so following; but I will not eat with you, drink with you, nor pray with you' [1.3.33-5]. He is nervous about going to dine with the Christians, and even more appalled when he hears there will be revels: 'What, are there masques? Hear you me Jessica: lock up my doors…but stop my house's ears—I mean my casements; let not the sound of shallow fopp'ry enter my sober house' [2.5.28-36].

---

[63] Kitch, *Political Economy*, 2009: 107–10; Adelman, 'Her Father's Blood', 2003: 9ff.

Shakespeare here can be read as articulating a justification of Christian anti-semitism—'they scorn and reject us', they do not assimilate into the society in which they live. But the tension between the assertion of universal values and the assertion of community solidarity is not easily resolved. Shakespeare's Shylock takes a stand, as an excluded member of the Venetian society, as in the society but not of it, a position that gives him a critical place from which to evaluate the Christian trading republic.[64] Shylock sees how the institutions of property as control and alienability (saleability) makes property of human beings who can accordingly be treated in exactly the same way that asses, dogs, and mules are [4.1.87-100]. Objections that slaves should be treated better invite the response 'the slaves are ours' [4.1.96-7]. By that account of property, and control, there can be no doubt that Shylock has entitlement to his pound of flesh. 'The villainy you teach me I will execute' [3.1.67-78].

There is also a tension between this interpretation of Shylock as a critical evaluator and his own desire for revenge, for physical, material, and symbolic payback for the insults and injuries he has suffered. His insistence on his pound of flesh is reminiscent, as G.W.F. Hegel (1770-1831) remarks, of systems in which the dismemberment and distribution of enemies', wrongdoers', and debtors' body parts is considered rightful recompense to sufferers.[65] The problem with revenge, of course, is that the avenger is likely to exact dismemberment of himself as much as of his enemy. On one account, this is the point of political pacification, which brings antagonistic parties and groups into shared power to organize the society, the polity, the sovereignty, that enables them to resolve hostilities without bloodshed: to do enemies down without doing them in, to find political assent to distributions of rights and duties, benefits and burdens. But how are the antagonisms of structured societies— such as the Venice in which sovereign power permits the Jews to settle, to remain as denizens of the city but in a segregated space, excluded from the political institution—to be overcome politically? In particular, could there really be the civic friendship in Venice, that permits just polity, given the nature of the antagonisms between groups, and the effectiveness with which women are excluded and dominated, and the Jews are tolerated but reviled?

---

[64] Nancy C.M. Hartsock. 1983/1998. 'The Feminist Standpoint: Developing the ground for a specifically feminist historical materialism', The Feminist Standpoint Revisited and other Essays (Westview Press: Boulder, CO); Gayatry Chakravorty Spivak. 1988. 'Can the Subaltern Speak?', in C. Nelson and L. Grossberg (eds.), Marxism and the Interpretation of Culture (Macmillan Education Basingstoke); Michael Walzer. 1989. The Company of Critics: Social Criticism and Political Commitment in the Twentieth Century (Basic Books: New York).

[65] G.W.F. Hegel. 1821/1977. The Philosophy of Right, trans. T.M. Knox (Oxford University Press: Oxford), pp. 18-19.

The boundaries of the society of *Merchant of Venice* separate individuals and groups from each other. The clear boundary between Christians and Jews is symbolized most obviously by the walls and gates of the ghetto, and made visible by sartorial distinctions and performances, including Shylock's 'Jewish gabardine' [I.3.109]. The clear boundary between women and men is excessively symbolized and represented in spatial segregation (Portia at Belmont, Bassanio and his friends out in the city, Jessica at home, Shylock at the Rialto). In traditional and not so traditional societies alike sartorial distinctions are marked—girls' and boys', women's and men's clothing are quite distinct and rule-governed. The women violate these boundaries—disguised as men. Their presence in public is deviant—they should not be there, should not be dressed in male garb, should not be breaking moral rules. Jessica, Shylock's friend Tubal reports to him, has been seen in Genoa, and he has heard reports that she spent eighty ducats in one night [3.1.101–2].

The boundaries, then, are such that there can be transactions across them (betrothals, elopements); financial exchanges; and successful 'passings' of women as men. These are transactions and exchanges that blur distinctions. At the heart of *Merchant of Venice*, though, are crossings that are in one direction, preserving more than transgressing boundaries, and evading miscegenation. Jessica converts, voluntarily, to Christianity. Shylock is sentenced to convert.[66] Excluded, disadvantaged communities can exclude in their turn. Jessica will be excluded from the world of the Jews by her disobedience to patriarchy as much as by her entry into a new religion. We can only speculate on Shylock's fate in Venice after the action closes.

Marx looks forward to a world without class distinctions (differences in relationship to capital and labour power), and he also looked for the collapse of the religious distinctions that paradoxically exaggerated and mystified institutions of capitalism such as financial capital.[67] The normative question of which categories should be blurred or dissolved, and which should be safeguarded from transgression or corruption can't be addressed as such here. We can only appreciate how Shakespeare's antitheses and paradoxes, his observations of transformations in exchange and circulation hold together in unsteady balance, I think, both endorsement of human freedom and ethical (non-violent, non-exploitative, non-oppressive) connections, and a zestful taste for mixing and bending.

---

[66] Hall, 'Guess Who's Coming to Dinner?', 1992/2004: 209–10.
[67] Karl Marx. 1867/1954. *Capital*, Vol. 1 (Lawrence and Wishart: London), pp. 212–15.

Political Economy and the Political Way

The depth of the social divisions and exclusions in *Merchant of Venice* casts doubt on the possibility of a just polity premissed on friendship. *Timon of Athens* focuses on the fragility of the egalitarian, reciprocal, human relations that must underpin any civic friendship, and their liability to corruption by inequality, by hypocrisy, and by countervailing material antagonisms. In the course of his argument with the senate, Alcibiades argues for particular distinction rather than uniform laws that operate in a way that people cannot understand. Open violence is preferable to sneaking surreptitiously; we engage in open warfare and pitched battle; we don't go round the enemy camp's tents and quietly cut all their throats while they sleep [3.5/S.10: 42–5]. If we deny this, then we assert that women, who stay at home, are more valiant than the men who go to war. The altercation goes on for many lines, and the senators stick to their view that 'the law is strict…we are for the law; he dies' [3.5/S.10: 84–5]. But the senators who face Alcibiades down are already compromised by the way they themselves have undermined the culture of citizenship equality with their betrayal of Timon.

Merchant of Venice shows the loss, or failure, of civic friendship in a structurally segregated society, and one in which personal profit from exchange is defended and justified, and losses are seen, also, as justified or as evidence of desert. *Merchant of Venice*, like *Timon of Athens*, is a significant contribution to the genre of theatrical performance that played with new characters and new classes, new ways of living, and explored 'trade' as a metaphor for human relations.[68]

---

[68] Kitch, *Political Economy*, 2009: 2–4.

7

Politics and Magic

Macbeth and *Tempest*

Politics and Magic

The idea that politics and magic are deeply intertwined with one another is both preposterous and commonsensical. The identification of politicians as magicians is certainly commonplace in many political cultures. It can have diverse meanings. In many settings, sovereigns, monarchs in particular, connected as they are with divinity, with the supernatural, or with the occult, are surrounded by sacred objects, are themselves sacred, and are dangerous, sometimes taboo. Always power and distinction lend them charisma, making them dazzling creatures.[1] There is a contrast between the aura that surrounds the person of a monarch, president, or prime minister, and the commonplace indistinction of their staff. In cultures where occult, supernatural, or otherwise magical power is accepted and taken seriously as an explanation of fortune, good or bad, and of the domination of some individuals over others, it can be taken for granted that powerful individuals use magic power, for good or for ill, depending on your point of view, in order to achieve and maintain their positions.[2]

Elizabethan and Jacobean England were like this: magic loomed large, as a factor of the everyday, as an element of state rule, and as a matter for sovereign concern. Understanding the occult powers of substances, achieving mastery of them, is the outcome of study which, accordingly was thought to be a proper pursuit for monarchs.[3] Because magic is dangerous, even evil, it was a matter of sovereign concern, the monarch having the duty to safeguard the

---

[1] David I. Kertzer. 1988. *Ritual, Politics and Power* (Yale University Press: New Haven), pp. 46–8; Stephen Ellis and Gerrie ter Haar. 2004. *Worlds of Power: Religious Thought and Political Practice in Africa* (C. Hurst: London), pp. 90–9.

[2] Elizabeth Frazer. 2018. 'Political Power and Magic', *Journal of Political Power*, 11(33): 359–77.

[3] Stephen Orgel. ed. 1987. 'Introduction', William Shakespeare, *The Tempest* (Oxford University Press: Oxford), pp. 7–14; Douglas Brooks-Davies. 1983. *The Mercurian Monarch: Magical Politics from Spenser to Pope* (Manchester University Press: Manchester), pp. 4–5.

Shakespeare and the Political Way. Elizabeth Frazer, Oxford University Press (2020). © Elizabeth Frazer.
DOI: 10.1093/oso/9780198848615.001.0001

state and the people.[4] Powerful people themselves are sanguine about the idea that they have to be seen to have some kind of magic power, to have a reputation as a sort of magician, and that that is a necessary and inevitable aspect of their role. Nelson Mandela, for instance, said: 'I am not a god or a prophet, but I have to act like one'.[5]

However, equally commonsensical is the view that this is a corruption of politics. An otherwise admirable figure like Mandela is here taking a dangerous step away from the principle that political power is the property of people together, given the right circumstances and conditions. It is a human capacity of which we should all have a grasp. We have seen that politics is susceptible to being overwhelmed, or captured, by economic motivations and exchanges, by violence, by forms of domination and exploitation like patriarchy or racism. It can also be destroyed by belief that the rights, authorities, and capacities of those who rule have a supernatural origin.

On the other hand, in sceptical and anti-political times, the idea of politician as magician is also an unmasking device, revealing politicians to be charlatans, tricksters, who use sleight of hand, and dazzling appearances to conceal mendacity and manipulation. All politicians as such, but especially those who gain office, use an essentially magical style of performance, and are 'by definition dishonest', say critics.[6] In current cultures, being likened to 'a wizard', when applied to sports stars or musicians, is entirely approbatory. But, strikingly, when politicians are associated with wizardry, it is evil, or commonplace criminality, or at best mendacity that is invoked. The term 'Welsh wizard', applied to footballer Gareth Bale is a comment on his genius; when it is used in respect of David Lloyd George (1863-1945; British prime minister, 1916-1922) it is much more ambiguous. 'Welsh wizard' is also used of John Dee (1527-1608), sometime adviser to Elizabeth I, of whom more below.

There is analogy, or perhaps continuity, between these discourses and phenomena of supernatural, occult, and magic powers, and the more mundane transformations that are the stuff of everyday social life, where we step into and out of roles and statuses. These transformations—from unemployed person to an individual with a task, a job title, and a place in an organization; from single to married; from candidate to president of a republic—are frequently marked with changes in clothing and insignia, and are felt, albeit in

[4] Orgel, 'Introduction', 1987: 20.
[5] Deborah Posel. 2014. '"Madiba Magic": Politics as enchantment', in Rita Barnard (ed.), *The Cambridge Companion to Nelson Mandela* (Cambridge University Press: Cambridge), p. 371.
[6] David Graeber. 2012. 'Can't Stop Believing: Magic and politics', *The Baffler*, https://thebaffler.com/salvos/cant-stop-believing 21.

elusive ways by the transformed individual, often having an effect on bodily comportment. Of course, such transformations have a good deal to do with the way persons are treated very differently by others after their change of status. Often, though, the rituals and symbols that mark, that actually constitute, the transformation are decidedly solemn, or festive, out of the ordinary. Often a power which transcends the social scene is invoked—the power of gods or other supernatural beings, or organized religious authority, or the power of the state—the power by which you are made a citizen, or married, or registered as an arrival in the society as a baby. Ritual and symbol are inextricable elements of magic—they are how spells are cast and magic transformations achieved. But they are also inextricable elements of social life and, in particular, of political life, and especially the transformations and passages from heir to monarch, or candidate to elected officer, from policy proposal to law, and so on.

So there seems to be a deep tie between magic and politics; at the same time as it is important for us to hold onto the social, material nature of political capacity. There are clear differences between a stage conjurer cutting an audience member in half and a judge administering the oath of office to an incoming president and handing over a symbolic object that signifies presidential power. These are different from one person using threats or rituals of spells or magic in order to dominate or exploit another. But it is terribly difficult to draw bright lines between rational, intelligible, materially and socially based processes of categorization and ordering (like distinguishing between who is married and who is not, who is a real citizen and who only a denizen of a state); what look from a secular materialist point of view like non-rational claims (for instance, that the harm being visited on one person by another goes beyond the usual methods of theft, assault, slander or libel, bullying or intimidation to spells or magic); or what look like bogus tricks or fraud rather than genuine transformations.

The monarch's, and the judges' and clergy's duties to tackle the potential dangers of witchcraft, which were clear enough in early modern European states (and are still a preoccupation for law[7]) raise analogous difficulties. The first is how to distinguish between good, well-intentioned *magia*, and *maleficium* or witchcraft used for evil purposes. *Maleficium* conjures with evil spirits, even the devil himself, to aid with the control of occult powers. If the magus has contact with the spiritual or supernatural world at all (as opposed to gaining understanding of occult powers by way of human wisdom) he

---

[7]   Frazer, 'Political Power and Magic', 2018: 368.

engages with angels.[8] The second difficulty is how to distinguish between genuine magic powers (whether *maleficium* or *magia*) and the bogus trickery of charlatans and hoaxers.[9] The third is how to tell the difference between scholarly and lofty, forward looking, study of natural properties (which can be understood as a kind of proto-modern science) and commonplace traditional purveyance of spells, forecasts, potions, and amulets in the market place (folk superstition, which becomes less salient in societies as levels of uncertainty, risk. and want decrease).[10]

In Shakespeare, magic practices are both taken for granted as a reality and are the object of scepticism. Forty years after Shakespeare's *Tempest* scepticism was unambiguously expressed by Thomas Hobbes (1588-1679), who lamented that ordinary people don't understand science—they think of geometry as conjuring, a magic art.[11] Skinner understands Hobbes to be echoing a complaint of writers of the previous (that is, Shakespeare's) generation—he quotes John Dee (1527-1608) making much the same point. More subtly, Hobbes deploys magic as a metaphor for the hierarchy of the Roman church under the pope which 'may be compared not unfitly to the kingdom of fairies; that is to the old wives' fables in England, concerning ghosts and spirits, and the feats they play in the night.'[12] Hobbes's own aim is to account for absolute sovereignty without recourse to divine right or magic, as a construction of analytic reason and logic alone, repudiating metaphysics and metaphor.[13] Yet, in writing *Leviathan* Hobbes recognizes that logic alone will not do; if he tries to avoid metaphysics, his metaphor of the absolute state as a creature of mythical proportions and moral status goes well beyond physics.[14]

---

[8] Ian Seymour. 1989. 'The Political Magic of John Dee', *History Today*, 39: 30; Orgel, 'Introduction', 1987: 20-1.

[9] Stephen Greenblatt. 1988. 'Shakespeare and the Exorcists', *Shakespearean Negotiations: The Circulation of Social Energy in Renaissance England* (University of California Press: Berkeley, CA), pp. 98-9; Emily Butterworth. 2008. 'The Work of the Devil? Theatre, the supernatural, and Montaigne's public stage', *Renaissance Studies*, 22(5): 705-22.

[10] Keith Thomas. 1971. *Religion and the Decline of Magic: Studies in Popular Beliefs in Sixteenth and Seventeenth Century England* (Weidenfeld and Nicholson: London); John Henry. 2008. 'The Fragmentation of Renaissance Occultism and the Decline of Magic', *History of Science*, xlvi: 1-48; Lauren Kassell. 2005. 'The Economy of Magic in Early Modern England', in Margaret Pelling and Scott Mandelbrote (eds.), *The Practice of Reform in Health, Medicine and Science 1500-200* (Ashgate: Aldershot); Alan Macfarlane. 2000. 'Civility and the Decline of Magic', in Peter Burke, Brian Harrison, and Paul Slack (eds.), *Civil Histories: Essays Presented to Sir Keith Thomas* (Oxford University Press: Oxford).

[11] Thomas Hobbes. 1651/1996. *Leviathan* (Oxford University Press: Oxford), Ch. 5, S.18; Quentin Skinner. 2002. *Visions of Politics: Hobbes and Civil Science* (Cambridge University Press: Cambridge): 82.

[12] Hobbes, *Leviathan*, 1651/1996: Ch. 47, S.21.

[13] Hobbes, *Leviathan*, 1651/1996: Ch. XII, S.12; Skinner, *Visions of Politics*, 2002: 78.

[14] Skinner, *Visions of Politics*, 2002: 80-6; Robert E. Stillman. 1995. 'Hobbes' Leviathan: Monsters, metaphors, magic', *ELH*, 62: 791-819.

Some of Shakespeare's representations of sovereign power can inform-atively be brought into relation with Hobbes's theory of absolute sovereignty. Hobbes explicitly set out to repudiate views of sovereignty—that it can or should be shared, that it cannot be 'absolute', that the bearer of sovereign office is themself subject to the law—which were explicitly articulated and argued, for instance, against the claims of James I, by Edward Coke (1552-1634; Lord Chief Justice of England, 1613-16).[15] That for Shakespeare, and in the polit-ical culture, the source, the nature, and the limits of sovereignty were open questions is clear from his dramatic treatments of monarchy.[16] These open questions are also salient in *Tempest* and *Macbeth*.

Political thinkers since early modern times have dealt with the centrality to politics of transformations, with the dazzling charisma of monarchs and other high office holders, and with the commonplace understandings of these in terms of magic, religion, and the supernatural.[17] Late modern theories of polit-ical domination and legitimation recognize and analyse magic performances and reputation.[18] According to this view, there are continuities between ideas of the sacred as determining and immanent in the material world and social rela-tions, and the norms that govern social ritual and symbolism in modern secular societies. Whether these are thought of in terms of supernatural power, divine ordination, or tradition, they have the effect of sacralizing society and, espe-cially, authoritative institutions.[19] This means, as Max Weber (1864-1920) insists, that under certain circumstances the authority of magi and prophets, relatively unconstrained by norms or laws, can be sufficient to enforce, and to legitimize judgements or pronouncements.[20] Charismatic authority results from the intersection of an individual's special qualities, their successful claim to, and audiences' attribution to them of 'supernatural, superhuman, excep-tional' powers. Typically in history (not always, not everywhere) such powers are regarded as divine in origin, and the person as having magical capabilities.[21] Importantly, Weber's analysis constantly emphasizes the intersection of forms

---

[15] Larry May. 2012. 'Hobbes against the Jurists: Sovereignty and artificial reason', *Hobbes Studies*, 25: 226.

[16] David Scott Kastan. 1986. 'Proud Majesty Made Subject: Shakespeare and the spectacle of rule', *Shakespeare Quarterly*, 37(4): 459-75.

[17] Giorgio Galli. 2004/2012. *La Magia e il potere* (Lindau s.r.l: Torino).

[18] Max Weber. 1921/1978. *Economy and Society*, trans. and ed. Geunther Roth and Claus Wittich (University of California Press: Berkeley, CA), pp. 53-6, 215, 242, 647; Michael Mann. 1986/2012. *The Sources of Social Power*. Vol. 1: *A History of Power from the Beginning to AD 1760* (Cambridge University Press: Cambridge), pp. 341-71.

[19] Emile Durkheim. 1912/2001. *The Elementary Forms of Religious Life* (Oxford University Press: Oxford): esp. 'Conclusion'; Kertzer, *Ritual, Politics and Power*, 1988: 37-9, 61-6.

[20] Weber, *Economy and Society*, 1921/1978: 647.

[21] Weber, *Economy and Society*, 1921/1978: 242.

of power: religion can be used as a means of intimidation, spirit manifest-
ations to dazzle, and magic power as a threat—'magic' can be a mask for
violence.[22]

A notable, highly salient example is Julius Caesar (100-44 BCE), and his
use of ideas of divinity to secure personal power. There is a long tradition of
discourse about what was wrong and right about Caesar's power, with its
roots in the classical sources themselves, particularly developed in the republican tradition, notably by Machiavelli.[23] Weber understood 'Caesarism' to be
a distinctive style of political domination.[24] Shakespeare's own representation of
Julius Caesar (composed 1599) has decisively made its way into popular understandings and representations of uses of divinity, charisma, political manipulation, and military distinction as the basis for sovereign claims. In Shakespeare's
play it is Caesar's encouragement of associations of himself with divinity that is
at the heart of Brutus's and Cassius's fear that he is plotting to be king, and for
an end of republican power [*Julius Caesar* 1.1.64-75; 1.2.59-62, 115-18].

This chapter focuses on a range of questions regarding the liminal relation
between magic and political power. In *Macbeth* and *Tempest*, Shakespeare
plays a number of bases and dynamics of the power to govern against one
another. In what follows we shall see how Macbeth's, the weird sisters', and
Prospero's uses of magic in pursuit of domination or, in the case of the weird
sisters, subversion, come into relation with alternative bases of political power
and ways of ruling—with visions of Christian kingship, and with the violences
of tyranny, but notably also with an ideal of open, just, political government.
The plays explore the problems—to put it mildly—that dog those who deploy
magic as a shortcut to rule. Weber's characterization of politics as work,
labour, 'slow, strong drilling through hard boards'[25] is less spectacular than
politics as machiavellian scheming, ducking and diving, or princely riding of
the wave; and more mundane than the exercise of military brilliance to legitimate domination, as well as less dazzling than magic. But all these shortcuts
to ruling power mean that something is lost. What is lost, when the magic

[22] Weber, *Economy and Society*, 1921/1978: 907.
[23] Plutarch. 1919. 'Caesar', *Plutarch's Lives*, Vol. VI, trans. Bernadotte Perrin (William Heinemann:
London); Walter W. Skeat. ed. 1875. *Shakespeare's Plutarch: Being a Selection from The Lives in North's
Plutarch which Illustrate Shakespeare's Plays* (Macmillan and Co: London), S.4: 45–6, S.39: 92–5, S.43:
97–8; Niccolo Machiavelli. 1531/1970. *The Discourses on the First Decade of Titus Livy*, ed. Bernard
Crick, trans. Leslie J. Walker SJ (Penguin: Harmondsworth), e.g. Ch. X, XVII, XXIX.
[24] Weber, *Economy and Society*, 1921/1978: 1125–7; Peter Baehr. 2008. *Caesarism, Charisma and
Fate: Historical Sources and Modern Resonances in the Work of Max Weber* (Transaction Publishers:
New Brunswick).
[25] Max Weber. 1919/1994. 'The Profession and Vocation of Politics', in Peter Lassman and Ronald
Speirs (eds.), *Weber Political Writings* (Cambridge University Press: Cambridge), p. 369.

shortcut is resorted to, is a question posed by the plays. Considering that question brings into view what kind of political actors—genuine or bogus—as well as what kind of magicians, Prospero and Macbeth are. More generally, the questions are posed of how we should understand magic in relation to political power—as the sign of credulity and confusion in the polity? As the work of charlatans and tricksters? Or as a deeper metaphor for a certain ineffable quality of political power itself? Both *The Tempest* (composed 1611) and *Macbeth* (composed 1606) focus on the central character's struggle for the power to govern.

Macbeth, Sovereignty, and Magic

Macbeth seeks to achieve kingship, and, having achieved it by regicide, to maintain it. His enemies suffer under his violence and tyranny, regroup to consider their options, pool forces, or don't quite manage to, and eventually overcome him with military power, enabling Malcolm the rightful heir to the murdered King Duncan to take the throne with the promise of better rule to come. The political setting for *Macbeth* is a feudal world in which thanes—landlords who hold their lands by grant of the king in virtue of their military service—are in a relationship of allegiance with and service to the king. King Duncan's grip on sovereignty is in crisis, as he has lost the allegiance of some thanes, including Macdonald and Cawdor, who have rebelled and joined forces with an external enemy, the King of Norway. Duncan receives reports of Macbeth's courageous military service and declares that Macbeth will be Thane of Cawdor [1.2.64-6]; subsequently Cawdor is defeated and executed [I.4.1-7]. We first meet Macbeth, with Banquo, on their way home from battle. They meet three 'witches', also referred to in the list of 'persons of the play' as the 'Weird Sisters'. The witches predict that Macbeth will be Thane of Cawdor, and king [1.3.50-67], a prophecy that is bemusing to Macbeth and Banquo, but seems uncanny when they discover from Ross and Angus, sent by King Duncan to find him, that Macbeth is now Thane of Cawdor [1.3.100-9]. Lady Macbeth receives Macbeth's news before he reaches home, and also notice that the King is on his way to stay at their house. On reading his letter she determines that Macbeth must be king, although she doubts that he is ruth-less enough [1.5.1-40].

   When Macbeth arrives home the idea that they should kill Duncan, and hasten the eventuality of the witches' prophecy, is more or less agreed between them [1.5.56-72] although Macbeth—who is to do the killing—has misgivings, and is disturbed in his mind [1.7.1–50, 2.1.31–66]. But he does kill Duncan, stabbing him as he sleeps. On discovery of the body, the Macbeths blame servants [2.3.102–10]; Duncan's sons Malcolm and Donalbain flee, to England and to Ireland respectively [2.3.137–43]. Banquo suspects that Macbeth has 'played foully' in bringing the witches' promise to fruition. Macbeth, now as king, is naturally uneasy as regards his security although the witches have told him that he cannot be killed by anyone 'of woman born', and not until Birnam Wood comes to Dunsinane. Macbeth's mind is increasingly disordered. His bewilderment begins when he meets the weird sisters, and increases when he learns that he is Thane of Cawdor. He is disturbed by his argument with Lady Macbeth about the wisdom or sense of murdering Duncan, and her challenges to his courage. Disturbance turns into full-blown psychological distress as he 'sees' a dagger he knows not to be there [2.1.34–40], and has a vision of Banquo's ghost [3.4.37–59] (Banquo has been killed by him) not shared by guests at the banquet [3.4.37], and then sees a procession of apparitions conjured by the witches [4.1.83–149].

The country is in fear of his violent tyranny. Banquo's son Fleance escapes when the assassins come. Macbeth's hired assassins pursue Macduff, murdering Lady Macduff and their children. Macduff is in England with Malcolm when he hears the news about his family. Meanwhile, Lady Macbeth, assailed with guilt, takes her own life. Macduff, Malcolm, and Ross, supported by English forces, invade Scotland; the troops move towards the battlefield at Dunsinane camouflaged with branches, so it appears that the wood is on the move. Macbeth is isolated and so enmeshed in violence that he cannot see any way out but his own death [3.4.137–9, 5.3.30–2]. He engages in combat with Macduff, learning that Macduff had not been 'born of woman' but by caesarian section. Macbeth is killed; and Malcolm succeeds to the throne of Scotland, reinstituting the relationships between king and thanes.

The simple political story of usurpation and restoration of kingship is made complex by the way the drama rehearses a range of alternative ways of ruling, juxtaposed and contrasted within the action. Macbeth's struggle for sovereignty, his tyrannical power, and his dealings with the witches (and thereby Satan), contrast both with the saintly Christian kingship of Edward the Confessor of England and with the military feudal kingship of Duncan in Scotland. The web of established feudal relationships of obligation, allegiance, and personal service between Duncan and the thanes is shown to be fragile and subject to a number of disruptions. Individual military distinction and heroism, the kind exemplified by Macbeth during the war at the beginning of the action, gives him personally a claim to greatness which disrupts the feudal order just as it is central to the logic of that order. Most significantly, feudalism is disrupted by treachery and rebellion—exemplified by Macdonald and then Cawdor (1.2), and then by Macbeth's regicide and usurpation (2.1). The corollary of terror and tyranny is surveillance, spying, and the destruction of social trust and open political dialogue—dramatized in 3.6 when two lords cautiously discuss the state of Scotland.[26] The dispersed power and authority, webs of allegiance, and rights of feudal loyalty contrast, in turn with the pushes to centralized, unified sovereign power over the state (in Macbeth's aspirations and actions). The ideal of stable, sovereign domination of a centralized territorial state, of course, brings with it problems of legitimacy and of succession, and the question of how new forms of political allegiance can be established.[27]

Macbeth, in particular in partnership with Lady Macbeth with her lauding of strategy, opportunism, and ruthlessness, can be counted among Shakespeare's machiavellians—an ironized version of the prince envisioned by Machiavelli himself who will use exemplary violent power only in the service of the good and the glory of the state itself, not simply for his own aggrandizement.[28] Neither Macbeth nor Lady Macbeth articulate any aspirations for the good of the state, as opposed to their own good of supremacy. Machiavelli contrasts his ideal prince explicitly with the Christian prince who, in Machiavelli's view, will be insufficiently martial and strategic to the extent that he really conducts himself according to pious Christian standards. Malcolm, for his part, is assailed by doubt about his capacity to find Christian virtues and capacities in himself should he be called upon to rule [4.3.50-99, 141-59]. The courage of Machiavelli's prince involves taking chances, being alive to *kairos* or the critical moment, as well as aware of *chronos*, the way over time fortune ebbs and flows.[29] This theme of *kairos* is ironized in *Macbeth*, where Macbeth's aspiration to timely and decisive action 'if it were done when 'tis done, then 'twere well 'twere done quickly' [1.7.1-5] runs up against the reality that actions have unpredictable, uncontrollable ramifications.[30]

---

[26] Nicholas Brooke. ed. 1606 (comp.)/1990. 'Introduction', in William Shakespeare, *The Tragedy of Macbeth* (Oxford University Press: Oxford), p. 22.

[27] Bryan Lowrance. 2012. 'Modern Ecstasy: Macbeth and the meaning of the political', *ELH*, 79: 823–49.

[28] Niccolo Machiavelli. 1532/1961. *The Prince*, trans. George Bull (Penguin: Harmondsworth), Chs. VIII, XIX.

[29] Machiavelli, *Prince*, 1532/1961: Chs. XXI, XXV.

[30] Stephen Greenblatt. 2009. 'Shakespeare and the Ethics of Authority', in David Armitage, Conal Condren, and Andrew Fitzmaurice (eds.), *Shakespeare and Early Modern Political Thought* (Cambridge University Press: Cambridge), p. 72; Philippa Berry. 1997. 'Reversing History: Time, fortune, and the doubling of sovereignty in Macbeth', *European Journal of English Studies*, 1: 367–87.

Most important for this chapter, though, is the way *Macbeth* is a play about characters who are embroiled in the uses of magic to achieve and maintain their power to govern. The weird sisters can be interpreted as opponents of Macbeth, perhaps of the class of thanes altogether, perhaps of all social and political order. They use magic as a way to victimize Macbeth, to sabotage rule, to undermine the order of the state. Macbeth chooses to be guided by their prophecies into acting to seize the kingship he thinks they have foretold. Throughout the action, the theme of the intersection, and the confusion between supernatural power and forces with natural order is prominent. The beauty of the Scottish landscape, and the nature of the country, is explicitly invoked [1.6.1-10]. But the category 'natural' is more than weather, glens, and moors. Shakespeare consistently intersects that kind of nature with material technologies—equally natural to human societies, although artificial. Weapons are used for killing. The attacking forces use camouflage to confound Macbeth's military strategy—what kind of natural? The supernatural and the natural both intersect, further, with magic as a special kind of technology. The weird sisters summon winds from 'all quarters' [1.3.11-17], and conjure up apparitions [4.1]. Even more importantly for the thesis of this book, we must take into account the intersection, with both natural and supernatural, of the political and the social worlds. These are the worlds in which human relationships are established, institutions built, social norms enforced and violated, orders of inequality challenged and refashioned.

Like other Shakespeare dramas, *Macbeth* features a proliferation of alternative and competing ideas of how this order should work and what are the sources of the power to rule. For Macbeth, in particular, they are a source of bewilderment; he does not understand what he sees and senses, and cannot get a grip on, let alone control, the power that he takes hold of and attempts to wield. Most importantly, perhaps, Macbeth is confused about the material phenomena of natural experience, the social relationships that alone make a world and a life, the psychological effects of his own imagination and disordered mind, and the magic effects conjured up by the witches. Shakespeare pushes at the boundaries between magic, social materiality, and politics.

The Tempest and Magic Rule

In *The Tempest* Prospero has been deprived of the dukedom of Milan. This, by his own admission, is partly because he did not attend to the discharge of his duties in government nor to maintaining his power to govern effectively. He was displaced, and the governing power usurped, by his scheming brother Antonio, in collusion with Alonso, King of Naples. Excluded from his homeland, Prospero and his little daughter Miranda are put on a ship, on which they eventually arrive on the island [1.2. 65-174]. Caliban, described as 'savage and deformed' in the list of characters, and Ariel, an 'airy spirit', both live on the island when he and Miranda arrive. There, Prospero continues with his book study and the augmentation of his powers. Effectively he exchanges unsuccessful republican rule as duke in Milan for authoritarian and absolutist rule in his new island domain.[31] Prospero enslaves Caliban, exploiting his bodily labour, and punishing him for an attempted assault on Miranda [1.2.340-50] and keeps Ariel in bondage [1.2.242-51], exploiting his spiritual magic. He dominates his daughter, both as a child and then later by planning— and arranging—that she marry Ferdinand, the son of Alonso, heir to Naples. Following the deal in which Antonio had secured Alonso's support in his overthrow of Prospero, Milan now pays tribute to Naples. Prospero's plan, politically, therefore, involves bringing about the marriage and simultaneously regaining the dukedom of Milan—thus securing a lasting alliance, but based on marriage, not on a plot between sovereign and client, between Milan and Naples.

The first scene of *The Tempest* shows us a shipwreck; in the second scene it is clear that Prospero has raised the tempest that wrecks the ship [1.2.1-15] The shipwrecked party, cast ashore on the island, include Antonio, the usurper Duke of Milan; Alonso the king of Naples, his brother Sebastian, and his son Ferdinand; and courtiers and servants. On the island, they are subject to Prospero's power—in thrall to his, and Ariel's, capacities to conjure up illusions, visual, auditory, and tactile; to send them to sleep and to wake them; to confuse them and seduce them. Ferdinand—son of Alonso—is subjected by Prospero, by the use of punitive spells, and set to work, just as Ariel and Caliban are. Prospero's plan brings his political plot to regain his dukedom together with a revenge plot against his enemies.

Tempest, like *Macbeth*, can be read for the way distinct patterns and ideals of rule crowd together. The basic generative political theme of usurpation (Antonio's usurpation of Prospero's authority and office) is made ambiguous by Prospero's own testimony that his rule as duke had been inadequate, while Antonio was the cannier political operator [1.2.66-105].[32] Sovereignty and

---

[31] Coppelia Kahn. 1981. *Man's Estate: Masculine Identity in Shakespeare* (University of California Press: Berkeley, CA), p. 222.
[32] Orgel, 'Introduction', 1987: 15.

legitimacy are one thing, political skill and capacity are quite another, and there can be a conflict between them. The ideal of an autonomous state presided over by sovereign rule—the desideratum of machiavellian princely politics and the republican tradition, as well as the ideal of modern state formation—also is compromised by inter-state relations. Deals have to be done with other sovereigns, and Milan is in a relation of tribute with Naples [1.2.110-16, 121-7]. In the end Prospero regains his dukedom but secures a future in which Milan will still be tied to Naples.[33]

On the island Prospero's rule is authoritarian; it is totalitarian. More generously, he might be (and often is) seen as a wise 'philosopher king', or the statesman whose power orders all others.[34] He designs, controls, and determines lives and territory. Those who are ruled by him are unable to evade that rule—his power is greater than theirs, whether it perpetrates the violence visited on Caliban, or Ariel's inability to free himself, or Miranda's happy obedience. According to such a view, the usurper is doubly condemned—those who wish for political power are the least fitted to rule; while the wise, those who are indifferent to it, are the best rulers, and will rule for the sake of the polity and out of duty. Thomas More makes this point, in *Utopia*; it is consistent with Aristotle's model of turn taking in office, ruling and also being ruled; and is a plausible reading of Plato's *Republic*, and the motivations and duties of the philosopher kings.[35] According to such a picture, when Prospero—the wise, book learned monarch—regains the dukedom, the proper order of things has been restored.

It's notable that, according to this view, Prospero's political design is more important than his practices of magic and domination which are instrumental means to his political ends. Such a politically instrumental account of Prospero's magic is plausible; but interpretation of his governing technique as the exemplary legitimate operation of wisdom is far less so. Prospero's domination of Miranda is straightforwardly patriarchal. The enslavement of Caliban, and the uses of pain and torment to keep him subjugated and working, irresistibly raise the picture of 'new worlds' in which new forms of extraction are possible if sufficient ways of dominating labour are organized.[36] Early

[33] Orgel, 'Introduction', 1987: 3.
[34] Patrick Coby. 1983. 'Politics and the Poetic Ideal in Shakespeare's The Tempest', *Political Theory*, 11: 215–43.
[35] Thomas More. 1516/2002. *Utopia* (Cambridge University Press: Cambridge), Bk 1 esp. 42, l; Bk. II *passim*.
[36] Orgel, 'Introduction', 1987: 32–6; Paul Brown. 1985. '"This Thing of Darkness I Acknowledge Mine": The Tempest and the discourse of colonialism', in Jonathan Dollimore and Alan Sinfield (eds.), *Political Shakespeare: New Essays in Cultural Materialism* (Manchester University Press: Manchester).

modern imagination of 'primitive' people went together with justifications of violent colonization—religious, by way of reason of state, ideas of racial superiority, or European world destiny. Colonial invasions and settlements were achieved, as well as by straightforward uses of military style organized violence, by spectacular uses of gunpowder and the achievement of a reputation for magical or supernatural power.[37]

Greenblatt relates Prospero's style of government to sixteenth-century discourses of royal pardon, and interprets him as 'generating and distributing anxiety' (like, I argued, Duke Vincentio in *Measure for Measure).*[38] Whether Prospero is modelled on medieval monarchs with their reputations for magic power; or whether he is like the invading colonists, with their new, deadly technologies and their ruthlessness, which can only be understood as supernatural, the inhabitants of the island and the shipwrecked party are in his thrall. The shipwrecked newcomers are confused in their senses: they hear music and disembodied voices, smell strange scents, see apparitions, sleep and wake in strange rhythms [3.2.40-50, 122-3; 3.3.17-20ff]. Their clothes are dry and clean when they come to consciousness, just as if there had been no shipwreck [2.1.61-70]. They are in the control of a power they cannot understand.

From the point of view of republican politics, Prospero wields arbitrary power over those around him—they are dependent on him for good will, kindness (or absence of cruelty, at any rate), and pardon and freedom. Whether these will be delivered by him is quite unpredictable. In the terms of neo-republican normative political theory, he is far from being a legitimate authority.[39] And in a further Shakespearean twist, freedom and pardon, when they are delivered by Prospero, are ambiguous. His forgiveness of Antonio is as much withheld as delivered [5.1.126-9, 130-4]; Ariel—finally—is set free (5.1.316-18), but Caliban can be interpreted as simply abandoned [5.1.290-9].[40] From the point of view of right and justice in property and territory, Prospero's uncompromising denial of Caliban's claims—whether these are couched in terms of Caliban's prior occupation of the island or of his property in it [1.2.331-2],[41]—can only be interpreted as an assertion of the so-called 'right' of the stronger. To be sure, that 'right' is elaborated, and justified, by Prospero,

[37] Brown, 'This Thing of Darkness', 1985; Deborah Willis. 1989. 'Shakespeare's Tempest and the Discourse of Colonialism', *Studies in English Literature 1500-1900*, 29(2): 277-89.

[38] Stephen Greenblatt. 1988. *Shakespearean Negotiations: The Circulation of Social Energy in Renaissance England* (University of California Press: Berkeley, CA), pp. 129-30, 142-4, 147.

[39] Philip Pettit. 1997. *Republicanism: A Theory of Freedom and Government* (Clarendon Press: Oxford); Frank Lovett. 2010. *A General Theory of Domination and Justice* (Oxford University Press: Oxford).

[40] Orgel, 'Introduction', 1987: 26.   [41] Orgel, 'Introduction', 1987: 25.

by reference to Caliban's devilish parentage and dangerous nature [1.2.282-4, 1.2.319-20]. Prospero's sovereignty over the island is shadowed by the erstwhile rule of Sycorax, Caliban's witch-like mother.

Prospero's use of his magic arts to control the island's spirits, eventually to control the weather, and to control Ariel, Miranda, and Caliban is also juxtaposed with utopia. The theme of ideal government is raised explicitly by Gonzalo (one of the shipwrecked party), who dilates on the possibilities of ideal social and political relations in a new land [2.1.145-66].[42] Shakespeare here is following Montaigne's 'Of the Caniballes'.[43] But he never articulates a utopian vision without revealing its shadow side. Gonzalo's vision, his companions point out, is contradictory to begin with [2.1.154-5, 164-5]. Similarly, themes of utopian 'new' forms of voluntaristic love and marriage are debunked by the reality of Prospero's control of Miranda, by his arrangement of her marriage [3.1.92-4, 4.1.5-11]. There is Cockaignian material plenty—but the feasts and cornucopia, the pageants and revels are illusions [4.1.148-58].[44]

Magic and Politics

Three ways of reading 'magic' in relation to politics in the two plays can all be supported interpretively. First, magic, or at least a reputation for it, are straightforward resources for domination or for maintaining sovereignty. This is the way modern social theorists approach magic and related phenomena, and there are instances ready enough in political cultures, including Shakespeare's own and others nearer to our own time. Second, 'magic' can be approached sceptically, as trickery or delusion. What looks like the effect of magic can be explained as the effect of something else—psychology or rigged appearances. Third, magic can operate metaphorically in relation to politics. The power of the ruler, the political competitor, and even of democratic actors (although *Macbeth* and *Tempest* are not among Shakespeare's plays that feature claims of popular sovereignty) is 'like magic'. Where it works, political power has a mysterious quality—and 'magic', in texts like Shakespeare's, and in political comment and discourse, emphasizes this.

---

[42] Orgel, 'Introduction', 1987: 31.
[43] Orgel, 'Introduction', 1987: App. D; Michel de Montaigne. 2006c. 'Of the Caniballes', in John Florio (trans. and ed.), *The Essayes*, Vol. 1 (The Folio Society: London).
[44] Robert Weimann. 1978. *Shakespeare and the Popular Tradition in Theater: Studies in the Social Dimension of Dramatic Form and Function* (Johns Hopkins University Press: Baltimore), pp. 20, 106f.

Let's take magic as a political resource first. Prospero can be understood, and in performance has often been played, as a magus-ruler, whose wisdom and book study have enabled him to develop the powers over natural substances and phenomena that will enable him to regain his political status as ruler [1.2.72–7, 5.1.106–11]. Caliban and some of the shipwrecked party determine to take over Prospero's island: Caliban recommends that they destroy his books first [3.2.86–97]. The magus is a recognizable figure in early modern politics and culture. John Dee (1527–1608) advised Elizabeth I from 1555, when 'he performed angelic magic' to divine the immediate political future and to assist Princess Elizabeth's preparations for a succession crisis threatened by the apparent fulfilment of Queen Mary's phantom pregnancy.[45] He later wrote manuscripts which collectively set out a vision of a 'British empire' presided over by Elizabeth as empress. This vision was based on his reading of the Arthurian precedent, and generated the expectation that Elizabeth would reveal the philosopher's stone.[46] Elizabeth and her ministers sponsored alchemy, including Dee's work; and during the crisis of discovery of a catholic/witch plot against Elizabeth in 1578 he performed counter-magic on her behalf.[47]

We can see Dee's magic as an important resource for him politically, gaining him centrality in the court and proximity to the monarch. But we must emphasize also his usefulness to the Elizabethan government. His reputation for magic, and his participation in magic practices and study opened up opportunities for the government to employ Dee in intelligence gathering, under the guise of consulting experts in other countries on witchcraft and counter-magic, affording ways and means in foreign policy.[48] So neither Dee's imperial writings nor his magic writings can be understood independently of Elizabethan domestic and international politics.[49]

The case of Dee also reveals a route between the role of magus and that of purveyor or hawker of magic goods and services. When changes in court opinion marginalized his ideas of empire, as far as English policy was concerned, he too was marginalized. He continued to try to secure a hearing from the monarch—by publishing new angelic revelations. But, out of favour, he had to revert to a traditional trade, making a living by scrying, astrology,

---

[45] Glyn Parry. 2006. 'John Dee and the Elizabethan British Empire in its European Context', *The Historical Journal*, 49: 645.

[46] Parry, 'John Dee', 2006: 645–7, 665; Brooks-Davies, *Mercurian Monarch*, 1983: 3.

[47] Parry, 'John Dee', 2006: 668.

[48] Parry, 'John Dee', 2006: 668–9; Stuart Clark. 1997. *Thinking with Demons: The Idea of Witchcraft in Early Modern Europe* (Clarendon Press: Oxford).

[49] Parry, 'John Dee', 2006: 674.

and other kinds of natural magic.[50] From one point of view we can see this as a loss of his position in the practices that were continuous with the development of modern science and reversion to superstition. But the idea that the one is a 'rational' and the other a 'superstitious' practice, and that Dee didn't make it as a rational practitioner cannot hold. Isaac Newton (1643–1727) could be lambasted by nineteenth-century romantics for having destroyed mystery and beauty with his rationalist analysis—reducing the rainbow with the prism. But it is notable that alchemy was subjected, by him, to all his considerable powers of reason, scientific record keeping, and mathematical analysis for his whole working life.[51] Both are rational to the extent that they bring a return, or profit to the practitioner.[52]

Macbeth and Prospero both deploy 'magic' as a political resource, for their political ends as dominators, as sovereign rulers. They are members of a large class of rulers and would-be rulers who deal with the power, and the ambiguity, of a reputation for magic, bad or good. The weird sisters, for their part, are engaged with oppositional political ends. They seek to undermine the political and social order using magic means. It is important to acknowledge the significance of magic politics of this kind, which is much in evidence in modern times. In numerous episodes from the history of persecuted or dispossessed peoples, resort to apocalyptic thinking which generates culture and ritual to urge on the end times, and to refuse or evade the material and political power of the oppressors, is common.[53] As examples of power of the powerless, rituals to curse governments and the like are a frame that makes sense of the marginality and the seeming malice of women like Shakespeare's weird sisters.[54]

A second way of thinking about *Tempest* and *Macbeth* is via Shakespeare's sceptical voices—sceptical about the pretensions of rulers, and the prospects of politics, and, especially, sceptical about the claims of magicians. Many readings of Shakespeare's tragedies and late dramas emphasize that character is key. The individual and political drama is complex, and also plausible, and dramatic enough without magic. Macbeth's downfall is a result of his complex

---

[50] Glyn Parry. 2012. 'Occult Philosophy and Politics: Why John Dee wrote his Compendious Rehearsal in November 1592', *Studies in History and Philosophy of Science*, 43: 480–8.

[51] Henry, 'Fragmentation', 2008: 1.

[52] Kassell, 'Economy of Magic', 2005; Lauren Kassell. 2007. *Medicine and Magic in Elizabethan London* (Oxford University Press: Oxford).

[53] Anne Tagonist. 2017. '2016: The year magic broke into politics', http://dark-mountain.net/blog/2016-the-year-magic-broke-into-politics/ (accessed May 2017).

[54] Lyndal Roper. 1994. *Oedipus and the Devil: Witchcraft, Religion and Sexuality in Early Modern Europe* (Routledge: London); Ellis and ter Haar, *Worlds of Power*, 2004; Frazer, 'Political Power and Magic', 2018.

relationship with his wife and with himself, of his failures of insight and fore-sight, and, indeed, from the political theory point of view, of his neglect of the critical political relations of action in concert, shared deliberation, forgiveness and trust, and his error in mistaking extreme violence for political action.[55] According to such rationalist readings, the plots can be disenchanted, practic-ally without loss.

In *Macbeth*, the question whether the weird sisters are women who are strange and malicious or witches, which is to say in touch with the supernat-ural via techniques such as spells, is arguably answered within the play by 4.1 when they meet with Hecate, who is associated with sorcery and necromancy. But 4.1 is generally agreed to be an addition—a response to the popularity of witch plays—and it is not clear that Shakespeare is the author.[56] The fact that the weird sisters are referred to as just that suggests that Shakespeare's inten-tion is to be non-categorical about them. The foul weather might have been conjured up by the weird sisters. Equally, it might be nothing more than weather, which contributes to Macbeth's confusion about what is apparent and what is real. In *The Tempest*, the nature of the storm is also ambiguous. Prospero is presented as having conjured it, while ensuring that its victims are not really physically harmed. Yet he also says: 'By accident most strange, bountiful Fortune, now my dear lady, hath mine enemies brought to this shore' [1.2.178-80]. He could be a normal, dominating, ruthless, manipula-tive, character, who by a combination of trickery, violence, and—crucially—luck, overthrows the usurper.

Prospero and Macbeth can also be read as characters whose actions are constrained by the social and material worlds, and by the non-optionality of politics. Prospero fell short as duke; but political life comes with him to the island, where he takes the tempting course of absolute authority, tyranny over those around him, and the use for domination of the ordinary social and psy-chological powers which enable him to enslave Caliban and to punish him, and later to dazzle and confuse the bewildered shipwreck victims. The play is about political failure, and about the evils of domination—what happens when one person has too much power over others, as colonialists have too much power over the people whose lands they dominate.[57] Macbeth experi-ences the dagger—but he knows it is not there [2.1.38-40]. He sees, but the

[55] Brooke, 'Introduction', 1606 (comp.)/1990: 23; Mildred Tonge. 1932. 'Black Magic and Miracles in Macbeth', *Journal of English and Germanic Philology*, 31: 236, 244–6.

[56] Brooke, 'Introduction', 1606 (comp.)/1990: 64–6; Geoffrey Bullough. ed. 1973. 'Macbeth', *Narrative and Dramatic Sources of Shakespeare*, Vol. 7 (Routlege and Kegan Paul: London), p. 424.

[57] Brown, 'This Thing of Darkness', 1985: 59–68.

other characters do not, Banquo's ghost [3.4.60-4]. Birnam Wood does seem to come to Dunsinane, but in an instance of perfectly ordinary military tactics [5.5.44-6, 5.6.1-2]. In the end, Macbeth must fully understand the material basis of his downfall—the ambiguous meaning of a caesarean 'birth' and military subterfuge. He also must understand its political basis—as king he loses all loyalty and allegiance, and his violence spreads fear, mistrust, and enmity. Macbeth is too unfocused to engage in political work; he relies on his capacity for violence, and on the promise of the women who seem to speak with the authority of the supernatural. Politics requires relationships that sustain action in concert. Like Prospero, Macbeth has avoided the work they demand.

So, we can understand magic—or a reputation for it, at any rate—as a material resource; or we can understand magic as an illusion, a confusion of material, social, military, and political power with something uncanny. Between these two, we must take seriously how the metaphor of magic has an unshiftable place in political discourse, including the study and the practice of politics, in modern and postmodern societies. Accordingly, we can read Prospero's domination and regaining of sovereignty, the weird sisters' mischief, and Macbeth's downfall in a third way as comments on the nature of political power.

Political power can be said to be like magic because 'politicians lie'—dishonesty and deception are at the heart of political relationships and processes, so critics say. Rhetoric, verbal art, double talk and occult meanings, incantations have magic—and subordinating—effects on audiences, whose attention is distracted from the true mechanisms of the trick.[58] The politician-magician dominates by falsehood. In politics, just as in conjuring shows, and in the weird sisters' bringing Macbeth's downfall about, ritual performance brings to 'reality'—by way of an incantation, an oath, a spell—a 'new' state of affairs which people ambivalently believe. Success depends on willing suspension of disbelief on the part of the audience, but this suspension itself is cleverly brought about by the magician, or the politician, their support teams, and those who invest in them. It's not so much 'magic' as 'conjuring' and trickery, then, that carries the analogical weight in the politics as magic metaphor.

Ethically, magic and trickery are all one. Voodoo economics, spin doctors: such epithets signify disapprobation—it's all superficial, smoke and mirrors; politicians and their advisors are charlatans. These are dangerous phenomena, too—people are taken in by them. This runs counter to ideals of citizenship, and governmental power based on publicly achieved assent. It also runs

---

[58] Plato. *c.*330 BCE/2008. 1925. *Gorgias, or On Rhetoric—Refutative*, Vol. III, trans. W.R.M. Lamb (William Heinemann: London), pp. 452-5.

counter to the ideals of authoritarian systems. Authoritarian political rule requires obedience—but obedience following from the legitimacy, and the power of authority. If people are obedient because of magic that's a failure of authority. So voodoo economists and political wizards do harm, the reasoning goes, because they compromise the legitimacy of authority. They are also reckless as to the effects of their magic, by definition. Just as in politics the responsibility to be as far-sighted as possible about the effects of decision and action goes hand in hand with the irreducible fact that in politics the future is open because events and, critically, the reactions and actions of other people cannot be wholly controlled, so in magic the magician is always at risk of setzzpoints up the 'conjuring' aspect of politics, and also its danger and injuriousness.

Macbeth can be read as a tragic political character whose 'politics' is enmeshed with violence—both the military violence of courageous open battle, and the criminal violence of clandestine assassination and murder. According to Max Weber, who more than other modern thinkers insists on this association between politics and violence, and who takes magic seriously, the passionate, tragic politician must perforce become 'involved with the diabolical powers that lurk in violence'.[59] In Macbeth's case the devilry and violence are unconstrained by any other standards of politics than the lies, deceits, and dangers of illusion and conjuring. His tragedy is intensified by the fact that, under the influence of, deceived by, diabolical powers, he goes deep into violence for sovereignty, and into the violence of sovereignty: 'I am in blood stepped in so far, that should I wade no more, returning were as tedious to go o'er' [3.4.137-9]. Prospero's torment of Caliban can be seen as a straight instance of the kind of physical violence that we associate with torture (and, thereby, with political purposes): the pain is unpredictable, and therefore feared the more by Caliban; and it is varied [2.2.3-14].

The weird sisters, too, exert the diabolical power that gives politics such a bad name. Think of the helplessness and consternation, as well as the disgust, that people express when they are faced with politics that they are not equal to nor party to, whether that is at the state level, or when they are victims of political manoeuvring in personal or work life. But an alternative way of understanding the weird sisters' politics, more consonant with ideas of the capacity of the relatively powerless to disrupt and to put into crisis the comfortable assumptions and power play of the relatively powerful, is that they fight the authoritatively clear distinctions between 'symbolic' and 'real', between

---

[59] Weber, 'Profession and Vocation', 1919/1994: 365.

programmatic control and spontaneous genuine human capacity.[60] This takes us back to the idea of magic as an important political resource. Among the ideals of movement politics, whether the class movements, actions, and protests against dearth and injustice represented in Shakespeare's dramas, or the later twentieth-century movements for peace, liberation, and equality is a vision of a new society which rests on the appeal, and the efficacy, of the spontaneous. Against the machinations, and the overt uses of violent power, of statecraft and sovereign authority is pitted a complex network of social relationships, which permits freedom. In many contexts (we can cite, for instance, anti-war movements of the second half of the twentieth century) these ideals have recourse to motifs of weaving, or witchcraft, or magic symbols, which ambiguously work directly against the violent power of military, industrial, governmental complexes, by disarming security operations for instance, and, in any case, stand as a symbolic focus of opposition.[61] In this frame, the dancing of the witches, the spectacles they conjure up, their riddling teasing of Macbeth and Banquo precisely represent the social and the magical power that cannot be contained by statecraft, and that evades sovereignty. It also is disruptive of efforts to build allegiance and assent by way of public—visible, audible, inclusive—debate and contention. In that sense, it is anti-political.

On the other hand, Hobbes's and Shakespeare's deprecation of alleged magic is pressing. Macbeth is credulous. Prospero dominates characters who believe in his magic and can't see how it's done. People readily believe that dominators must have supernatural powers—what else can explain the enormity of their deeds?[62] Misunderstandings of politics, and how it's really done result in misattributions of magic powers. I don't believe that we have to decide, in reading *Macbeth* and *Tempest*, between the understandings of magic as a political resource, magic as a metaphor for politics, and the debunking sceptical denigration of magic. It would be difficult to do so, as elements of plot and dialogue draw our attention to each of these; and, famously, Shakespeare's plays are intelligible at multiple levels, with metaphor and symbolism being always prominent. He takes for granted the pervasiveness of daily commonsensical beliefs about magic power and witchcraft in sixteenth-century Britain. Political

---

[60] Sean McCann and Michael Szalay. 2005. 'Do You Believe in Magic? Literary thinking after the New Left', *Yale Journal of Criticism*, 18: 435–68.

[61] McCann and Szalay, 'Do You Believe in Magic?', 2005: 435–8; Tim Cresswell. 1994. 'Putting Women in Their Place: The Carnival at Greenham Common', *Antipode*, 26: 35–58; Elizabeth Frazer and Kimberly Hutchings. 2014. 'Feminism and the Critique of Violence: negotiating feminist political agency'. *Journal of Political Ideologies*: 19: 143–163.

[62] Ellis and ter Haar, *Worlds of Power*, 2004: 92–3.

actors do exploit magic, and the reputation for it, in their rivalries and allegiances with others. So Shakespeare straightforwardly reflects back to his audiences their sense of their world.

Theatrical Magic

The practical problem of the susceptibility of 'magic' to being unmasked as mere trickery was generating a sceptical approach to the supernatural, one that it seems plausible to judge Shakespeare as sharing in.[63] Scepticism about magic is clearly articulated in *Macbeth*, with its deep psychological and epistemological themes of the appearance-reality distinction. The more ambiguous *Tempest* also has to be read in light of the themes of the shows of pageant [3.3.18-82] and masque [4.1.60-142], and the magic of theatre. The analogy of politics with magic is complicated enough—but we can't avoid adding into the analysis this further, theatrical technology. The technology of the theatre, and the King's Men's abilities and resources to mount spectacular effects, developed over time, with the *Macbeth*, *Lear*, and *Tempest* storms being among the company's great achievements.[64] Politics deploys technologies too—from Machiavelli's recommendation of invisible ink for risky communications[65] to uses of magic for political ends. The practice and projects of the magus involves calming storms, controlling the seasons, controlling persons.[66] Part of Prospero's magic relies on its theatrical nature. His spectacles dazzle and bemuse his audiences, narrowing, as Carlson puts it, his enemies' options until they have 'no choice'.[67]

But politics, magic, and theatre are linked more deeply in two ways. First, is the association of theatre itself with the kind of conjuring and illusion that is diabolical.[68] Just as simultaneously witchcraft and magic are explicable as material (explicable by psychological propensities to see what one believes, and by straightforward trickery and hoax) as well as diabolical, so also theatre

---

[63] Michel de Montaigne. 1588/2006d. 'Of the Lame or Cripple', *The Essays*, Vol. 3, trans. John Florio (The Folio Society: London); Greenblatt, 'Shakespeare and the Exorcists', 1988: 97–100; Butterworth 'The Work of the Devil?', 2008: 705–6; William M. Hamlin. 2013. *Montaigne's English Journey: Reading the Essays in Shakespeare's Day* (Oxford University Press: Oxford).

[64] Donald Carlson. 2015. '"Tis New to Thee": Power, magic and early science in Shakespeare's Tempest', *The Ben Jonson Journal*, 22: 2–4.

[65] Niccolo Machiavelli. 1521/1965. *The Art of War*, ed. Neal Wood, trans. N. Farnsworth (Perseus Books: Cambridge, MA), Bk 7.

[66] Orgel, 'Introduction', 1987: 20; Clark, *Thinking with Demons*, 1997.

[67] Carlson, 'Tis New to Thee', 2015: 18.

[68] Butterworth 'The Work of the Devil?', 2008: 712–13.

can be deceptive and illusory, and also a rational site of citizen sociability, with participation in drama as a valuable training in memory, speech, rhetoric, and comportment. This is Montaigne's argument in his essay on education.[69] But, second, obviously, theatrical performance introduces ambiguity and complexity into the question of speech and meaning. Ambiguity regarding what is said and done, and ambivalence on the part of characters, theatre audiences, and readers alike, regarding their assuredness about what is meant, suffuse both these plays. The problem of who is saying what, to whom, pervades *Macbeth*. Macbeth is haunted by the ambiguity of the weird sisters' words, and their nature [e.g. 3.1.56-71]. He knows that what has happened is not what he foresaw or intended [3.4.135-41]. An implicit adversion to politics can be read here. In speaking together, political actors—especially, but definitely not only, in conditions of sovereign terror—can never be sure how they will be heard or interpreted, and what will be the fate of their utterances later. This is dramatized in the circumspect political speech between thanes in 3.6 and 4.3. The philosophical point is made by Stanley Cavell: words exceed a speaker's grasp, we are incapable of being fully responsible for what we say.[70] Political speech and consequent actions or outcomes do not stand in any clear, predictable, or controllable relation of cause and effect. There is no stable relationship between the uttered symbol and the signified that is taken up by others.

Here, political speech can be compared to the magic spell or incantation that conjures up the magician's production. Both can be intended to bring about effects; both, though, have to be cogitated, interpreted. In particular, both are implicated in riddle and wordplay which, while puzzling, might, or might not be resolved.[71] In politics, any expectation that what is said and what is meant will unfailingly bring about intended consequences is disappointed. This is true in magic too: a curse alone will not bring about an enemy's downfall. The curse, the spell, or the magic word has to be engaged in a series of social transactions for the harm to transpire. The curser can expect to be held accountable for their animus, in the event that harm befalls their enemy—but not because the curse directly brings about the harm. The political

---

[69] Michel de Montaigne. 1580/2006b. 'Of the Institution and Education of Children', in John Florio (trans. and ed.), *The Essayes*, Vol. 1 (The Folio Society: London), p. 175; Hamlin, *Montaigne's English Journey*, 2013; Hugh Grady. 2000. 'Shakespeare's Links to Machiavelli and Montaigne: Constructing intellectual modernity in early modern Europe', *Comparative Literature*, 52: 119–42.

[70] Stanley Cavell. 1987/2003d. 'Macbeth Appalled', *Disowning Knowledge in Seven Plays of Shakespeare*, updated edn (Cambridge University Press: Cambridge), p. 233.

[71] Weimann, *Shakespeare and the Popular Tradition*, 1978: 137.

actor's responsibility for the outcome of their speech—what they are responsible for—exceeds their intention, is despite its ambiguity.

The theatrical, as opposed to the political and the magical, actor's responsibility for what is said and done is even more ambiguous. Shakespeare's drama has been argued to take its own political power seriously. The plays stage political power, and invite the audience to judge the legitimacy and justifiability of power and authority on the stage, and, by implication, power and authority outside the theatre too.[72] In theatre, audiences negotiate between the framework of the play and the framework of the everyday. They comment on characters' actions and conduct, and on actors playing roles. In politics, participants comment on individuals in offices and their actions in office in relation to their actions in the everyday. Citizens negotiate what political actors say, what they mean, and the multiplicity of their effects.

Prospero's epilogue adverts to himself as ruler, who did use magic power but no more, and now has to leave the enchantment of the island and journey back, under the power of sail, to the world of the rule of men [5.1.319-38]. His request to the audience 'Let your indulgence set me free' can be read as a supplication for forgiveness. But more than that, the speech contrasts the island, where he had 'spirits to enforce, art to enchant' with the political world to which he is returning, the one of freedom, mercy, crimes, and pardons; of rule and being ruled. That is, at this point Prospero, and we, can disavow the link between politics and magic and emphasize political power as that human, social, normal, power that we have to rule rule, and to evade it, and to oppose it, and to participate in it. Nothing magic about this. Nevertheless, Prospero also draws attention to himself as actor, bound by the script and the production to the stage and to the audience, whose indulgence—applause—at the end of the performance will set him free. The actor on the stage, playing the part is only a human being with human, not supernatural, powers.

[72] Jean Howard. 2006. 'Dramatic Traditions and Shakespeare's Political Thought', in David Armitage (ed.), *British Political Thought in History, Literature and Theory 1500-1800* (Cambridge University Press: Cambridge); Alan Finlayson and Elizabeth Frazer. 2010. 'Fictions of Sovereignty: Shakespeare, theatre and the representation of rule', *Parliamentary Affairs*, 64: 235; Alain Badiou. 2008. 'Rhapsody for the Theatre: A short philosophical treatise', *Theatre Survey*, 49: 187-238.

8

Politics and Theatre

Hamlet

Political Theatre

In this final chapter, I develop the points about politics and theatre, and bring
them into relationship with the stories of political power that we have met in
this book. All the plays discussed, including *Hamlet*, pose questions to do
with sovereign power and authority—where it comes from, what it does, what
makes it real as opposed to illusory. Economy—the activity and institutions of
trading, accumulation, finance, property, and rent, and the social and cultural
power that is both a direct product and a by-product of market position and
success—sometimes relies on, and sometimes undermines or opposes the
authority of sovereign institutions. In many traditions of political thinking
divine or magical, supernatural power ordains sovereign authority.

In others, sovereign institutions are an articulation, and a specific institu-
tionalization of the political power that is an inevitable feature of human societies. Human beings are inclined not only to submit to or contest the authority
and the domination of those who rule—they are inclined also to argue about
matters, such as by what right those who rule rule, whether rule is being done
in the best way, and whether those who are excluded from governing positions should be permitted, or able to take them up. They also have a distinctive
capability to set up institutions, to argue about and reorganize organizations.
They have the distinctive capability of conducting themselves in a friendly
fashion, permitting disagreement and cooperation. Appearing and speaking
publicly means that in a polity voices are heard or muted, messages processed or
ignored, persons included or excluded.

On that basis, sovereign power is nothing more nor less than the power to
organize power. It is deeply intertwined with the social, economic, cultural,
and religious power that individuals and groups exercise, negotiate, or contest, and comply with in their daily lives. Individuals are subject to power, not
only other people's overt coercion or violence, and not only the constraints or
opportunities that follow from resources or the lack of them, but also the

Shakespeare and the Political Way. Elizabeth Frazer, Oxford University Press (2020). © Elizabeth Frazer.
DOI: 10.1093/oso/9780198848615.001.0001

more deeply settled commonsense, goes without saying, understandings of who is who, and what is what. The proverbs, the jokes, the permissions to pass certain judgements, the metaphors and tropes that make sense, and have descriptive validity in their context—these all disclose the structure of power that arranges the members of the community of these discourses, those who share a language. The forms of power are always subject to political contestation; and established patterns of authority and power—sovereign or otherwise—are also always subject to reflexive challenge.

A prominent theme in Shakespeare criticism is how the language and the plots of the plays rest on a range of taken for granted views of proper social and political relations—notably, patriarchy and the dominance of men over women; the social distinctiveness of ruler from ruled; the stability of the sovereign state; the clarity of the social structural distinctions of race, ethnicity, class, and religion. Such distinctions are often binary—man v. woman, black v. white, good v. evil, natural v. artificial. They often structure plots symbolically: Juliet and her father v. Romeo and his friends; in *Measure for Measure* the Duke and his political appointees v. the common people of the taverns and street; Macbeth v. the witches; Martius's military distinction v. the political canniness of the tribunes; Shylock v. Antonio; Desdemona v. Othello. These distinctions are articulated by characters in ways that takes their reality and rightness for granted—the characters speak of each other as different or the same. In productions, of course, contrasts can be emphasized symbolically, visually, in costume and face paint. They are also articulated in other aspects of speech, in metaphors, styles of address, in jokes, in allusions, which are repetitively emphasized in ways that elicit affective responses from audiences, whether collusive laughter or horror. The repetition problematizes them as they are recycled. These are distinctions that go without saying; but that they are said so often shows that they don't go without saying.

We have, so far, several broad accounts of Shakespearean theatre and politics. First, the plays stage politics—telling stories of the rise and fall of rulers, of the circulation of dominating and resistant power, of the intersection of inter-personal and social relations with politics and government.[1] The Elizabethan theatre can be understood as a place of political education in its broadest meaning. It was not didactic or exhortatory, as the churches were; it was free of the literacy qualification needed to read and discuss treatises and

---

[1] Wilhelm Hortmann. 2002. 'Shakespeare on the Political Stage in the Twentieth Century', in Sarah Stanton and Stanley Wells (eds.), *The Cambridge Companion to Shakespeare on Stage* (Cambridge University Press: Cambridge); David Scott Kastan. 1986. 'Proud Majesty Made Subject: Shakespeare and the spectacle of rule', *Shakespeare Quarterly*, 37(4): 459–75.

other literary works in universities. It played with the principles and rules expounded in grammar schools. In theatrical productions, politics is performed; questions such as who should rule, whether resistance is justified, how trickery and manipulation work, how power is achieved are rehearsed. This can be in an explicitly informative way, as when characters explain to each other or to the audience the relationship between their personal position or dilemma and the background conditions of law, authority, or culture. More elliptically, the importance of keeping women out of public space and from positions of authority is rehearsed and reiterated, and symbolized, in stories and the endless jokes about cuckoldry and whoredom, even as women's capacity for public participation is plotted.[2] The imperative of unified sovereignty is emphasized to an audience transfixed by the spectacles of rape, murder, and torture, and by the victories of honourable violence.[3]

Second, the plays offer commentary, more or less daring and satirical, on political and social life outside of the theatre. The performance of a historical story of a king can be read as a series of comments on the current state, the society, the monarch. Allusions to contemporary events and controversies can be seen as a form of political discussion, whether overt—theatre as political comment and political intervention—or, as political comment so frequently is, safely encoded as jesting and clowning, securely deniable, a matter of coincidence rather than design if any of the characters of the plays bear any resemblance to real people living or dead.

Third, the theatre purveys, in its language, in the incorporation of the audience into the action, in the collusion between playwright, actors, and audience in making meaning, an enactment of politics that goes further than showings, tellings, or symbolizations of it. Theatre audiences are called upon to suspend disbelief—to enter the world of the play, ignoring or bracketing the economic and physical materiality of the theatre, the staff, the catering, the seating. They have to engage with the characters, both as such and also as productive performances by an actor, whose success in the performance is judgeable, just as the character is judgeable. Audience members also have to treat with their fellow audience members. Annabel Patterson emphasizes the Elizabethan and Jacobean theatre as a social 'heterocosm'—in this it is like the city streets.[4] One interpretation of this is that the early modern theatre achieved a unity of

    [2] Lisa Jardine. 1983/1989. *Still Harping on Daughters: Women and Drama in the Age of Shakespeare* (Columbia University Press: New York); Marilyn L.Williamson. 1986. *The Patriarchy of Shakespeare's Comedies* (Wayne State University Press: Detroit, MI).
    [3] Leonard Tennenhouse. 1986/2005. *Power on Display: The Politics of Shakespeare's Genres* (Methuen: London).
    [4] Annabel Patterson. 1989. *Shakespeare and the Popular Voice* (Basil Blackwell: Oxford), p. 17.

taste, a publically endorsed culture of 'mingle-mangle of all sorts and conditions'.[5] Robert Weimann quotes Hamlet: 'The toe of the peasant comes near the heel of the courtier' [5.1.132-4] (Hamlet is talking about changing times, and about death—the leveller that means (via burial, decay, and growth) that the body of a king passes through the guts of a beggar [4.3.20-31]). More sceptically, we can observe the social mechanisms for separation rather than for mingling, in the theatre. Tiers divide the audience by money and class. Cities can be zoned so as to minimize heterogeneity; some streets, but only some, are truly open to all. Perhaps rather than mingle-mangle we have juxtaposition. Perhaps, as Patterson suggests, rather than mixing we have self-conscious 'slumming it' by the rich, and, ironically or not, consciously joining in a 'superior' cultural form by the poor.[6]

This indeterminacy of the nature of the tie between the co-participants in theatrical audience serves to reinforce the analogy with polity. The votes of the tribes contribute to the votes of the polity; the tribes are intact. Members of classes, or party members, or, sometimes, individuals speak or vote or pass judgement from a particular standpoint, confirming the differentiated nature of the general polity, the society, the state. The audience to theatre are distanced from the spectacular glimpses of glamour for which they have paid, glamour that they know, at some level, to be show, to be dazzlement, to be underpinned by a perfectly ordinary body like their own, a person somewhat like themselves. Similarly, political participation—whether it's disagreement or deliberation about policy, or judgement about who rules, or protest—requires suspension of disbelief. We focus on candidates and officers, their conduct and action; we also think about the human individuals who are entwined in their roles.

Thomas Hobbes was thinking of the classical theatre, with its masks and 'personae', as he emphasized this artificial nature of political ties and political power.[7] For Hannah Arendt, the theatre is the political art, par excellence. It is the only one 'whose sole subject is man in his relationship to others'. The actors are play-acting, to be sure. But in so doing they are imitating acting, which all of us must do. It is this repetition that reveals, to audiences, and to the actors themselves, what it is to be related to others publicly.[8] Persons as audience members, or as polity members, are actors in character, just as much as they are persons, relating to actors in character and to the persons.

[5] Robert Weimann. 1978. *Shakespeare and the Popular Tradition in Theater: Studies in the Social Dimension of Dramatic Form and Function* (Johns Hopkins University Press: Baltimore), pp. 172–4.
[6] Patterson, *Shakespeare*, 1989: 18.
[7] Thomas Hobbes. 1651/1996. *Leviathan* (Oxford University Press: Oxford), Ch. XXI.
[8] Hannah Arendt. 1958. *The Human Condition* (University of Chicago Press: Chicago), pp. 186–8.

Of course, the nature and depth of this participation varies with the play, and the kind of political and social reflection that is enjoined varies with the nature of the production. Witnessing a performance of sovereign violence, and of the powerlessness, abjection, and reduction of its victims, is a different way of engaging with the nature of state than is a spectacular song and dance routine. Both prompt reflection on the ethics and politics of the characters, but in a different style from listening to and trying to understand soliloquy and dialogue. Special effects such as storms and action sequences of battle or riot inflect political relationships differently from perfect poetry.

But, clowning or melodrama, social realism or stripped down human bodies—none of these theatrical styles eclipses politics. The plays are still about who rules, who wins, how they hold onto or lose dominance; how rights, legitimacy, justification can be achieved, and the nature of the power and authority that characters wield over one another and that hold them in their relative places. On the other hand, theatrical effects—the theatre company's capacity to make a storm, or to produce an apparition, or to act a scene of violence—are always appreciated by the audience by way of the suspension of disbelief and also judged in terms of success. The audience thinks about the storm, or the battle, or the apparition, or the violence in the context of the drama; and they also evaluate whether or not the storm, battle, apparition, or fight was convincing, realistic; whether it had the effect of an actual one, or whether it was symbolically successful. There are parallels here with our judgements of a politician's speech and their actions, of the effectiveness of a policy or a government. We think about what they did, and how they did it, and what they really, not ostensibly, did, and what they seemed to do.

My further consideration of theatricality and politics—the place of theatre in politics, the theatrical representation and discussion of politics, the analogies between theatrical production and performance, and the practice of politics itself—is going to be in the context of readings of *Hamlet* (about 1602). In *Hamlet*, all the themes so far discussed—friendship, violence, speech, affect and emotion, the body politic, popular sovereignty, patriarchy, territory, social and supernatural power, confidence and uncertainty, appearance and reality, political roles and action—are present in the text.

Hamlet and Politics

Prince Hamlet has returned from university to Elsinore, the royal court in Denmark, on the death of the king, his father, old Hamlet. The old king's brother, Claudius, who has married Hamlet's mother Gertrude, has become king. The play begins with the appearance of a ghost to the guards of the fortifications of Elsinore [1.1], and our introduction to Hamlet's very unhappy place in the court—he is overtly grieving, appalled that his mother has remarried so soon after his father's death [1.2.63-159]. His friend Horatio believes the ghost to be that of Hamlet's father [1.1.40-59], and duly the ghost and Hamlet meet [1.4.17-61]. The ghost condemns his widow for her sexual depravity, tells Hamlet that Claudius had murdered him, and demands that Hamlet exact vengeance [1.5.1-91]. Claudius and Gertrude are concerned at Hamlet's conduct—his grief, his anger and anti-social behaviour. They invite Hamlet's university friends—Rosencrantz and Guildenstern—to Elsinore hoping they will cheer Hamlet up [2.2.1-36]. Hamlet also has a romantic love relationship with Ophelia, the daughter of privy council member Polonius. Ophelia is, of course, under the emotional and authoritative control of her father and her brother Laertes, who both believe that a marriage is impossible because of differences in Hamlet's and Ophelia's status. Accordingly, they both instruct her to reject Hamlet's advances [1.3.1-44, 89-136]. Laertes leaves Denmark to travel to France [1.2.50-63].

So, to begin with, we see Hamlet in a typically complex social context. He is angry with his mother and dislikes his step-father. He is connected in egalitarian friendship with Horatio, Rosencrantz, and Guildenstern; is alienated from the culture of the court; and has been politically displaced from sovereign authority. There is an ostensible puzzle, given monarchical conventions of primogeniture and male succession, why Hamlet has not automatically inherited the throne. In some systems, including Denmark, traditionally succession was a matter of election, although as heir to the old king, Hamlet does have a claim. Commentators see in *Hamlet* allusion to the interest of the Danish monarch, and significance of the Danish constitution in questions about James I's succession to Elizabeth 1.[9] The court is the site of Claudius's political skill, statesmanship, and authority. He has evidently constructed allegiances and secured assent to his accession [1.2.1-16]; and is skilfully managing a difficult foreign policy challenge. Old Fortinbras, king of Norway, had been killed by old Hamlet in a challenge which saw exchange of territory from Norway to Denmark [1.1.80-107]. Young Fortinbras, nephew of the current king of

---

[9] Stuart M. Kurland. 1994. 'Hamlet and the Scottish Succession?'. *Studies in English Literature 1500-1900*, 34(2): 279–300; Ronald B. Jenkins. 2015. 'Prince Hamlet and the Problem of Succession', *ANQ: Quarterly Journal of Short Articles, Notes and Reviews*, 28(2): 63–7.

Norway, opportunistically taking advantage of the unsettlement of Denmark on the death of the old king, now wants the territory back [1.2.16-41].

Hamlet's grief and anger about the marriage will strike modern audiences as intelligible. His conviction mingled with doubt about Claudius's guilt, the emotional and psychological pressure following his encounter with the ghost, his wish to avenge his father's death, his distaste for the politics and government of the country develop into a strategy of acting mad (madder than he really is) in order to evade the efforts of his mother and friends to normalize him, to try to establish more clearly Claudius's guilt or innocence, and to further his project of vengeance. Polonius (who is by instinct a gossip and a plotter, a purveyor of hackneyed versions of social convention and humanist ethics, and not insightful about other people) is determined to get to the truth about the causes of Hamlet's conduct, and recruits Claudius and Gertrude into a series of stratagems to observe Hamlet and catch him out. One of these involves setting Ophelia, secretly observed by her father and Claudius, into converse with Hamlet. In the course of this encounter Hamlet is misogynistically insulting to Ophelia [3.1.91ff]. This performance determines Claudius and Polonius that Hamlet should be sent away to England. A theatrical troupe comes to Elsinore [2.2.312-15, 414f]; and Hamlet hits upon the device of asking them to perform a play about a regicide and the usurper's seduction of the murdered king's wife. His hope is that the shock of this performance will cause Claudius's bad conscience to be revealed. Indeed, at the critical point in the performance—when the murderer pours poison into the king's ear—Claudius does, of a sudden, rise and exit together with his attendants [3.2.249-54].

In this telling, I have set out motivations and reasons for Hamlet's conduct, actions, and speech, and emphasized the theme of machiavellian subterfuge as an individual strategy to gain advantage. But a deep feature of this play, one that makes it so significant in literature, is that we are very uncertain about both motivation and meaning. Critics vary between thinking of Hamlet as a procrastinator (assuming that he has a duty, which he accepts, to avenge his father's murder) and focusing on his deep sexual ambivalence, which is reflected in his relationships with and conduct to both Ophelia and his mother. We don't know whether Hamlet's conduct is evidence of his real emotional instability and social untrustworthiness, or is feigned.[10] I have described his relationships of friendship with Horatio, Rosencrantz, and Guildenstern. *Hamlet* can be cited for its adversion to the ideal of the humanistically educated prince who combines 'courtier, soldier, scholar', and for

---

[10] Jenkins, 'Hamlet and Succession', 2015: 66-7.

whom friendship is significant.[11] But it can also be read as Shakespeare's unmasking of the pretensions of humanist ethics and philosophy.[12] The text has been read as suggesting that Hamlet had not actually been at the university studying at all, but had been leading a dissolute life with theatrical people.[13] Among the evidence adduced for this interpretation is that Hamlet, at the outset, is unsure of Horatio's name [I.2.161-2]; his relationship with Rosencrantz and Guildenstern is the opposite of trusting friendship [2.2.270-310]; by contrast, he knows the players individually and greets them like comrades [2.2.413-21]. This deflation of Hamlet as a virtuous prince dismantles, also, classical theories of political relations. Friendship, the social networks that empower individuals vis-à-vis the authorities that govern them are irrelevant when individuals are as unstable and uncertain as Hamlet is, or when overweening violence governs the world.

Similarly, the players' performance of 'The Murder of Gonzago' and the trap to catch the king [2.2.577-94] is often thought to evidence Claudius's guilt. After the play Hamlet believes Claudius to be guilty. The ethic of revenge prescribes that he now should kill him, preferably in a manner that makes it clear to Claudius, as he dies, why [3.3.72-7]. But, of course, there is still doubt. There are grounds to believe that the ghost is a ghost, that its testimony is veridical, that its wishes are prescriptions. But there are also grounds for scepticism that such apparitions can really be a guide to truth, can really exert authority.[14] Similarly, human social actions, what they mean and signify are dubious. Leaving a theatrical performance in the middle is notable; but the point of sovereign monarchy is that the king can do what he feels like doing: his whims as well as his judgements are authoritative. The audience, but not Hamlet himself, later hear Claudius confess: 'O, my offence is rank, it smells to heaven. It hath the primal eldest curse upon't—a brother's murder'... [3.3.36-72]. Hamlet sees Claudius at this moment, but there is no textual hint that he hears his words; Claudius is kneeling as if in prayer but 'pray I cannot' [3.3.38]. Hamlet hesitates—he believes that Claudius is at prayer, so in a state of grace, and the point of revenge against a murderer is that the murderer must go to hell [3.3.73-82].

---

[11] Quentin Skinner. 1978. *The Foundations of Modern Political Thought*. Vol. 1: *The Renaissance* (Cambridge University Press: Cambridge), p. 91.

[12] Rhodri Lewis. 2017. *Hamlet and the Vision of Darkness* (Princeton University Press: Princeton), pp. 10, 18.

[13] Jenkins, 'Hamlet and Succession', 2015.

[14] Stanley Cavell. 1987/2003c. 'Hamlet's Burden of Proof', *Disowning Knowledge in Seven Plays of Shakespeare*, updated edn (Cambridge University Press: Cambridge), pp. 180–2.

In any case, Hamlet, like the ghost of his father, is conflicted between obsession with Claudius's guilt and Gertrude's.[15] Polonius, still intent on catching Hamlet out [3.3.27-9] is concealed in Gertrude's room when Hamlet confronts her, urged on by a further appearance of the ghost. Detecting a spy hidden behind a curtain, Hamlet kills Polonius (he does not know who he has killed—it might be Claudius [3.4.26-8]). Claudius now has reason to send Hamlet away immediately, and we know—he discloses it to the theatre audience—that he has asked the king of England to have Hamlet assassinated [4.3.60-9]. Ophelia is broken hearted and deranged by her father's death, and dies by drowning [4.7.137-58]. Luckily—or simply because he does not trust Rosencrantz or Guildenstern, or Claudius—on board the ship that is carrying him to England, Hamlet discovers Claudius's letters to England and rewrites them with instructions that Rosencrantz and Guildenstern, who are accompanying him, be killed [5.2.1-60]. Luckily, pirates overrun the ship, and he escapes and returns to Elsinore [4.6.11-29]. He is challenged to a duel, a fencing match, by Laertes who has returned to Denmark on the death of his father, and has planned with Claudius that he will use a poisoned foil that will kill Hamlet [4.7.58-137]. Claudius poisons a cup of the wine to be drunk at the match, which Gertrude, in error, drinks [5.2.239-44]. The poisoned rapier wounds Hamlet; in the course of the fight he and Laertes exchange rapiers and it then wounds Laertes also [5.2.253-75]. Hamlet stabs Claudius, and forces him to drink from the poisoned cup and, in order to prevent Horatio committing suicide, also drinks from it [5.2.279-302]. As he dies, Hamlet, who is Claudius's named heir [I.2.108-12], prophesies that 'th'election lights on Fortinbras. He has my dying voice' [5.2.306-11]. Into this scene of death come English ambassadors to report to Claudius that Rosencrantz and Guildenstern are dead; young Fortinbras arrives with them [5.2.315].

Hamlet can be interpreted as one of Shakespeare's peerless humanist creations: the educated prince whose father dies in doubtful circumstances, whose mother marries his father's brother, whose consequent emotional and psychological anguish generates an extraordinary study of a human individual in relationship with himself—with the confusion of his emotions, with his wish for revenge, with his conflicted relation with his own capacity for violence. Hamlet challenges the ethics of the court presided over by his uncle the new king, condemning the hypocrisy of politics in the name of authenticity and truth on the part of individuals. However, he has to act a part in order to find and act on the truth. So Hamlet, the character, is a crucial instance not

---

[15] Jardine, *Still Harping on Daughters*, 1983/1989: 71, 92, 127-8.

only of self-consciousness and interiority, but also of the individual struggling with the compromises of social norms and of political logic. The play is also received as an extraordinarily insightful study of intimate family conflict, especially a child's contradictory feelings about mother, and father, and his mother's attachments to others. Hamlet's fascinated disgust with Gertrude's sexuality can be interpreted in the terms of Sigmund Freud's construction of the Oedipal myth and its place in human psychic development. This, actually, is by the authority of Freud himself, for whom *Hamlet*, together with Sophocles' *Oedipus Rex*, is a primary source in *The Interpretation of Dreams* (1900).[16] Obviously, it would be perverse to ignore the story of *Hamlet* as a family drama, as a study of sexuality, and of generational and parental relations.

Like *Macbeth* and *Tempest*, *Hamlet* is also a story of the intersection of the natural, social, and political worlds with supernatural forces, the occult powers that are hidden from our usual daily view of the world we inhabit but which may be understood by 'philosophers' [1.1, 1.4] In *Hamlet* it is not the magical, but the ghostly, the spectres of human lives past which linger on, in communication with us in the present.[17] Banquo's ghost reproaches and terrorizes Macbeth, reminding him of his guilt. The ghost of Hamlet's father demands that he be avenged, for his wife's sexual betrayal and viciousness, and for his brother's crime of murder. The appearance of the ghost on the battlements of Elsinore makes Horatio politically apprehensive: 'in the gross and scope of mine opinion, this bodes some strange eruption to our state' [1.1.68-9], echoed later by Marcellus's 'something is rotten in the state of Denmark' [1.4.65]. Both of them signal the relationship between the supernatural and the political; at least, politics gone wrong. Whether we interpret these themes as a realistic theatrical depiction of Shakespeare's society, with its beliefs in supernatural phenomena, or as a comment on, an instance of the emerging materialist scepticism about the supernatural, the ghost symbolizes the disorder of a wrongful succession, the wrongful politics of the court that keeps the usurper in power, and the sexual disorder of the early marriage of the old king's widow. It foreshadows the violence and the deaths. Horatio is afraid that the ghost is a diabolical manifestation to make Hamlet mad [1.4.43-54]. Structurally and symbolically this foreshadows Hamlet's subsequent actions and conduct—whether it is genuine disorder of mind or acting out that dominates Hamlet's mad behaviour.

---

[16] Sigmund Freud. 1900/2010. *The Interpretation of Dreams*, trans. James Strachey (Basic Books: New York), pp. 282-3.

[17] Cavell, 'Hamlet', 1987/2003c: 188-9; Jacques Derrida. 1993/1994. *Specters of Marx: The State of Debt, the Work of Mourning and the New International* (Routledge: London), pp. 1-16.

According to these interpretations, *Hamlet* is a play about which we should say that the political setting—state, court, foreign policy, elected monarch, alleged usurpation, and regicide—is simply the frame for a tragic psychological and ethical drama, which might just as well take place entirely within the confines of a household and family. Shakespeare's sources supply the setting of monarchy and court; but, in his work, state, government, and politics is the frame only for emotions and feelings, for truth and dishonesty, for violence and sex, love and hate. *Hamlet* is very long, and does not fit nicely into the conventional timeframe of much late modern theatre performance, so cuts are necessary.[18] Obvious candidates are the relatively long speeches and conversations about the political and diplomatic ins and outs of the relationships and arguments between the king of Norway, his nephew Fortinbras, Claudius who is now king of Denmark, his predecessor Hamlet's father, and the Poles about territory [1.1.80-107, 1.2.17-41, 2.2.58-85]. Productions which de-emphasize this foreign policy problem mean that Fortinbras can seem to arrive like a stranger who just happens upon a dreadful scene, and is in a position to make externally based judgement about what's happened, while lacking the internal understanding that makes the awful so intelligible [5.2.302-56].[19]

Such interpretations can also emphasize the existential, absurdist aspect of the tragic deaths, and the themes of 'accident' and 'coincidence' which structure the play. The players just happen to arrive at an opportune moment. The ship happens to be overrun by pirates. Gertrude picks up the wrong cup of wine. In their fencing match the foils of Laertes and Hamlet are unintentionally swapped. These themes of accident or temporal coincidence just like the themes of psychological pressure, emotional pain and grief, parental control of children and children's desire for parents, and supernatural interventions and signs operate to depoliticize the play.

I certainly don't want to argue that the loss and gain of territories in Poland is centrally what Shakespeare tells us a story about in *Hamlet*. But, as Bullough argues, it equally can seem that, rather than focusing at the individual level, Shakespeare expands the scope and focus of the story, compared to his sources, away from inter-personal passion and violence, to take in the courtly society and culture, international connections, and the political challenges to

    [18] G.R. Hibbard. ed. 1987. 'Introduction', William Shakespeare, *Hamlet* (Oxford University Press: Oxford), pp. 1, 19f.
    [19] Jan Kott. 1964. *Shakespeare our Contemporary*, trans. Boleslaw Taborski (W. W. Norton: New York), pp. 72-3.

rule.[20] Horatio and Marcellus, for instance, interpret the ghost's appearance as a sign that wrong or disaster is devolving on the state. Perhaps this focus on politics conceals from them the more ethically significant evil and disaster that is about to befall individuals and social relationships; what seems to them to be a matter of state and society could really be a matter of personality and inter-personal relationships. That is the line of Freud's reasoning. He saw in Hamlet, as he saw in the tale of Oedipus, a deeply located symptom of emotional and sexual conflict, one which warrants focusing on the individual characters of Hamlet, Claudius, Gertrude, both in relation to each other and in relation to their inner lives. But equally we can see that there are independent ethical reasons for individuals to be cognizant of the structures, the systems, and the authorities that govern, and to cultivate the capacities to challenge, participate in, and cooperatively shift those structures, systems, and authorities in the direction of justice. There is a 'character' dimension to this political imperative.

This way of putting it points to a fundamental problem of political theory—one with a history, the exact puzzle about which changes over time and across contexts. The early modern period is often, plausibly, read as seeing a displacement of consciousness from mysterious power—whether of the monarch or of god, or of supernatural forces and apparitions—to the personal, inner life of individuals and their effects on each other. Shakespeare is identified as a key figure, of course, in this 'emergence of individualism', with a new ethics, new forms of freedom (and new forms of subjection). In the modern period and late modernity the puzzle has been rather the other way. Individuals are more likely to attribute to personal circumstances and characteristics what is more properly seen as political—social facts like differential wealth, earning, educational achievement, propensity to violence, health, etc., are likely to be attributed to individual virtues and vices, although they should be seen, according to materialist analyses, as a function of social and political structures of power. Those who challenge injustice and hierarchy fight to establish that 'natural', or 'divinely ordained', or individual facts are political constructions. The history of social movements is a history of individuals coming to see class disadvantage, or racism, or sexism as characteristics of system and structure, not matters of individual capacity or failing.[21]

---

[20] Geoffrey Bullough. ed. 1973. 'Hamlet', *Narrative and Dramatic Sources of Shakespeare*, Vol. 7 (Routlege and Kegan Paul: London), p. 59; Lewis, *Hamlet and the Vision of Darkness*, 2017: 1–9.

[21] Mary Wollstonecraft. 1792/1994. 'A Vindication of the Rights of Woman', in Janet Todd (ed.), *Mary Wollstonecraft: Political Writings* (Oxford University Press: Oxford), Ch. IX; Cecil Wright Mills. 1959. *The Sociological Imagination* (Oxford University Press: Oxford), Ch. 1.

Shakespeare's insights contribute to this quizzical questioning. Among the political theory questions that *Hamlet* poses are how, exactly, supernatural, social, and political powers and forces interact and intersect. These stories raise, in very direct form, the question of whether acting politically really is admirable and what vicious forms of political action do to individuals and to polities. And, more directly than other plays discussed in this book, *Hamlet* puts before us the theatrical nature of political power, posing the question of the ethical meaning and value of that.

Politics and Sovereignty

Claudius is in a very vexed situation vis-à-vis his own claims of sovereignty. Obviously, the problem is that he is a regicide, and therefore has by definition usurped sovereign power. Even absent the regicide, if the play is read in terms of the English, and Scottish, constitutions then he is definitely a usurper, as Hamlet is the normally rightful heir, and is of an age to rule.[22] Judged by the Danish constitution it is not so clear, as the monarchy was elective. But the electoral body observed the convention that it would usually elect the heir of the deceased monarch.[23] Unlike Macbeth, Claudius is not a tyrant: he is a statesman. Macbeth the regicide and usurper is quickly enmeshed in extreme violence. By contrast Claudius—the regicide, the fratricide, the usurpation, and the attempted assassination of Hamlet notwithstanding—undoubtedly has political resources. He maintains the allegiance of key actors—the court, the queen, political advisors.

For some interpreters this fact of conciliation and the maintenance of allegiance contributes to the theme of 'something rotten in the state'. It is evidence enough to support the interpretation of a corrupt court culture. Murder, usurpation or not, crime to be concealed or no, there is that deep duplicity to politics and political speech such that it is a kind of crime, whether or not it conceals a legal crime or an evil act like murder. G.R. Hibbard focuses on Claudius's logical, deliberative, efficient speech, his circumspection and insertion of caveats into his remarks, seeing these as signs of the corruption—the hypocrisy, the falsity, the artfulness and double talk—of the court. Claudius's assumption, as he tries to deal with the Hamlet problem among others, is that all, like him, seek favour, are ambitious. In the case of the obsequious courtier Osric (reviled by

[22] Lewis, *Hamlet and the Vision of Darkness*, 2017: 315–24; Jenkins, 'Hamlet and Succession', 2015: 64.
[23] Jenkins, 'Hamlet and Succession', 2015: 63–4; Kurland, 'Hamlet and Scottish Succession?', 1994: 298–9n.53.

Hamlet and Horatio) this is confirmed [5.2.104-45]; and Rosencrantz and Guildenstern, on one interpretation, readily enough take the opportunity to serve the monarch, rather than working with the grain of trust and friendship to find out what Hamlet's really thinking and up against. Claudius's presiding over this political culture is sign enough of his ethical shortcomings.[24]

More significant than this generalized suspicion of political action and reason, Claudius has a problem with sovereignty. He knows, obviously enough, that he is not sovereign in the sense of 'god's anointed'; nor has his route to the succession been the conventional one of being heir to the old king, unless there is something we don't know about old Hamlet's will.[25] If he really believes in divinely ordained sovereignty, then he must know that he is not sovereign. If he does not believe in it, then he must know that governing power is based on something else. But Claudius continues to play the part of sovereign. In a breathtaking episode, Laertes, seeking vengeance for the death of his father, and having gathered supporters from among the people (some of whom are evidently liable to rise up against the regime which features this death rate, the departure of Hamlet, and so on) arrives at the court 'with his followers' [4.5.108-9]. Gertrude lays hold of him. Claudius stays calm:

> Let him go, Gertrude. Do not fear our person. There's such divinity doth
> hedge a king that treason can but peep to what it would, acts little of his will.
>
> [4.5.120-3]

Hibbard observes that this is 'supremely ironical', which it is, and identifies it as 'true hypocrisy on a grand scale'[26]—which it, kind of, is. But, we can observe, if there is such a thing as sovereignty, it must always be performed; its ontological and ethical status is always supremely doubtful; and if it has any foundation or source of validity that must be political power, albeit frequently parading as something else—as the will of god or as natural law. So perhaps Claudius's performance of sovereignty is more veridical than, say, James I's—for Claudius knows what James really cannot acknowledge, that final power is never final, always fragile, always a performance, and if it is held in place by anything it has to be political power, backed up with violence. Among Claudius's forms of political power are competent and canny statesmanship. Like the Duke of Venice in *Othello*, Claudius capably deals with ambassadors and staff, organizes and deploys defensive military force. His

---

[24] Hibbard, 'Introduction', 1987: 42–3; Hortmann, 'Shakespeare on the Political Stage', 2002.
[25] Jenkins, 'Hamlet and Succession', 2015: 64.
[26] Hibbard, 'Introduction', 1987: 304n.

communication with the king of Norway is successful; Claudius's hunch about his, and Fortinbras's, motivations and relationships, prove to be well-founded [2.2.60-79].

It's certainly the case that Hamlet himself is angry at the court culture as much as at his mother's and uncle's marriage. When we first meet him, he contrasts court hypocrisy and dissimulation with his own authenticity and truth. He is not 'seeming' to grieve, he *is* grieving [I.2.75-86]. He justifies sending Rosencrantz and Guildenstern to their deaths not only because he doesn't trust them, but because those who live by spying will die by spying. They need not have taken the job that Claudius offered them [5.2.58-9]. Similarly, when he kills Polonius—not meaning, exactly, to kill Polonius—he quickly justifies the deed by Polonius's conduct [3.4.32-3] and condemns him as a 'prating knave' [3.4.193-5]. But of course, Hamlet himself engages in trickery to catch the king—speaking with ambiguous meaning; playing on others' weaknesses in order to infuriate and outwit them. It is part clowning (he gets all the best comic lines), and part machiavellian scheming. As soon as he protests that where the courtiers dissimulate he is what he seems, it becomes clear that he does not know what he is. His ruthlessness with his enemies—Claudius, Polonius, Rosencrantz, and Guildenstern—of course is intelligible in the light of the fact that they are his enemies. In political terms, we must know who is with us, who against us; in the context of regicide, and Claudius's hold on power, it would not be wrong to Hamlet to fear for his own life. Such considerations stem from the reality of sovereign monarchy, the interests and conduct of courtiers and claimants, friends and foes, in a context in which opposition and dissent are intelligibly and justifiably counted as treachery, and in which treachery is repayable with death.

Another kind of politics is also at work in the play—the popular sovereign power or claims of the populace.[27] In Denmark, a council or body of electors decides who has sovereign office. But there are also the common people to be considered. The stability of sovereign monarchy based on an aristocratic class hierarchy can never be wholly secure; a critical aspect of political power is that it is the power that maintains a pattern of rule, but it must perforce be a constant process of negotiating the challenges to that rule. These come from forces external to it—as, the people in an aristocratic, monarchical system. Or from within it, as, in an elite system, Claudius has to look to the threats from Hamlet, or from Laertes. A democracy is a more or less precarious balance between the

---

[27] Tennenhouse, *Power on Display*, 1986/2005: 88–91.

citizenry and others.[28] After Polonius's death, Laertes returns and, because suspicion regarding Polonius's death has fallen on the court in general, on Claudius as much as on banished Hamlet, he succeeds in generating popular support for his claims: 'The rabble call him lord;...they cry "Choose we, Laertes shall be king"..' [4.5.95-105]. The facts of the Danish constitution, just like the facts of the hereditary monarchical constitution of England, cannot remove the fact of popular political power and the propensity, from time to time, of the people to assert it, or attempt to, whether in proclamation or in protest. The means that governors can deploy in order to evade the voices of the populace—defining popular requests as impertinence, popular protest as treason, suggestions of constitutional change as treachery, or, as Claudius does, neutralizing the leaders—varies, according to constitution, obviously, but also according to political circumstances. Claudius does successfully neutralize Laertes. His assertion of divine protection notwithstanding, he successfully persuades Laertes of his (Claudius's) innocence in the matter of Polonius's death, of Hamlet's guilt, and he recruits Laertes into the plan to challenge Hamlet to a public duel, and to ensure Hamlet's death by that means.

In *Hamlet*, then, in familiar Shakespearean style, we have numerous accounts of politics. First, we have politics as the achievement and deployment of sovereignty, with all the dilemmas and difficulties that that involves. Connectedly, we have political power in the sense of the power that some dominators achieve and maintain to dominate a territory, and the people and resources in it. But the achievement of this dominance, whether under the guise of sovereignty, as with Claudius, or simply under the guise of might and influence, as with the patriarchs in *Romeo and Juliet*, always has to be shored up by attention to the threats against it. Politics is the process by which individuals and groups are counted, in or out, as adversaries worth reckoning with or as irrelevant. We have politics—the achievement and maintenance of the power to govern—as mendacity, trickery, cunning, and manipulation; we have sneaky uses of deadly violence. We have politics as an essentially public matter, in which—notwithstanding how formal, constitutionally mandated, functional powers and authority are distributed between institutions and offices—the voices and the conduct of those who are governed are as much to be taken into account as those of the governors. We also have politics in the sense of domination by parental, patriarchal, power.

---

[28] Tennenhouse, *Power on Display*, 1986/2005: 91.

Patriarchy and Misogyny

Polonius is a key political character in *Hamlet*, the kind who gives politics—in the sense of participation in a court setting around a ruler, the function of advice and service to a sovereign—a bad name. Polonius is present when Claudius meets with ambassadors and other councillors, forwarding his son Laertes's request for permission to leave the court and travel to France [1.2.42-62]. This permission is one bit of sovereign business for Claudius; it follows his discussions and transactions with councillors and ambassadors; and precedes his turning to Hamlet to see what's the matter with him. Structurally, we can see a parallel with the opening scene in *Othello*, where the Duke deals with foreign policy, and turns to deal with Brabantio's complaint about his daughter's elopement. The family structures of the polity are the business of government. Hamlet, we can infer, is justifiably resentful at being treated as a bit of business; and his reply to Claudius is quite in contrast with Laertes's and Polonius's supplication to their monarch. Polonius serves Claudius—bringing in the ambassadors on their return from their Norwegian envoy [2.2.40] and offering his opinion [2.2.85]; he brings the news of the actors' arrival to Hamlet [2.2.384-7]. Polonius is a councillor—a stereotypically hair-splitting, non-sequitur-uttering 'advisor' whose advice comes well wrapped up in self-regarding irrelevance.

We see Polonius mainly in relation to his son and his daughter; his relationship with them is mediated by his relation with the monarch, but equally his relationships with Claudius and with Gertrude are mediated by his paternal relationships with his children. He subjects Laertes and Ophelia to the kind of advice that we hope he does not offer to the king, although we fear that his unselfconsciousness might mean that he does. He lists for Laertes instructions on how to speak, how to act with friends and with strangers, how to spend his money, what the French are like [1.3.55-81]. Laertes might well resent this long disquisition, but he is the inheritor of his father's peremptory prescriptive style and authority when it comes to his sister. Before he has to endure Polonius's advice to him, he treats Ophelia to a similar litany of advice about how she should behave to Hamlet, what Hamlet's attitude and motivations regarding her must be, about Hamlet's station in life compared with hers [I.3.6-44]. Ophelia is spirited enough to reproach him with hypocrisy: 'Do not…show me the steep and thorny way to heaven, whilst like a puffed and reckless libertine himself the primrose path of dalliance treads and recks not his own rede' [1.3.47-51].

The political style of advice, and the parental and patriarchal styles, intersect and interact. They can both be reproached for the way the message is couched: uninterrupted speech, with many points.[29] Popular understanding of boring political speech is one reason why politics as such is disliked. And speakers can be charged with hypocrisy: offering advice about conduct which the speaker can hardly live up to. Polonius precedes his admonition to Laertes: 'to thine own self be true, and it must follow, as the night the day, thou canst not then to be false to any man' [I.3.78-82] by being true to himself, and false to his son. He sets a spy—Laertes's companion Reynaldo—to report back on Laertes's conduct [2.1.1-70]. This pattern of exercise of patriarchal power by spying, concealment, secret communication, tricks, and traps, contrasts both with an ideal of open political conduct and with Laertes's openly authoritarian, judgemental, and domineering approach to his sister.

Patriarchal power is inherited from fathers by sons, and is exerted over sisters as much as over daughters. It is, in Pateman's word, fraternal.[30] Father power can be displaced, legally, and the systematic oppression of women continue. Laertes's admonitions to Ophelia tell the familiar story of the probability that Hamlet would besmirch and despoil Ophelia—attributing weakness to women and sexual predation to men, and putting all the responsibility on Ophelia: Hamlet cannot be trusted with Ophelia's virtue or her well-being; it is up to Ophelia to guard herself and keep out of reach [I.3.10-44]. Patriarchal power is a matter of right and authority: who has the right and the authority to give orders to whom? Ophelia's riposte to Laertes is spirited and just; but any moral right she has on her side does not imply that she has authority in the matter. Second, though, there is a content to patriarchal power: the definition of gender in terms of sexuality (not just sex), the association of male sexuality with predation or at least dominance, and women's with susceptibility, and further than this the association of female body and sexuality with corruption. This story of female weakness and susceptibility to being seduced is, though, given a number of twists by Hamlet himself, first in his encounter with Ophelia and then in his confrontation with Gertrude. His misogynistic discourse about, and to, Ophelia and Gertrude outdoes Lear's diatribes about and to Regan and Gonoril.

Ophelia obeys Polonius's and Laertes's wish that she should refuse Hamlet's advances. Hamlet is affecting, or is uttering, difficult to comprehend,

---

[29] Hibbard, 'Introduction', 1987: 34.
[30] Carole Pateman. 1989. 'The Fraternal Social Contract', *The Disorder of Women* (Polity Press: Cambridge).

pressured speech—either a symptom of his disturbance or a strategy to confuse and torment his foes. In an encounter with Polonius, whom he has already insulted in sexual terms [2.2.174], he associates Ophelia, seemingly, with sexual and physical decay and corruption [2.2.181-90]. The point, strategically, is to upset Polonius; the manner of doing so is damaging to Ophelia, and to women generally. If Hamlet's anger or distress at being separated from Ophelia is motivation enough for insulting Polonius, this does not sufficiently account for his insult to Ophelia—except that, in patriarchy, this is an insult to her father more than to her.[31] In the staged encounter with Ophelia, when she has been instructed to return Hamlet's gifts, they begin speaking gently enough, but Ophelia's meanings are misunderstood by Hamlet, he immediately shifts to questioning her honesty, the relationship between honesty and beauty, and he interprets her words, and the dilemma between them, in terms of sexual depravity—prostitution, the breeding of sinners, culminating in the celebrated 'get thee to a nunnery' [3.1.91-141].[32]

In the frame of patriarchal political power, the insult to Ophelia is insult to her father and brother. In the frame of psychoanalysis, Hamlet's obsession with sexuality and depravity is focused on Gertrude whose fault is not only in marrying his father's brother very soon after his father's death, and in conniving at a wrongful transfer of sovereign power, but is focused on the sexual, intimate, physical relations between Gertrude and Claudius.[33] The ghost emphasizes this: 'Let not the royal bed of Denmark be a couch for luxury and damned incest' [1.5.82-4] echoing what Hamlet himself has already articulated: 'O most wicked speed, to post with such dexterity to incestuous sheets!' [1.2.156-7]. At the performance of *The Murder of Gonzago*, Hamlet joins Ophelia in the audience: 'shall I lie in your lap?' incepting a string of sexual innuendo which deliberately mocks Ophelia's gravity and nervousness.

Hibbard reads Hamlet's rejection of Ophelia, and his performance of madness by way of constant use of misogynistic innuendo and accusation, and the revelation of his obsession with women's sexuality in general, Gertrude's and Ophelia's in particular, as evidence that he is 'genuinely mad.'[34] The theme of madness, the confusion between appearance and reality, the instability of meaning and language are played with through the plot. The appearance of the ghost is interpreted by Horatio as a possible apparition of the devil,

[31] Hibbard, 'Introduction', 1987: 213n.
[32] Janet Adelman. 1992. *Suffocating Mothers: Fantasies of Origin in Shakespeare's Plays* (Routledge: London): 14–15.
[33] Adelman, *Suffocating Mothers*, 1992: 15ff, 247-50nn.5–16.
[34] Hibbard, 'Introduction', 1987: 50–1.

tempting Hamlet to madness and suicide [1.4.48–54]. The arc of the story begins and ends with Horatio, whose fears about the state, and about the people at the court, of course are realized—Hamlet does indeed pass through madness to suicide. But we don't need any supernatural explanation. The human psyche itself, the child's deeply conflicting desires regarding mother's and father's bodies and beings, generates the kind of confusion of feeling that Hamlet evidently is suffering from.[35] Further, Hamlet's testing and trapping of others into revealing their guilt is a perfectly ordinary and intelligible strategy on the part of a person suffering extreme pain and conflicting emotion. Individuals in severe pain can either withdraw from the world, into themselves and their relationship with their pain, or they can act it out, frequently aggressively, in their relations and interactions with others.[36] Pressured speech, riddling questions, barely intelligible narratives that either are oriented towards an 'aha, gotcha' moment or subside into inconclusiveness are patterns of communication and interaction that are familiar to any who care for and interact with individuals who, in modern, rationalistic, medically-based cultures are categorized as suffering from mental ill-health to some degree, or who in spiritually or supernaturally oriented cultures are thought of as having special relationships with the supernatural.

On the other hand, as numerous feminist commentators across centuries and places have remarked, there's nothing 'mad' about this level of misogyny at all. It is, rather, a depressingly commonplace element of sexist, homophobic, patriarchal cultures which insist on a rigid, hierarchical, binary, sex-gender structure from which any deviation must be exemplarily punished. We can safely reject the interpretation that the extremity of the misognyistic insults is, itself, evidence that Hamlet is unhinged; it is, rather, evidence of his secure place in his culture. As Lisa Jardine points out, scatological, sexual imputations of viciousness to women are a pervasive aspect of Shakespearean jest, and the audience laughter that is generated is in part collusion in an established sexual culture premised on sexual inequality.[37] That, for her, is the politics of Shakespeare's theatre. Shakespeare's extraordinary stock of inventive puns and new adjectival nouns, and his virtuosic rhythm and rhyme make his speakers of invective stand out in literature. But the certainty that misogynistic innuendo and witty allusions to sexual organs and acts will either raise a laugh from an audience or will make violence or extremity of emotion intelligible is not

[35] Freud, *The Interpretation of Dreams*. 1900/2010: 282–3.
[36] Elaine Scarry. 1985. *The Body in Pain: The Making and Unmaking of the World* (Oxford: Oxford University Press), pp. 18ff, 143.
[37] Jardine, *Still Harping on Daughters*, 1983/1989: 121–2, 133.

itself the mark of, or evidence of, his genius. Both of these functions of misogynistic, obscene gags, tropes, and allusions are evident in *Hamlet*. When
'mad', Hamlet plays the fool. Where the Fool in *Lear* speaks truth to power,
Hamlet questions the truth of normality—subverting the everyday standards of
politeness and civility, and therefore unsettling his interlocutors, in a way that
is familiarly comic, but also, of course, in a way that asks acutely how it is that
'normal' standards of interaction come to be that way.

Popular and elite political anxiety and preoccupation with the imminent
death of Queen Elizabeth, and speculation about the succession, itself, Steven
Mullaney argues, carried deep within it a misogynistic current.[38] A number
of sexual ambivalences in the popular and elite representations of Elizabeth
add up to a familiarly misogynistic, complex product. Allegiance and loyalty
to the monarch had frequently been articulated and practiced through the
conventions of chivalry, in particular the more modern conventions of avow-
als of adoration from a (male) lover to his (female) object. The development
of the Petrarchan sonnet form into a quintessential kind of English language
love poem has a complex cultural history and various contexts of production,
but adoration of the unattainable woman-monarch was a key element.[39]
Edmund Spenser's (1552-99) *Faerie Queen* was received as celebratory of
Elizabeth and the Tudors, although later it could be read as ambiguously critical.[40] Plastic representations of Elizabeth—'paintings, gravings and print-
ing'—were closely policed by the state.[41] The depictions of the beautiful,
beautifully dressed monarch symbolizing world, heaven, and earth, and
divine sanction for sovereign authority were matched later by a historical
idealization of Elizabeth as a wise ruler.[42]

But as Mullaney shows, these idealizations were contrasted with scurrilous
discourses and critical descriptions of the aging queen's bizarre appearance
and decaying physical body, in a context of political near-disloyalty, more or
less overt impatience with her long decline, and explicit celebration at the
prospect of a male successor when she died. These dissenting, critical

---

[38] Steven Mullaney. 1994. 'Mourning and Misogyny: Hamlet, The Revenger's Tragedy, and the final
progress of Elizabeth I', *Shakespeare Quarterly*, 45: 139–62.

[39] Levenson, Jill L. ed. 2000. 'Introduction', in William Shakespeare, *Romeo and Juliet* (Oxford
University Press: Oxford), pp. 52–6.

[40] Edmund Spenser. 1590/2001. *The Faerie Queen*, ed. A.C.Hamilton (Pearson Education Limited:
Harlow); Donald Stump. 2019. *Spenser's Heavenly Elizabeth: Providential History in the Faerie Queen*
(Palgrave Macmillan: London).

[41] P.L. Hughes and J.F. Larkin. eds. 1964–9. 'Prohibiting Portraits of the Queen (Westminster,
1563)', *Tudor Royal Proclamations: Vol II: The Later Tudors 1553–1587* (Yale University Press: New
Haven), p. 19.

[42] Mullaney, 'Mourning and Misogyny', 1994: 145.

(circumspectly so, of course, in a context in which opposition or dissent of any degree amounted to treason) judgements, communications, and remarks cannot be dissociated from the misogyny that is both their vehicle and their content, and which reached a significant level around 1600. The queen's appearance is repulsive, and that repulsion cannot be separated from a fascinated speculation about her sexual organs. Her use of cosmetics to mask her aging face contrasts with the impossibility of disguising the lost teeth and aging body. The oil portraits of the idealized beauty of majesty—the body of the sovereign—contrast with the use of paint as an idolatrous violating disguise of the corruption of the physical body of the queen. The cosmetics paradoxically serve to accentuate and reveal what they are supposed to conceal.[43] The woman's part taken by a male actor on the theatrical stage represents the female body as grotesque.

Mullaney also connects this misogyny with ambivalent practices and discourses of grief. In Protestant thinking, grieving for the dead is frowned upon as an ungodly denial of resurrection.[44] Such moral judgement is caught in Claudius's reproaches to Hamlet: 'to persever in obstinate condolment is a course of impious stubbornness, 'tis unmanly grief, it shows a will most incorrect to heaven' [I.2.92–106]. Of course, such discourses do not tell us how bereavement and grief were actually felt and practised at times and in contexts contemporaneous with these judgements. In particular grief can be a liminal state between holding onto (incorporating) and letting go (introjecting).[45] This frame can make sense of a good deal of the imagery of Hamlet's speech (Freud cites Hamlet in his essay on grief). When Hamlet returns to Denmark after his near-death experiences—his journey to England was supposed to end in his death by orders of his uncle; the ship was attacked by pirates, and wrecked—he encounters the gravedigger, preparing the graves for Polonius and Ophelia. The gravedigger uncovers a skull from an earlier buried body—Yorick, a clown or court jester who had played with and entertained Hamlet the child [5.1.170–85].

This scene, opening the final act, explicitly thematizes the death, corruption, and decay that, whether or not masked by the appearances of court manners, have been dominant throughout; and also relates them to the circle

---

[43] Mullaney, 'Mourning and Misogyny', 1994: 147–8; cf. also Ernst H. Kantorowicz. 1957/1997. *The King's Two Bodies: A Study in Medieval Political Theology* (Princeton University Press: Princeton, NJ).

[44] Mullaney, 'Mourning and Misogyny', 1994: 153–4.

[45] Mullaney, 'Mourning and Misogyny', 1994: 152–4; Sigmund Freud. 1917/2005. 'Mourning and Melancholia', *On Murder, Mourning and Melancholia*, trans. Shaun Whiteside (Penguin Books: Harmondsworth); Derrida, *Specters of* Marx, 1993/1994: Ch. 5.

of life, and to laughter. Yorick the clown—with open licence to mock, to laugh, to say the unsayable—contrasts with Hamlet the antic riddler whose words and actions cannot be deciphered by his interlocutors. Hamlet the antic riddler obsessively plays with ideas of sex, death, burial, and decay, and the unseemliness of feasting and happiness. When Claudius and Gertrude want to know what he has done with Polonius's body (Hamlet lugs it away out of Gertrude's room after the killing [3.4.191-96]), he speculates that perhaps 'politic worms' are feasting on it [4.3.20-5]. The theme of feasting recalls the untimely 'funeral baked meats' which confounded the wedding celebrations with the funerary solemnities [1.2.180-1]. But in his grief for what should not have died, Hamlet is obsessing about the dissolution of boundaries, the mingling of materiality: 'Your fat king and your lean beggar is but variable service—two dishes, but to one table. That's the end' as far as the worms that eat the bodies in the graves are concerned [4.3.20-5]. This same dissolution of boundaries is what obsesses him about his mother's sexuality; and about the slippage between 'the king' and a particular body. 'The king', for Hamlet, is his dead father; but according to the conventions of sovereign inheritance, the king is Claudius.

Theatricality

Hamlet is a play in which the metaphor of theatricality does a good deal of creative work. First, there is Hamlet's and Claudius's respective agonies over the parts they have to play, and the question of the relation of their authentic selves to their acting selves. Each of them is wrestling to keep control of their lines, their demeanour, and the carrying off of the action of the drama in which they are enmeshed. We can interpret this as comment on what it is to be a human agent—how difficult it is to continue to play a part in full con-sciousness of it as a part; but conversely how difficult to assert an authentic identity between one's self, one's utterances, and one's actions. Hamlet's gab-bling and quibbling, his impertinence and insult familiarly puts him into the position of the creative player with language, the licenced clown. But the play with insanity, the clown who has lost touch with himself, so long has he been clowning, is uncomfortably close to the loss of self that we associate with mental unwellness, or the loss to their human community of the person who enters the altered state of the divine, or the devilish. In the character and fate of Hamlet, the problem is maintenance of a proper distance between self and the part he has to play. At least, we the audience, we the readers are not sure where the boundary lies. In the case of Claudius, the scheming villain plays the part of the gracious sovereign hedged about with divinity and exerting his wise rule. Ostensibly, at any rate, there is a clear enough line between the player and the played—Claudius and sovereign king. The player has to inhabit the role of competent ruler—and this Claudius does well enough, because he is one. But now the boundary between the player and the played is blurred.

Robert Weimann comments on the Shakespearean stage's unique capacity to simultaneously widen and close the gap between the actor and the role.[46] My point about a normative account of politics is that it must take full account of this ambiguity of actor and acted part: whether we are participating in protest, representing others in political office, exercising authority in some capacity or another, or simply watching, listening, and reading controversies about public policy, we have to be cognizant of the tense relationship between self and political self—both with respect to the political performer we are watching and to ourselves as political judge.

Second, the *Hamlet* plot focuses on the clever use of the play within a play as a trap, within a wider drama of sovereignty and inheritance, murder and revenge. The revenge story is complicated by the avenger's uncertainty about the guilt of the murderer. To begin with, to get this story going, of course, theatricals have to be a social institution. The role and place of the theatrical troupe in city and in courtly life is a taken for granted bit of realism in Shakespeare's art; theatrical skill is a skill that real people can acquire, from which a living can be made.[47] They are part of the economy and they have a part in political power—power that determines how the world goes. Shakespeare can rely on his audience recognizing the topical allusion to the dynamics of theatrical performance, in cities, in more or less permanent theatre structures with paying admission, and the periodic closure of the theatres, for public health, or for censorship, or other social control reasons. During such times of closure, theatrical companies would take to the road, seeking taverns, open spaces, and other venues for performances, as do the troupe in *Hamlet*.

Hamlet seizes upon the performance as a trap, deploying the familiar device of showing—in pageant form, often, or as a series of visions—a life, and a future, to a person, for their edification. The theatrical company, by

[46] Robert Weimann. 1988. 'Bifold Authority in Shakespeare's Theatre', *Shakespeare Quarterly*, 39: 411.
[47] Louis Montrose. 1996. 'Shakespeare, the Stage and the State', *SubStance*, 25: 59, 61.

material and social means, can stage the series of visions that in the earlier medieval tradition are conjured by angels and demons showing an Everyman character the temptations of vice and the attractions of virtue, the possibility of a heavenly way.[48] In the work of Shakespeare and his contemporaries, the witness to the apparitions is a complexly individuated character; the apparitions are personally meaningful, the response is as much confusion about self as about the possibility of a future life. *The Murder of Gonzago* is designed to be horrifying to Claudius and to touch his conscience, but also to confuse and punish him as the ghost's appearance to Hamlet is confusing and punishing. Theatre, the point is, makes you think, and the thinking is painful.

Hamlet uses the theatrical performance as a political stratagem—it outs Claudius as guilty and deserving of punishment, and it displaces him from sovereign authority. The court has acquiesced, and Gertrude, widow of the old king, has connived in his usurpation, under the guise of rightful accession. Politics as usual cannot be trusted to deliver the right result—the moral, the proper result. Political decision making in a council setting can be swayed by the persuasive power of a focal individual, or by expediency, or by the hopes and aspirations for personal advancement and advantage of the council members. It can be captured by group think. All of these intelligible, social, and psychological factors get in the way of ideal decision making, in which all principles are rightly ranked, all facts are open and rationally weighed, in which principles and premisses are in the correct logical relationship of implication and entailment with the conclusion, the decision and outcome. So Hamlet, in order to enforce the right result, has recourse to trickery, to sleight of hand, to acting a part that is not truly his. He also agrees to an ordeal by combat, a duel, in order symbolically to reestablish the order of honour after the wrongful death of Polonius. In the end, of course, he has recourse to violence, forcing Claudius to drink the poison intended for Hamlet himself.

All of these forms of action—council politics, play-acting and pretence, the performance trick, ordeal by combat, violence—all serve, structurally, to challenge, and to undermine, Claudius's claims to sovereign authority. They all reveal, to the audience, a representation of complex 'political reality'—this is what politics really is. The monarch is a player, just as courtiers, the populace, rivals, and allies, all play roles. In *Hamlet*, 'all the world's a stage' [*As You Like It*, 2.7.139-66]. The worlds of human beings are theatres. For war, for operations, for power plays, a platform for action is needed, a rostrum, a stage. Young Fortinbras marches across the regions of Scandinavia, northern and

---

[48] Weimann, *Shakespeare and the Popular Tradition*, 1978: Ch. IV.

into eastern Europe,[49] across territories which are the theatres of war, of state policy and would-be control. His armies march across the territory of Denmark into Poland [4.4], that is to say across the platform stage, or the other space of performance. The theatrical place of performance is demarcated and bounded. It is a space reserved for actors and players. Audience and onlookers must remain outside it. Violating the stage boundary destroys, permanently or temporarily, the play.[50] A few actors, with some soldierly apparel and some theatrical props, stand synecdochally for, and are seen by the audience as, the Norwegian army; just as the Norwegian army is understood synecdochally as the power of the state of Norway, and just as Danish state sovereignty is put into crisis by the presence of foreign forces on its territory.

Shakespeare's theatre, then, represents politics theatrically and in so doing brings into sharp relief the theatricality of politics. The question of authority, as well as the basis of action in concert, is raised by the play within a play, and by Hamlet's, Polonius's, Claudius's, and Gertrude's playing of their parts as passed over heir, councillor to the monarch, sovereign authority, widow queen.[51] The question is raised, where is the authority that can say, of Polonius's sentential speech, or of the ghost's assertion of Gertrude's corruption and of Claudius's murderousness, what is true, and what is false? What is good, politically speaking, and what bad? The audience knows things—because we are told them by Hamlet, or by Claudius—that the characters do not know. We draw conclusions from our own observations of the ghost. We are witness to partial, partially strategic disclosure of elements of selves. We are both authoritative, and obedient to, or compliant with, the action that the playwright and the actors delineate for us. In the case of Hamlet, with the length of the written text, the story we are told in the theatre depends on the production. As readers, it depends on the patience and attention with which we read the text. We are both ruler and ruled, as in the doubling of politics itself.

---

[49] Stuart Elden. 2018. *Shakespearean Territories* (University of Chicago Press: Chicago).
[50] Weimann, *Shakespeare and the Popular Tradition*, 1978: Ch. VI.
[51] Weimann, 'Bifold Authority', 1988; Robert Weimann. 1992. 'Representation and Performance: The uses of authority in Shakespeare's theatre', *PMLA*, 107: 506.

Conclusion

The Political Way

People are fed up with the political way. It's all talk talk talk; and we need action. Compromise is all very well, but principles, truth, are at stake—we can't compromise them. There's deadlock, gridlock; and then it turns out that the parties are thinking, and acting, more for factional advantage than they are for the good of the polity. These complaints run through Shakespeare's dramas as they do through modern and contemporary polities. On the other hand, there is also a good deal of disquiet at the alternatives. A world in which everything is for sale, and in which people are conscious of price and have lost sight of value, is demoralizing. If we leave everyone free to exchange as best they can and make their own way we have societies that are so unequal that the rich simply don't see the poorest, and the poor are just as injured as they would be if they were subject to physical violence. Those who are victorious in physical combat take their victory to deliver them rights and authority, as well as material prizes; but if we know anything about violence it is that it generates more of itself; everyone is hurt, even if they don't die. It might be nice if societies were to be run by wise magicians, or divinely ordained sovereigns with omnipotent capacities, or benevolent dictators. But, who are they? They are only people like those they govern.

Anyway, who can believe that having no choice, having no real space for dissent, or no prospect that the dissenters might prevail is an acceptable way for human beings—with their taste for arguing the toss, their ability to weigh up not only the effects of the rules but also the rules by which the rules became rules? It's vanishingly unlikely that the members of any ideal society, governed by any set of rules, would not start questioning and arguing about that—'who wrote those rules?' 'Really?'—'but that's only myth, or tradition, or theory; and anyway, who gave them—that author, that thinker, that ruler, that philosopher—the authority?' All of these questions, and more, also run through Shakespeare's dramas, as they do through political societies before and after.

One problem is deep ambiguity in the concept of politics, the adjective political, the thing (if you like) 'the political'. As we have seen, the concept of

Shakespeare and the Political Way. Elizabeth Frazer, Oxford University Press (2020). © Elizabeth Frazer.
DOI: 10.1093/oso/9780198848615.001.0001

prudential, far-sighted, wise decision making and conduct is generally posi-tively evaluated. However, of course such decision making and conduct might be exercised as much for evil ends as for good ones. So perhaps 'politic' itself is ethically neutral. But worse, it seems always to teeter towards the negative: it shades so easily into dodgy, manipulative, sly tricksterism. Game playing, but devoid of innocence. And from here we move seamlessly to the occult world where mysteries are hidden, actors disguised, appearances manipulated by sleight of hand. The lack of any clear distinctions between politic action and evil trickery alarms critics into thinking that politics, itself, has a deeply dubious ethical (or unethical) quality. But the problem with this line of infer-ence and implication is that it lacks any reference to openness, visibility, audi-bility, accountability—publicity. The first ambiguity, then, is between either the idea that politics is ethically neutral or negative and suspect, or the idea that politics, proper, is constrained by goodness, and by justice; this by way of its public nature, which means that, in becoming political, in participating in politics, we are committed already to taking everyone into account.

It is by no means the case that 'publicity', just like that, can do all the ethical work that needs to be done if politics and political rule are to be worthy of their human, and humane, source. Shakespeare's theatre emphasizes the ambi-guities, but also more importantly the complexities, of 'appearance' and 'action'. What we see—in theatre, in a good chunk of our social worlds, in politics—is not what we get. As we have seen, speakers can't control the uptake of their words, and are hardly in command of all that they mean. The speaking actor on the public stage is—has to be—costumed, embodied, and lit; and that goes for us too in our social and public lives. In any case, we disagree about the rules and norms that ought to govern what we say and how we say it, and what we do and what we try to get the others to do with us, or how we oppose the words and the actions of those we are competing with. These disagreements are articulated in the course of our evaluations of other people's performances, actions, and speeches. That goes for our criticisms of theatre and other cultural productions, and for our evaluations of social events we participate in; and for our evaluations of the political process of competition for the power to govern. They are articulated in the course of our engagements with the authorities, the powers, the decision makers who are engaged in the production of the worlds we inhabit, and who make such a difference to our interactions and relation-ships with others. Here is the second ambiguity. Public life is often thought of in terms of community, what is shared; and it is that basic sharing and agree-ment that anchors its ethical quality. But, actually, public life, public places are the sites of misunderstanding, of disagreement and conflict.

One way that dissent from rules, and disagreement about the rules that regulate rules, and downright scepticism or disbelief about the authority behind rules can be mellowed is by institutions that are thought of as sovereign. Shakespeare's dramas don't resolve the deep disagreements about what that amounts to. If we begin with free and equal individuals, with needs that should be met—as modern thinkers including Shakespeare himself do, up to a point— then final authorities, and their pronouncements and actions should be bounded by people's assent, as well as their needs. That is, there is an inference from the sovereignty of the individual, to popular (that is shared or aggregated) sovereignty. Popular sovereignty governs the 'sovereignty' of governments, law makers, judges. The sovereignty of state entities, or of the constitutions and committees of clubs or associations, on this account, is functional. But thinking of it as a jolly handy device to solve a certain kind of human social problem does not quite capture it. The power to regulate, or to constitute, power, the laws that regulate laws, can't, after all, be powers and laws just like any other ones. So it has seemed anyway.

Accordingly, sovereign power is thought of as having divine origins or ordination, or having a potency which transcends the normal web of norms and counter-norms, compliance and transgression, infractions and punishments, that is the stuff of human life in organized society. As we have seen, this allegedly extraordinary nature of sovereign power can be expressed best, seemingly, by extraordinary violence. Concomitantly, extraordinary violence - execution (not murder); torture (the power of life and death with a further turn (the power to withhold both life and death from the victim); depriving human beings of what they need as humans—extraordinary violence, and the reduction or snuffing out of human life that is its corollary, is understood by many thinkers to be the essence of sovereign power.

A third ambiguity in the concept politics is that it is frequently identified, associated at least, in ordinary discourses, in political theories, and in art, with sovereignty. In Shakespeare's dramas, as we have seen, sovereignty in this extraordinarily violent sense is played against popular sovereignty, the claims that the people should choose and decide and authorize. A problem is that popular sovereignty can itself turn to extraordinary violence. That's the story that the aristocratic, or monarchical, or otherwise hierarchical investors in unified sovereignty will tell, in order to justify their domination. But, it does not have to happen. Telling how properly political power can constitute and regulate an order, without violence, has been the work of political thinkers in many traditions. These accounts all have to get to grips with the relationship between political power, properly speaking, and the sovereign, final power that has to reside somewhere (although not, necessarily, in one place).

These ambiguities account for the way politics as such is widely distrusted—either because it is futile, only ever self-serving, and impotent against the real forces of material and technological change; or because it harbours violence—sovereign violence—at its heart. Politics, political action and roles are distrusted by those who think it would be better if the world were run by generals and social actors subjected to a bit of military discipline. It is distrusted by those who think that business people—entrepreneurs, the executive officers of large corporations, with their alleged capacities for doing deals, for efficiency and budgetary discipline—would do a better job of administering states and inter-state organizations. Or that those with religious authority should rule, bringing states, or the globe, to godly ways. One problem, among many, with such proposals is that they are premissed on the elimination of dissent.

That takes us back to our opening puzzlement. So, I won't go round the circuit again. Shakespeare's dramas, as I remarked earlier, do many things. They offer a series of canny observations on political power and sovereignty. They weigh, and repeatedly advert to the principle that all should count, and that those who get to do the counting should themselves be held to account (including by the uncounted). They dramatize acerbic evaluations of the prospects of friendship as the generator of political justice, divinity as the source of sovereign rule, or the wilderness as a place to escape the machinations of political and social norms and authority. Shakespeare was not a political theorist in the way that many of his sources were. He was sceptical about the method of drawing an ideal society and then wondering about how it might be realized, or how its standards might be applied to real social worlds. He tended to home in on the paradoxes of such idealizations: to press on the puzzles not seek to resolve them.

There is something of this in political life itself. I know—sovereign authority sentences people to death, and their lives can never be restored; it deals with transgression, or processes of exclusion, by dehumanizing and killing. All this is final in the worst sense of the term. But political power—proper political power—resurfaces. There is no finality: a sentence of death is executed; the injustice is articulated and rearticulated; campaigns are got up; and a new agreement that the death was wrongful is pronounced. No good, I agree, for the person executed, or for their suffering friends and family. But better than a world in which power really is final. This repetitive nature of politics—it's all talk talk talk and nothing is ever, really, decided; no sooner is a decision made than those who dissented from it (whose assent was commanded, but who withheld their consent) re-open the question—this repetitive endless indecisive provisional nature of political power maddens and enrages people. No doubt it maddened and enraged Shakespeare as well. But the play of power, the repetition of performance, and, in the course of repetition, the transformations and shifts of meaning—these are the subject (among other subjects) of his drama, and its substance. Our participation and the participation of other audiences distant and near are an enactment of something like the political power whose puzzles Shakespeare, endlessly, dramatizes.

References

Adelman, Janet. 1992. *Suffocating Mothers: Fantasies of Origin in Shakespeare's Plays* (Routledge: London).

Adelman, Janet. 2003. 'Her Father's Blood: Race, conversion and nation in The Merchant of Venice', *Representations*, 81: 4–30.

Adelman, Janet. 2008. *Blood Relations: Christian and Jew in The Merchant of Venice* (University of Chicago Press: Chicago).

Agamben, Giorgio. 1995/1998. *Homo Sacer: Sovereign Power and Bare Life*, trans. Daniel Heller-Roazen (Stanford, CA: Stanford University Press).

Agamben, Giorgio. 2003 (in Italian)/2005. *State of Exception* (University of Chicago Press: Chicago).

Ahmed, Sara. 2014. *The Cultural Politics of Emotion* (Edinburgh University Press: Edinburgh).

Alexandra, Andrew. 1993. 'Militarism', *Social Theory and Practice*, 19: 205–23.

Alighieri, Dante (1265–1321). 1939. *The Divine Comedy*. Vol. 2: *Purgatorio*, trans. and ed. John D. Sinclair (Oxford University Press: New York).

Allen, J.W. 1938. *English Political Thought 1603–1660* (Methuen and Co. Ltd: London).

Alulis, Joseph, and Vickie Sullivan. eds. 1996. *Shakespeare's Political Pageant: Essays in Literature and Politics* (Rowman and Littlefield: London).

Anglo, Sydney. 2005. *Machiavelli—The First Century: Studies in Enthusiasm, Hostility and Irrelevance* (Oxford University Press: Oxford).

Arendt, Hannah. 1951. *The Origins of Totalitarianism* (Harcourt Inc: San Diego).

Arendt, Hannah. 1954/1990. 'Philosophy and Politics', *Social Research*, 57: 427–54.

Arendt, Hannah. 1958. *The Human Condition* (University of Chicago Press: Chicago).

Arendt, Hannah. 1969. *On Violence* (Harcourt Brace: New York); also in Hannah Arendt. 1972/1973. *Crises of the Republic* (London: Penguin Books, 1973).

Aristotle (384–322 BCE). 1932. *Politics*, trans. H. Rackham (Harvard University Press: Cambridge, MA).

Aristotle. 1934. *Nicomachean Ethics*, trans. H. Rackham (Harvard University Press: Cambridge, MA).

Armitage, David, Conal Condren, and Andrew Fitzmaurice. eds. 2009. 'Introduction', *Shakespeare and Early Modern Political Thought* (Cambridge University Press: Cambridge).

Arneson, Richard. 1985. 'Shakespeare and the Jewish Question', *Political Theory*, 13: 85–111.

Augustine, St (354–430). *c.*426 CE/1984. *The City of God*, trans. Henry Bettenson, ed. and intro. John O'Meara (Oxford University Press: Oxford).

Augustine, St. 1958. 'De Sermone Domini in Monte Secundum Matthaeum', in Geoffrey Bullough (ed.), *Dramatic and Narrative Sources of Shakespeare*, Vol. 2 (Routledge and Kegan Paul: London).

Bacon, Francis (1607–10). 1753. 'Of Friendship', *The Works of Francis Bacon*, Vol. I (London: A. Millar).

Badiou, Alain. 2008. 'Rhapsody for the Theatre: A short philosophical treatise', *Theatre Survey*, 49: 187–238.

Baehr, Peter. 2008. *Caesarism, Charisma and Fate: Historical Sources and Modern Resonances in the Work of Max Weber* (Transaction Publishers: New Brunswick).

Baldwin, T.W. 1944. *Shakspere's Small Latine and Lesse Greek* (University of Illinois Press: Champaign, IL).

Banfield, Edward C. 1958. *The Moral Basis of a Backward Society* (Chicago: The Free Press).

Bartels, Emily C. 2006. 'Too Many Blackamoors: Deportation, discrimination, and Elizabeth I', *Studies in English Literature 1500–1900*, 46: 305–22.

Barton, Anne. 1985/2004. 'Livy, Machiavelli and Shakespeare's *Coriolanus*', in Catherine M.S. Alexander (ed.), *Shakespeare and Politics* (Cambridge University Press: Cambridge), pp. 69–70.

Bate, Jonathan. 1993. *Shakespeare and Ovid* (Clarendon Press: Oxford).

Bawcutt, N.W. 1971. 'Policy, Machiavellianism, and the Earlier Tudor Drama', *English Literary Renaissance*, 1: 195–209.

Bawcutt, N.W. 1991. 'Introduction', *Shakespeare Measure for Measure* (Oxford University Press: Oxford).

Beechey, Veronica. 1979. 'On Patriarchy', *Feminist Review*, 3: 66–82.

Bejan, Teresa M. 2017. *Mere Civility: Disagreement and the Limits of Toleration* (Harvard University Press: Cambridge, MA).

Bermel, Albert. 2001. *Artaud's Theatre of Cruelty* (Methuen: London).

Berry, Philippa. 1997. 'Reversing History: Time, fortune, and the doubling of sovereignty in Macbeth', *European Journal of English Studies*, 1: 367–87.

Bickford, Susan. 1996. 'Beyond Friendship: Aristotle on conflict, deliberation and attention', *The Journal of Politics*, 58(2): 398–421.

Blits, Jan H. 2016. 'Philosophy (and Athens) in Decay: *Timon of Athens*', *The Review of Politics*, 78(4): 539–50.

Bloom, Allan. 2000. *Shakespeare on Love and Friendship* (University of Chicago Press: Chicago).

Bloom, Allan, and Henry Jaffa. 1964. *Shakespeare's Politics* (Chicago University Press: Chicago).

Bodin, Jean. 1576/1992. *On Sovereignty*, ed. Julian Franklin (Cambridge University Press: Cambridge; selection from *Six Livres de la Republique*, trans. Richard Knolles, 1606).

Bodin, Jean. 2010. *Colloquium of the Seven about Secrets of the Sublime*, trans. Marion Leathers Kuntz (Pennsylvania State University Press: University Park, PA).

Brayton, Dan. 2003. 'Angling in the Lake of Darkness: Possession, dispossession and the politics of discovery in King Lear', *ELH*, 70: 399–426.

Breight, Curtis C. 1996. *Surveillance, Militarism and Drama in the Elizabethan Era* (Macmillan Press Ltd: Basingstoke).

Brett, Annabel S. 2011. *Changes of State: Nature and the Limits of the City in Early Modern Natural Law* (Princeton University Press: Princeton).

Brett, Annabel S. 2018. 'Is There Any Place for Environmental Thinking in Early Modern European Political Thought?', in Katrina Forrester and Sophie Smith (eds.), *Nature, Action and the Future: Political Thought and the Environment* (Cambridge University Press: Cambridge).

Brooke, Arthur. 1562/1977. 'The Tragicall Historye of Romeus and Juliet', in G. Bullough (ed.), *Narrative and Dramatic Sources of Shakespeare*, Vol. 1 (Routledge and Kegan Paul: London), pp. 269–363.

Brooke, Nicholas. ed. 1606 (comp.)/1990. 'Introduction', in William Shakespeare, *The Tragedy of Macbeth* (Oxford University Press: Oxford), pp. 1–90.

Brooks-Davies, Douglas. 1983. *The Mercurian Monarch: Magical Politics from Spenser to Pope* (Manchester University Press: Manchester).

Brown, Carolyn E. 1996. 'Duke Vincentio of "Measure for Measure" and King James of England: The poorest princes in Christendom', *Clio: A Journal of Literature, History and the History of Philosophy*, 26: 51–79.

Brown, Paul. 1985. '"This Thing of Darkness I Acknowledge Mine": The Tempest and the discourse of colonialism', in Jonathan Dollimore and Alan Sinfield (eds.), *Political Shakespeare: New Essays in Cultural Materialism* (Manchester University Press: Manchester), pp. 59–68.

Budelmann, Felix, Laura Maguire, and Ben Teasdale. 2013. 'Audience Reactions to Greek and Shakespearean Tragedy' (Oxford: Oxford University Research Archive), http://ora.ox.ac.uk/objects/uuid:da99b8a5-1102-4d47-aabb-118ca658722d

Bull, George. ed. 1532/1961. 'Introduction', in Niccolo Machiavelli, *The Prince* (Penguin: Harmondsworth), pp. 9–26.

Bullough, Geoffrey. ed. 1957. 'Romeo and Juliet', *Narrative and Dramatic Sources of Shakespeare*, Vol. 1 (Routledge and Kegan Paul: London), pp. 269–82.

Bullough, Geoffrey. ed. 1957. 'Merchant of Venice', *Narrative and Dramatic Sources of Shakespeare*, Vol. 1 (Routledge and Kegan Paul: London), pp. 445–62.

Bullough, Geoffrey. ed. 1958. 'Measure for Measure', *Narrative and Dramatic Sources of Shakespeare*, Vol. 2 (Routledge and Kegan Paul: London), pp. 399–416.

Bullough, Geoffrey. ed. 1964. 'Coriolanus', *Narrative and Dramatic Sources of Shakespeare*, Vol. 5 (Routledge and Kegan Paul: London), pp. 453–95.

Bullough, Geoffrey. ed. 1966. 'Timon of Athens', *Narrative and Dramatic Sources of Shakespeare*, Vol. 6 (Routledge and Kegan Paul: London), pp. 225–50.

Bullough, Geoffrey. ed. 1973. 'King Lear', *Narrative and Dramatic Sources of Shakespeare*, Vol. 7 (Routledge and Kegan Paul: London), pp. 296–308.

Bullough, Geoffrey. ed. 1973. 'Hamlet', *Narrative and Dramatic Sources of Shakespeare*, Vol. 7 (Routlege and Kegan Paul: London), pp. 3–59.

Bullough, Geoffrey. ed. 1973. 'Othello', *Narrative and Dramatic Sources of Shakespeare*, Vol. 7 (Routlege and Kegan Paul: London), pp. 193–237.

Bullough, Geoffrey. ed. 1973. 'Macbeth', *Narrative and Dramatic Sources of Shakespeare*, Vol. 7 (Routlege and Kegan Paul: London), pp. 423–527.

Butterworth Emily. 2008. 'The Work of the Devil? Theatre, the supernatural, and Montaigne's public stage', *Renaissance Studies*, 22(5): 705–22.

Caesar, Julius (100–44 BCE). 1917. *The Gallic War*, trans. H.J. Edwards (Harvard University Press: Cambridge, MA).

Cameron, Deborah. 1985. *Feminism and Linguistic Theory* (Macmillan: London).

Cameron, Deborah, and Elizabeth Frazer. 1987. *The Lust to Kill: A Feminist Investigation of Sexual Murder* (Polity: Cambridge).

Cantor, Paul A. 1996. 'King Lear: The tragic disjunction of wisdom and power', in Joseph Alulis and Vickie Sullivan (eds.), *Shakespeare's Political Pageant: Essays in Literature and Politics* (Rowman and Littlefield: London).

Carlson, Donald. 2015. '"Tis New to Thee": Power, magic and early science in Shakespeare's Tempest', *The Ben Jonson Journal*, 22: 1–22.

Cavell, Stanley. 1969/2003. 'The Avoidance of Love: A reading of King Lear', *Disowning Knowledge in Seven Plays of Shakespeare*, updated edn (Cambridge University Press: Cambridge), pp. 39–124.

Cavell, Stanley. 1979/2003. 'Othello and the Stake of the Other', *Disowning Knowledge in Seven Plays of Shakespeare*, updated edn (Cambridge University Press: Cambridge), pp. 125–42.

Cavell, Stanley. 1987/2003b. 'Coriolanus and the Interpretations of Politics (Who Does the Wolf Love?)', *Disowning Knowledge in Seven Plays of Shakespeare*, updated edn (Cambridge University Press: Cambridge), pp. 143–77.

Cavell, Stanley. 1987/2003c. 'Hamlet's Burden of Proof', *Disowning Knowledge in Seven Plays of Shakespeare*, updated edn (Cambridge University Press: Cambridge), pp. 179–92.

Cavell, Stanley. 1987/2003d. 'Macbeth Appalled', *Disowning Knowledge in Seven Plays of Shakespeare*, updated edn (Cambridge University Press: Cambridge), pp. 223–50.

Cavell, Stanley. 2003. *Disowning Knowledge in Seven Plays of Shakespeare*, updated edn (Cambria Press: Cambridge).

Cicero (106–43 BCE). 1913. *On Duties (De Officiis)* (Harvard University Press: Cambridge, MA).

Cicero. 1923. 'Laelius: On friendship', *Cicero*, Vol. XX, ed. and trans. W.A. Falconer (Harvard University Press: Cambridge, MA).

Cicero. 1949. *De Inventione* (Harvard University Press: Cambridge, MA).

Clark, Stuart. 1997. *Thinking with Demons: The Idea of Witchcraft in Early Modern Europe* (Clarendon Press: Oxford).

Clausewitz, Carl von. 1832/1976. *On War*, ed. and trans. Michael Howard and Peter Paret (Princeton University Press: Princeton, NJ).

Coby, Patrick. 1983. 'Politics and the Poetic Ideal in Shakespeare's The Tempest', *Political Theory*, 11: 215–43.

Cohen, Derek. 1993. *Shakespeare's Culture of Violence* (Macmillan Press Ltd: Basingstoke).

Condren, Conal. 2009. 'Unfolding the Properties of Government: The case of *Measure for Measure* and the history of political thought', in David Armitage, Conal Condren, and Andrew Fitzmaurice (eds.), *Shakespeare and Early Modern Political Thought* (Cambridge University Press: Cambridge), pp. 157–75.

Cooper, John M. 1977. 'Aristotle on the Forms of Friendship', *Review of Metaphysics*, 30: 619–48.

Corrigan, Philip, and Derek Sayer. 1985. *The Great Arch: English State Formation as Cultural Revolution* (Basil Blackwell: Oxford).

Cresswell, Tim. 1994. 'Putting Women in Their Place: The Carnival at Greenham Common', *Antipode*, 26: 35–58.

Crick, Bernard. 1962/2013. *In Defence of Politics* (Bloomsbury: London).

Delany, Paul. 1977. 'King Lear and the Decline of Feudalism', *PMLA*, 92: 429–40.

Delphy, Christine. 1978/1984. *Close to Home: A Materialist Analysis of Women's Oppression* (Hutchinson: London).

Derrida, Jacques. 1988. 'The Politics of Friendship', *Journal of Philosophy*, 85: 632–44.

Derrida, Jacques. 1993/1994. *Specters of Marx: The State of Debt, the Work of Mourning and the New International* (Routledge: London).

Derrida, Jacques. 1994/1997. *Politics of Friendship* (Verso: London).

Descartes, Rene. 1641/1954. 'Meditations on First Philosophy: Wherein are demonstrated the existence of God and the distinction of soul from body', in Elizabeth Anscombe and Peter Thomas Geach (eds.), *Descartes Philosophical Writings* (Thomas Nelson and Sons: Sunbury on Thames).

Dessen, Alan C. 1978. 'The Logic of Elizabethan Stage Violence: Some alarms and excursions for modern critics, editors, and directors', *Renaissance Drama*, 9: 39–69.

Dobski, Bernard J., and Dustin A. Gish. 2012. 'Shakespeare, the Body Politic, and Liberal Democracy', *Perspectives on Political Science*, 41: 181–9.

Dollimore, Jonathan. 1984/2004. *Radical Tragedy: Religion, Ideology and Power in the Drama of Shakespeare and His Contemporaries* (Palgrave Macmillan: Basingstoke).

Dollimore, Jonathan. 1985a. 'Introduction: Shakespeare, cultural materialism, and the new historicism', in Jonathan Dollimore and Alan Sinfield (eds.), *Political Shakespeare: New Essays in Cultural Materialism* (Manchester University Press: Manchester).

Dollimore, Jonathan. 1985b. 'Transgression and Surveillance in Measure for Measure', in Jonathan Dollimore and Alan Sinfield (eds.), *Political Shakespeare: New Essays in Cultural Materialism* (Manchester University Press: Manchester).

Dollimore, Jonathan, and Alan Sinfield. eds. 1985. *Political Shakespeare: New Essays in Cultural Materialism* (Manchester University Press: Manchester).

Drury, Shadia B. 1988. *The Political Ideas of Leo Strauss* (St. Martin's Press: New York).

Durkheim, Emile. 1912/2001. *The Elementary Forms of Religious Life* (Oxford University Press: Oxford).

Elden, Stuart. 2013. 'The Geopolitics of King Lear: Territory, land, earth', *Law and Literature*, 25: 147–65.

Elden, Stuart. 2018. *Shakespearean Territories* (University of Chicago Press: Chicago).

Ellis, Stephen, and Gerrieter Haar. 2004. *Worlds of Power: Religious Thought and Political Practice in Africa* (C. Hurst: London).

Elshtain, Jean. 1987/1995. *Women and War* (Chicago University Press: Chicago).

Enloe, Cynthia. 2000. *Maneuvers: The International Politics of Militarising Women's Lives* (University of California Press: Berkeley).

Erasmus, Desiderius (1466–1536). 1536/1946. *The Complaint of Peace*, trans. Thomas Paynell, Early English Books Online, https://eebo.chadwyck.com

Esslin, Martin. 1968. *The Theatre of the Absurd* (Penguin: Harmondsworth).

Faderman, Lilian. 1981. *Surpassing the Love of Men: Romantic Friendship and Love between Women from the Renaissance to the Present* (Morrow: New York).

Filmer, Robert. 1680/1991. 'Patriarcha', in Johann P. Sommerville (ed.), *Patriarcha and other Writings* (Cambridge University Press: Cambridge).

Finlayson, Alan, and Elizabeth Frazer. 2010. 'Fictions of Sovereignty: Shakespeare, theatre and the representation of rule', *Parliamentary Affairs*, 64: 233–47.

Fitter, Chris. 2016. '"The Art of Known and Feeling Sorrows": Rethinking capitalist transition, and the performance of class politics, in King Lear', *Early Modern Literary Studies*, 19: 1–23.

Flaumenhaft, Mera J. 2017. 'Romeo and Juliet for Grownups', *Review of Politics*, 79: 545–63.

Fontaine, Laurence. 2018. 'Prodigality, Avarice and Anger: Passions and emotions at the heart of the encounter between aristocratic economy and market economy', *European Journal of Sociology*, 59: 39–61.

Forrester, Katrina, and Sophie Smith. 2018. 'History, Theory and the Environment', in Katrina Forrester and Sophie Smith (eds.), *Nature, Action and the Future: Political Thought and the Environment* (Cambridge University Press: Cambridge).

Foucault, Michel. 1973/1978. *I, Pierre Riviere, Having Slaughtered My Mother, My Sister, and My Brother: A Case of Parricide in the 19th Century* (Penguin: Harmondsworth).

Foucault, Michel. 1976/1980. 'Two Lectures', in Colin Gordon (ed.), *Power/Knowledge: Selected Interviews and other Writings 1972-1977* (Pantheon Books: New York).

Foucault, Michel. 1983/1985. 'The Meaning and Evolution of the Word Parrhesia', *Discourse and Truth: The Problematization of Parrhesia. Six Lectures at the University of California at Berkeley CA Oct–Nov 1983*, ed. Joseph Pearson, https://foucault.info/parrhesia/

Foucault, Michel. 1983/1985. *Discourse and Truth: The Problematization of Parrhesia. Six Lectures at the University of California at Berkeley CA Oct–Nov 1983*, ed. Joseph Pearson, https://foucault.info/parrhesia/

Foucault, Michel. 1997/2003. *Society Must Be Defended: Lectures at the College de France 1975-76* (Penguin: Harmondsworth).

Foucault, Michel. 2002. *Essential Works of Foucault 1954-1984*. Vol. 3: *Power*, ed. James D. Faubion (Penguin: Harmondsworth).

Franklin, Julian H. 1992. 'Introduction', *Jean Bodin: On Sovereignty* (Cambridge University Press: Cambridge), pp. ix–xlii.

Fraser, Nancy. 1989. 'Struggle over Needs', *Unruly Practices: Power, Discourse and Gender in Contemporary Social Theory* (Polity Press: Cambridge), pp. 161–87.

Frazer, Elizabeth. 2008. 'Mary Wollstonecraft on Politics and Friendship', *Political Studies*, 56(1): 237–56.

Frazer, Elizabeth. 2016. 'Shakespeare's Politics', *Review of Politics*, 78: 503–22.

Frazer, Elizabeth. 2018. 'Political Power and Magic', *Journal of Political Power*, 11(3): 359–77.

Frazer, Elizabeth, and Kimberly Hutchings. 2011. 'Virtuous Violence and the Politics of Statecraft in Machiavelli, Clausewitz and Weber', *Political Studies*, 59: 56–73.

Frazer, Elizabeth, and Kimberly Hutchings. 2014. 'Feminism and the Critique of Violence: Negotiating feminist political agency', *Journal of Political Ideologies*, 19(2): 143–63.

Frazer, Elizabeth, and Kimberly Hutchings. 2020. *Violence and Political Theory* (Polity Press: Cambridge).

Freud, Sigmund. 1900/2010. *The Interpretation of Dreams*, trans. James Strachey (Basic Books: New York).

Freud, Sigmund. 1917/2005. 'Mourning and Melancholia', *On Murder, Mourning and Melancholia*, trans. Shaun Whiteside (Penguin: Harmondsworth), pp. 203–18.

Fricker, Miranda. 2007. *Epistemic Injustice* (Oxford University Press: Oxford).

Galli, Giorgio. 2004/2012. *La Magia e il potere* (Lindau s.r.l: Torino).

Genesis (The first book of Moses called Genesis). n.d. *Holy Bible*, Authorised (King James) version (Cambridge University Press: Cambridge).

Gentillet, Innocent. 1576/1602. *A Discourse upon the meanes of wel governing and maintaining in good peace, a kingdome, or other principalitie, against N. Machiavell (in his Il Principe]*, trans. S. Patericke (A. Islip: London).

George, David. 2000/2004. 'Plutarch, Insurrection and Dearth in *Coriolanus*', in Catherine M.S. Alexander (ed.), *Shakespeare and Politics* (Cambridge University Press: Cambridge).

Gil, Daniel Juan. 2013. *Shakespeare's Anti-Politics: Sovereign Power and the Life of the Flesh* (Palgrave Macmillan: Basingstoke).

Goldstein, Joshua S. 2001. *War and Gender* (Cambridge University Press: Cambridge).

Goleman, Daniel. 1995. *Emotional Intelligence: Why It Can Matter More Than IQ* (Bloomsbury Publishing: London).

Grady, Hugh. 2000. 'Shakespeare's Links to Machiavelli and Montaigne: Constructing intellectual modernity in early modern Europe', *Comparative Literature*, 52: 119–42.

Graeber, David. 2012. 'Can't Stop Believing: Magic and politics', *The Baffler*, https://thebaffler.com/salvos/cant-stop-believing

Green, Jeffrey. 2010. *The Eyes of the People: Democracy in an Age of Spectatorship* (Oxford University Press: Oxford).

Greenblatt, Stephen. 1988. *Shakespearean Negotiations: The Circulation of Social Energy in Renaissance England* (University of California Press: Berkeley, CA).

Greenblatt, Stephen. 1988. 'Shakespeare and the Exorcists', *Shakespearean Negotiations: The Circulation of Social Energy in Renaissance England* (University of California Press: Berkeley, CA).

Greenblatt, Stephen. 2009. 'Shakespeare and the Ethics of Authority', in David Armitage, Conal Condren, and Andrew Fitzmaurice (eds.), *Shakespeare and Early Modern Political Thought* (Cambridge University Press: Cambridge), pp. 64–79.

Greenblatt, Stephen. 2018. *Tyrant: Shakespeare on Power* (Penguin Random House: London).

Greg, W.W. 1940. 'Time, Place and Politics in King Lear', *The Modern Language Review*, 35: 431–46.

Habermas, Jurgen. 1970. 'On Systematically Distorted Communication', *Inquiry: An Interdisciplinary Journal of Philosophy*, 13: 205–18.

Habermas, Jurgen. 1977. 'Hannah Arendt's Communications Concept of Power', *Social Research*, 44: 3–24.

Habermas, Jurgen. 1995. 'Reconciliation through the Public Use of Reason: Remarks on John Rawls' political liberalism', *Journal of Philosophy*, XC11: 109–31.

Hadfield, Andrew. 2004. *Shakespeare and Renaissance Politics* (Thomson Learning: London).

Hadfield, Andrew. 2005. *Shakespeare and Republicanism* (Cambridge University Press: Cambridge).

Halio, Jay L. ed. 1993. 'Introduction', William Shakespeare, *The Merchant of Venice* (Oxford University Press: Oxford).

Hall, Kim F. 1992/2004. 'Guess Who's Coming to Dinner? Colonisation and miscegenation in The Merchant of Venice', in Emma Smith (ed.), *Shakespeare's Comedies* (Blackwell Publishing: Oxford).

Hamlin, William M. 2013. *Montaigne's English Journey: Reading the Essays in Shakespeare's Day* (Oxford University Press: Oxford).

Hartsock, Nancy C.M. 1983/1998. 'The Feminist Standpoint: Developing the ground for a specifically feminist historical materialism', *The Feminist Standpoint Revisited and other Essays* (Westview Press: Boulder, CO), pp. 105–32.

Hegel, G.W.F. 1821/1977. *The Philosophy of Right*, trans. T.M. Knox (Oxford University Press: Oxford).

Heinemann, Margot. 1992. 'Demystifying the Mystery of State: King Lear and the world upside down', *Shakespeare Survey*, 44: 75–83.

Henry, John. 2008. 'The Fragmentation of Renaissance Occultism and the Decline of Magic', *History of Science*, xlvi: 1–48.

Hibbard, G.R. ed. 1987. 'Introduction', William Shakespeare, *Hamlet* (Oxford University Press: Oxford), pp. 1–137.

Hirschman, Albert O. 1977/1997. *The Passions and the Interests: Political Arguments for Capitalism before Its Triumph*, Twentieth Anniversary edn (Princeton University Press: Princeton, NJ).

Hobbes, Thomas. 1651/1996. *Leviathan* (Oxford University Press: Oxford).

Holbrook, Peter. 2000. 'The Left and King Lear', *Textual Practice*, 14: 343–62.

Holland, Norman N. 1959. 'Measure for Measure: The duke and the prince', *Comparative Literature*, 11: 16–20.

Hortmann, Wilhelm. 2002. 'Shakespeare on the Political Stage in the Twentieth Century', in Sarah Stanton and Stanley Wells (eds.), *The Cambridge Companion to Shakespeare on Stage* (Cambridge University Press: Cambridge), pp. 212–19.

Howard, Jean. 2006. 'Dramatic Traditions and Shakespeare's Political Thought', in David Armitage (ed.), *British Political Thought in History, Literature and Theory 1500–1800* (Cambridge University Press: Cambridge).

Hulliung, Mark. 1974. 'Patriarchalism and Its Early Enemies', *Political Theory*, 2: 410–19.

Hughes, P.L., and J.F. Larkin. eds. 1964–9. 'Prohibiting Portraits of the Queen (Westminster, 1563)', *Tudor Royal Proclamations: Vol II: The Later Tudors 1553–1587* (Yale University Press: New Haven), p. 19.

Hume, David. 1741-2. *Essays, Literary, Moral and Political* (Ward, Lock and Co: London).

Hume, David. 1751/1975. 'Enquiry Concerning the Principles of Morals', in L. A. Selby-Bigge (ed.), *Enquiries Concerning Human Understanding and the Principles of Morals* (Clarendon Press: Oxford), pp. 169–323.

Huntingdon, Samuel P. 1957/1967. *The Soldier and the State: The Theory and Politics of Civil-Military Relations* (Harvard University Press: Cambridge, MA).

Hutter, Horst. 1978. *Politics as Friendship: The Origins of Classical Notions of Politics in the Theory and Practice of Friendship* (Wilfried Laurier University Press: Waterloo, Ontario).

Jaffa, Harry V. 1957. 'The Limits of Politics: An interpretation of King Lear, Act I, Scene 1', *The American Political Science Review*, 51(2): 405–27.

James VI and I, R. 1598/1982. 'The True Law of Free Monarchies; or the Reciprock and mutuall duetie betwixt a free King and his natural subjects', in James Craigie (ed.), *Minor Prose Works of James VI and I* (Scottish Text Society: Edinburgh), pp. 57–82.

James VI and I, R. 1603/1944. *Basilicon Doron*, ed. James Craigie, 2 vols (William Blackwood and Sons Ltd: Edinburgh).

Jardine, Lisa. 1983/1989. *Still Harping on Daughters: Women and Drama in the Age of Shakespeare* (Columbia University Press: New York).

Jay, Martin. 2010. *The Virtues of Mendacity: On Lying in Politics* (University of Virginia Press: Charlottesville, VA).

Jenkins, Ronald B. 2015. 'Prince Hamlet and the Problem of Succession', *ANQ: Quarterly Journal of Short Articles, Notes and Reviews*, 28(2): 63–7.

Jensen, Pamela K. 2006. 'Vienna Vice: Invisible leadership and deep politics in Shakespeare's Measure for Measure', in John A. Murley and Sean D. Sutton (eds.), *Perspectives on Politics in Shakespeare* (Lexington Books: Oxford), pp. 155–87.

Jowett, John. ed. 2004. 'Introduction', William Shakespeare and Thomas Middleton, *Timon of Athens* (Oxford: Oxford University Press), pp. 1–153.

Kahn, Coppelia. 1977. 'Coming of Age in Verona', *Modern Language Studies*, 8(1): 5–22.

Kahn, Coppelia. 1981. *Man's Estate: Masculine Identity in Shakespeare* (University of California Press: Berkeley, CA).

Kantorowicz, Ernst H. 1957/1997. *The King's Two Bodies: A Study in Medieval Political Theology* (Princeton University Press: Princeton, NJ).

Kassell, Lauren. 2005. 'The Economy of Magic in Early Modern England', in Margaret Pelling and Scott Mandelbrote (eds.), *The Practice of Reform in Health, Medicine and Science 1500–200* (Ashgate: Aldershot), pp. 43–57.

Kassell, Lauren. 2007. *Medicine and Magic in Elizabethan London* (Oxford University Press: Oxford).

Kastan, David Scott. 1986. 'Proud Majesty Made Subject: Shakespeare and the spectacle of rule', *Shakespeare Quarterly*, 37(4): 459–75.

Kertzer, David I. 1988. *Ritual, Politics and Power* (Yale University Press: New Haven).

King, Preston. 1999. 'Introduction: The challenge of friendship in modernity', *Critical Review of International Social and Political Philosophy*, 2: 1–14.

King, Preston. 2007. 'Friendship in Politics', *Critical Review of International Social and Political Philosophy*, 10: 125–45.

Kitch, Aaron. 2009. *Political Economy and the States of Literature in Early Modern England* (Ashgate: Farnham).

Knapp, Jeffrey. 2016. 'Hamlet and the Sovereignty of Reasons', *The Review of Politics*, 78: 645–62.

Kott, Jan. 1964. *Shakespeare our Contemporary*, trans. Boleslaw Taborski (W. W. Norton: New York).

Kurland, Stuart M. 1994. 'Hamlet and the Scottish Succession?'. *Studies in English Literature 1500–1900*, 34(2): 279–300.

Laertius, Diogenes (180–140 BCE). *c.*220 BCE/1925. 'Diogenes', in *Lives of Eminent Philosophers* (London: William Heinemann and Co.).

Lakoff, George, and Mark Johnson. 1980/2003. *Metaphors We Live By* (University of Chicago Press: Chicago).

Ledwith, Sean. 2016. 'Marx's Shakespeare', *Counterfire*, https://www.counterfire.org/articles/analysis/18300-marx-s-shakespeare

Leopold, David. 2014. 'Karl Marx and British Socialism', in W. J. Mander (ed.), *The Oxford Handbook of British Philosophy in the Nineteenth Century* (Oxford University Press: Oxford).

Levenson, Jill L. 1995. 'Alla Stoccado Carries It Away: Codes of Violence in Romeo and Juliet', *Shakespeare's Romeo and Juliet: Texts, Contexts and Interpretation*, ed. Jay L. Halio (University of Delaware Press: Newark, NJ), pp. 83–96.

Levenson, Jill L. ed. 2000. 'Introduction', in William Shakespeare, *Romeo and Juliet* (Oxford University Press: Oxford), pp. 1–134.

Levi, Carlo. 1947/1963. *Christ Stopped at Eboli*, trans. Frances Frenaye (Farrar, Strauss, Inc.: New York).

Lewis, C.S. 1960. *The Four Loves* (Geoffrey Bles: London).

Lewis, Rhodri. 2017. *Hamlet and the Vision of Darkness* (Princeton University Press: Princeton).

Lilla, Mark. 2016. *The Shipwrecked Mind: On Political Reaction* (New York Review Books: New York).

Limon, Jerzy. 1995. 'Rehabilitating Tybalt', in Jay L. Halio (ed.), *Shakespeare's Romeo and Juliet: Texts, Contexts and Interpretation* (University of Delaware Press: Newark, NJ), pp. 97–106.

Livy (Titus Livius, 59 BCE–17 CE). 1919–22. *Annales*, Books 1–4 (a.k.a. *Ad Urbe Condita*), trans. B.O. Foster (Harvard University Press: Cambridge, MA).

Lloyd, Genevieve. 1984. *The Man of Reason: 'Male' and 'Female' in Western Philosophy* (Methuen: London).

Locke, John. 1690/1960. *Two Treatises of Government* (Cambridge University Press: Cambridge).

Lovett, Frank. 2010. *A General Theory of Domination and Justice* (Oxford University Press: Oxford).

Lowrance, Bryan. 2012. 'Modern Ecstasy: Macbeth and the meaning of the political', *ELH*, 79: 823–49.

Macfarlane, Alan. 2000. 'Civility and the Decline of Magic', in Peter Burke, Brian Harrison, and Paul Slack (eds.), *Civil Histories: Essays Presented to Sir Keith Thomas* (Oxford University Press: Oxford).

Machiavelli, Niccolo. 1521/1965. *The Art of War*, ed. Neal Wood, trans. N. Farnsworth (Perseus Books: Cambridge, MA).

Machiavelli, Niccolo. 1525/1988. *Florentine Histories*, trans. Laura F. Banfield and Harvey C. Mansfield (Princeton University Press: Princeton, NJ).

Machiavelli, Niccolo. 1531/1970. *The Discourses on the First Decade of Titus Livy*, ed. Bernard Crick, trans. Leslie J. Walker SJ (Penguin: Harmondsworth).

Machiavelli, Niccolo. 1532/1961. *The Prince*, trans. George Bull (Penguin: Harmondsworth).

Mack, Peter. 2010. *Reading and Rhetoric in Montaigne and Shakespeare* (Bloomsbury Academic: London).

Mann, Michael. 1986/2012. *The Sources of Social Power*. Vol. 1: *A History of Power from the Beginning to AD1760* (Cambridge University Press: Cambridge).

Marcus, George E. 2000. 'Emotions in Politics', *Annual Review of Political Science*, 3: 221–50.

Marlowe, Christopher. c.1590/1978. *The Jew of Malta*, ed. N.W. Bawcutt (Manchester University Press: Manchester).

Marx, Karl. 1843/1975. 'On the Jewish Question', in Lucio Colletti (ed.), *Early Writings* (Penguin: Harmondsworth).

Marx, Karl. 1843/1975. 'Critique of Hegel's Doctrine of the State', *Karl Marx Early Writings*, trans. Rodney Livingstone and Gregor Benton (Penguin: Harmondsworth).

Marx, Karl. 1844/1975. 'Economic and Philosophical Manuscripts', *Karl Marx Early Writings*, trans. Rodney Livingstone and Gregor Benton (Penguin: Harmondsworth).

Marx, Karl. 1852/1897. *The Eighteenth Brumaire of Louis Bonaparte* (Kessinger Publishing, Whitefish, MT).

Marx, Karl. 1867/1954. *Capital*, Vol. 1 (Lawrence and Wishart: London).

Marx, Karl, and Friedrich Engels. 1848/1977. *Manifesto of the Communist Party* (Progress Publishers: Moscow).

Marx, Stephen. 1992. 'Shakespeare's Pacifism', *Renaissance Quarterly*, 45: 49–95.

Matheson, Mark. 1995/2004. 'Venetian Culture and the Politics of *Othello*', in Catherine M.S. Alexander (ed.), *Shakespeare and Politics* (Cambridge University Press: Cambridge), pp. 169–84.

Matthew, St (The Gospel According to St Matthew). n.d. *Holy Bible*, Authorised (King James) version (Cambridge University Press: Cambridge).

May, Larry. 2012. 'Hobbes against the Jurists: Sovereignty and artificial reason', *Hobbes Studies*, 25: 223–32.

Mbembe, Achille. 2003. 'Necropolitics', *Public Culture*, 15: 11–40.

McAlindon, Tom. 1991. *Shakespeare's Tragic Cosmos* (Cambridge University Press: Cambridge).

McAlindon, Tom. 1992. 'Tragedy, King Lear, and the Politics of the Heart', *Shakespeare Survey*, 44: 85–90.

McCandless, David. 1994. 'Helena's Bed-trick: Gender and performance in All's Well that Ends Well', *Shakespeare Quarterly*, 45: 449–68.

McCann, Sean, and Michael Szalay. 2005. 'Do You Believe in Magic? Literary thinking after the New Left', *Yale Journal of Criticism*, 18: 435–68.

McLuskie, Kathleen. 1985. 'The Patriarchal Bard: Feminist criticism and Shakespeare—King Lear and Measure for Measure', in Jonathan Dollimore and Alan Sinfield (eds.), *Political Shakespeare: New Essays in Cultural Materialism* (Manchester University Press: Manchester), pp. 88–108.

Meilaender, Peter C. 2012. 'Marriage and the Law: Politics and theology in Measure for Measure', *Perspectives on Political Science*, 41: 195–200.

Meron, Theodor. 2018. 'Shakespeare: A dove, a hawk, or simply a humanist', *American Journal of International Law*, III: 936–57.

Miles, Geoffrey. 1996. *Shakespeare and the Constant Romans* (Oxford University Press: Oxford).

Mill, John Stuart. 1859/1989. 'On Liberty', in Stefan Collini (ed.), *On Liberty and other Writings* (Cambridge University Press: Cambridge).

Mills, Cecil Wright. 1959. *The Sociological Imagination* (Oxford University Press: Oxford).

Mohanty, Chandra Talpade. 1984. 'Under Western Eyes: Feminist scholarship and colonial discourses', *Boundary*, 2(12): 333–58.

Montaigne, Michel de. 1580/1603 (in English)/2006a. 'On Friendship', *The Essays*, Vol. 1, trans. John Florio (The Folio Society: London), pp. 180–93.

Montaigne, Michel de. 1580/2006b. 'Of the Institution and Education of Children', in John Florio (trans. and ed.), *The Essayes*, Vol. 1 (The Folio Society: London), pp. 134–75.

Montaigne, Michel de. 2006c. 'Of the Caniballes', in John Florio (trans. and ed.), *The Essayes*, Vol. 1 (The Folio Society: London), pp. 202–21.

Montaigne, Michel de. 1588/2006d. 'Of the Lame or Cripple', *The Essays*, Vol. 3, trans. John Florio (The Folio Society: London), pp. 270–81.

Montrose, Louis. 1996. 'Shakespeare, the Stage and the State', *SubStance*, 25: 46–67.

More, Thomas. 1516/2002. *Utopia* (Cambridge University Press: Cambridge).

Mullaney, Steven. 1994. 'Mourning and Misogyny: Hamlet, The Revenger's Tragedy, and the final progress of Elizabeth I', *Shakespeare Quarterly*, 45: 139–62.

Murley, John A., and Sean D. Sutton. eds. 2006. *Perspectives on Politics in Shakespeare* (Lexington Books: Oxford).

Neill, Michael. ed. 2006. 'Introduction', William Shakespeare, *Othello* (Oxford University Press: Oxford), pp. 1–179.

North, Thomas. 1595/1998. *Plutarch: The Lives of the Noble Grecians and Romans*, ed. Judith Mossman (Wordsworth Editions: Ware).

Nussbaum, Martha. 2001. *Upheavals of Thought: The Intelligence of Emotions* (Cambridge University Press: Cambridge).

Nuttall, A.D. 2007. *Shakespeare the Thinker* (Yale University Press: London).

Orgel, Stephen. ed. 1987. 'Introduction', William Shakespeare, *The Tempest* (Oxford University Press: Oxford), pp. 1–87.

Ovid (Naso, Publius Ovidius, 43 BCE–c.17 CE). 1916/1977. *Metamorphoses* (Harvard University Press: Cambridge, MA).

Parker, R.B. ed. 1994. 'Introduction', William Shakespeare, *Coriolanus* (Oxford University Press: Oxford), pp. 1–148.

Parker, R.B. ed. 1994. 'Appendix', William Shakespeare, *Coriolanus* (Oxford University Press: Oxford), pp. 1–148.

Parry, Glyn. 2006. 'John Dee and the Elizabethan British Empire in its European Context', *The Historical Journal*, 49: 643–75.

Parry, Glyn. 2012. 'Occult Philosophy and Politics: Why John Dee wrote his Compendious Rehearsal in November 1592', *Studies in History and Philosophy of Science*, 43: 480–8.

Pateman, Carole. 1988. 'Wives, Slaves and Wage-slaves', *The Sexual Contract* (Polity Press: Cambridge), Ch. 5.

Pateman, Carole. 1989. 'The Fraternal Social Contract', *The Disorder of Women* (Polity Press: Cambridge).

Patterson, Annabel. 1989. *Shakespeare and the Popular Voice* (Basil Blackwell: Oxford).

Peltonen, Markku. 2009. 'Political Rhetoric and Citizenship in Coriolanus', in David Armitage, Conal Condren, and Andrew Fitzmaurice (eds.), *Shakespeare and Early Modern Political Thought* (Cambridge University Press: Cambridge).

Pettit, Philip. 1997. *Republicanism: A Theory of Freedom and Government* (Clarendon Press: Oxford).

Philp, M. 1994. 'On Politics and its Corruption', *Political Theory Newsletter*, 6: 1–18.

Philpott, Daniel. 2011. 'Sovereignty', in George Klosko (ed.), *The Oxford Handbook of the History of Political Philosophy* (Oxford University Press: Oxford).

Plato (c.429–c.348 BCE). 1925. 'The Statesman/Politicos', *Plato*, Vol. VIII, trans. Harold N. Fowler (Harvard University Press: Cambridge, MA).

Plato. 1930–1935. *Republic* (Harvard University Press: Cambridge, MA).

Plato. 1938. 'Symposium', *Plato: Five Dialogues*, trans. Michael Joyce (J.M. Dent and Sons: London).

Plato. *c.*330BCE/2008. 1925. *Gorgias, or On Rhetoric—Refutative*, Vol. III, trans. W.R.M. Lamb (William Heinemann: London).

Platt, Peter G. 2009. *Shakespeare and the Cuture of Paradox* (Ashgate: Farnham).

Plutarch (*c.*46–*c.*120 CE). 1916a. 'Alcibiades', *Plutarch's Lives*, Vol. IV, trans. Bernadotte Perrin (William Heinemann: London).

Plutarch. 1916b. 'Caius Martius Coriolanus', *Plutarch's Lives*, Vol. 4, trans. Bernadotte Perrin (William Heinemann Ltd: London).

Plutarch. 1919. 'Caesar', *Plutarch's Lives*, Vol. VI, trans. Bernadotte Perrin (William Heinemann: London).

Plutarch. —. 'Antony', *Plutarch's Lives*, Vol. VI, trans. Bernadotte Perrin (William Heinemann: London).

Plutarch. 1931. 'Sayings of Spartan Women', *Plutarch, Moralia*, Vol. III (Loeb Classical Library, Harvard University Press: Cambridge, MA).

Pocock, J.G.A. 1975. *The Machiavellian Moment: Florentine Political Thought and the Atlantic Republican Tradition* (Princeton University Press: Princeton).

Posel, Deborah. 2014. ' "Madiba Magic": Politics as enchantment', in Rita Barnard (ed.), *The Cambridge Companion to Nelson Mandela* (Cambridge University Press: Cambridge).

Prokhovnik, Raia. 1999. *Rational Woman: A Feminist Critique of Dichotomy* (Routledge: London).

Prokhovnik, Raia. 2008. *Sovereignty: History and Theory* (Imprint Academic: Exeter).

Putnam, Robert D., Robert Leonardi, and Raffaella Nanetti. 1993. *Making Democracy Work: Civic Traditions in Modern Italy* (Princeton University Press: Princeton, NJ).

Quintilian (35–100 CE). 2001. *The Orator's Education*, Books 1–12 (Loeb Classical Library, Harvard University Press: Cambridge, MA).

Ranciere, Jacques. 1995/1999. *Disagreement: Politics and Philosophy*, trans. Julie Rose (University of Minnesota Press: Minneapolis, MN).

Rawls, John. 1993. *Political Liberalism* (Columbia University Press: New York).

Rawls, John. 1995. 'Political Liberalism: Reply to Habermas', *Journal of Philosophy*, 92: 132–80.

Raymond, Janice. 1986. *A Passion for Friends: Towards a Philosophy of Female Affection* (Women's Press: London).

Renato Rizzoli. 2017. 'Shakespeare and the Ideologies of the Market', *European Journal of English Studies*, 21(1): 12–25.

Roper, Lyndal. 1994. *Oedipus and the Devil: Witchcraft, Religion and Sexuality in Early Modern Europe* (Routledge: London).

Rousseau, Jean-Jacques. 1755/1997. 'Discourse on Political Economy', in Victor Gourevitch (ed.), *Rousseau: The Social Contract and Other Later Political Writings* (Cambridge University Press: Cambridge).

Rousseau, Jean-Jacques. 1762/1997. 'The Social Contract', in Victor Gourevitch (trans. and ed.), *The Social Contract and Other Later Political Writings* (Cambridge University Press: Cambridge).

Rousseau, Jean-Jacques. 1762/1997. *The Social Contract and Other Later Political Writings*, trans. and ed. Victor Gourevitch (Cambridge University Press: Cambridge).

Runciman, David. 2008. *Political Hypocrisy: The Mask of Power, from Hobbes to Orwell and Beyond* (Princeton University Press: Princeton, NJ).

Sanders, Lynn M. 1997. 'Against Deliberation', *Political Theory*, 25: 347–76.

Sargent, Gerard. 2015. 'Timon, Sir Thomas North, and the Loup-Garou', *Notes and Queries*, 62: 572–4.

Sartre, Jean-Paul. 1946/2007. *Existentialism Is a Humanism*, trans. Carol Macomber (Yale Univeristy Press: New Haven).

Scarry, Elaine. 1985. *The Body in Pain: The Making and Unmaking of the World* (Oxford: Oxford University Press).

Schmitt, Carl. 1922/1985. *Political Theology: Four Chapters on the Concept of Sovereignty*, trans. George Schwab (MIT Press: Cambridge, MA).

Schmitt, Carl. 1927/1996. *The Concept of the Political*, trans. George Schwab (Chicago University Press: Chicago).

Schochet, Gordon J. 1969. 'Patriarchalism, Politics and Mass Attitudes in Stuart England', *The Historical Journal*, 12: 413–41.

Schochet, Gordon J. 1975/1988. *The Authoritarian Family and Political Attitudes in 17th Century England: Patriarchalism in Political Thought* (Transaction Books: New Brunswick).

Schwarzenbach, Sybil. 1996. 'On Civic Friendship', *Ethics*, 107(1): 97–128.

Seymour, Ian. 1989. 'The Political Magic of John Dee', *History Today*, 39: 29–36.

Shakespeare, William. 1591 (comp.)/2003. *Henry VI*, part 1, ed. Michael Taylor (Oxford University Press: Oxford).

Shakespeare, William. 1592? (comp.)/2003. *Henry VI*, part 2, ed. Roger Warren (Oxford University Press: Oxford).

Shakespeare, William. 1593 (comp.)/2000. *Romeo and Juliet*, ed. Jill H. Levenson (Oxford University Press: Oxford).

Shakespeare, William. 1594–6(?) (comp.)/2001. *Henry VI*, part 3, ed. Randall Martin (Oxford University Press: Oxford).

Shakespeare, William. 1595 (comp.)/2011. *Richard II*, ed. Anthony B. Dawson and Paul Yachnin (Oxford University Press: Oxford).

Shakespeare, William. 1595 (comp.)/1993. *The Merchant of Venice*, ed. Jay L. Halio (Oxford University Press: Oxford).

Shakespeare, William. 1596/1997. *Henry IV*, part 2, ed. Rene Weis (Oxford University Press: Oxford).

Shakespeare, William. 1598/1987. *Henry IV*, part 1, ed. David Bevington (Oxford University Press: Oxford).

Shakespeare, William. 1598/1993. *Much Ado about Nothing*, ed. Sheldon P. Zitner (Oxford University Press: Oxford).

Shakespeare, William. 1599 (comp.)/1984. *Julius Caesar*, ed. Arthur Humpreys (Oxford University Press: Oxford).

Shakespeare, William. 1599/1982. *Henry V*, ed. Gary Taylor (Oxford University Press: Oxford).

Shakespeare, William. 1599/1993. *As You Like It*, ed. Alan Bressenden (Oxford University Press: Oxford).

Shakespeare, William. 1601/1994. *Twelfth Night*, ed. Roger Warren and Stanley Wells (Oxford University Press: Oxford).

Shakespeare, William. 1602 (comp.)/1987. *Hamlet*, ed. G.R. Hibbard (Oxford University Press: Oxford).

Shakespeare, William. 1604 (comp.)/1991. *Measure for Measure* (Oxford University Press: Oxford).

Shakespeare, William. 1604 (comp.)/2004. *The Life of Timon of Athens*, ed. John Jowett (Oxford University Press: Oxford).

Shakespeare, William. 1604 (comp.)/2006. *Othello*, ed. Michael Neill (Oxford University Press: Oxford).

Shakespeare, William. 1605/1996. *The First Quarto of King Lear*, ed. Jay L. Halio (Cambridge University Press: Cambridge).

Shakespeare, William. 1605/1997. *King Lear*, ed. R.A. Foakes (Bloomsbury Academic: London).

Shakespeare, William. 1605 (comp.)/2000. *The History of King Lear*, ed. Stanley Wells (Oxford University Press: Oxford).

Shakespeare, William. 1606 (comp.)/1990. *The Tragedy of Macbeth*, ed. Nicholas Brooke (Oxford University Press: Oxford).

Shakespeare, William. 1608 (comp.)/1994. *The Tragedy of Coriolanus*, ed. R.B. Parker Oxford University Press: Oxford).

Shakespeare, William. 1611 (comp.)/1987. *The Tempest*, ed. Stephen Orgel (Oxford University Press: Oxford).

Shklar, Judith. 1989. 'The Liberalism of Fear', in Nancy L. Rosenblum (ed.), *Liberalism and the Moral Life* (Harvard University Press: Cambridge, MA).

Shortland, Michael. 1988. 'Setting Murderous Machiavel to School: Hypocrisy in politics and the novel', *Journal of European Studies*, xviii: 93–120.

Shrank, Cathy. 2003. 'Civility and the City in Coriolanus', *Shakespeare Quarterly*, 54: 406–23.

Shuger, Debora Kuller. 2001. *Political Theologies in Shakespeare's England: The Sacred and the State in Measure for Measure* (Palgrave: Houndmills).

Siegel, Paul N. 1961. 'Christianity and the Religion of Love in Romeo and Juliet', *Shakespeare Quarterly*, 12(4): 371–92.

Skeat, Walter W. ed. 1875. *Shakespeare's Plutarch: Being a Selection from The Lives in North's Plutarch which Illustrate Shakespeare's Plays* (Macmillan and Co: London).

Skinner, Quentin. 1978. *The Foundations of Modern Political Thought*. Vol. 1: *The Renaissance* (Cambridge University Press: Cambridge).

Skinner, Quentin. 1996. *Reason and Rhetoric in the Philosophy of Hobbes* (Cambridge University Press: Cambridge).

Skinner, Quentin. 2002. *Visions of Politics: Hobbes and Civil Science* (Cambridge University Press: Cambridge).

Skinner, Quentin. 2014. *Forensic Shakespeare* (Oxford University Press: Oxford).

Smith, Adam. 1776/1974. *The Wealth of Nations* (Penguin: Harmondsworth).

Spenser, Edmund (1552?-99). 1590/2001. *The Faerie Queen*, ed. A.C. Hamilton (Pearson Education Limited: Harlow).

Spivak, Gayatry Chakravorty. 1988. 'Can the Subaltern Speak?', in C. Nelson and L. Grossberg (eds.), *Marxism and the Interpretation of Culture* (Macmillan Education Basingstoke), pp. 271–313.

Stillman, Robert E. 1995. 'Hobbes' Leviathan: Monsters, metaphors, magic', *ELH*, 62: 791–819.

Strauss, Leo. 1952. *Persecution and the Art of Writing* (The Free Press: Glencoe, IL).

Stump, Donald. 2019. *Spenser's Heavenly Elizabeth: Providential History in The Faerie Queen* (Palgrave Macmillan: London).

Tagonist, Anne. 2017. '2016: The year magic broke into politics', http://dark-mountain.net/blog/2016-the-year-magic-broke-into-politics/ (accessed May 2017).

Tennenhouse, Leonard. 1986/2005. *Power on Display: The Politics of Shakespeare's Genres* (Methuen: London).

Thaler, Mathias. 2019. *Naming Violence: A Critical Theory of Genocide, Torture, and Terrorism* (Columbia University Press: New York).

Thomas, Keith. 1971. *Religion and the Decline of Magic: Studies in Popular Beliefs in Sixteenth and Seventeenth Century England* (Weidenfeld and Nicholson: London).

Thucydides (c.460-c.400 BCE). 1972. *History of the Peloponnesian War*, ed. and intro. M.I. Finley, trans. R. Warner (Penguin: Harmondsworth).

Tonge, Mildred. 1932. 'Black Magic and Miracles in Macbeth', *Journal of English and Germanic Philology*, 31: 234–46.

Tovey, Barbara. 1996. 'Wisdom and the Law: Thoughts on the Political Philosophy of Measure for Measure', in Joseph Alulis and Vickie Sullivan (eds.), *Shakespeare's Political Pageant: Essays in Literature and Politics* (Rowman and Littlefield: London), pp. 61–75.

Traub, Valerie. 1992/2004. 'The Homoerotics of Shakespearian Comedy', in Emma Smith (ed.), *Shakespeare's Comedies* (Blackwell Publishing: Oxford), pp. 164–91.

Vagts, Alfred. 1959. *A History of Militarism: Civilian and Military* (Hollis and Carter: London).

Walker, R.B.J. 1993. *Inside/Outside: International Relations as Political Theory* (Cambridge University Press: Cambridge).

Walzer, Michael. 1989. *The Company of Critics: Social Criticism and Political Commitment in the Twentieth Century* (Basic Books: New York).

Ward, Angela. 2017. 'Symbols of the Sacred: Religious tension in Act I Scene 1 of Romeo and Juliet', *Literature and Theology*, 31(1): 64–77.

Weber, Max. 1919/1994. 'The Profession and Vocation of Politics', in Peter Lassman and Ronald Speirs (eds.), *Weber Political Writings* (Cambridge University Press: Cambridge).

Weber, Max. 1921/1978. *Economy and Society*, trans. and ed. Geunther Roth and Claus Wittich (University of California Press: Berkeley, CA).

Weimann, Robert. 1978. *Shakespeare and the Popular Tradition in Theater: Studies in the Social Dimension of Dramatic Form and Function* (Johns Hopkins University Press: Baltimore).

Weimann, Robert. 1988. 'Bifold Authority in Shakespeare's Theatre', *Shakespeare Quarterly*, 39: 401–17.

Weimann, Robert. 1992. 'Representation and Performance: The uses of authority in Shakespeare's theatre', *PMLA*, 107: 497–510.

Wells, Robin Headlam. 2009. *Shakespeare's Politics* (Continuum: London).

Wells, Stanley. ed. 1605 (comp.)/2000. 'Introduction', in William Shakespeare, *The History of King Lear* (Oxford University Press: Oxford).

Whitehorne, Peter. 1521/1964. 'Dedicatory Epistle to Elizabeth I', in Niccolo Machiavelli, *Art of War*, ed. Neal Wood (Perseus Books: Cambridge, MA).

Willett, John. 1959/1977. *The Theatre of Bertold Brecht: A Study from Eight Aspects* (Methuen: London).

Williamson, Marilyn L. 1986. *The Patriarchy of Shakespeare's Comedies* (Wayne State University Press: Detroit, MI).

Willis, Deborah. 1989. 'Shakespeare's Tempest and the Discourse of Colonialism', *Studies in English Literature 1500–1900*, 29(2): 277–89.

Winter, Yves. 2018. *Machiavelli and the Orders of Violence* (Cambridge University Press: Cambridge).

Wollstonecraft, Mary. 1792/1994. 'A Vindication of the Rights of Woman', in Janet Todd (ed.), *Mary Wollstonecraft: Political Writings* (Oxford University Press: Oxford).

Wollstonecraft, Mary. 1796/1987. *A Short Residence in Sweden, Norway and Denmark* (Penguin: Harmondsworth).

Index

For the benefit of digital users, indexed terms that span two pages (e.g., 52–53) may, on occasion, appear on only one of those pages.